THE ART OF

ASSET

ALLOCATION

SECOND EDITION

Principles and Investment Strategies for Any Market

DAVID M. DARST

New York Chicago San Francisco Lisbon
London Madrid Mexico City Milan
Montreal New Delhi San Juan
Seoul Singapore Sydney Toronto

1 2 3 4 5 6 7 8 9 0 FGR/FGR 0 9 8

ISBN: 978-0-07-159294-9
MH ID: 0-07-159294-6

This publication is designed to provide accurate and authoritative information in regard
to the subject matter covered. It is sold with the understanding that the publisher is not
engaged in rendering legal, accounting, or other professional service. If legal advice or
other expert assistance is required, the services of a competent professional person should
be sought.
—*From a Declaration of Principles Jointly Adopted by a Committee of the American Bar
Association and a Committee of Publishers and Associations*

McGraw-Hill books are available at special quantity discounts to use as premiums and
sales promotions, or for use in corporate training programs. To contact a representative,
please visit the Contact Us pages at www.mhprofessional.com.

This book is printed on acid-free paper.

This book is dedicated

To those who have gone before

Guy Bewley Darst
James McGinnis Darst
Susan McGinnis Darst
Kimberly Lawrence Netter
Eleanor Humphrey Wassman
Edward Robert Wassman

and

To those who are going forward

David Martin Darst, Jr.
Elizabeth Mathews Darst
Diane Wassman Darst

CONTENTS

SECTION 2

THE MECHANICS OF ASSET ALLOCATION

Chapter 3

Asset-Allocation Tools and Concepts   41

Chapter 4

Asset-Allocation Rebalancing   95

SECTION 3

UNDERPINNINGS OF ASSET ALLOCATION

Chapter 5

Individual Investor Behavior   151

SECTION 4

ASSET CLASS CHARACTERISTICS

Chapter 6

Distinguishing Qualities of Asset Classes   201

Chapter 7

Analyzing Assets' Rates of Return   255

FOREWORD

The objective of investing is to increase the purchasing power of capital. This means that the total return after taxes from the portfolio must exceed the inflation rate. How high this "real" return is, and how risky the means of achieving it, are what asset allocation is all about.

Asset allocation is the most important factor in the performance equation of a multiasset portfolio. Huge amounts of time and money are devoted to the selection and evaluation of investment managers, but far less attention is paid to asset allocation. This book is designed to remedy that oversight.

David Darst and I believe that regression to the mean, or the tendency of returns to gravitate toward their long-term averages, is one of the most powerful forces in investing. Any asset allocation process must have an abiding respect for history. As Winston Churchill said, "the farther backward you can look, the farther forward you can see."

Brinson, Singer, and Beebower have published several scholarly studies in *The Financial Analysts Journal* on the determinants of portfolio performance. They found that differences in allocation policy accounted for 91.5% of the variations of returns across a sample of 82 large, multiasset U.S. pension fund portfolios from 1977 to 1987. An analysis by SEI of 97 large pension funds showed that 87% of differential performance was related to asset class selection. A Hamilton Johnson study demonstrated that by correctly alternating between stocks, bonds, and cash, over 10 years, annual returns three times those of the typical balanced fund can be realized.

It makes sense that asset allocation, rather than manager selection, should account for around 90% of the performance differentials in diversified, multiasset portfolios. At various times in the 1980s, the difference in the annual return between owning U.S. and international equities was around 1,000 basis points per year for as long as three to five years. The performance gap between a first quartile manager and a third quartile manager in either category was around 300 basis points per annum.

Good asset allocation can result in the return on the whole being more than the sum of the returns on the parts. Large pension funds, such as General Electric's, have achieved total fund returns in excess of sector returns by astute asset allocation. By contrast, a Department of Labor study suggests that annual total returns of the average pension plan over the last 20 years have been less than the returns of the individual sectors. These funds tended to have maximum weightings in stocks and bonds after good performance rather than before. This is like steering a fast car down a winding mountain road by looking through the rear-view mirror at the bends in the road over which the car just traveled.

I believe that asset allocation will get much more attention, and that the investment stars of the future will be the individuals, fiduciaries, fund officers, and committees who make the correct asset allocation calls. Manager selection, which receives so much focus today, will be de-emphasized. A diversified mix of managers results in varying styles that tend to cancel each other out. When growth stock investing is hot, good performance by growth stock managers is offset by poor relative performance by value managers and vice versa.

No one is as deep a student, as much a disciple of asset allocation, or a more intense practitioner, as my friend David Darst. It is not an easy profession. It is an art, a science, and much more. I have worked with David as an investor for years, and this book will always be on my "special" bookshelf.

Barton M. Biggs
Founder and Former Chairman
Morgan Stanley
Investment Management
Founder and Managing Partner
Traxis Partners

PREFACE

The book you are now holding contains a great deal of practical information to help investors allocate their assets in any kind of financial market environment. As shown in Figure P.1, *The Art of Asset Allocation* furnishes a comprehensive array of tools, charts, illustrations, matrices, worksheets, and practical guidance designed to illuminate: (i) the *basic principles* of asset allocation; (ii) the *mechanics* of asset allocation; (iii) the behavioral *underpinnings* of asset allocation; (iv) the *essential characteristics* of each of the 17 major asset classes; and (v) a *series of approaches* to financial markets analysis. In addition, investors will benefit from (vi) *matrices and worksheets* designed to carry out asset allocation successfully on an ongoing basis.

In response to changing asset prices, broadening investment goals, and an increasing desire to know more about and exert influence over their investments, investors want sound, pragmatic advice on asset allocation and investment strategy. *The Art of Asset Allocation* has been designed specifically to enhance the financial thinking and actions of individual investors across the wealth spectrum, ranging from: (i) the *96 million U.S. households* with $100,000 or less in discretionary financial assets totaling $3.4 trillion; (ii) the *16 million U.S. households* with between $100,000 and $1 million in discretionary financial assets totaling $5.6 trillion; (iii) the *2.2 million households* with between $1 million and $10 million in discretionary financial assets totaling $6.0 trillion; and (iv) the *100,000 households*

F I G U R E P.1

Important Themes of *The Art of Asset Allocation*

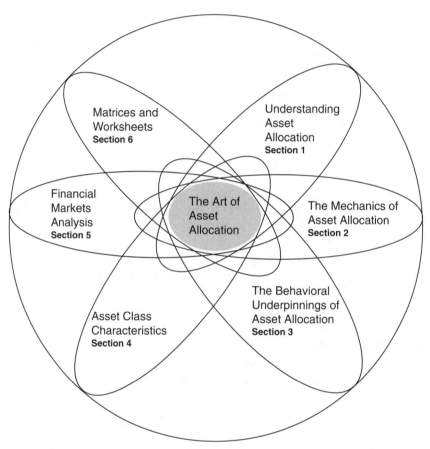

Source: The Author.

with more than $10 million in discretionary financial assets totaling $2.2 trillion.

Many other investors, intermediaries, issuers, regulators, educators, and students also will benefit from this book, including professional investors, non-U.S. investors, corporate and governmental financial officers, and supervisory authorities. As far as is known, no other work in the financial literature is quite like this book.

One Approach to Reading *The Art of Asset Allocation*

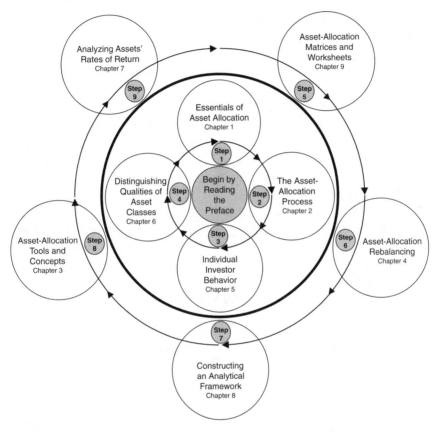

Source: The Author.

Although many investors may prefer to read this book in chapter sequence from cover to cover, a number of other investors may wish to begin with the four core chapters and fill in as they go along. Figure P.2 sets forth one efficient method for using *The Art of Asset Allocation*.

In Figure P.2, four core chapters of this book, Chapters 1, 2, 5, and 6, are grouped together to offer the investor a quick yet thorough treatment of the most important asset-allocation themes and practices.

Having read these chapters, the investor is then in a position to: (i) begin the process of asset allocation; (ii) continue reading Chapters 9, 4, 8, 3, and 7 (in clockwise sequence around the outside of the four core chapters shown in Figure P.2), before beginning to allocate assets; or (iii) pursue (i) and (ii) simultaneously.

Table P.1 shows nine special features, where to find them in this book, and why they are of use, relevance, and value to the investor. These special features include: (i) asset-allocation basics; (ii) how to proceed in asset allocation; (iii) insights into individual investor behavior; (iv) key characteristics of each of the 16 major asset classes; (v) asset-allocation worksheets; (vi) asset-allocation-rebalancing techniques; (vii) analytical frameworks for allocating assets; (viii) asset-allocation tools and concepts; and (ix) how to analyze assets' rates of return.

In writing this book, I have been fortunate to be able to draw upon the wisdom and insight of a great many members of the

T A B L E P.1

Special Features of *The Art of Asset Allocation*

Chapter in Which to Find the Features	Features to Be Found	Why the Features Are of Use, Relevance, and Value to Investors
1	Asset-allocation basics	Describes the steps, meanings, and foundations of asset allocation, and indicates when asset allocation does and does not work.
2	How to proceed in asset allocation	Examines differing investor needs according to wealth levels and the various types of asset allocations according to style, orientation, and inputs.
5	Insights into individual investor behavior	Explores many key behavioral factors that affect individuals' investment decisions and patterns of thinking, action, and reflection.
6	Asset class characteristics	Summarizes the key features, choices, advantages, and risks of investing in 17 major asset classes, lists assets that act like other assets, and addresses issues of asset allocation and asset protection in conditions of extreme stress or duress.

T A B L E P.1 (Continued)

Special Features of *The Art of Asset Allocation*

Chapter in Which to Find the Features	Features to Be Found	Why the Features Are of Use, Relevance, and Value to Investors
9	Asset-allocation worksheets	Reviews mentality-, outlook-, and age-based allocation guidelines and asset-allocation cycles, and profiles investors, their investment outlook, and the potential investment universe.
4	Asset-allocation rebalancing techniques	Investigates the advantages, disadvantages, means, and circumstances for rebalancing all types of assets, including conventional and alternative assets, concentrated positions, and personal holdings.
8	Analytical frameworks for allocating assets	Evaluates a variety of analytical constructs to help investors assess the efficacy of societal analysis, market-cycle analysis, scenario analysis, investor-satisfaction analysis, strategy-implementation analysis, comparative financial analysis, and financial-climate analysis.
3	Asset-allocation tools and concepts	Explains in practical terms how market prices reflect information, how assets' returns relate to each other, how an asset's return compensates the investor for bearing risk, and how portfolio optimization models work.
7	Analyzing assets' rates of return	Provides important perspective on how specific assets and asset classes have performed by groups of years, on a year-to-year basis, and in different kinds of economic environments.

professional, managerial, and support resources of Morgan Stanley, Goldman Sachs, Citigroup, Merrill Lynch, UBS, Credit Suisse, JP Morgan Chase, HSBC, Fidelity, Vanguard, PIMCO, Lehman Brothers, Wells Fargo, Deutsche Bank, Wachovia, Bank of America, and several other outstanding financial organizations. For reasons of space, I deeply regret that I am not able to cite each valued colleague by name; my debt is great to the asset managers, economists, portfolio managers, quantitative strategists, financial advisors, investment representatives, research analysts, legal and compliance personnel, human resources and marketing officers, investment bankers, institutional sales and trading professionals, graphics and creative services staff members, operations and technology specialists, branch managers, and the highly capable assistants, administrators, and staff members who so ably support these individuals.

Of particular value have been the advice and counsel provided by: *Ausaf Abbas, Teresa Abbate, Alan Abelson, Yuki Adachi, Melissa Adamson, Kpate Adjaoute, Carlye Adler, Rich Adler, Ulrich Adler, Anwar Ahmed, Ariel Aisiks, Dave Albrecht, Basel Algadhib, Peter Aliprantis, Darya Allen-Attar, Steve Alley, Marsha Alleyne, Jim Allwin, Bruce Alonso, Tatiana Alonso, Jeff Alvino, Greg Amadon, Effie Anagnostopoulos, Carol Anderson, Steve Anderson, Michael Appleton, Ariel Arazi, Lee Archer, Carlos Arias, Michael Armstrong, Tom Armstrong, Sigurdur Arngrimsson, Matt Arpano, Jim Ash, Paul Ashby, Steven Ashley, Suzy Assaad, Rich Atlas, Tom Aydelotte, Ellen Babby, Lon Babby, Miguel Bacal, Gunther Bacher, Hans-Ueli Bachofen, Deepanshu Bagchee, Jim Baker, Carla Bakker, Michelle Baldwin, Jack Ball, Elyssa Baltazar, Charles Banta, Nick Bapis, Vinny Barile, Janet Barnes, Bob Bauman, Stephen Baumgarten, Mark Bavoso, Marina Behr, Beverly Bell, Jim Bell, Jamie Bennett, Lewis Bernard, Peter Bernstein, Sharon Bess, Eric Best, Chuck Biderman, Jerry Bierbaum, Linda Bierds, Barton Biggs, Ted Bigman, Frank Biondo, Mag Black, Scott Black, David Blair, Rick Blosser, Harris Blum, Jess Bobier, Leslie Bocskor, Sonya Bogaars, Mitchell Bompey, Walter Bopp, Andy Boszhardt, Eric Boutin, Francine Bovich, Emily Boyd, Alex Bradford, Ben Bram, Gary Brandwein, Jeffrey Brattain, John Breglio, Roli Breitenecker, Ed Brennan, Michelle Brew, Simon Brewer, Alex Bridport, Felipe Britto, Bill Broadbent, Matthew Bronfman, John Paul Broussard, Anne Brown, Danielle Brown, Rob Brown, Jennifer Browne, Rich Brownstein, Adolf Brundler, John Brynjolfsson, Ravi Bulchandani, Norm Burger, Adriana Burke, Dan Burke, Cam Burns, Clarissa Bushman, Martin Bussmann, Ray Cameron, Elizabeth Camp, John Campbell, Peter Canelo, Angelica Cantlon, Mac Caputo, Christina Caras, Peter Carman, Ty Carmichael, Ronan Carr, Sam Carroll, Roger Carter, Louise Casanova, Tony Casanova, Eva Castillo,*

Bob Castrignano, Dollaya Chaibongsai, Abhijit Chakrabortti, Jill Chanin, Jacky Charboneau, Erica Chau, Vivian Chen, Atrice Cherie, Tiffany Cherie, Nicole Cheslock, Tracy Chesman, Lulu Chiang, Alexandra Christiansen, Mayree Clark, Kelly Close, Lori Cohane, Bruce Cohen, Rita Colella, Robert Coleman, Heather Comero, Susan Conroy, Dan Cook, Lee Cooperman, Scott Copenhaver, Doug Coppola, Hernando Cortina, Jon Corzine, Jim Cramer, Nigel Cree, Ron Crismon, Zoe Cruz, Larry Cunningham, Ellie Currie, Rachelle Curry, Andy Cushman, Liza D'Souza, Chris Daifotis, Sonia Dandona, Jonathan Darnell, Parthie Darrell, David Wise Darst, Michael David, Richard Davidson, Barry Davis, Marguerite Day, Mark Dayton, Ernesto de la Fe, Christina de Marval, Matteo De Nora, Nathaniel de Rothschild, Robert de Rothschild, Gael de Roquefeuil, Guillaume de Toulouse-Lautrec, Dick Debs, Michelle Debusschere, Dan Dechant, Guy DeChazal, Elizabeth Del Prete, Jeannine Deloche, Tom DeLong, Melinda DeMaio, Rich DeMartini, Alex Denner, John Devlin, Sarah Devlin, Brit Dewey, Madhav Dhar, Jon Diamond, Spencer Hellstrom Diamond, Jeff Diermeier, David Dineen, Michelle Doig, Danielle Donovan, Kerry Dowd, Patrick Downs, Laura Dox, Patty Doyle, Craig Drill, Tom Driscoll, Kelly Drop, Ray Drop, Liza D'Souza, Alexander Duff, Turney Duff, Renee Dugan, Baker Duncan, Townes Duncan, Robert Dunn, David Dwek, Ken Ebbitt, David Edwards, Duncan Edwards, John Egan, Carl Eifler, Joe Eisler, Gregory Elinsky, Barry Elkins, Amy Elliott, Charley Ellis, Lincoln Ellis, Timothy Emanuels, Jennifer Schoellkopf Emanuelson, Catherine Eristoff, Amy Esposito, Lior Evan, Susan Everly, Carolyn Everson, Frank Fabozzi, Charles Fago, Caroline Falk, Amy Falls, and *Cara Fanning.*

Major encouragement, insight, and support have also been faithfully rendered by: *Catherine Farmer, Bill Farrell, Michael Fascitelli, Alex Fash, Ali Fayed, Tracy Fayed, Rebecca Fender, Kerry Ferguson, Henry Fernandez, Alf Field, Doug Fields, David Fife, Gene Fife, Michael Finkbeiner, Edwin Finn, Dan Finnegan, Pat Finnegan, Ben Firestein, Dick Fisher, Jim Fisher, Simon Flannery, Bill Flatley, Eugene Flood, Rose Ford, Wolf Forster, Bernardo Fort-Brescia, Tom Frame, Irene Francis, Cedric Francois, Carlos Frederico, Bobby Frist, Julie Frist, Annemarie Froehner, Ken Froewiss, Robert From, Glenn Fuhrman, Jack Gabarro, Dilip Gadkar, Steve Galbraith, Ernst Gall, Fran Gallagher, Bret Gallaway, Gary Gannaway, Jorge Garcia-Garcia, Stretch Gardiner, Virginia Garmendia, Jonathan Garner, Neal Garonzik, James Gatto, Claire Gaudiani, Michael*

Gellert, Stephen George, James Geraghty, Roselle Gerber, Gordon Getty, Heinz Geyer, Pat Geyer, Khalid Ghayur, Debra Gill, Godfrey Gill, Gaspare Gioia, Drita Gjidoda, Jeanne Glasser, Mark Glasser, Alexis Glick, Bob Goldfarb, Marc Goldman, Diana Gomez, Rolando Gonzalez-Bunster, Marian Goodell, Gary Goodenough, John Goodwin, Berry Gordy, Rick Gould, Andie Grace, Jim Grant, Pansy Grant, Richard Grant, Tone Grant, Jeff Graves, Scott Gregorchuk, Linda Greub, Bill Griffiths, Jimmy Griscom, Bill Gruver, Carmen Guarini, Josh Gully, Raj Gupta, Urs Guthmann, Jerry Guthrie, Claudio Haddad, Freddy Hahne, Judith Halabrin, John Halasz, Katy Hall, James Halligan, Curtis Hammond, Julie Hammond, Ted Hampel, Shelley Hanan, Harry Handler, Tracy Hanyak, Lisle Harding, Ray Harris, Andy Hart, Larry Harvey, Kim Hatchett, Jennifer Hausler, John Havens, Kathryn Hay, Marianne Hay, Sam Hayes, David Haynes, Mary Healey, Tom Healey, Steven Hefter, Stuart Hendel, Eleni Henkel, Charles Henneman, Katherine Hennessey, Tom Herman, Mike Hertz, Jim Higgins, Mike Higgins, Calvin Hill, Grant Hill, Janet Hill, Jamie Hirsch, Bill Hobi, Eileen Hod, Manuela Hoelterhoff, Bonnie Hoff, David Hogan, Bob Holcomb, Greg Hoogkamp, Catherine Hooper, David Horn, Michael Horowitz, Sue Hostetler, John Howard, Patsy Howard, William Huffman, Yolanda Humbel, Kevin Hunt, Liz Iannone, Jennifer Ioli, Honsum Ip, Anand Iyer, William Jackman, John Jacob, Matt Jagoda, Aldon James, Calvin James, Rene Jaquet, Angela Jelmolini, Dan Jick, Paul Jingozian, Eric Johnson, Janice Johnson, Robin Joines, Kia Joorabchian, Sharzad Joorabchian, Tannaz Joorabchian, Marc Jourdren, Alois Jurcik, Patricia Kakounis, Joe Karas, Allison Karayanes, Peter Karches, Skip Karetsky, Mark Kary, Mahdy Katbeh, Shannon Kates, Steve Kay, Tom Kazazes, Theodore Keith, David Kelso, Don Kempf, Olivier Khalil, Bob Kidder, Chloe Kiernan, Paul Kimball, Carey King, Christina King, Ellen King, Norman King, Peter King, Andrew Kirk, Barbara Kirk, Dallas Kirk, Kathy Kirk, Skip Kirk, Terry Kirk, Seth Klarman, Sheila Klehm, Victoria Klein, Jennifer Kloppenborg, Paul Klug, Josh Knechtel, Chuck Knight, Jeff Kobernick, Maya Koenig, Anita Kolleeney, George Kozmetsky, Joyce Kramer, David Kratovil, Kimberly Kravis, Fred Krom, Gailen Krug, Chuck Krysieniel, Larry Kudlow, Gina Kuhlenkamp, Elizabeth Kuo, Eiichiro Kuwana, Halvard Kvaale, Alexander Kwok, Raymond Kwok, Robert Lamb, Eddie Lampert, Kinga Lampert, Nicholas Lampert, Nina Lampert, Ed Landry, Christian Lange, Robert Lanigan, Kathy LaPorte, Ruth Laredo, Rick Larkin, Judy Lawhorn,

Jenny Lawrence, Pierre Le Gal de Kerangal, Noreen Leahey, Liz Lee, Ben Leewak, Willy LeGagneur, Marty Leibowitz, Willi Leimer, Harold Fitzgerald Lenfest, Bob Lenzner, Megan Lesko, and *Robert Lesko.*

Of great help have been: *Rick Levin, David Lew, Katelyn Lewis, Lisha Li, Aaron Liberman, Jay Light, Gretchen Lilyholm, Ching-Shan Lin, Jamie Linden, Richard Lindquist, Diana Lindsay, Nelly Linggi, Ferdinand Lips, Jim Little, Joseph Lizzio, Monique Lodi, John Loeb, Dan Long, Vickie Longo, Jonathan Lonske, Henry Looser, Kent Lorentzen, Brianna Lorenz, Robert Louis-Dreyfus, Thierry Lovenbach, Dannette Lowe, Lisa Luca, Scott Lurding, Alex Lynch, Liz Lynch, Will Lyon, Coleman Lyons, Alec Machiels, John Mack, Cheryl MacLachlan, Lois Macri, Rick Madden, John Madigan, Eric Madoff, Paul Madoff, Jeff Madrick, Jim Mahon, Dominic Maister, Georges Makouhl, Lauren Male, Burt Malkiel, Ted Malloch, Tim Maloney, Sean Marani, Jeff Marcus, Nancy Marcus, Joanne Marini, Terry Markey, Michael Markland, Kim Markowitz, Jack Markwalter, Miles Marsh, Richard Marston, Ron Masci, Fariborz Maseeh, Carol Massar, Gail Massey, Leena Mathew, Cecile Mattei, Robin Maynard, Susan Mayring, Alighiero Mazio, Joe McAlinden, John McArthur, Kathy McAvey, Tara McCabe, Dan McCarthy, Tom McConnell, David McCreery, Sarah McDaniel, Keith McDermott, Jack McDonald, Melody McDonald, Kathy McDonough, Ray McGuire, Katherine McKinnon, Tim McLaughlin, Dennis McLeavey, Tom McManus, Catherine McRae, Ellen McRedmond, Linda McRedmond, Matthew Mead, Sarah Meehan, Mary Meeker, Terry Meguid, Steve Memishian, Leslie Menkes, Richard Menschel, Robert Menschel, Mitch Merin, Mitzi Meriwether, Jack Merriman, Cory Mervis, Chrissy Messia, William Messner, Trish Metz, Danny Meyer, Diana Meyer, Doris Meyer, Jack Meyer, Karen Meyer, Bill Michaelcheck, Aaron Michel, Paul Middendorf, Brooke Mifflin, Allison Mignoni, Mike Miles, Fred Miller, Ira Miller, Lea Miller, Steve Miller, Theodore Miller, Daniel Minerbo, Sabby Mionis, Robert Mischel, Leah Modigliani, Marie Mole, Sal Monastero, Michelle Montague, Missy Moore, Juliet Moran, Shannon Moran, Peggy Moreland, Sue Morelli, Rick Morgan, Jim Moriarity, John Morris, Tom Morrow, Averell Mortimer, Bill Morton, George Moseley, Kirsten Moss, Cyril Moulle-Berteaux, Wendy Moy, Jim Moye, Robert Mueller, Vreni Mueller, Cynthia Muller, Peter Muller, Linda Munger, Steve Munger, Robert Murchison, Jennifer Murphy, Michael Nahass, Reid Nahm, Ray Nasher, Donald Nelson, Joseph*

Neubauer, Steve Newhouse, Eric Newman, Gina Nguyen, Que Nguyen, Laura Nicholson, Christopher Niehaus, Gerry Noejovich, Laura Norman, Jane Norris, Joan Norton, Amr Nosseir, Michael Novick, Richard O'Connell, Tim O'Connell, Bridget O'Daly, Ray O'Rourke, Walter Ochsner, Stephanie Oesch, Morris Offit, Pilar Frank O'Leary, Daniela Oliveira, Terri O'Neill, Valerie O'Neill, Fabian Onetti, Jocelyn Ong, Jon Orseck, John Osbon, Kathryn Osborne, James O'Shaughnessy, Miguel Osio, Mac Overton, Gary Pacarro, Gwen Kahoku Pacarro, Kahi Pacarro, Noel Pacarro, Steve Paine, Susan Paine, Emilie Paisley, David Pakman, Cheryl Palmerini, Patty Palumbo, Jessica Pancoe, Vikram Pandit, Mercedes Paratje, Michael Parekh, Maggie Parent, Joan Park, Beth Pasciucco, Miro Pasic, Nandu Patel, Nicholas Pavle, Andy Peake, Elizabeth Peck, Steve Pedersen, Jay Pelosky, Joe Perella, Don Perlyn, Marilyn Perlyn, Mark Peters, Jack Petersen, Wayne Peterson, Chris Petrow, Brian Pfeifler, John Phelan, Keith Phillips, Todd Phillips, Raul Pineda, Dina Pinos, Jerry Pinto, Tom Piper, Rick Pivirotto, Scott Pofcher, Christine Pollak, Lisa Polsky, Stephen Pond, Dick Powers, Manoj Prasad, Skip Pratt, Diana Propper de Callejon, Phil Purcell, Becky Quick, Kimberly Quinones, and Richard Radke.

Special thanks are also extended to: Richard Rainwater, Narayan Ramachandran, Zelle Reams, Madelyn Reddin, Alan Reid, Edna Reid, Hank Reiling, Jaclyn Reindorf, Doug Rentz, Paolo Revelli, Neri Reyes, Vicki Reyes, Eileen Reynolds, Linden Rhoads, Larry Ricciardi, Lucy Ricciardi, Nick Ricciardi, Rachel Richards, Kevin Richardson, Carolyn Ridgway, Ramzi Rishani, Peter Riva, Jose Rivera, Steve Roach, Ron Robison, Janice Rodriguez, Christina Roedema, Robert Roethenmund, Chase Rogers, Jack Rogers, Jim Rogers, Rich Rogers, Sally Rogers, Dick Rogoff, Sarah Rolston, Bryan Romano, Amy Rosmarin, Christina Rossi, Michelle Roth, Bob Rubin, Owi Ruivivar, Peter Rukeyser, Regina Rule, Jim Runde, Diana Ryan, Don Ryan, Arnold Saltzman, Ammanda Salzman, Jeff Salzman, Blanca Sanabria, Arif Sarfraz, Richard Sass, Kimi Sato, Anthony Scaramucci, John Schaefer, Gene Schatz, Robert Scherer, Matt Scherrer, Susan Scheuble, Alan Scheuer, Jim Schlueter, Olivia Schmied, Barry Schneider, Alan Schroder, Bill Schuck, Jacqui Schwab, Rick Schwartz, Brent Schweisberger, Jim Schweitzer, Rosanna Scimeca, Robert Scott, Sharon Kay Scott, Bob Sculthorpe, Dan Sears, Rob Sechan, Dick Seidlitz, Greg Semkow, Hayedeh Sepahpur, Paul Servidio, Camilla Seth, Griff Sexton, Omar Seymour, Ghazala Shabbir, Palak Shah, Ruchir

Sharma, Carol Shasha, Dennis Shea, Thaddeus Shelly, Stephanie Shen, Jack Shepard, Jack Shepherd, Nicole Sherwood, Peter Sherwood, Ruby Sherwood, Robert Shiller, Liz Shook, R. J. Shook, Joe Siegman, David Silfen, Ron Silver, Bruce Simon, Jennifer Simonian, David Singer, Dianna Smith, Nadine Smith, Roy Smith, John Snyder, Arthur Soter, Rod Speidel, Amy Speranza, Ed Spiegel, Sven Spiess, Susan Squires, Sara Stenson, Douglas Stern, Andrew Stevens, Jackie Stewart, Janet Stewart, Karen Stewart, Milton Stewart, Henry Stifel, Mike Stone, John Stowe, Anna Stratman, John Straus, Scott Stuart, Silvia Suarez, Serge Suleimani, Paul Sullivan, Rodney Sullivan, Grayson Sumner, Denise Sussman, David Swensen, Bibi Swenson, Geoffrey Tabin, Daniel Tafur, Sukanto Tanoto, Edgar Taplin, Janet Tavakoli, Todd Taylor, Louise Teeple, Sarah Teller, Jocelyn Tetel, Barbara Theodorellis, Jonathan Thomas, Patricia Thomas, Patric Thusius, Robert Thwaites, Andrew Tobias, Jason Todd, Granville Toogood, Louis Toscano, Steven Townsend, Bill Tugurian, Laura Tyson, Michael Urias, Nick Valenti, Henry Valera, Chris Van Aeken, George van Amson, Gail van Lingen, Laura Van Orden, Karen Van Petten, David Vanrenen, Renee Vara, Keith Vass, Itche Vasserman, Jennifer Vaughan, Helen Vendler, John Verble, Jessica Verdejo, Jason Vickery, Alex Viner, Mary Viviano, Jon Von Planta, Norb Vonnegut, Peggy Wager, Sir David Walker, Patrick Wall, Anne Wallace, David Wallace, Gardner Wallace, Jean Wallace, Paris Wallace, Ginger Ward, Louise Wasso-Jonikas, Steve Weber, John Weinberg, Benjamin Weir, Matthew Wells, Steven Wheeler, Martha Wheldon, Andy White, John Whitehead, Bruce Whitman, Wheelock Whitney, Fred Whittemore, Marna Whittington, Kirk Wickman, Byron Wien, James Wiggins, Barrie Wigmore, Alex Williams, Ben Williams, Dan Wimsatt, Kathleen Winger, Phil Winters, Jacques Wittmer, Ursula Wittwer, Forest Wolfe, Kent Womack, Jim Wombles, Iris Wong, Nadine Wong, Sandy Wong, Stella Wong, Rick Woolworth, Richard Worley, Bill Wright, Edwin Wydler, Xiyan Xie, Eric Yamin, Sam Ye, James Yellen, Tucker York, Amanda Young, Diana Young, Pat Young, Betty Yum, Drew Zager, Ardeshir Zahedi, Shama Zehra, Lei Zeng, Jing Zhao, Jennifer Zimmerman, Shelley Zimmerman, Barbara Zuckerberg, Dina Zuckerberg, Lloyd Zuckerberg, and *Roy Zuckerberg.*

Particular energy, creativity, and diligence have characterized all the input from my teammates: *Michelle Ahn, Christen Brown, Yi Ding Chen, Caroline Chu, Denise D'Alberto, Natalie Dillon, Hal Goltz,*

Charlotte Greenough, John James, Alex Kwok, Wei-Kai Lang, Celine Ma, Mike Mascetti, Joan Park, Lily Rafii, Kyelim Rhee, Ilana Seidel, Stephanie Shen, Irene So, Elizabeth Wells, and *Richard Whitworth.*

Words cannot express the depth of my gratitude to several of my partners in this work. In many ways, this book could not have become a reality without their affirmation, persistence, patience, intelligence, enthusiasm, guidance, character, perspective, diligence, dedication, clarity of thinking, pragmatism, and high ideals. I want to thank: *Ela Aktay, Judy Brown, Annie Chang, Catherine Dassopoulos, Dave El Helou, Frances Drake, Jeanne Glasser, Jennifer King, Barbara Luxenberg, Regina Maher, Sarah Nelson, Barbara Reinhard, Josephine Giovanniello Rosenberg, Annie Rusher, Stephanie Whittier,* and *Catherine Willingham.*

It gives me great joy to here salute, love, and appreciate my family, who have unfailingly cheered me and cheered me on. In respectful homage this book is presented with my embrace to: my wife, *Diane Darst,* our children, *Elizabeth Darst* and *David M. Darst,* my brothers, *Guy Darst, Chuck Darst,* and *Dan Darst,* as well as *Kitty Darst, Josie Darst, Mary Darst, Jackson Darst, Elaine Woodall, Allison Eden, Tom Woodall, Valerie Belmont, Debra Lanman, Jonathan Lanman, J.T. Lanman, Nell Lanman, Donald Netter, Bob Wassman, Bobby Wassman,* and *Susan Wassman.*

The word "art" can be traced through the Latin language, ultimately to its ancient Indo-European root "ar," meaning "to fit together." Among our numerous modern-day dictionary definitions of art are: (i) the expression of what is beautiful, appealing, or of more than ordinary significance; (ii) the principles or methods governing a craft or branch of learning; and (iii) skill in conducting any human activity. In addition to these senses of the term "art," an important reason for naming this book *The Art of Asset Allocation* relates to the use of more than 130 illustrations and charts intended to help investors quickly grasp and retain important asset allocation and investment concepts. I wish investors much success in all market environments with the help of the art, not to mention the science, within these pages.

David M. Darst

S E C T I O N

UNDERSTANDING ASSET ALLOCATION

CHAPTER 1

ESSENTIALS OF ASSET ALLOCATION

OVERVIEW

The purpose of this chapter is to introduce the subject of asset allocation, why it is important, some of its ramifications, and how asset allocation should fit into an investor's financial thinking.

This chapter also contains a number of introductory ideas and insights about asset allocation. We first explore several of the fundamental meanings of asset allocation, including blending assets' different characteristics to produce a strong composite, recognizing tradeoffs, setting constraints on the amount of a given asset class, and diversification. Next, we diagram and review, one by one, the sequential steps involved in the asset-allocation process.

This chapter spells out the key asset-, market-, and investor-based foundations of asset allocation; later chapters discuss each of these topics in more detail. Here we pay attention to the risks and rewards of asset allocation, contrasting financial market environments in which asset allocation works best with financial circumstances in which asset allocation appears not to add much value. The chapter concludes with a review of the effects of inflation on purchasing power and the chief influences that tend to guide investors toward either of the two major groupings of assets—principal-protection assets versus principal-growth assets.

MEANINGS OF ASSET ALLOCATION

Asset allocation may mean different things to different types of investors. For many *professional investors*, asset allocation often means: (i) calculating the rates of return from, standard deviations on, and correlations between various asset classes; (ii) running these variables through a mean-variance optimization program to select asset mixes with different risk-reward profiles; and (iii) analyzing and implementing some version of the desired asset allocation in light of the institution's goals, history, preferences, constraints, and other factors.

For *individual investors*, asset allocation may or may not include these formal calculations. In general, individual investors need to pursue asset allocation with special attention to: (i) the tax status and after-tax implications of investments in a given asset class; and (ii) the investor's individual motivations, personal circumstances, and cyclical and secular market outlook.

Some of the strategic issues affecting individual investors' asset-allocation decisions include: the timing and magnitude of intergenerational income requirements; the ability to measure, withstand, and be adequately compensated for bearing risk or loss; absolute and relative performance goals and benchmarks for measuring returns; the influence of one or more concentrated investment positions; personal holdings in the form of art, jewelry, or collectibles; and meaningful financial liabilities such as mortgage debt or margin borrowing.

After a thorough review of the investor's financial profile and objectives, a disciplined asset-allocation process tends to proceed in a series of sequential steps, depicted in Figure 1.1.

First, the investor and his or her advisor examine and then spell out assumptions with regard to future expected returns, risk, and the correlation of future returns between asset classes. Second, the investor and advisor may select asset classes that best match

F I G U R E 1.1

Sequential Steps in Asset Allocation

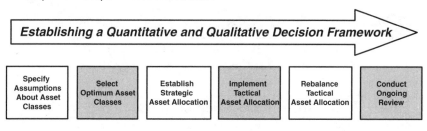

Source: The Author.

the investor's profile and objectives and that together have the maximum expected return for a given level of risk or, stated another way, the minimum risk for a given level of return. Third, the investor may establish a long-term asset-allocation policy (some investors refer to this as "Strategic Asset Allocation"), which reflects the optimal long-term standard around which future asset mixes might be expected to vary. Fourth, the investor may decide to implement Tactical Asset Allocation decisions against the broad guidelines of the Strategic Asset Allocation. Fifth, the investor will, in many instances, periodically rebalance the portfolio of assets, with sensitivity to the tax and transaction-cost consequences of such rebalancing, taking account of the Strategic Asset Allocation framework. Finally, from time to time, the investor may carefully review the Strategic Asset Allocation itself to ensure overall appropriateness given the investor's current circumstances and frame of mind, the outlook for each of the respective asset classes, and overall expectations for the financial markets.

For many investors, asset allocation has several deeper meanings beyond the mathematical optimization of returns, standard deviations, and correlations. Some of these meanings are set forth in Figure 1.2.

Very importantly, asset allocation is about *blending* the underlying characteristics of various types of asset classes to produce a type of financial alloy that possesses a more favorable risk-reward profile than any of its component elements. Further, asset allocation is about *recognizing and balancing tradeoffs*, chief among

F I G U R E 1.2

Fundamental Meanings of Asset Allocation

 Blending underlying characteristics
of various asset classes to produce a stronger
composite than any single element.

 Recognizing and balancing tradeoffs
including time horizon, capital-preservation goals,
and expected sources of return.

 Setting minimum and maximum constraints
to ensure sufficient representation, but not
overconcentration.

 Diversifying asset classes
to align portfolio and personal risk/reward
profiles, and to be compensated for bearing
nondiversifiable volatility.

Source: The Author.

them being the investor's time horizon, capital preservation goals, and expected sources of return.

Asset allocation is also about *setting minimum and maximum tradeoffs* to ensure sufficient representation, but not overconcentration, of various kinds of investments. Finally, asset allocation is centrally about *diversification* among asset classes and specific investments to align the expected risk profile of the investor's portfolio with his or her own risk profile. Rather than attempting to time the market in a limited number of asset classes, asset allocation seeks, through diversification, to provide higher returns with lower risk over a sufficiently long time frame and to compensate the investor appropriately for bearing nondiversifiable volatility.

Distilled to its essentials, asset allocation addresses four fundamental questions: (i) What is the proper mix between equities and fixed-income securities? (ii) What is the proper mix between domestic and international assets? (iii) What is the proper reference currency, and the proper degree of non-reference currency exposure? and (iv) What is the proper division of assets between conventional and alternative investments? With these questions as a backdrop, asset allocation also focuses on two key investor decisions: (i) How much price risk and purchasing-power risk is the investor prepared to take? and (ii) Does the investor intend to rebalance the portfolio with any degree of regularity, only on an occasional basis, or not at all?

FOUNDATIONS OF ASSET ALLOCATION

To increase the odds of success in asset allocation, the investor needs to take a rigorous, consistent, and thoughtful approach toward the foundations of asset allocation. Several of the most important of these foundations are set forth in Figure 1.3.

F I G U R E 1.3

Foundations of Asset Allocation

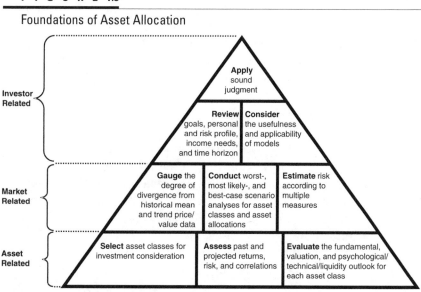

Source: The Author.

The *asset-related* foundations of asset allocation include:

- **Selection of Asset Classes:** The investor must determine which asset classes will be considered for the portfolio and, by extension, which asset classes will be excluded from consideration. For example, *within the fixed-income universe*, the investor needs to decide whether to include taxable, tax-exempt, or both kinds of these securities in the portfolio, and to determine quality (investment-grade, high-yield, or both), maturity (short-term, intermediate-term, long-term, or some combination of these), and other characteristics. Characteristics affecting the selection of *broad asset classes* include: (i) the amounts available for investment; (ii) how much time the investor can devote to asset allocation; (iii) the investor's own profile, experience, market outlook, preferences, and aversions; and (iv) other criteria, including cost, efficiency, liquidity, and perceived social impact.

- **Assessment of Asset Characteristics:** The investor needs to examine the past history of and projected outlook for the risks, return, or correlations of each asset class under consideration. The investor also must devote particular scrutiny and reflection to cases in which any of these measures—risk, return, or correlations—are projected to continue, or move counter to, historically high or low values.

- **Evaluation of the Outlook for Each Asset Class:** Asset classes should be evaluated according to rigorously applied measures that provide insight into: (i) their underlying economic and financial fundamentals; (ii) their valuations according to historical levels and relative to other assets; and (iii) the psychological, technical, and liquidity factors affecting asset prices. *Fundamental factors* include: the economic, monetary, and fiscal environment; the outlook for corporate profits and for inflation or deflation; and governmental, exchange rate, or geopolitical developments. *Valuation factors* include: the types, inputs, and applicability of asset valuation models; and specific measures of valuation (such as—for equities—price-earnings, price-to-book, price-to-sales, and dividend yield ratios, and yield gaps). *Psychology/technical liquidity factors* include: investor ownership profiles and capital flows into and out of various asset classes; sentiment measures; corporate and insider buying and selling activity; and other influences reflecting investor behavior, such as cash ratios and margin borrowing activity.

The *market-related* foundations of asset allocation include:

- **Gauging Divergence:** Charts and graphs can help investors evaluate where an asset's price and valuation levels stand in relation to cyclical and secular trends, and assess how close or how divergent such prices and valuations are from their long-term averages. For example, many financial market participants look at how long and by how much an asset class has deviated from its historical pattern of return and risk.

- **Scenario Analysis:** The purpose of conducting a series of scenario analyses is to help the investor realistically assess the probabilities of various sets of economic and financial conditions coming to pass. In this way, a variety of worst-case, most likely, and best-case events, and their resulting effects on specific assets and blends of assets, can mentally prepare the investor for some of the emotional and investment responses that may ensue.

- **Risk Estimation:** At a deep and visceral level, many investors think about risk in terms of realized or unrealized losses in the value of their assets and their net worth. Risk estimation, risk assessment, and risk control should play a prominent role in any asset-allocation activity. Among the most commonly encountered measures of risk are: (i) the standard deviation of investment returns; (ii) the worst-case loss over a given time period, ranging from one day, to one week, one month, one quarter, one year, or longer; (iii) the worst-case decline from peak to trough; and (iv) how long it takes for prices to recover to their previous peak levels.

The *investor-related* foundations of asset allocation include:

- **Investor Circumstances Review:** Investors need to reflect on and analyze their own circumstances as a crucial part of asset allocation. These circumstances include: (i) the investor's goals, experience, mentality, and psychological characteristics; (ii) the investor's demographic, income, and wealth profile, present and future family relationships, and other anticipated capital inflows and outflows through time; and (iii) the time horizon of the investing activity for which assets are being allocated.

- **Models Efficacy Analysis:** Financial, investment, and asset-allocation models serve a useful purpose in that they bring logical procedures, quantitative methods, and analytical discipline to the asset-allocation process. At the same time, overreliance on investment models can present serious drawbacks. The investor needs to probe as deeply as possible into prior and future financial conditions, extreme events, and other circumstances: (i) when the models are most applicable and useful; and (ii) when the same models are found to be of limited value.

- **Application of Judgment:** Perhaps the most important foundation element in asset allocation is the application of sound judgment and rationality to every phase of portfolio construction and ongoing investment activity. In this effort, investors should maintain a healthy skepticism and strive to look for fallacious reasoning, inappropriate and/ or inaccurate assumptions, and weak points in the asset mix, both as a whole and throughout its constituent parts.

THE RISKS AND REWARDS OF ASSET ALLOCATION

Advantages and Disadvantages of Asset Allocation

One of the chief *advantages* of asset allocation is to improve the risk-reward tradeoff of an investment portfolio. As stated earlier in this chapter, investors usually pursue this objective by selecting an appropriate mix of asset classes and underlying investments based on: (i) the investor's needs and temperament; (ii) the characteristics of risk, return, and correlation coefficients of the assets under consideration for the portfolio; and (iii) the financial market outlook. A core objective of asset allocation is to increase the overall return from a portfolio for a given degree of risk, or to reduce the overall risk from the portfolio for a targeted level of return. For asset allocation to achieve successful investment results for a given investor over any meaningful time frame, the *right asset classes* and the *right properties* need to be blended together in the *right proportions.*

A major perceived *disadvantage* of asset allocation stems from missed opportunities to participate in significant, sustained price advances in one or more of the major asset classes—a form of asset envy. In many respects, the growth of the Standard & Poor's 500 index from 1995 through 1999—with annual gains of 37.5%, 22.9%, 33.4%, 28.6%, and 21.0%, respectively—caused numerous investors to focus increasingly on U.S. large-capitalization equities and, at the same time, lose faith in the wisdom and efficacy of asset allocation. Ironically, historical perspective on many extraordinary upward (or downward) price moves in equities, bonds, commodities, real estate, and other asset classes indicates that an opportune time to pursue asset allocation, with its attendant portfolio rebalancing and diversification, comes just at that point when widespread investor opinion is highly biased in favor of prices continuing to extend their winning (or losing) streak.

When Asset Allocation Works

The opportunities for asset allocation to produce improved risk control and investment performance may be better in some financial market environments than they are in others. Allocation activity generally yields successful investment results when one or more of the following conditions are present:

♦ **Rotating Price Leadership:** Asset allocation tends to add value when no single asset class dominates other asset classes year after year. The diversification or exposure that asset allocation provides across different groups of assets in multiyear periods of rotating price leadership helps the portfolio gain from the results of outperforming assets and avoid overreliance on the results of underperforming assets.

- **Stable Relationships:** If the returns, risks (as measured by the variance in returns, or standard deviation), and performance interrelationships among asset classes remain reasonably stable over time, the financial outcomes of asset allocation may have a better chance of approximating predicted results.

- **Low Correlations:** One of the fundamental assumptions underlying asset-allocation theory is that the prices of many major asset classes do not all move in the same direction and in roughly similar magnitude at the same time. Asset allocation is usually beneficial when the prices of some financial assets zig while others zag, and vice versa.

- **Stable Ingredient/Result Profile:** One mark of a good recipe is the resilience of the quality of the finished product to small errors in the proportions of ingredients used by the chef. Similarly, successful results in asset allocation need to be reasonably forgiving as to the range of financial outcomes that are produced by small variations in the investor's mix of assets. When the investor exercises care in the selection and weighting of asset classes, the *overall* portfolio's risk-return profile should be reasonably stable, even when one or more of the specific underlying asset classes' outcomes varies from those predicted by past history or the investor's own projections.

- **Appropriate Rebalancing Activity:** An important but frequently overlooked element in the asset-allocation process is the need to monitor and make any needed adjustments to the shifts in asset weighting that result from asset classes' differing price changes. It is usually wise to follow rebalancing rules that appropriately take advantage of cyclical asset class price shifts. At the same time, the investor's portfolio rebalancing activity should avoid prematurely curbing exposure to asset classes experiencing strong *secular growth* and also avoid the excessive redeployment of capital into asset classes that are continuing to exhibit *secular price erosion.*

◆ **Investor Judgment and Skill:** The ultimate outcome of asset allocation depends highly on the investor's own judgment and skill in selecting and weighting asset classes, asset managers, and, in some cases, specific investments. Mastery of this skill set is not easy and requires, among other traits, patience, perception, insight, courage, resolution, realism, flexibility, and, not least, self-control and self-knowledge.

When Asset Allocation Does Not Work

Under certain conditions, asset allocation may produce investment results that widely diverge from the investor's original intentions. When this occurs, one or more of the following conditions may have contributed to the shortfall:

◆ **Unusual Financial Environments:** When one asset class (such as large-capitalization U.S. growth equities) outperforms another asset class (such as mid-capitalization equities, value equities, emerging markets equities, or bonds) by a meaningful margin for several years in a row, investors may take a dim view of asset allocation. In such circumstances, investors: (i) tend to fixate on and want the outperformance of the most successful asset class; (ii) look askance at the lower blended returns generated by a mix of high-performing and low-performing asset classes; and (iii) generally focus on the *returns* component of asset allocation, rather than on the equally important *risk management* and *risk control* features of asset allocation. In short, asset allocation tends to depend on asset classes' valuations and annual returns reverting to their long-term mean, and in the late stages of a protracted bull (or bear) market, divergences from the mean may very well persist far beyond historical norms.

◆ **Unstable Relationships:** Another basic tenet of asset allocation is the expectation that the returns, risk (as measured by standard deviation), and correlation coefficients of the principal asset classes will remain within some reasonable bounds of their historical performance and, further, that the relationships among these measures for different asset classes will hold true over time. When these relationships break down, or exhibit abnormal patterns of behavior for lengthy periods, the blended results produced by a given asset allocation may diverge sharply from expected outcomes.

- **Rising Correlations:** When the correlations between groups of assets are high, they tend to move up or down in price together, and the risk-reducing benefits of diversification are considerably reduced or even nullified. During eras when markets and market participants in different regions of the world and in different asset classes become increasingly linked through such media as the Internet, electronic communications networks, global television, multi-location financial intermediaries, and various kinds of asset-bridging derivatives markets, price correlations tend to rise in many cases. This phenomenon has at times occurred during episodes of market instability or exogenous financial shocks, precisely when investors might rely most heavily on diversification and asset allocation to cushion against such turbulence. A number of worldwide-focused investors may view their portfolios on a sectoral basis by industry group (such as energy, pharmaceuticals, or consumer staples), by currency bloc, or by pan-national fixed-income-instrument category (such as sovereign debt or mortgage paper). As a result, asset prices in these global groupings may show signs of rising correlations and coincident price movements. In such periods, asset-allocation activity that assumes and relies on geographical price divergence may yield disappointing results.

- **Unstable Ingredient/Result Profile:** The asset-allocation process tends to not produce satisfying results if small variations in the mix of assets in the investor's asset allocation produce wide swings in the portfolio's expected outcomes. It is often helpful to test the expected risk and return of several slightly varying asset allocations under a range of possible financial scenarios. In simple cases, this can be done by hand with a pocket calculator, and in more complex scenarios, it can be accomplished with one of the asset-allocation optimization programs available through a financial services firm or on the Web through various investing services sites. Through this process, called sensitivity analysis, the investor can determine the strengths and weaknesses of an array of asset-allocation frameworks.

- **Inappropriate Rebalancing Activity:** When contemplating whether and how to rebalance a portfolio's asset alloca- tion, investors should keep two crucial decisions in mind. First is the frequency of rebalancing activity. Some investors consider rebalancing an asset allocation as frequently as quarterly, whereas others do not make shifts in their targeted asset allocation more than every one to three years, or even less often than that. Second is the set of rebalancing guidelines for readjusting the portfolio in response to shifts in asset weightings that are brought about by upward or downward price moves in each asset class. Significant detractions from the hoped-for benefits of asset allocation may occur when the investor rebalances the asset weightings too frequently (or too infrequently) and lets asset price losses or gains trigger responses that are not in the investor's long-term best interests.

- **Investor Error:** Human beings are fallible, and often allow excessive feelings of confidence or certainty to cause them to minimize or ignore risk. Conversely, excessive caution may cause investors to avoid altogether the prudent assumption of risk. In some ways, asset allocation rests upon the expectation that no one can predict the invest- ment performance of several asset classes with certainty year in and year out. Investors can, however, reduce the gap between intended and actual results by devoting time and care to matching their asset allocation to their risk tolerance, time horizon, income needs, and tax status.

PRINCIPAL-PROTECTION ASSETS AND PRINCIPAL-GROWTH ASSETS

For long-term investors, *purchasing-power risk* is at least as important as multi-period market-price volatility risk. In contrast, for short-term investors who may not have the opportunity for good and bad years of investment performance to offset one another, *market-price volatility risk* tends to be more important than purchasing-power risk.

The implications of time duration and purchasing-power risk for asset allocation thus generally lead to greater emphasis: (i) in *longer-term* portfolios, on equities and equity-like assets that have relatively higher long-term returns and higher volatility; and (ii) in *shorter-term* portfolios, on principal-protection, interest-generating assets that have relatively lower long-term returns and lower volatility. These investor asset-allocation guidelines are summarized in Figure 1.4.

F I G U R E 1.4

Principal-Protection Assets and Principal-Growth Assets

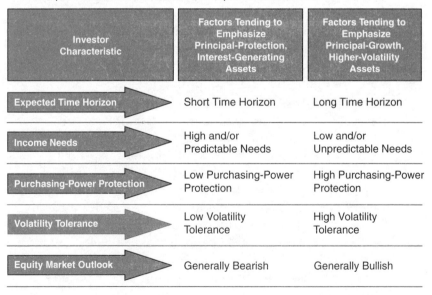

Investor Characteristic	Factors Tending to Emphasize Principal-Protection, Interest-Generating Assets	Factors Tending to Emphasize Principal-Growth, Higher-Volatility Assets
Expected Time Horizon	Short Time Horizon	Long Time Horizon
Income Needs	High and/or Predictable Needs	Low and/or Unpredictable Needs
Purchasing-Power Protection	Low Purchasing-Power Protection	High Purchasing-Power Protection
Volatility Tolerance	Low Volatility Tolerance	High Volatility Tolerance
Equity Market Outlook	Generally Bearish	Generally Bullish

Source: The Author.

Investors who have specific income requirements, and who can also adopt a long-term investment horizon, may: (i) prefer to spend small amounts of principal from the body of the portfolio and/or from capital gains to augment dividend and interest income, rather than (ii) constructing a portfolio that attempts to meet specified income targets strictly through dividend and interest income. Such investors believe that an overemphasis on assets that generate a high proportion of their total annual return from dividend and interest payments (such as bonds, preferred stocks, and utility and real estate investment trust shares) may in the long run give up the opportunity for significant capital growth offered by equities and equity-like alternative assets such as real estate, venture capital, and private equity. The so-called *total return approach*, which takes capital gains into account as well as dividend and interest income, has been followed by a number of university endowments, many of which have formulated spending rules to keep any disbursements of income plus designated amounts of principal well below their portfolios' projected annual total return.

THE EFFECTS OF INFLATION ON PURCHASING POWER

Two of the most fundamental, yet least appreciated, aspects of asset allocation are the role of time and the magnitude of purchasing-power risk. Investors who can construct and manage their wealth with a longer time frame have many more chances to use the gains earned in good years to offset the damages wrought by short-term volatility.

History shows that for most mainstream asset classes, including bonds and stocks, as the investor's actual holding period lengthens, from 1-year holding periods, through 5-year and 10-year holding periods, to 20-year holding periods, the realized rate of return tends to converge toward the asset's long-term average rate of return (approximately 10.6% for the Standard & Poor's 500 index and approximately 5.4% for long-term U.S. Treasury bonds).

Even at relatively modest annual rates of *inflation*, over a 20-year time period, the effective loss in an investment's purchasing power can be debilitating. Figure 1.5 presents the ratio of remaining purchasing power to the investor's original purchasing power for

F I G U R E 1.5

Ratio of Remaining Purchasing Power to Original Purchasing Power

Annual Inflation Rate	After 1 Year	After 5 Years	After 10 Years	After 20 Years
1%	0.99	0.95	0.90	0.82
2%	0.98	0.90	0.82	0.67
3%	0.97	0.86	0.74	**0.54** *
4%	0.96	0.82	0.66	0.44
5%	0.95	0.77	0.60	0.36
6%	0.94	0.73	0.54	0.29
7%	0.93	0.70	0.48	0.23
8%	0.92	0.66	0.43	0.19
9%	0.91	0.62	0.39	0.15
10%	0.90	0.59	0.35	0.12
12%	0.88	0.53	0.28	0.08
15%	0.85	0.44	0.20	0.04

* On a pretax basis, an investor would need an asset value of 1.85 times the original value merely to maintain purchasing power.

Source: The Author.

average annual inflation rates ranging from 1% to 15% and for time periods of 1, 5, 10, and 20 years.

As shown in Figure 1.5, at an annual inflation rate of 3%, after 20 years, the investor has lost 46% (1.00 minus the 0.54 of *remaining* purchasing power) of his or her *original* purchasing power on an investment whose principal value is assumed to remain unchanged. Under such a scenario, the investor needs the asset value to grow to 1.85 times its original value merely to maintain its original purchasing power (1.85 times 0.54 equals 1.00). If taxes have to be paid, the required growth will be even larger.

Throughout modern financial history, the rate of inflation has not remained constant, but has risen, fallen, and at times even turned negative (deflation) in response to monetary conditions, the state of the domestic and global economy, currency movements, supply-demand conditions for goods and services, producer and consumer expectations, and other factors. Although there is no assurance that the average annual inflation rate will remain at a certain positive level over long stretches of time, varying amounts of purchasing-power erosion have for many years in the past been a fact of life and represent a significant risk that the investor should address squarely and prepare for.

CHAPTER 2

THE ASSET-ALLOCATION PROCESS

OVERVIEW

To better understand the asset-allocation process, investors need to think about their evolving financial requirements, the various types of asset allocation, and how asset allocation interacts with other investment disciplines. Investors' asset-allocation needs tend to change as their wealth levels change over time. This chapter explores some ways to meet these needs as investors seed, build, and realize their fortunes.

The main *types* of asset allocation—style, orientation, and inputs—are also discussed here. An asset allocation *style* may be conservative, moderate, or aggressive; the *orientation* of an asset allocation may be strategic, tactical, or a blend of the two; and the main *inputs* to an asset allocation may be quantitative, qualitative, or both. This chapter also introduces a process known as *performance-attribution*, which shows how to deconstruct the specific sources of contribution to an investor's strategic benchmark return versus his or her actual tactical results.

The chapter concludes with a description of how the process of allocating assets informs the selection of style and sector, region and country, industry and security, investment managers, currency, and market timing.

MATCHING ASSET CLASSES WITH WEALTH LEVELS AND INCOME NEEDS

As investors progress through the main stages of wealth creation and wealth realization, their needs and concerns evolve, as does the array of asset classes appropriate for their investment portfolios. This progression is depicted in Figure 2.1.

In Figure 2.1, investors are shown to generally progress through one or more of the following wealth stages during their lifetime:

*   **Wealth-Seeding Phase:** Investors at the beginning—or wealth-seeding—stage are concerned primarily with basic

F I G U R E 2.1

Matching Asset Classes with Wealth Levels and Investor Needs

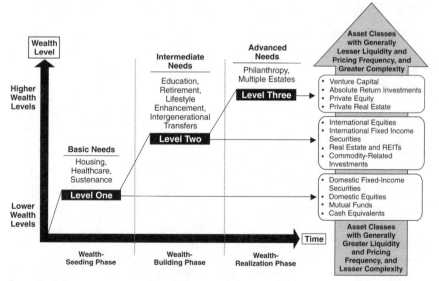

Source: The Author.

needs such as housing, healthcare, food, clothing, and insurance. If surplus capital is available for investments, such investors should consider asset classes that are easy to understand and that offer a reasonable degree of liquidity. These asset classes generally include cash equivalents, domestic equities, and domestic fixed-income securities, held directly or through mutual funds.

- **Wealth-Building Phase:** As investors progress through the growth—or wealth-building—phase, their needs expand to include education, lifestyle enhancement, retirement, and intergenerational transfers of assets. At the same time, their range of investable asset classes may expand in many cases to include not only the asset classes described in the wealth-seeding phase, but also international equities, international fixed-income securities, real estate and REITs, and perhaps commodity-related investments.

- **Wealth-Realization Phase:** In those cases where investors acquire significant wealth—in the wealth-realization phase—possibly through a liquidity event such as a merger or acquisition, a securities offering, or inheritance, their needs may expand yet again, to include philanthropy and the maintenance of multiple estates. In this phase, investors may contemplate investing in an even broader range of asset classes in addition to those considered by investors in the wealth-seeding and wealth-building phases. These more advanced asset classes also may be characterized by a lower level of liquidity, possibly less frequency of valuation and pricing, and a somewhat greater degree of complexity. These assets include venture capital, absolute return investments such as certain kinds of hedge funds and fund of funds structures, private equity, and private real estate.

Please be aware that the asset matchings illustrated in Figure 2.1 are merely general guidelines. In many cases, investors in the wealth-realization phase will want to give full consideration to the investments normally encountered in the wealth-building and wealth-seeding phases. However, as a general rule, investors in the early stages of wealth development should most often avoid investing a meaningful portion of their fortunes in asset classes intended for high-wealth investors in the wealth-realization phase.

TYPES OF ASSET ALLOCATION

The *scope* of investors' asset allocation essentially describes and defines their universe of investment activity. This investment universe may include *all* geographic regions and asset classes, or it may be limited to *one* country or region (such as North America, Europe, Latin America, or Asia) and be relatively confined to equities, bonds, and cash. After delineating the scope of their asset allocation, investors can properly consider the *types* of asset allocation in their portfolios. Asset-allocation types may be classified according to their style, their orientation, and their inputs, and they may be combined in a variety of ways, as shown in Figure 2.2.

Asset Allocation Styles

The *style* of an asset allocation may be described as conservative, moderate, or aggressive. It is difficult to characterize any particular asset or investor temperament as strictly conservative, moderate, or aggressive in all market climates, as these styles have some degree of interaction with and dependency on prevailing investment norms and the financial market environment. A top-quality asset-allocation style may be considered *highly conservative* (such as

F I G U R E 2.2

Types of Asset Allocation

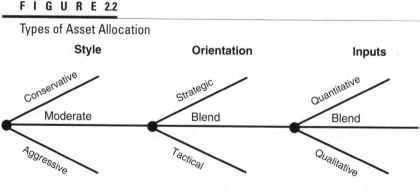

high weightings in bonds and cash) under stable financial markets with low inflation, yet be deemed *highly aggressive* under other circumstances, such as volatile financial markets with high inflation and wide swings in interest rates and bond prices.

At the turn of the new millennium, a conservative asset-allocation style had: (i) relatively *lower* levels of exposure to equities, equity-like investments (such as high-yield and emerging-markets debt, real estate, absolute return investments, certain hedge funds, private equity, and venture capital investments); and foreign investments and currencies; possibly combined with (ii) relatively *higher* levels of exposure to cash and short-term investments, fixed-income securities, and domestic investments and currencies.

Under the same financial circumstances, an aggressive asset-allocation style had: (i) relatively *higher* levels of exposure to equities, equity-like investments, and foreign investments; possibly combined with (ii) relatively *less* exposure to cash and short-term investments, fixed-income securities, and domestic investments.

In a similar financial environment, a moderate asset allocation would be positioned somewhere between the description of a conservative asset allocation and the description of an aggressive asset allocation.

Other features of asset-allocation styles include the objectives and intended price behavior of the portfolio. In general, a conservative asset-allocation style should exhibit lower price volatility (as measured by the standard deviation of returns from the portfolio) and, possibly, generate a somewhat greater proportion of its returns in the form of dividend and interest income rather than primarily through capital gains. By contrast, an aggressive asset-allocation style may exhibit higher price volatility and generate a somewhat greater proportion of its returns in the form of capital gains rather than income. A moderate asset-allocation style attempts to exhibit price volatility below that of the aggressive style and above that of the conservative style, and generate returns from a mixture of income and capital gains.

Asset-Allocation Orientation

As shown in Figure 2.2, the *orientation* of an asset allocation can be described as strategic, tactical, or a blend of these orientations.

A strategic asset allocation attempts to establish the best long-term mix of assets for the investor, with relatively less focus on short-term market fluctuations. The strategic asset allocation should reflect: (i) the investor's intermediate and long-term perspective on financial markets and specific asset classes; (ii) distinctive aspects of his or her long-term goals for the assets that might tilt the asset allocation in a particular direction (such as toward a certain currency or lower investment liquidity, greater variability in returns, or less certainty as to the timing of potential returns); and (iii) various means, and the reliability thereof, for monitoring and managing long-term risk.

Strategic asset allocation serves several purposes. It helps determine which asset classes to include in the long-term asset mix. For example, some investors may decide to identify and spell out in writing their preferences for long-term exposures to asset class subgroups, such as small-capitalization equities, emerging markets equities, convertible securities, or real estate investment trusts (REITs). Usually, strategic asset allocation changes relatively infrequently, primarily in response to: (i) meaningful changes in the investor's risk profile and returns objectives; (ii) altered expectations about assets' returns, standard deviations, and/or correlations; and (iii) the emergence of a new class of assets that the investor had not considered previously.

The overall strategic asset allocation may find expression in a written document, on a stand-alone basis or as part of an Investment Policy Statement, and can serve as a guidepost for effecting any tactical asset-allocation moves. Through the use of policy ranges, the investor can indicate how closely or loosely any tactical asset shifts may vary from the strategic allocation. For example, an investor's strategic asset allocation may call for a 30% weighting in high-grade bonds, with a 10% allowable band (i.e., as high as 40% and as low as 20%).

To enhance the usefulness of the strategic asset allocation, investors may select appropriate indices for each asset class in the strategic asset allocation, to create a blended benchmark return against which the overall tactical investment results of the asset allocation may be measured. An example of this calculation methodology is shown in Table 2.1.

In the sample comparison of the *strategic* asset-allocation *benchmark* (column 5) returns with the investor's *tactical* results *actually generated* (column 6), the portfolio's actual return exceeded the strategic blended benchmark return for the year by 440 basis points, or 4.4% (20.9% versus 16.5%, or column 6 minus column 5).

Columns 7, 8, and 9 in Table 2.1 deconstruct the specific sources of this outperformance through a process known as *performance-attribution analysis.* Performance-attribution analysis seeks to identify the specific positive or negative contributions to the difference between: (i) the *strategic* allocation benchmark return (produced by the strategic asset-allocation weightings for each asset class multiplied by the total return for the index representing each asset class); and (ii) the investor's *tactical* return (produced by the investor's tactical asset allocation multiplied by the total return actually earned by the investor's designated vehicle or manager for each asset class).

Simply expressed, performance-attribution analysis helps determine: how much of the difference in returns is due to (i) strategic versus tactical asset-allocation decisions; and (ii) outperformance or underperformance by the investor (or his or her asset manager) compared with the performance of the benchmark index representing each specific asset class. Similar methodologies may be used within a given asset class. For example, performance-attribution analysis may be employed within the Large-Capitalization U.S. Equities class to determine: how much of the investor's actual performance is due to (i) industry sector-weighting decisions versus the S&P 500 benchmark; and (ii) specific security selection within each industry sector versus the benchmark security composition for that sector.

In Table 2.1, of the +4.4% difference between the strategic allocation benchmark return and the investor's tactical return, +2.0% is attributable to the *asset-allocation decision* and +2.4% to the *investor's tactical return* versus the benchmark index return. Of the +4.4% total return differential: +3.4% came from large-capitalization U.S. equities (of which +1.6% was due to the decision to tactically allocate 50% to this asset class, versus 45% for the investor's strategic asset allocation, and +1.8% was due to the fact that the investor's own—or externally hired—asset management results, while

T A B L E 2.1

Strategic and Tactical Benchmark Returns for Representative Strategic Asset Allocation

(Total Nominal Returns in U.S. Dollars)

		(1)	(2)	(3)	(4)
Asset Class	Index	Investor's Strategic Asset Allocation	Investor's Tactical Asset Allocation	Latest Year's Index Total Return for Strategic Allocation	Latest Year's Tactical Return for Investor
Large-Capitalization U.S. Equities	S&P 500	45%	50%	28.6%	32.5%
Japanese Equities	MSCI Japan	5%	3%	5.1%	4.0%
Emerging Markets Equities	MSCI Emerging Markets Free	5%	2%	−22.0%	−17.0%
U.S. Long-Term Treasury Bonds	Ibbotson Associates Long-Term Government Bonds	30%	30%	13.1%	14.6%
High-Yield Bonds	High-Yield (Credit Suisse Upper/Middle Tier) Index	5%	5%	0.6%	−1.0%
Cash	30-Day U.S. Treasury Bills	10%	10%	4.9%	5.2%
Total		100%	100%		

Total Blended Strategic Benchmark Return

Total Blended Investor's Tactical Return

Total Difference in Strategic vs. Tactical Return

Source: The Author.

+32.5%, outperformed the S&P 500 Index's 28.6% return for that year). Meanwhile, +0.8% of the return differential owes to emerging markets equities (of which +0.5% was due to the tactical asset-allocation decision to put only 2% of the portfolio in this class,

(5) = (1) × (3) Contribution of Asset Class to Strategic Allocation Blended Benchmark Return	(6) = (4) × (2) Contribution of Asset Class to Investor's Tactical Return	(7) = (6) − (5) (7) = (8) + (9) Total Difference Between Strategic Allocation Benchmark Return and Investor's Tactical Return	(8) = [(2) − (1)] × 4 Difference Attributable to Tactical Asset Allocation Decision	(9) = (1) × [(4) − (3)] Difference Attributable to Tactical Return vs. Index Return
12.9%	16.3%	3.4%	1.6%	1.8%
0.3%	0.1%	−0.2%	−0.1%	−0.1%
−1.1%	−0.3%	0.8%	0.5%	0.3%
3.9%	4.4%	0.5%	0.0%	0.5%
0.0%	−0.1%	−0.1%	0.0%	−0.1%
0.5%	0.5%	0.0%	0.0%	0.0%
		4.4%	2.0%	2.4%
16.5%				
	20.9%			
4.4%		4.4%	= 2.0%	+ 2.4%

versus 5% in the investor's strategic asset allocation; another +0.3% can be traced to the investor's own [or externally hired] asset management results, −17.0%, which outperformed the IFCI Composite Index's −22.0%). Another +0.5% of the return came from U.S. Long-Term Treasury Bonds (of which 0.0% was due to the tactical asset-allocation decision, as the investor's 30% allocation to this asset class exactly matched the 30% strategic asset allocation, and +0.5% was due to the investor's own [or externally hired] asset management results, +14.6%, which outperformed the results of the Ibbotson Associates Long-Term Government Bond Index). The asset classes consisting of Japanese Equities, High-Yield Bonds, and Cash made negligible or slightly negative contributions to the difference between the strategic-allocation benchmark return and the investor's tactical return.

A strategic asset allocation can also be an important reference guide, when extremes of market enthusiasm or despondency tempt investors to shift their asset allocation dramatically. Although times of financial upheaval often present attractive buying or selling opportunities, these are generally best addressed from a tactical standpoint rather than changing the overall strategy in response to short-term market swings. A strategic asset allocation may help bring a certain degree of reflection, reason, and a disciplined, methodical pace to important asset-deployment decisions.

A tactical asset allocation may take different forms and serve somewhat different purposes than a strategic asset allocation. Whereas some investors may adopt a primarily tactical approach to asset allocation, viewing the long term as an effectively ongoing series of short-term time frames, others use the tactical asset allocation to either reinforce or counteract the portfolio's strategic-allocation polices. A common tactical asset-allocation time horizon may be one year, although some large professional and individual investors with adequate resources and the mentality to do so may make tactical asset-allocation adjustments (or at least hold meetings to consider such adjustments) as frequently as quarterly, monthly, or even weekly.

Tactical asset allocation tends to be utilized when investors have a reasonably firm conviction that an asset class is strongly overvalued (or undervalued), and are willing to back up that conviction on a short- to intermediate-term basis by underweighting (or overweighting) the asset class in question. In some cases, investors may use exchange-traded basket products, index futures, options, or other derivative instruments to adjust their exposure quickly. Owing to the price-aware, opportunistic nature of tactical asset allocation, special forms of tactical risk management can include price alerts, limit and stop-loss orders, simultaneous-transaction techniques, and value-at-risk (VAR) models.

As a matter of practice, many investors use a combination of tactical and strategic allocation. Tactical allocation helps investors anticipate and respond to significant shifts in asset prices (akin to making short-term corrections in a trans-oceanic sailboat race). Strategic allocation allows investors to map out a long-term plan for deploying assets to attain multiyear or even multidecade goals (in trans-oceanic sailing terms, akin to charting a course, navigating, and executing the large-scale maneuvers required to sail from starting point to destination).

Asset-Allocation Inputs

Figure 2.2 also focuses on the types of inputs that investors use to formulate the percentages of the overall portfolio that they will invest in each asset class. They can determine these percentages with the aid of quantitative models, qualitative judgments, or a combination of these approaches.

The *quantitative* approach generally involves several steps, most of which have been rendered easier and more accessible by the broader distribution of asset-allocation software on disk, CD-ROM, or the Internet. First, investors might select asset classes and sub-classes for the portfolio. One such list of 25 asset classes and sub-classes, in Table 7.1 in Chapter 7, together with an index or source of the benchmark, can help investors track investment perform-ance. Table 7.1 also shows the asset classes' annual investment returns and standard deviations of performance for a variety of long time intervals, with shorter time periods when data covering the entire period are not available.

Second, investors can spell out their assumptions about: (i) future expected returns; (ii) risk (expressed in standard deviation terms) of the asset classes being considered; and (iii) correlations of future expected returns between each pair of asset classes. As a starting point, many investors consider past investment perform-ance, standard deviations, and returns correlations during varying time frames, ranging from a few years to 5-, 10-, 20-, and 30-year periods.

Third, a so-called portfolio-optimization program can generate a set of possible asset allocations, each with its own level of expected risk and return. From these results, investors can select a series of what are known as Efficient Frontier asset allocations, showing portfolios with the minimum risk for a given level of expected return, as well as portfolios with the maximum expected return for a given level of risk.

Fourth, after reviewing the asset allocations suggested by the portfolio-optimization modeling software, investors may very well decide to set upper and/or lower percentage limits on the maximum and minimum amounts allowed in the portfolio. In this last step, investors impose constraints on the optimization software.

As a practical matter, many investors who use portfolio-optimization modeling software do not rely strictly on the software's outputs. Like pilots who use a combination of automatic controls and manual guidance, these investors realize that program-determined results are determined by *projections* of return, risk, and correlation assumptions. These projections may or may not resemble past history, and may or may not need to be adjusted in some cases for higher transaction costs, taxes, custody, and reporting. As a result, these results need to be reviewed carefully for soundness and consistency with investors' own preferences and aversions.

As has been noted, the *qualitative* approach can play a role in portfolio construction, working in tandem with quantitative tools, or as the primary input to portfolio design. The qualitative elements of asset allocation often rely heavily on the analysis of historical data, charts, statistical tools, and other models. But what sets the qualitative approach apart from the quantitative approach is its primary reliance on the investor's own informed judgment and other sources of investment counsel, rather than mathematical algorithms or software programs, to establish initial portfolio weightings and then alter them at judicious intervals.

Generally speaking, qualitative asset-allocation methodologies assess *fundamental* measures (such as economic indicators and earnings estimates, monetary conditions, and changes in wage, price, and productivity trends), *valuation* measures (such as real interest rates, the slope of the yield curve, price-earnings ratios, and price-to-book ratios), and *psychology/technical/liquidity* measures (such as funds flows, investor sentiment indicators, volatility indices, and price and volume charts). These assessments, carried out on an absolute basis and relative to long-term historical averages, are often expressed in terms of the number of standard deviations above or below their long-term mean.

Another important component of the qualitative approach involves discussion and consultation with trusted sources about assumptions, past and projected returns, and cross-asset relationships to test their soundness, consistency, and practical validity. It is difficult to overemphasize the importance of reflection, common sense, and rational thinking in selecting and developing the qualitative and quantitative inputs to asset allocation. All the models, theoretical constructs, and rules-based allocation packages available to the investor are of little value if they are not leavened with wit, will, and wisdom.

INTERSECTIONS OF ASSET ALLOCATION WITH OTHER DISCIPLINES

For asset allocation to produce successful investment results over time, skill in selecting and rebalancing assets must be harnessed to certain other disciplines. In many cases, all but the most multi-talented, experienced, and polymathic investors may rely to some degree on resources such as asset managers, consultants, rating organizations, newsletters, and financial intermediaries for expertise and advice.

Figure 2.3 sets forth selection decisions affecting asset allocation. Several of these disciplines are described in the following paragraphs.

Style and Sector Selection

If asset allocation can be described as the process of deciding which forests to select, *style and sector selection* can be described as deciding which species of trees to select. Style and sector selection also encompasses so-called theme, industry, or group selection. This discipline

F I G U R E 2.3

Selection Decisions Affecting Asset Allocation

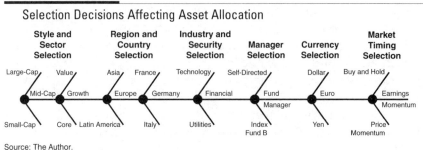

Source: The Author.

applies to a great many of the major asset classes besides equities. In some financial market environments, most sectors within a given asset class tend to move roughly together, whereas under other financial market conditions, sectors may exhibit a considerable degree of returns divergence. Investors therefore should pay attention to these distinctions, whether or not they are in fact employed to demarcate separate subdivisions within specific asset classes.

For instance, within the bond asset class, investors can allocate assets by *credit rating* (ranging from investment grade, or higher-rated bonds, to high-yield, or lower-rated bonds), by *maturity or duration* (ranging from short-, to intermediate-, to long-maturity issues), and by *sector* (ranging from government, to government agency, to corporate, to tax-exempt municipal bonds).

Within the equities asset class, investors can allocate assets by *market capitalization* (ranging from large-, to mid-, to small-capitalization stocks), by *style* (including growth, value, and core styles, the latter being an opportunistic blend of the growth and value approaches), by *theme* (ranging from defensive to aggressive, or from so-called New Economy to Old Economy), or even by *pan-sectoral themes* (such as environmentally sensitive, demographically driven, or export-oriented equities). The aggregate multiyear investment returns from investing in various sectors and styles, as well as in selected countries and regions, are shown in Tables 7.2, 7.3, and 7.4 in Chapter 7.

Within the alternative investments class, investors can allocate assets, among other classifications, by sector (such as real estate, venture capital, private equity, and hedge funds) and by style (including merger arbitrage, convertible arbitrage, options-based strategies, distressed investments, LBO activity, or mezzanine-round investments).

Region and Country Selection

For many investors, international investing represents the initial step toward broader diversification. Depending on where, when, and for how long such trans-national investment forays are made, the results can span the spectrum from highly successful, to merely acceptable, to regrettable.

As with sectors and styles, in some financial market environments, asset classes within a particular region or country may move in the same direction and in roughly the same magnitude, whereas at other times, a region or country may decidedly march to its own tune and not move in sync with returns in other parts of the world. For example, at times during the 1980s, the 1990s, and after the turn of the new millennium, when Japanese fixed-income and equities prices rose or fell, prices for similar assets in other regions and countries moved in a different direction. Investors need to assess the short-term and long-term probability that regional or country-based diversification actually will produce diversification in returns and results that are relatively uncorrelated across geographies. When *geographically different* markets produce *highly correlated* results, regional and country selection may not be as important as style, sector, and industry selection.

Industry and Security Selection

Continuing to use the field of forestry as an analogy, the selection of individual industry groups and securities is akin to the selection of specific trees. Investors commit funds to industries and/or securities as discrete investments, as separate account management by an investment advisor, or through pooled vehicles such as mutual funds, closed-end funds, unit investment trusts, or private partnerships.

Although numerous studies have emphasized the importance of asset allocation in explaining the variation of total returns from investing over time, these findings do not diminish the significance of industry and security selection for the investor. For example, Table 7.7 in Chapter 7 shows that performance of the 10 major industry subgroups of the Standard & Poor's 500 index have diverged widely year to year from 1991 through 2006.

Manager Selection

In many respects, manager selection is one of the most important disciplines affecting asset allocation, particularly for investors who allocate funds across a wide range of asset classes. Investors may decide to manage some portion of the assets themselves—either directly or through index funds and/or exchange-traded funds such as SPDRs (known as "Spiders") (S&P 500-based), Diamonds (Dow Jones Industrial Average-based), Cubes (Nasdaq 100-based), or Webs (World Equity Benchmark Shares, which track 17 different foreign markets). Even though not all asset classes and their principal subgroups have easily locatable and tradable index funds or exchange-traded funds, their number and usage by all types of investors grew during the 1980s and especially in the 1990s. In a related trend, some large professional investors employ futures and other types of derivative instruments as a quick, efficient, and low-cost means of increasing or decreasing index-based exposure to a specific asset class.

Relative to the 1970s and early 1980s, the amount and quality of information available to investors about asset managers have increased significantly. At the same time, the number of asset managers also has expanded dramatically. Reflecting these developments, the manager-selection process has steadily improved through: (i) standardization of performance-reporting methods; (ii) broader dissemination channels through print media and Internet-based distribution systems; and (iii) various financial firms' asset-manager access programs that provide due diligence and selection of managers, periodic reporting, and formalized manager inclusion and retention procedures, for a fee.

Currency Selection

After choosing a reference or base currency, investors should decide whether to hedge the portfolio's currency exposure arising from currencies outside the base currency. Although hedging can reduce overall volatility of returns generated by a given asset allocation, such hedging can have significant costs.

Although investors can find powerful and plausible arguments for and against hedging any external currency asset in the portfolio, in the short term, unanticipated and unhedged currency shifts can add to or detract from external assets' investment returns. It therefore behooves investors to evaluate the degree and likely impact of any currency revaluations or devaluations on the foreign currency-denominated returns from a given asset, as well as how these possible currency changes might affect the base-currency equivalent of the foreign-currency returns.

Market Timing

The attractiveness and perceived utility of market-timing methods tend to be influenced by investors' expectations for price behavior in the specific asset class in which they invest. For instance, when asset prices have been steadily rising, and are expected to continue doing so, investors tend to downplay the usefulness of market timing, preferring instead to invest any available funds immediately rather than attempting to do so on a phased basis, or on market-price retrenchments. In contrast, if asset prices have been moving in an up-and-down or sideways pattern, and are expected to persist in this fashion, investors and asset managers tend to accentuate market-timing methods. In attempting to time the market, investors may add funds to or withdraw funds from the asset class in question according to a periodic schedule, seeking to take advantage of downward or upward price fluctuations.

Another intersection of market timing and asset allocation involves the mentality and objectives of investors. Investors who view asset allocation as a means of preserving and growing the value of their portfolios in a risk-controlled manner over the long term probably will utilize a buy-and-hold policy. Versions of this policy can be structured around the principles of letting the winning asset classes continue to grow while pruning the losing asset classes. This policy generally works when the winning asset class performs well over a sustained period of time. But this approach can also produce highly disappointing results when funds that increasingly are shifted to the high-performing asset classes later suffer magnified losses if and when the concentrated-weighting asset classes decline in value.

Within the equity asset class, some investors have at times pursued various momentum-based incarnations of market timing. *Earnings-momentum strategies* involve buying the shares of companies that are exhibiting strong growth in reported results and analysts' earnings forecast revisions, and selling the shares of companies experiencing a slowdown in the rate of growth in earnings and analysts' earnings forecast revisions. In a similar vein, *price-momentum strategies* are based on buying shares of companies whose prices are advancing and selling the shares of companies whose prices are declining. Such momentum-based methods, involving high rates of portfolio turnover and trading activity, can be risk-prone and quite removed from the basic principles and goals of asset allocation. As a result, investors who construct their portfolios on the basis of sound asset allocation principles tend to restrict their momentum-based market-timing techniques to a fairly constrained proportion of their total asset allocation, if they use them at all.

S E C T I O N

THE MECHANICS OF ASSET ALLOCATION

CHAPTER 3

ASSET-ALLOCATION TOOLS
AND CONCEPTS

OVERVIEW

Many of the underpinnings of asset-allocation theory and practice build upon the highly evolved, but relatively straightforward, principles of statistics, economics, and finance. A general appreciation of how this body of learning informs the mechanics of asset allocation can help investors understand the advantages, as well as the limitations, of the theories, concepts, and tools that drive and define the inner workings of these investing disciplines. Armed with this knowledge, investors can approach the real-world applications of asset allocation with more realistic expectations.

This chapter explores the origins, evolution, and practical uses of Modern Portfolio Theory and Efficient Market Theory, and provides perspective on the long-term returns and risks of various asset classes and portfolios of assets. Next, some analytical ideas will help investors understand the long-term distribution of assets' returns and various measures of how assets' returns can vary, or exhibit risk, compared with their average historical returns.

This chapter explains, calculates, and applies the concepts of standard deviation and correlation to the asset-allocation and investment process. Other helpful concepts also are described here, including the Efficient Frontier, beta, alpha, and various return-per-unit-of-risk measures such as the Sharpe ratio, Sortino ratio, and Treynor ratio. After reviewing some of the main features of the Capital Asset Pricing Model (CAPM) and diagramming the Capital Market Line and Security Market Line, this chapter explores the processes, outputs, advantages, and disadvantages of asset-allocation mean-variance optimization models.

MODERN PORTFOLIO THEORY/EFFICIENT MARKET THEORY

During the late 20th Century, a number of important new concepts and investment insights emerged. Many of these ideas were evolutionary, some were revolutionary enough to win Nobel prizes in economics for their progenitors, and quite a few are still being enhanced and extended. Investors who familiarize themselves with these intellectual breakthroughs can apply these powerful tools to asset allocation. Just as a skillful driver does not need to comprehend the workings of an internal-combustion engine and drive-train operations to operate an automobile, an investor does not have to understand the mechanics of asset allocation's theoretical and practical nuances to take advantage of their key tenets and principles. However, investors can benefit greatly from a basic awareness of how asset-allocation models work and their statistical and mathematical underpinnings, strengths and weaknesses, and applications in the real world in varying market environments.

Several economic, statistical, and financial principles affecting asset allocation are set forth in Figure 3.1, ranging from general market concepts to asset-specific concepts.

The arrow in Figure 3.1 summarizes and traces the approximate progression of many theoretical and practical constructs affecting asset allocation. Modern Portfolio Theory and one of its cornerstones, Efficient Market Theory, deal with how market prices reflect and react to information. Normal Probability Distribution and z-score, and the Mean, Variance, Semi-Variance, and Standard Deviation of Distribution draw upon the discipline of statistics and

F I G U R E 3.1

Selected Economic, Statistical, and Financial Concepts Affecting Asset Allocation

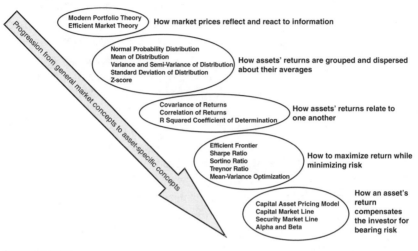

Source: The Author.

address how assets' returns are grouped and dispersed about their mean or statistical averages. Two additional principles applied to asset allocation are the Covariance and the Correlation of assets' returns. The R Squared (R^2) Coefficient of Determination measures the degree to which movements in the overall market determine fluctuations in portfolio returns.

Several other concepts—including the Efficient Frontier, Mean-Variance Optimization, the Sharpe ratio, the Sortino ratio, and the Treynor ratio—help investors evaluate the tradeoff between risk and return and offer potential means of minimizing risk while maximizing return. The Capital Asset Pricing Model, the Capital Allocation Line, the Security Market Line, and the measures known as beta and alpha measure how an asset's return compensates the investor for bearing risk. The following sections discuss each of these building blocks.

Modern Portfolio Theory and Efficient Market Theory

At its deepest level, Modern Portfolio Theory (MPT) and one of its chief branches, Efficient Market Theory (EMT), relate to asset allocation by asserting that the only way for an investor to earn higher returns is by taking on more risk. According to EMT, asset prices in an efficient market reflect all relevant, available, *known* information, as well as the market's consensus expectations concerning *unknown* information. In an efficient market: (i) asset prices quickly and appropriately respond to new information; (ii) alert investors rapidly take advantage of any mispricings of assets until they are eliminated; (iii) future cash flows of assets are properly predicted on the basis of all relevant information; and (iv) the interest rates used to discount these future cash flows correctly reflect the degree of risk of these projected streams of capital.

Based on the chief assertions of EMT, a number of market observers have concluded that asset prices follow a random pattern, also called a *random walk.* The *strong form* of EMT maintains that asset prices reflect all public and private information for the past, present, and consensus-forecast future. In an even stronger version of the strong form of EMT, the discount rate for an asset is not posited to change over time, and asset prices in such an efficient market demonstrate random-walk behavior. In practice, many observers hold that the discount rate for a given asset *does* vary over time, thus negating the random character of asset prices. The *semi-strong form* of EMT asserts that asset prices reflect only *public* information about the past, present, and consensus future, and the *weak form* of EMT indicates that asset prices only incorporate public, *past* information.

In an efficient market, investors are said to receive no compensation for bearing risk or volatility that can be easily dissipated or avoided through diversification. Stated another way, diversifiable risk earns no compensation. As a result, investors need to pay at least as much attention to *risk reduction* through diversification as they pay to the quest for high asset returns. In the early 1950s, the economist Harry Markowitz quantitatively explored the notion that diversification is not achieved merely through an increased *number* of investments. Instead, diversification requires investing in assets whose *patterns of returns* are distinct and different enough from one another to partially or wholly offset one another's returns and thus reduce overall portfolio volatility. The asset-allocation process thus draws upon and ties into MPT and EMT by focusing on the effects that including, limiting, or excluding a specific asset class will have on the risk (volatility) and return characteristics of the portfolio as a whole.

The combination of EMT with analysis of investor behavior and the practice of asset allocation yields several important implications. First, the basic attractiveness of an asset derives not merely from its potential to generate a high expected return but also from a *blend* of characteristics, including its expected return, its volatility of returns (risk), and, not least, the degree to which its returns relate to the returns of other assets in the portfolio. Second, history has witnessed substantial variability in the returns generated by various asset classes, and appropriate asset-allocation strategies can help reduce the effects of these price fluctuations on the overall portfolio. Third, the compression of a large proportion of the broad, long-term upward or downward movements in asset prices into a relatively limited number of actual trading days underscores the difficulty, if not the futility, of market-timing tactics for most investors.

Fourth, the mechanics of asset allocation can be marshaled to help the investor: (i) measure and monitor risk; (ii) make decisions about whether it may be worthwhile to increase or decrease the aggregate risk level of the portfolio; and (iii) scientifically evaluate how a new or existing asset will add to or detract from the overall character of the portfolio. Fifth, many investors often expect to achieve higher returns with less volatility (risk) than is in fact the case. By directing attention to the *range* of returns generated by assets in different subperiods, and to the interrelationships among different assets within the portfolio, EMT helps asset allocation balance the desire for gain against fear of loss. Sixth, one study[1] makes the case that asset-allocation policy explains: (i) 90% of the *variability* of portfolio returns *across time*; (ii) 40% of the *variation* of portfolio returns *across funds*; and (iii) 100% of the *amount* of absolute return of the *portfolio.*

ASSET AND PORTFOLIO RETURNS

Asset Class Returns

Investors hold assets to generate returns in the form of: (i) changes in capital value (capital gains or losses, also known as price return);

---

[1] "Does Asset Allocation Policy Explain 40%, 90%, or 100% of Performance?" by Roger G. Ibbotson and Paul D. Kaplan, *Financial Analysts Journal*, January/February 2000, available at *www.aimr.org/knowledge/pubs/faj/*.

(ii) income (primarily in the form of current and reinvested dividends and interest); or (iii) a combination of the two. Figure 3.2 shows the geometric and arithmetic mean returns, standard deviation of returns, and distribution of returns for selected stocks, bonds, bills, and inflation for the years 1926 through 2006.

F I G U R E   3.2

Annual Total Returns, 1926–2006

Series	Geometric Mean	Arithmetic Mean	Standard Deviation	Frequency Distribution[1]
Large Company Stocks	10.4%	12.3%	20.1%	
Small Company Stocks[2]	12.7	17.3	33.2	
Long-Term Corporate Bonds	5.8	6.1	8.6	
Long-Term Government Bonds	5.3	5.7	9.4	
Intermediate-Term Government Bonds	5.3	5.5	5.7	
U.S. Treasury Bills	3.8	3.9	3.2	
Inflation	3.1	3.1	4.4	

Annual Total Return
(In 5% Ranges)

Notes: [1]The horizontal axis represents the annual total return in increments of 5% ranges. The vertical bars represent the frequency distribution of the number of years, from 1926 to 2006, falling within each specific percentage range.
[2]The single data point for the 1933 Small Company Stock Total Return, 142.9%, is not shown in the distribution diagram.

Source: *Stocks, Bonds, Bills, and Inflation: 2007 Yearbook*, Ibbotson Associates, Morningstar; The Author.

For large company stocks from 1926 through 2006, the *arithmetic mean* annual total return was 12.3%, representing a *simple average* (also known as the *mean*) of all the returns, high and low, positive and negative, generated over this 81-year time frame. The *final value* of an asset's growth is calculated by compounding the *arithmetic mean*, not the geometric mean. The *geometric mean* for the large company stocks, 10.4%, is the compound rate of return over the years from 1926 through 2006. Reflecting the real-world uncertainty inherent in the above- and below-average returns that constitute average results, the arithmetic mean is used as the discount rate and the rate to or from which the standard deviation of returns (explained more fully below) is added or subtracted.

For holding periods of 1 year, 5 years, 10 years, 15 years, and 20 years, Table 3.1 displays the highest and lowest single-period compound rates of return for selected stocks, bonds, bills, and inflation.

For *20-year holding periods*, the highest compound annual rate of return from investing in large company stocks was 17.87% per annum, achieved during the 1980–1999 interval. By contrast, the lowest compound 20-year annual rate of return from investing in large company stocks was 3.11% per annum (of which a considerable portion may have been represented by annual dividend payments), from 1929 through 1948. Out of 62 overlapping 20-year time periods, large company stocks generated positive returns in each period, and were the highest returning asset class nine times among the asset groupings shown in Table 3.1, with small company stocks the highest 20-year return generator in the remaining 53 of the 62 twenty-year time periods.

Portfolio Returns

Holding *various combinations* of U.S. asset classes can yield meaningful investment insights about their returns. Figure 3.3 shows the *one-year* portfolio returns generated by a variety of asset mixes.

Based on the results of 673 sample *one-year* portfolios from January 1950 through December 2006, an asset allocation consisting of *90% stocks, 0% bonds, and 10% cash* produced an average return of 12.2%. During this period, the best one-year result of this

T A B L E 3.1

Multiperiod Compound Annual Returns, 1926–2006

Series	Maximum Value Return	Maximum Value Year(s)	Minimum Value Return	Minimum Value Year(s)	Number of Years Positive Returns (Out of 81 Years)	Number of Years Highest Returning Asset
Annual Returns						
Large Company Stocks	53.99%	1933	−43.34%	1931	58	16
Small Company Stocks	142.87	1933	−58.01	1937	57	36
Long-Term Corporate Bonds	42.56	1982	−8.09	1969	64	6
Long-Term Government Bonds	40.36	1982	−9.18	1967	60	9
Intermediate-Term Government Bonds	29.10	1982	−5.14	1994	73	2
U.S. Treasury Bills	14.71	1981	−0.02	1938	79	6
Inflation	18.16	1946	−10.30	1932	71	6
5-Year Rolling Period Returns					(Out of 77 Overlapping 5-Year Periods)	
Large Company Stocks	28.55%	1995–99	−12.47%	1928–32	67	23
Small Company Stocks	45.90	1941–45	−27.54	1928–32	68	42
Long-Term Corporate Bonds	22.51	1982–86	−2.22	1965–69	74	7
Long-Term Government Bonds	21.62	1982–86	−2.14	1965–69	71	2
Intermediate-Term Government Bonds	16.98	1982–86	0.96	1955–59	77	2
U.S. Treasury Bills	11.12	1979–83	0.07	1938–42	77	0
Inflation	10.06	1977–81	−5.42	1928–32	70	1
10-Year Rolling Period Returns					(Out of 72 Overlapping 10-Year Periods)	
Large Company Stocks	20.06%	1949–58	−0.89%	1929–38	70	20
Small Company Stocks	30.38	1975–84	−5.70	1929–38	70	42
Long-Term Corporate Bonds	16.32	1982–91	0.98	1947–56	72	6
Long-Term Government Bonds	15.56	1982–91	−0.07	1960–59	71	0
Intermediate-Term Government Bonds	13.13	1982–91	1.25	1947–56	72	2
U.S. Treasury Bills	9.17	1978–87	0.15	1933–42/ 1934–43	72	1
Inflation	8.67	1973–82	−2.57	1926–35	66	1
15-Year Rolling Period Returns					(Out of 67 Overlapping 15-Year Periods)	
Large Company Stocks	18.93%	1985–99	0.64%	1929–43	67	12
Small Company Stocks	23.33	1975–89	−1.31	1927–41	64	51
Long-Term Corporate Bonds	13.66	1982–96	1.02	1955–69	67	4
Long-Term Government Bonds	13.53	1981–95	0.40	1955–69	67	0
Intermediate-Term Government Bonds	11.27	1981–95	1.45	1945–59	67	0
U.S. Treasury Bills	8.32	1977–91	0.22	1933–47	67	0
Inflation	7.30	1968–82	−1.59	1926–40	64	0
20-Year Rolling Period Returns					(Out of 62 Overlapping 20-Year Periods)	
Large Company Stocks	17.87%	1980–99	3.11%	1929–48	62	9
Small Company Stocks	21.13	1942–61	5.74	1929–48	62	53
Long-Term Corporate Bonds	12.13	1982–01	1.34	1940–69	62	0
Long-Term Government Bonds	12.09	1982–01	0.69	1940–69	62	0
Intermediate-Term Government Bonds	9.97	1982–01	1.58	1930–59	62	0
U.S. Treasury Bills	7.72	1972–91	0.42	1929–50	62	0
Inflation	6.36	1966–85	0.07	1926–45	62	0

Source: *Stocks, Bonds, Bills, and Inflation: 2007 Yearbook*, Ibbotson Associates, Morningstar.

F I G U R E 3.3

One-Year Portfolio Returns for Selected U.S. Asset Allocations

U.S. Domestic Risk and Reward: One-Year Returns[1,2]

One-Year Return Summary: January 1950–December 2006

Portfolio Mix:	A	B	C	D	E	F	G	H	I	J
Stocks	90.0%	80.0%	70.0%	60.0%	50.0%	40.0%	30.0%	20.0%	10.0%	0.0%
Bonds	0.0%	10.0%	20.0%	30.0%	40.0%	50.0%	60.0%	70.0%	80.0%	90.0%
Cash	10.0%	10.0%	10.0%	10.0%	10.0%	10.0%	10.0%	10.0%	10.0%	10.0%
Year Ending Dec. 2006	14.8%	13.3%	11.9%	10.4%	9.0%	7.5%	6.0%	4.6%	3.1%	1.7%
Worst Return	−34.2	−30.9	−27.5	−24.2	−20.9	−17.5	−14.2	−10.8	−12.0	−14.3
Average Loss	−8.4	−7.4	−6.2	−5.0	−4.1	−3.4	−3.3	−3.2	−3.2	−3.6
Average Return	12.2	11.6	10.9	10.3	9.6	8.9	8.3	7.6	7.0	6.3
Average Gain	17.8	16.3	14.9	13.8	12.5	11.3	10.1	9.5	9.3	9.6
Best Return	55.8	52.9	50.1	47.2	44.4	43.1	44.8	46.4	48.1	49.7
% Negative	21.1	19.9	19.0	18.9	17.5	16.0	13.7	14.7	18.9	25.3
% Positive	78.9	80.1	81.0	81.1	82.5	84.0	86.3	85.3	81.1	74.7

Total Number of Portfolios: 673

Note: [1]Rolling one-year returns using 625 sample portfolios. [2]**Stocks**: S&P 500 Total Return; **Bonds**: Ibbotson U.S. Long-Term Government Total Return (20 years); **Cash**: U.S. 30-Day T-Bill Total Return.

Source: Ibbotson Associates, Inc.

asset allocation was a gain of 55.8%, while the worst one-year result was a loss of 34.2%. Overall, this asset allocation produced positive investment outcomes in 78.9% of the 673 one-year holding periods, with an average 17.8% gain. However, this asset allocation yielded negative investment results in 21.1% of the 673 one-year holding periods, with an 8.4% average loss.

Similarly, over the same 57-year time period, an asset allocation consisting of *0% stocks, 90% bonds, and 10% cash* produced an average return of 6.3%. The best one-year result of this asset allocation was a 49.7% gain, and the worst one-year result was a 14.3% loss. Overall, this asset allocation produced positive investment outcomes in 74.7% of the 673 one-year holding periods, with an average gain of 9.6%. However, this asset allocation yielded negative investment results in 25.3% of the 673 one-year holding periods, with an average loss of 3.6%.

Reflecting on the long series of one-year investment results produced by the *90% stocks* portfolio compared with the *90% bonds* portfolio yields several observations. First, the heavily equity-weighted asset allocation generated a significantly higher average return, 12.2%, than the 6.3% average return generated by the heavily bond-weighted asset allocation. Second, the range of annual returns for the 90% bonds portfolio, from a worst-case loss of 14.3% to a best-case gain of 49.7%, was wider than the range of annual returns for the 90% stocks portfolio, which was bounded by a worst-case loss of 34.2% and a best-case gain of 55.8%. Third, and perhaps counterintuitively, the percentage of negative one-year holding period results, 25.3%, was higher for the 90% bonds portfolio than the 21.1% of the time that the 90% stocks portfolio generated negative one-year returns.

Figure 3.4 contains similar returns data for the same population of U.S. asset allocations covering 625 *five-year* holding-period portfolios from January 1950 through December 2006.

As the U.S. asset-holding period stretches from one year to five years, (i) the high-low range of five-year annual returns is narrower than the high-low range of one-year returns; (ii) the percentage of time that the investment results ended up in negative territory is much less for the five-year holding periods than for the one-year holding periods; and (iii) the average return for each of the 10 U.S. asset allocations is reasonably close for the five-year holding periods to the returns for the same asset allocations for the one-year holding periods.

The methodology described above can be extended to international portfolio returns from a variety of global asset mixes—ranging from: 50% U.S. stocks, 40% international stocks, 0% U.S. bonds, 0% international bonds, and 10% cash; to 0% U.S. stocks, 0% international stocks, 80% U.S. bonds, 10% international bonds, and 10% cash. Ten of these representative asset mixes are shown in Figure 3.5.

Owing to the limited availability of data for several international asset classes stretching back beyond the 1980s or the mid-1970s, fewer sample portfolios can be used to calculate the average

F I G U R E 3.4

Five-Year Portfolio Returns for Selected U.S. Asset Allocations

U.S. Domestic Risk and Reward: Five-Year Returns[1,2]

□ Worst Return   ▨ Average Return   ■ Best Return

Five-Year Return Summary: January 1950–December 2006

Portfolio Mix:	A	B	C	D	E	F	G	H	I	J
Stocks	90.0%	80.0%	70.0%	60.0%	50.0%	40.0%	30.0%	20.0%	10.0%	0.0%
Bonds	0.0%	10.0%	20.0%	30.0%	40.0%	50.0%	60.0%	70.0%	80.0%	90.0%
Cash	10.0%	10.0%	0.0%	10.0%	10.0%	10.0%	10.0%	10.0%	10.0%	10.0%

Year Ending Dec. 2006	5.8%	5.9%	5.8%	6.1%	6.2%	6.3%	6.4%	6.5%	6.6%	6.7%
Worst Return	−3.1	−2.2	−1.9	−0.4	−0.6	−1.0	−1.3	−1.7	−2.1	−2.4
Average Loss	−1.3	−0.7	−0.5	−0.3	−0.4	−0.5	−0.5	−0.6	−0.7	−0.8
Average Return	11.1	10.6	9.5	9.5	8.9	8.4	7.9	7.3	6.8	6.3
Average Gain	11.9	11.0	9.7	9.5	9.0	8.5	8.0	7.4	7.0	6.7
Best Return	27.5	26.3	24.3	23.9	22.7	22.1	22.0	22.4	22.7	23.1
% Negative	6.2	4.0	2.1	0.3	0.3	0.5	1.0	1.4	2.4	6.1
% Positive	93.8	96.0	97.9	99.7	99.7	99.5	99.0	98.6	97.6	93.9

Total Number of Portfolios: 625

Note: [1]Rolling five-year returns using 625 sample portfolios. [2]**Stocks**: S&P 500 Total Return; **Bonds**: Ibbotson U.S. Long-Term Government Total Return (20 years); **Cash**: U.S. 30-Day T-Bill Total Return.

Source: Ibbotson Associates, Inc.

returns for *global* asset allocations than the number of sample portfolios containing *only U.S.* asset classes.

Based on the investment results of 192 sample *one-year* portfolios from January 1990 through December 2006, an asset allocation consisting of 50% U.S. stocks, 40% international stocks, 0% U.S. bonds, 0% international bonds, and 10% cash produced an average return of 9.9%. During this time period, the best one-year result of this asset allocation was a gain of 40.8%, and the worst one-year result was a loss of 24.2%. Overall, this asset allocation produced investment outcomes that were positive in 81.3% of the 192 one-year

F I G U R E 3.5

One-Year Portfolio Returns for Selected Global Asset Allocations

Global Risk and Reward: One-Year Returns[1,2]

Portfolio Mix:	A	B	C	D	E	F	G	H	I	J
U.S. Stocks	50.0%	45.0%	40.0%	35.0%	30.0%	25.0%	20.0%	15.0%	6.0%	0.0%
Global Stocks	40.0%	35.0%	30.0%	25.0%	20.0%	15.0%	10.0%	5.0%	4.0%	0.0%
U.S. Bonds	0.0%	8.0%	17.0%	27.0%	36.0%	45.0%	54.0%	63.0%	72.0%	80.0%
Global Bonds	0.0%	2.0%	3.0%	3.0%	4.0%	5.0%	6.0%	7.0%	8.0%	10.0%
Cash	10.0%	10.0%	10.0%	10.0%	10.0%	10.0%	10.0%	10.0%	10.0%	10.0%

One-Year Return Summary: January 1990–December 2006

Year Ending Dec. 2006	19.0%	17.1%	15.2%	13.2%	11.3%	9.4%	7.4%	5.5%	4.0%	2.2%
Worst Return	−24.2	−20.3	−16.2	−12.0	−8.0	−5.5	−3.8	−5.5	−7.0	−8.4
Average Loss	−12.4	−10.5	−8.8	−6.5	−3.8	−2.1	−1.8	−2.4	−3.1	−4.4
Average Return	9.9	9.8	9.7	9.6	9.5	9.4	9.3	9.2	8.9	8.7
Average Gain	15.1	14.2	13.2	12.5	12.0	11.2	10.2	10.1	10.2	10.5
Best Return	40.8	36.9	33.0	29.0	26.5	26.9	27.5	28.2	27.7	28.0
% Negative	18.8	17.7	16.1	15.1	15.6	13.5	7.8	7.3	9.9	12.0
% Positive	81.3	82.3	83.9	84.9	84.4	86.5	92.2	92.7	90.1	88.0

Total Number of Portfolios: 192

[1]Rolling one-year returns using 192 sample portfolios.

[2]U.S. Stocks: S&P 500 Total Return; U.S. Bonds: U.S. Long-Term Government Total Return (20 years); Cash: U.S. 30-Day T-Bill Total Return; International Stocks: MSCI EAFE Total Return; International Bonds: JP Morgan Global Bond Index Total Return.

Source: Ibbotson Associates, Inc.

holding periods, and in such circumstances, the average gain was 15.1%. However, this asset allocation yielded negative investment results in 18.8% of the 192 one-year holding periods, in which the average loss was 12.4%.

Figure 3.6 contains similar returns data for the same population of *global* asset allocations covering 144 *five-year* holding periods over the time span.

As the global asset holding period extends from one year to five years: (i) the range of five-year annual returns is narrower than the range of one-year returns; (ii) the worst five-year annual

F I G U R E 3.6

Five-Year Portfolio Returns for Selected Global Asset Allocations

Global Risk and Reward: Five-Year Returns[1,2]

	Worst Return	Average Return	Best Return
J	5.6%	8.4%	12.2%
I	5.0%	8.4%	12.3%
H	4.4%	8.6%	12.7%
G	3.7%	8.5%	12.9%
F	2.5%	8.5%	14.1%
E	1.1%	8.4%	15.2%
D	-0.2%	8.4%	16.4%
C	-1.6%	8.3%	17.6%
B	-3.0%	8.3%	18.7%
A	-4.3%	8.2%	19.9%

□ Worst Return ▨ Average Return ■ Best Return

Five-Year Return Summary: January 1990–December 2006

Portfolio:	A	B	C	D	E	F	G	H	I	J
U.S. Stocks	50.0%	45.0%	40.0%	35.0%	30.0%	25.0%	20.0%	15.0%	6.0%	0.0%
Global Stocks	40.0%	35.0%	30.0%	25.0%	20.0%	15.0%	10.0%	5.0%	4.0%	0.0%
U.S. Bonds	0.0%	8.0%	17.0%	27.0%	36.0%	45.0%	54.0%	63.0%	72.0%	80.0%
Global Bonds	0.0%	2.0%	3.0%	3.0%	4.0%	5.0%	6.0%	7.0%	8.0%	10.0%
Cash	10.0%	10.0%	10.0%	10.0%	10.0%	10.0%	10.0%	10.0%	10.0%	10.0%
Year Ending Dec 2006	9.3%	9.0%	8.7%	8.3%	8.0%	7.7%	7.3%	7.0%	7.0%	6.8%
Worst Return	-4.3	-3.0	-1.6	-0.2	1.1	2.5	3.7	4.4	5.0	5.6
Average Loss	-1.3	-0.9	-0.8	-0.2	N/A	N/A	N/A	N/A	N/A	N/A
Average Return	8.2	8.3	8.3	8.4	8.4	8.5	8.5	8.6	8.4	8.4
Average Gain	10.8	9.5	8.6	8.4	8.4	8.5	8.5	8.6	8.4	8.4
Best Return	19.9	18.7	17.6	16.4	15.2	14.1	12.9	12.7	12.3	12.2
% Negative	21.5	11.8	2.8	0.7	0.0	0.0	0.0	0.0	0.0	0.0
% Positive	78.5	88.2	97.2	99.3	100.0	100.0	100.0	100.0	100.0	100.0

Total Number of Portfolios: 144

[1]Rolling five-year returns using 144 sample portfolios.

[2]**U.S. Stocks**: S&P 500 Total Return; **U.S. Bonds**: U.S. Long-Term Government Total Return (20 years); **Cash**: U.S. 30-Day T-Bill Total Return; **International Stocks**: MSCI EAFE Total Return; **International Bonds**: JP Morgan Global Bond Index Total Return.

Source: Ibbotson Associates Inc.

returns are in positive territory for the majority of the portfolios; and (iii) there is a reasonably wide margin for each of the 10 global asset allocations between the one-year holding period returns and the five-year holding period returns, with the five-year group lower than the one-year group.

Normal Frequency Distribution of Returns

Examination of the annual returns from holding a single asset class, or a portfolio composed of several asset classes, usually reveals a pattern of distribution of returns. For example, Figure 3.2 earlier in this chapter shows the distribution of returns over the 1926–2006 period for six U.S. asset classes and inflation. This figure also illustrates that the returns for long-term corporate bonds, long-term government bonds, intermediate-term government bonds, U.S. Treasury Bills, and inflation tend to skew somewhat toward positive results and are fairly closely grouped around their mean. At the same time, the returns for large company stocks and small company stocks feature several periods of negative results and are scattered, or dispersed, more widely around their mean.

A pattern of all possible future returns from investing in an asset, or in a portfolio of assets, is said to follow *normal distribution* if it traces a continuous, symmetric, bell-shaped curve centered on its mean and described by the degree of its variance, or standard deviation from the mean. A schematic representation of two normal probability distributions, one with high dispersion of returns and another with low dispersion of returns, is shown in Figure 3.7.

According to the principles of statistics, the probability that a single observation of a normally distributed population will fall within plus or minus *one* standard deviation of its mean is 68.28%, within *two* standard deviations of its mean is 95.44%, and within *three* standard deviations of its means is 99.72%. Expressed in a different way, the probability that a single observation of a normally distributed population will be more than one standard deviation *above or below* its mean is 31.72%, more than two standard deviations *above or below* its mean is 4.56%, and more than three standard deviations *above or below* its mean is 0.28%.

The degree of asymmetry in a non-normal frequency distribution compared to a normal distribution is referred to as its *skewness*, and the state or quality of flatness or peakedness of the frequency distribution curve is called its *kurtosis*, from the Greek word for curvature. In practice, for some asset classes, such as equities, returns happen to occur with a frequency *toward each end of the bell-shaped curve* somewhat more often than would be the case if they followed a perfectly normal distribution of returns, a condition known as *leptokurtosis*. When this happens, the mean and variance of returns are no longer sufficient measures for asset-allocation

F I G U R E 3.7

Examples of Normal Probability Distribution of Returns

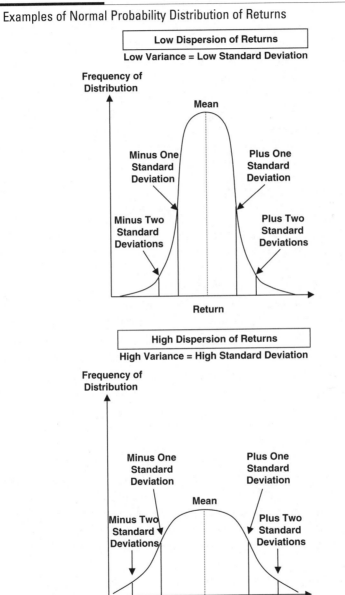

Source: The Author.

mean-variance optimization in the context of Modern Portfolio Theory.

Another useful and increasingly used term to describe the position of an observation (such as annual returns) in a frequency distribution is *z-score*. The z-score of a percentile ranking represents the number of standard deviations that an observation lies *above or below the mean of a normal frequency distribution*. For example, the z-score of the 95th percentile in a normal distribution is 1.645, indicating that the 95th percentile of the distribution is 1.645 standard deviations above the 50th percentile, or the mean of the distribution.

Estimating Expected Returns

Asset allocation involves the estimation and projection of *future* expected returns for each asset class. In general, but not in all cases, investors attempt to predict future returns by relying to a large extent on *past, historical*, patterns of arithmetic mean returns for asset classes, with appropriate adjustments reflecting an investor's expectations about financial market conditions, supply-demand factors affecting specific asset classes, and other circumstances. The use of previous years' returns as a guide to future returns assumes what is called the *stationarity* of return patterns over time. In fact, returns patterns do evolve over time, and investors need to treat data and forecasts with a generous admixture of care and realism.

One methodology for estimating expected returns involves a three-step process. In the first step, the investor selects, or calculates, a risk-free benchmark rate of return. In the second step, the investor calculates or derives a market-risk premium rate of return for each asset class. In the final step, the investor adds the risk-free benchmark rate to the risk premium rate to produce the expected rate of return for the asset class under consideration.

Two sample calculations of expected returns are set forth in Figure 3.8.

The first example shown in Figure 3.8 calculates the *expected* return from holding large company stocks by adding an equity risk premium of 6% to the 6% *expected* risk-free benchmark rate, in this case, of 30-year U.S. Treasury bonds. This produces an *expected*

F I G U R E 3.8

Estimating Expected Returns

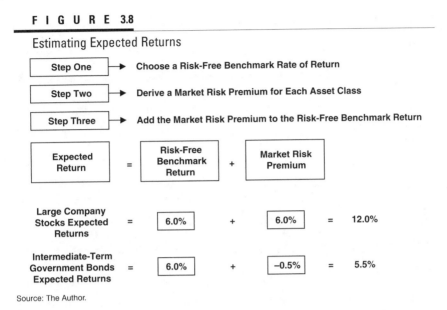

Source: The Author.

annual return of 12%. In recent years, a great deal of discussion has been generated about: (i) whether to use the U.S. Treasury 30-year bond, the U.S. Treasury 10-year bond, or another instrument for the risk-free benchmark rate of return; and (ii) whether the equity risk premium should be 6, 4, 2, or perhaps even 0%. Regardless of the investor's own views concerning these two issues, this commonly used procedure for estimating expected returns is worthwhile.

The second sample calculation in Figure 3.8 combines an intermediate government bond risk premium of –0.5% with the *expected* risk-free benchmark rate of 6% to produce an *expected* annual return of 5.5%. This example projects the market-risk premium of investing in intermediate government bonds to be 0.5% *less* than the annual return from investing in the benchmark risk-free asset.

Because of the potential fallibility of using historical data to express future results with a high degree of certainty, and the need to take account of *unexpected* future results, investors should forecast and express future returns and portfolio results in terms of *ranges* around expected returns.

ASSET AND PORTFOLIO RISK

Definitions and Types of Risk

There are several different and equally valid meanings and definitions of risk. Leslie Rahl of Capital Market Risk Advisors presented a list of 48 kinds of risk facing financial companies in the October 2000 issue of the Federal Reserve Board of New York *Economic Policy Review*. Some investors think of risk as the chance of loss or the actual experience of loss. Investors' tolerance for risk can vary substantially from one person to another, and even within the same person from one financial market environment to another or from one time period to another. Ironically, for the *long-term* investor, volatility of returns is not the primary risk; instead, the major risk is the diminution of purchasing power from the long-term erosive effects of consumer price inflation. In contrast, for *short-term* investors, volatility of returns may often take precedence over inflation. The worksheets (Figures 9.7, 9.9, and 9.11) and the risk mitigation matrix (Figure 9.12) in Chapter 9 present several practical aspects of risk management and risk control (pages 364–388).

Many commonly used risk measures rely on historical data, are subject to change as circumstances change through time, and thus need to be treated with care and considered together with a variety of different risk measures. Many investors consider some risks—ones that have a very low probability of occurring and/or a very low cost or consequence if they do take place—to be immaterial. Here are three resources for further exploring financial risk:

- The *Financial Times*'s comprehensive 10-part series "Mastering Risk," from April through June 2000, addresses the techniques used to identify, measure, and manage risk.
- **RiskMetrics** web site, *riskmetrics.com*, offers nine rules of risk management.
- **The Global Association of Risk Professionals'** web site, *garp.com*, provides several risk-related reference sources.

Viewed from a more formal, statistical standpoint, risk can be defined as the uncertainty—expressed as the variability, or standard deviation—of possible investment returns around the expected return of an asset or a portfolio of assets. Although *volatility* can be mathematically quantified, *an investor's volatility tolerance is subjective* and usually can be measured only with a fair degree of imprecision. In addition to capital price risk or volatility risk, investors face other forms of qualitative and quantitative risks, such as tracking and semi-tracking risk, and catastrophic or worst reasonable-loss risk. Still other risks include inflation or purchasing-power risk, business-cycle risk, currency risk, credit or default risk, event risk, liquidity risk, prepayment risk, reinvestment risk, and systemic risk. A number of financial market participants employ a measure of market risk called Value at Risk (VAR), which uses the assumed normal probability distribution of profit and loss for the assets in a portfolio to calculate the overall risk of the portfolio. For example, one gauge of VAR might be the percentage loss that would have been exceeded 5% of the time, based on historical returns over a certain time period such as one week. This measure would be referred to as the 95%/one-week VAR. An introduction to VAR can be found at *contingencyanalysis.com*.

An increasingly used measure of risk-adjusted investment performance is known as M-squared, named after its two developers, Franco Modigliani and Leah Modigliani. M-squared represents the return on an investment when that investment is adjusted to the same volatility (risk level) as the overall market with which the investment is being compared. M-squareds that exceed their benchmark market returns indicate that their investments returned more for their risk than the market did, and M-squareds which are less than their benchmark market returns indicate that their investments did not return as much as the market.

The market-wide, undiversifiable, *systematic* risk of investing in an asset class as a whole is considered to be market risk. The price risk that investors attempt to minimize or eliminate altogether is known as diversifiable, residual, or *unsystematic* risk. Another name for unsystematic risk is *idiosyncratic* risk. Every investment asset has elements of both systematic and unsystematic risk.

Variance and Standard Deviation

Investors can take account of the positive and the negative differences from the mean of an asset's returns over time by subtracting the average return (the mean) from each individual return. These differences, also known as deviations, are then squared to give equal treatment to positive and negative results, and they are then added together. The arithmetic average of the resulting total is known as the *variance*. The square root of the variance is known as the *standard deviation*, which is a key measure of the dispersion, variability, or volatility of a data series around its mean. Simply stated, standard deviation gauges the probability of a return being near the expected mean return. Table 3.2 calculates the variance and standard deviation for the 10-year returns of the Nasdaq Composite Index from 1997 through 2006.

To calculate the annual deviation of each individual year's return, just subtract the annual arithmetic mean return of 12.4% for

T A B L E 3.2

Calculation of Variance and Standard Deviation

Nasdaq Composite Index Price Return, 1997–2006

Calendar Year	Year	Return	Deviation from Mean	Squared Deviation from Mean
1997	1	21.6%	9.2	84.4
1998	2	39.6%	27.2	738.9
1999	3	85.6%	73.1	5,349.1
2000	4	−39.3%	−51.7	2,676.7
2001	5	−21.1%	−33.5	1,122.3
2002	6	−31.5%	−44.0	1,933.7
2003	7	50.0%	37.6	1,410.8
2004	8	8.6%	−3.9	14.9
2005	9	1.4%	−11.1	122.6
2006	10	9.5%	−2.9	8.6
Sum of 10 Years		124.47		1,346.2
Annual Arithmetic Average or Mean =		12.4%	Variance =	1,346.2

Standard Deviation = Square Root of $\sqrt{1,346.2}$ = 36.7%

Source: The Author and Bloomberg.

the 10-year period from each individual year's return. Then square and total the absolute value of each deviation to arrive at an average variance. The square root of the variance, 36.7% (the standard deviation of the series), has the benefit of being calculated and expressed in the same units (percentage points of return) as the underlying data population. Expressed in statistical terms, an investor in the Nasdaq Composite Index in this 10-year time frame had roughly a 67.1% probability of earning an annual return in any given year between −20.5% (the mean return, 12.4%, *less* one standard deviation, 36.7%) and 49.1% (the mean return, 12.4%, *plus* one standard deviation, 36.7%).

In general, a high standard deviation of returns indicates a high probability that the actual return from investing in an asset will differ from its expected return. The standard deviation of a series of data expresses the extent to which data points in that series differ from their arithmetic mean, not from their geometric mean. By statistical convention, investors measure standard deviation relative to the simple average (arithmetic) mean. Because of the higher degree of fluctuation in returns associated with a high standard-deviation measure, a *lower* rate of compound geometric returns, combined with a *high* level of standard deviation, produces the same mathematical outcome as a *higher* rate of compound geometric return combined with a *low* level of standard deviation. This relationship is shown in Figure 3.9.

As Figure 3.9 demonstrates, a compound geometric return of 8.9%, with a *relatively high* standard deviation of 25%, is the same as an arithmetic average return of 12%. At the same time, a compound geometric return of 11.5%, with a *relatively lower* standard deviation of 10%, also produces the same mathematical results as an arithmetic average return of 12%. In other words, a given average arithmetic annual return (such as 12%) results in a lower (or higher) compound geometric return the higher (or lower) the standard deviation of those returns.

A series of weekly, monthly, quarterly, or annual returns produces standard deviations that are weekly, monthly, quarterly, or annual standard deviations, respectively. Converting weekly, monthly, or quarterly standard deviations to annual standard deviations, sometimes known as the process of *scaling* standard

F I G U R E 3.9

Geometric Returns, Standard Deviation, and Arithmetic Returns

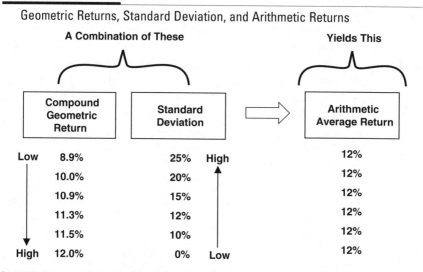

Source: The Author and "A Disciplined Approach to Global Asset Allocation," by R. D. Arnott and R. D. Henriksson, *Financial Analysts Journal*, May/June 1989.

deviations, is more complex than simply multiplying by 52, by 12, or by 4. Instead, investors must multiply the weekly, monthly, or quarterly standard deviation by the *square root* of the dimension by which time is changed—in these cases, by $\sqrt{52}$, by $\sqrt{12}$, or by $\sqrt{4}$, respectively.

Standard deviations may vary significantly depending on the time interval of measurement. For instance, weekly or monthly returns may exhibit greater volatility than annual returns. Several asset classes, such as Treasury bills or the appraised values of real estate, exhibit relatively lower month-to-month or quarter-to-quarter volatility than their long-term annual volatility. In practice, many investment sources utilize weekly or monthly data to capture as much information content as possible, and then annualize the returns and the associated standard deviations.

A specialized form of variance that focuses exclusively on negative returns, or returns below the mean, is known as *semi-variance*. This measure is useful when the distribution of returns is not symmetric about the mean, particularly when investors' reaction to, or the probability of, returns *below* the mean is higher than their reaction to, or the probability of, returns *above* the mean. Otherwise, the semi-variance is simply equal to one-half the variance. Calculation of semi-variance is similar to calculation of variance: add the squares of the differences of all the returns *below* the mean return. The square root of semi-variance is called *semi-deviation*. A more refined version of semi-variance, known as *downside variance*, calculates the degree of variability below a specifically chosen rate of return. Downside variance, or downside deviations, assesses the potential loss associated with a target rate of return. *Target semi-variance*, or *below-target risk*, quantifies the *magnitude* of potential shortfalls below a target rate of return by focusing only on downside deviations rather than on both upside and downside deviations. A related measure, *below-target probability*, estimates the *probability* of failing to meet a specified target rate of return and treats all shortfalls below this target rate in a similar manner, regardless of their actual magnitude.

Properly understood and utilized, the concept of standard deviation can be a powerful, although not an all-powerful, tool to help investors gauge one key element of risk—the volatility or dispersion of returns. Although it is theoretically possible for an asset to generate a high standard deviation of returns without any downside risk, most assets with a high standard deviation tend to have a reasonable probability of experiencing losses, or negative returns. Paying attention to standard deviation is one way investors focus on risk and their own tolerance for risk, rather than unduly concentrating on the pursuit of high returns.

Covariance

According to the principles of Modern Portfolio Theory, as well as ideas relating to the market portfolio, market efficiency, and other assumptions, the expected return on an asset is related to the risk of that asset. In other words, the return on an asset must be related to: (i) the covariance of that asset *with the rest of the investor's portfolio*; not (ii) the variance (or its square root, the standard deviation) of the asset's returns relative to that asset's own historical or projected returns data. Assuming that the rest of the investor's portfolio is the overall market of assets, the expected return on an asset depends in a linear fashion on the covariance of that asset with the overall market of assets.

Covariance measures the degree of variability of returns between two assets, or the extent to which the two assets' returns move together. Some investors use covariance to measure whether the returns in a given pair of assets have tended to move in the *same* direction (a *positive* number) or in the *opposite* direction (a *negative* number). In statistical terms, covariance is the product of two variables' deviations around their means. The covariance of two assets is calculated independently of the specific *amounts* of each of the two assets in a portfolio. The covariance of two investments' returns is an average of the products of the deviations of each asset's returns around its own expected mean return. By definition, covariance is calculated between asset *pairs*. As a result, increasing the number of assets in a portfolio can cause a much larger increase in the number of calculations. A two-asset portfolio requires one covariance calculation, a 10-asset portfolio requires 45 covariance calculations, and a 100-asset portfolio requires 4,950 calculations. In mathematical terms, the number of covariances equals $n/2$ times $(n - 1)$, where n = the number of assets in the portfolio.

Table 3.3 calculates the covariance and the correlation between total returns for a recent five-year period on the Standard & Poor's 500 Index and those on the Standard & Poor's 400 Midcap Index.

The lower the covariance between two assets is, assuming that the standard deviation of each underlying asset remains unchanged, the lower the correlation will be between those assets and the lower the volatility, or the standard deviation, of *the combined two assets* will be. To calculate the covariance, also known as the average product of deviations, investors must first calculate the average (mean) arithmetic returns for each index. Second, calculate the deviation of each year's return from its respective mean for each index. Third, multiply the deviations of each year's returns from their respective means. Fourth, add these products and divide by the number of years to obtain the average product of deviations, also known as the covariance. Fifth, divide the covariance of the returns of the two indices by the product of their standard deviations

T A B L E 3.3

Geometric Returns, Standard Deviation, and Arithmetic Returns

Calendar Year	Year	Total Return on S&P 500	Total Return on S&P 400 Midcap	Deviation of S&P 500 from Its Annual Arithmetic Average	Deviation of S&P 400 from Its Annual Arithmetic Average	Product of Deviations
2002	1	−22.1%	−14.5%	−29.7% ×	−26.6% =	0.0791
2003	2	28.7%	35.6%	21.1% ×	23.5% =	0.0495
2004	3	10.9%	16.5%	3.2% ×	4.4% =	0.0014
2005	4	4.9%	12.6%	−2.7% ×	0.5% =	−0.0001
2006	5	15.8%	10.3%	8.2% ×	−1.8% =	−0.0014
Annual Arithmetic Average Return		⬚7.6%⬚	⬚12.1%⬚			0.1284
Standard Deviation of Return		16.8%	16.0%			

Covariance = Average Product of Deviations = (0.1284 ÷ 5) = 0.0257

$$\boxed{\text{Correlation}} = \frac{\boxed{\begin{array}{c}\text{Covariance}\\\hline \boxed{\begin{array}{c}\text{Standard}\\\text{Deviation}\\\text{of}\\\text{S\&P 500}\end{array}} \times \boxed{\begin{array}{c}\text{Standard}\\\text{Deviation}\\\text{of}\\\text{S\&P 400}\end{array}}\end{array}}}{} = \frac{0.0257}{0.168 \times 0.160}$$

Correlation = 0.95

to arrive at the *correlation coefficient*. The example in Table 3.3 calculates the covariance as 0.0257 between the annual returns on the S&P 500 and the S&P 400, and the correlation coefficient between these two returns comes to 0.95. The use and meaning of the correlation measure are discussed below.

Correlation

The *cross-correlation coefficient*, often referred to as the correlation coefficient, or the correlation, is a useful way of denoting the degree of association between two series of data. In some ways, one of the deep meanings of asset allocation revolves around the search for pairs of assets and asset classes that have stable and low or, if possible, stable and negative correlations with one another.

The cross-correlation coefficient measures the strength or weakness of the *linear* relationship between two variables by calculating the covariance of two series of data divided by the product of their standard deviations. The pattern of one series of data and the correlation coefficient between it and a second data series determine the extent of predictability of the pattern of the second data series. A specialized form of correlation, also known as the *serial correlation coefficient,* or first-order auto-correlation, of a data series, denotes its degree of predictability relative to the *immediately preceding* values of the data. A data series with a low serial correlation coefficient will have a low degree of stability and predictability from period to period. A data series with a high serial correlation coefficient will have a high degree of stability and predictability from period to period. Further commentary on this condition is contained in the footnote to Table 3.4 (see page 67).

Stated in its most basic form, a *positive* correlation between two data series indicates that the data move in the *same* general direction at the same time (i.e., when the return on one asset *increases,* the return on the other asset tends to *increase*). In contrast, a *negative* correlation indicates that the data move in an *opposite* direction from each other at the same time (i.e., when the return on one asset *increases,* the return on the other asset tends to *decrease*). A *zero* correlation indicates that the two data series are *unrelated* in a linear manner to each other. Figure 3.10 shows these three kinds of correlation between the returns on two pairs of asset classes.

Correlation coefficients always range between a minimum of -1 and a maximum of $+1$. The positive correlation between the returns of asset class A and asset class B in the two *left-hand* panels of Figure 3.10 indicate that when the return on asset class A is above (or below) its average, the return on asset class B most likely will be above (or below) its average. The two *middle* panels of the exhibit show zero correlation—virtually no relationship—between the returns on asset class A and the returns on asset class B. The two *right-hand* panels display negative correlation between the returns on asset class A and asset class B. In this case, when the return on asset class A is above (or below) its average, the return on asset

T A B L E 3.4

Correlations of One-Year Returns, 1926–2006

Series	Large Company Stocks	Small Company Stocks	Long-Term Corp. Bonds	Long-Term Govt. Bonds	Intermediate-Term Govt. Bonds	U.S. Treasury Bills	Inflation
Large Company Stocks	1.00						
Small Company Stocks	0.79	1.00					
Long-Term Corporate Bonds	0.19	0.08	1.00				
Long-Term Government Bonds	0.12	−0.02	0.93	1.00			
Intermediate-Term Government Bonds	0.04	−0.07	0.90	0.90	1.00		
U.S. Treasury Bills	−0.02	−0.10	0.20	0.23	0.48	1.00	
Inflation	−0.02	0.04	−0.15	−0.14	0.01	0.40	1.00
Serial Correlations[1]	0.03	0.06	0.08	−0.08	0.15	0.91	0.65

Note: [1]The standard error for all estimates is 0.12. Given that the margin of error is 0.12, the longer-maturity, longer-duration assets shown in the table (Large Company Stocks, Small Company Stocks, Long-Term Corporate Bonds, and Long-Term Government Bonds) appear to have essentially zero or close to zero serial correlation, which supports the maxim that past investment performance is not indicative of future performance in the short run.

Source: *Stocks, Bonds, Bills, and Inflation: 2007 Yearbook*, Ibbotson Associates, Morningstar.

class B most likely will be just the opposite—below (or above) its average.

Correlations between pairs of assets or asset classes (e.g., between long-term government bond returns and large company stock returns) can vary considerably through time. Figure 3.11 shows the standard deviation (risk) and return of a combination of two asset classes for varying levels of correlation between these two asset classes' returns.

Point A in the exhibit shows the standard deviation (risk) and return of a portfolio with 100% of its assets invested in asset class A. Point B shows the risk and return of a portfolio with 100% of its assets invested in asset class B. The straight line stretching from A

F I G U R E 3.10

Schematic Representation of Positive, Zero, and Negative Correlations

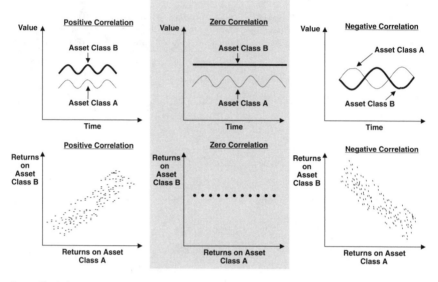

Source: The Author.

F I G U R E 3.11

Risk/Return Characteristics for Two-Asset Portfolios with Different Correlations

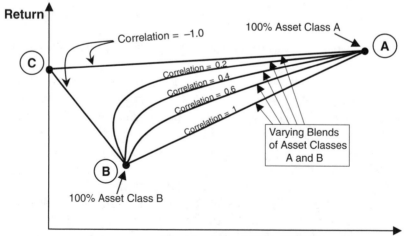

Source: The Author.

to B shows the risk and return characteristics of a portfolio of *varying blends* of investments between asset class A and asset class B, assuming that the correlation between these two asset classes is 1.0.

As *different* values are used for the correlation between asset class A and asset class B, such as 0.6, 0.4, 0.2, and –1.0 in the extreme instance, the risk-reward line for varying mixes of these two asset classes begins to shift toward the most favorable quadrant of the graph—the region of high returns and low risk in the upper left-hand quadrant. As the correlations become progressively lower in this example, mixes of asset class A and asset class B exhibit lower and lower risk (standard deviation) than either asset class A or asset class B independently. When the correlation between asset class A and asset class B is at its negative extreme, –1.0, Figure 3.11 shows that the investor can construct a blend of asset class A and asset class B at point C, which represents an essentially riskless portfolio, having a positive return and a standard deviation (risk) of zero. In practice, however, it is very difficult to find asset classes that are perfectly negatively correlated with each other.

To provide some perspective on the cross-correlation and serial correlations of asset class returns for one-year holding periods, Table 3.4 contains correlations for various pairs of six U.S. asset classes and inflation from 1926 through 2006.

For *one-year holding periods* over the 81-year time period covered by the table, large company stocks had a positive 0.79 *correlation coefficient* with small company stocks, on average, and a positive correlation of 0.19 with long-term corporate bonds, on average. Interestingly, the *serial correlation* coefficient of large company stock returns with themselves over the 1926–2006 period is practically zero, indicating that their one-year returns are virtually unrelated to one another from one year to the next.

Table 3.5 contains return, standard deviation, and asset-pair correlation data for *monthly holding* periods from 1997 through 2006 for 11 asset classes, including U.S. domestic and international equities, high-yield bonds, real estate investment trusts, commodities, and a proxy index for venture capital.

In Table 3.5, the range of correlations is noteworthy: from a very high 0.99, between U.S. large-capitalization equities and the broader market of all U.S. equities, to a rather low 0.01, between

T A B L E 3.5

Return, Standard Deviation, and Correlation Data, 1997–2006

| | | Annualized Returns | | 10-Year Correlation of Annual Returns | | |
| | | | | (1) | (2) | (3) |
Asset Classes		1997–2006	Risk (Std. Dev.)	U.S. Large-Cap Equities[a]	Broad Market U.S. Equities[b]	EAFE Equities[c]
(1)	U.S. Large-Capitalization Equities	8.4%	19.1%	1.00	–	–
(2)	U.S. Equities—Broad Market	8.5	18.6	0.99	1.00	–
(3)	Europe, Australasia, and the Far East (EAFE) Equities	7.7	20.8	0.78	0.82	1.00
(4)	Emerging Markets Equities	9.4	33.8	0.33	0.44	0.71
(5)	High-Yield Bonds	7.4	8.9	0.54	0.61	0.58
(6)	Real Estate Investment Trusts (REITS)	14.5	17.9	0.01	0.07	0.14
(7)	Venture Capital	17.7	87.2	0.38	0.40	0.39
(8)	Commodities	3.2	14.0	−0.26	−0.20	0.00
(9)	U.S. Investment-Grade Bonds	6.2	4.0	−0.39	−0.47	−0.74
(10)	Non-U.S. Government Bonds	3.9	10.6	0.21	0.20	0.37
(11)	Cash	3.7	1.8	0.14	0.05	−0.24

Sources:
[a]S&P 500 Index.
[b]Wilshire 5000 Index.
[c]Morgan Stanley Capital International (MSCI) Europe, Australasia, and the Far East (EAFE) Equity Total Return Index.
[d]Morgan Stanley Capital International (MSCI) Emerging Markets Free Gross Dividends Index.
[e]High Yield (Credit Suisse Upper/Middle Tier) Index.
[f]NAREIT (Real Estate Investment Trusts) Index.
[g]Cambridge Associates U.S. Venture Capital Index.
[h]Commodity Research Bureau Total Return Index.
[i]Lehman Brothers U.S. Aggregate Bond Index.
[j]J.P. Morgan Global ex-U.S. Bonds Index.
[k]Citigroup U.S. Treasury Bill (90-Day) Index.

U.S. large-capitalization equities and real estate investment trusts. The highest frequency of negative correlation during the period was for U.S. investment grade bonds versus each of the other asset classes. Cash (30-day U.S. Treasury bills) also exhibited negative

**10-Year Correlation of
Annual Returns**

(4)	(5)	(6)	(7)	(8)	(9)	(10)	(11)
Emerging Markets Equities[d]	High-Yield Bonds[e]	Real Estate Investment Trusts[f]	Venture Capital[g]	Commodities[h]	U.S. Investment Grade Bonds[i]	Non-U.S. Government Bonds[j]	Cash[k]
–	–	–	–	–	–	–	–
–	–	–	–	–	–	–	–
–	–	–	–	–	–	–	–
1.00	–	–	–	–	–	–	–
0.52	1.00	–	–	–	–	–	–
0.24	0.57	1.00	–	–	–	–	–
0.48	−0.16	−0.36	1.00	–	–	–	–
0.24	0.07	0.42	−0.04	1.00	–	–	–
−0.93	−0.29	−0.03	−0.60	−0.11	1.00	–	–
−0.03	0.45	0.03	−0.30	−0.13	0.14	1.00	–
−0.45	−0.53	−0.28	0.33	−0.47	0.27	−0.47	1.00

correlations during the 1997–2006 period with 6 of the other 10 asset classes.

In analyzing and reflecting on the data shown in Table 3.5, it is important to remember that these correlations represent *averages* for a 10-year period. Certain asset classes may show only a fairly modest correlation with other asset classes and thus represent attractive diversification candidates to reduce risk (standard deviation). For example, EAFE Equities and Emerging Markets Equities have correlations of 0.78 and 0.33, respectively, with large-capitalization U.S. equities. Investors should remember that in times of financial crisis, many of these indices' correlations may rise significantly, to the 0.75–0.80 range and above, thus vitiating or eliminating expected diversification benefits under normal circumstances.

Within a given asset class, a measure known as the *R Squared Coefficient of Determination* (R^2) shows the extent to which the performance of a selected index explains fluctuations in the returns. For example, an R^2 of 0.75 indicates that the returns of the specific index chosen to represent that asset class explain 75% of the fluctuation in the returns from investing in an asset class—such as through a mutual fund, an investment partnership, separate account management, a unit trust, or another vehicle. In such an instance, 25% of the fluctuation in returns from investing in the asset class might be attributable to non-index-related influences such as investment selection, market timing, investment overweighting or underweighting, or other factors.

RISK AND RETURN

Armed with the tools and concepts underlying risk and return, investors can combine these ideas to examine the tradeoffs and choices that arise in asset allocation and portfolio construction. Investors who aim to diversify by finding assets that are distinctly different from one another should examine: (i) how much additional risk (standard deviation) associated with an asset, or asset class, they must assume to earn higher rates of expected return; (ii) how much expected return they must give up to decrease risk to levels that they are comfortable with; and (iii) historical patterns of risk and return for the major asset classes.

Figure 3.12 shows the risk and return characteristics of selected asset classes for the 62 years extending from 1945 through 2006.

A line drawn through the points in Figure 3.12 is sometimes referred to as a *Capital Allocation Line.* Between 1945 and 2006,

F I G U R E   3.12

Historical Risk and Return for Selected Asset Classes, 1945–2006

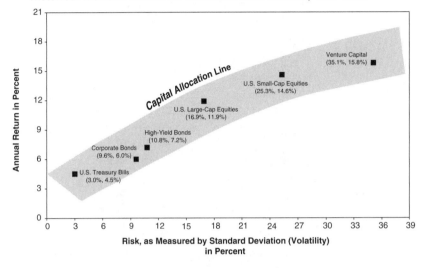

Note: Over the 1997–2006 time period, the respective risk (standard deviation) and return measures for the asset classes shown above were as follows: U.S. Treasury Bills, 1.8%, 3.7%; Corporate Bonds, 4.0%, 6.2%; High-Yield Bonds, 8.9%, 7.4%; U.S. Large-Capitalization Equities, 19.1%, 8.4%; U.S. Small-Capitalization Equities, 11.6%, 14.7%; and Venture Capital, 87.2%, 17.7%.

Source: Morgan Stanley Investment Research, Morgan Stanley Capital International, Dimensional Fund Advisors, Cambridge Associates, Standard & Poor's, Ibbotson Associates, Morningstar.

increasing levels of return are associated with an increased level of risk. U.S. Treasury bills exhibited a fairly narrow standard deviation of 3.0% and yielded an annual return of 4.5%. Corporate bonds had a 9.6% standard deviation and a 6.0% annual return, and high-yield bonds had a 10.8% standard deviation and a 7.2% annual return. U.S. equities exhibited a 16.9% standard deviation and an 11.9% annual return, and U.S. small-capitalization equities had a 25.3% standard deviation and a 14.6% annual return. Venture capital had a fairly wide standard deviation of 35.1% and a 15.8% annual return. A higher degree of risk generally produces a rise in the rate of annual return, as well as in the 10- and 20-year expected final values by holding each of these asset classes. Table 3.6 illustrates these facts of financial life.

For U.S. Treasury bills during 1945 through 2006, the standard deviation equals 3.0%, with a 4.5% average annual return. In a

T A B L E   3.6

Amount of Return per Unit of Standard Deviation

Asset Class	1945–2006		Units of Annual Return per Unit of Standard Deviation	Expected Final Value of $1 Invested for		Amount of Expected Final Value per Unit of Standard Deviation	
	Standard Deviation	Annual Return		10 Years Annual Return	20 Years Annual Return	10 Years Annual Return	20 Years Annual Return
U.S. Treasury Bills	3.0%	4.5%	1.50	$1.55	$2.41	$0.52	$0.54
Corporate Bonds	9.6	6.0	0.63	1.79	3.21	0.19	0.33
High-Yield Bonds	10.8	7.2	0.67	2.00	4.02	0.19	0.37
U.S. Large-Cap Equities	16.9	11.9	0.70	3.08	9.48	0.18	0.56
U.S. Small-Cap Equities	25.3	14.6	0.58	3.91	15.26	0.15	0.60
Venture Capital	35.1	15.8	0.45	4.34	18.80	0.12	0.54

Source: The Author.

crude way, this means that investors expect an average of 1.50 percentage points (units) of average annual return for each full percentage point of standard deviation as a measure of volatility.

Assuming that an investor earned the average rate for holding U.S. Treasury bills for a substantial time horizon, a $1.00 initial investment would grow to $1.55 after 10 years and to $2.41 after 20 years. The pretax monetary amount of expected final value *per unit* percentage point *of standard deviation* for U.S. Treasury Bills would be $0.52 after 10 years and $0.54 after 20 years.

At the other end of the risk and reward spectrum, if an investor earned the average rate for holding venture capital for a long time period, a $1.00 initial investment would grow to $4.34 after 10 years and to $18.80 after 20 years. The pretax monetary amount of expected final value *per unit* (percentage point) *of standard deviation* for venture capital would be $0.12 after 10 years and $0.54 after 20 years.

Beta

In addition to using *standard deviation* as one indicator of an asset's variance, or the risk specific to its own average returns, another measure, called the *beta* of the asset, has been developed to gauge an asset's degree of responsiveness to movements in the market as a whole. The beta helps divide an asset's *total risk* into its *market risk* and its *specific risk*, and represents that asset's contribution to the variance of the entire portfolio.

The beta of an asset is defined as the covariance of that asset divided by the variance of the market as a whole. Stated another way, beta is the same as the standard deviation of the asset times the asset's correlation with the market, divided by the standard deviation of the market. These relationships, shown in the following formulas, also demarcate how an asset's beta relates to and differs from its standard deviation:

$$\text{Beta of an Asset} = \frac{\text{Covariance of the Asset}}{\text{Variance of the Market}}$$

$$\text{Beta of an Asset} = \frac{\text{Standard Deviation of the Asset} \times \text{Correlation of the Asset with the Market}}{\text{Standard Deviation of the Market}}$$

The beta of an asset measures the degree of that asset's market-wide, undiversifiable, systematic risk. A beta of *greater than one* indicates that, for a percentage *price* movement in the market, the price of the asset will move by a *greater* percentage than the market price change, and is thus riskier than the market as a whole. A beta *equal to one* indicates that, for a given percentage *price* movement in the market, the price of the asset will move by *the same* percentage as the market price change, and is thus equal in risk to the market as a whole. A beta *less than one* indicates that for a given percentage price movement in the market, the price of the asset will move by a *lesser* percentage than the market price change, and is thus less risky than the market as a whole.

Because beta reflects the percentage upward or downward move of that asset when some broad market index moves upward or downward, a number of investors consider an asset's beta in conjunction with its R-Squared Coefficient of Determination (which spells out in specific percentage terms the extent to which fluctuations in a given index explain the fluctuations in an asset's returns).

Betas usually range between values of 0 and 2 or 3. Using equities as an example, during the late 1990s, high-beta stock industries (with betas in the 1.50 to 2.00 range) included airlines, electronics, and durable goods, and low-beta industries (with betas in the 0.60 to 0.90 range) included energy, utilities, and banking. Index funds (such as an S&P 500 index fund) usually exhibit betas of very close to 1 because they are set up to mirror an index of broad market movements.

The degree to which a portfolio or a fund such as an index fund does or does not closely follow the index it is set up to mimic is known as *tracking error*. *Tracking risk* is the standard deviation of returns between: (i) a portfolio or fund; and (ii) a selected index and, as such, represents the degree of variability between the returns on a portfolio or fund and the returns on a benchmark market index. Similarly, *shortfall risk* measures the probability of earning a return on an asset that is below a stated target return. For instance, investors who aspire to earn at least 5% with 85% certainty would seek to allocate the assets in their portfolio that present less than a 15% chance of the portfolio's returning below 5%.

Shortfall risk is also akin to *Value at Risk* (VAR), which takes into account the entire structure of an asset's returns distribution and measures the capital loss resulting from returns that fall below a specified percentile, or confidence level, such as 95%, 98%, or 99%. This means the investor would use VAR to project what the portfolio's loss in value would be if its results placed it in the 95th, 98th, or 99th percentile of returns, respectively. The VAR is used by a considerable number of financial market participants to focus on the magnitude and composition of negative occurrences in the extreme ends of a returns distribution.

Figure 3.13 depicts the beta and alpha (described in more detail on page 78) of an asset, as well as the calculations of alpha as a measure of the return that is not attributable to the market or the risk level of the investment.

Figure 3.13 shows that the beta of an asset is equivalent to the slope of the line—its vertical rise divided by its horizontal run—which relates the return *of the asset* to the return *of the market* as a whole. This line is also known as an *asset characteristic line.* Drawing upon the statistical concept introduced on page 72, the *R-squared* measure indicates how closely the data points are to the asset characteristic line and thus how closely an asset's return is correlated with the return of an asset class benchmark. An R-squared measure of zero indicates zero correlation between the return of an asset and the return of a market benchmark, and an R-squared measure of 100 indicates perfect correlation and is effectively the same as a correlation coefficient of +1.

Investors often use the R-squared concept to gauge how closely individual data points lie toward the regression line that is used in connection with a statistical procedure—called a *least squares linear regression*—to calculate the best fit for the calculation of beta from individual asset returns plotted on a graph against market benchmark returns.

Capital Asset Pricing Model

According to the Capital Asset Pricing Model (CAPM), the risk of an asset is equivalent to its beta, and differences in the average returns generated by different assets should be explained completely by

F I G U R E 3.13

Graphical Depiction of Beta and Alpha and Calculation of Alpha

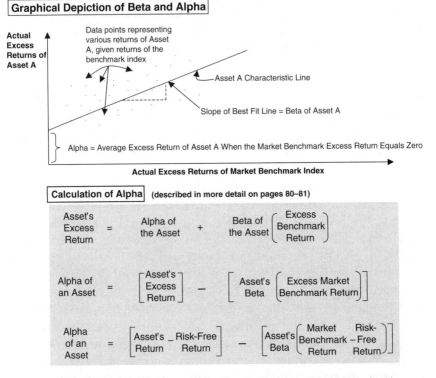

Graphical Depiction of Beta and Alpha

Actual Excess Returns of Asset A

Data points representing various returns of Asset A, given returns of the benchmark index

Asset A Characteristic Line

Slope of Best Fit Line = Beta of Asset A

Alpha = Average Excess Return of Asset A When the Market Benchmark Excess Return Equals Zero

Actual Excess Returns of Market Benchmark Index

Calculation of Alpha (described in more detail on pages 80–81)

$$
\begin{array}{ccc}
\text{Asset's Excess Return} & = & \text{Alpha of the Asset} & + & \text{Beta of the Asset}\left(\text{Excess Benchmark Return}\right)
\end{array}
$$

$$
\text{Alpha of an Asset} = \left[\text{Asset's Excess Return}\right] - \left[\text{Asset's Beta}\left(\text{Excess Market Benchmark Return}\right)\right]
$$

$$
\text{Alpha of an Asset} = \left[\text{Asset's Return} - \text{Risk-Free Return}\right] - \left[\text{Asset's Beta}\left(\text{Market Benchmark Return} - \text{Risk-Free Return}\right)\right]
$$

To calculate the alpha of an asset with a beta of 1.2 that returned 25% when the Market Benchmark Index returned 20% and the risk-free return (i.e., the 90-day Treasury Bill return) was 3.5%, these values can be inserted into the formula:

$$
\begin{aligned}
\text{Alpha} &= [25\% - 3.5\%] - [1.2(20\% - 3.5\%)] \\
&= 21.5\% - 1.2(16.5\%) \\
&= 21.5\% - 19.8\% \\
\boxed{\text{Alpha}} &= \boxed{+1.7\%}
\end{aligned}
$$

Source: The Author.

differences in their betas. This concept closely ties into Figure 3.8 shown on page 57, which addresses the process of estimating expected returns. The return on an asset should consist of an appropriate Risk-Free Benchmark Return plus an additional return, the market-risk premium, to compensate for the additional risk of the asset above or below the Risk-Free Benchmark Rate of Return. For example, because a high-beta asset produces *high* relative returns just when investors have least need of them—i.e., when the overall market is doing well—and produces *low* relative returns just when investors need them the most—when the overall market is faring poorly—investors deserve to be compensated for this risk.

The degree of asset-specific or security-specific risk is equal to the standard deviation of the term *epsilon*, or ε, in the equation in which the asset's total excess return (i.e., the return above a Risk-Free Benchmark Rate) equals the asset's beta times the index or benchmark excess returns, plus ε. This equation is expressed as:

$$\text{Asset's Total Excess Return} = \text{Alpha} + [(\text{Beta})$$
$$\times (\text{Market Benchmark Excess Return})] + \text{Epsilon}$$

According to this formula, if an asset had a beta of 1.4 and the market excess benchmark return increased by 3%, the asset's total excess return should increase by 1.4 times 3%, or 4.2%, plus the epsilon factor, which represents its asset-specific risk. In practice, for a *diversified portfolio as a whole*, the various positive and negative epsilons of the individual assets tend to cancel each other out. As a result, the beta of a diversified asset allocation is frequently considered to represent a good approximation of the degree of responsiveness of that asset allocation to overall movements in a benchmark market index.

In practice, the academic and investment communities have debated the degree of fit between historical asset returns and the returns predicted by the beta measure of CAPM. Although the results are not conclusive, it has been argued that higher-beta assets do in fact compensate investors for taking on additional risk; similarly, it has been argued that lower-beta assets produce somewhat higher returns on average than the returns forecast by the CAPM. One possible reason for this phenomenon is that the risk of assets, or their betas, may change over time. Investors should be attentive to how recent are the data used in calculating an asset's beta, as such data are perishable. Some respected financial scholars believe that beta is not the single factor describing asset returns' variability through time, thus opening the door for multifactor models.

Alpha

Many investors interpret the *alpha* of an asset as the difference between the *expected* excess returns on that asset and its *actual* return. As such, the alpha gives an indication of the degree to which that asset can generate returns that are higher than, equal to, or lower than normally expected returns, given the volatility of the asset relative to a market benchmark index. In this particular sense, alpha measures the outperformance or underperformance of an asset relative to the returns predicted by its beta. If an asset produces greater returns than its beta predicts, it is considered to have *positive alpha*, and if the asset produces lower returns than its beta predicts, it is said to have *negative alpha*. Some investors refer to alpha as *residual risk*, or *selecting risk*.

Figure 3.13 demonstrates how to calculate the alpha of an asset such as an individual security, a fund, or a portfolio of investments. The graph in the exhibit plots the various realized excess returns (i.e., returns that are greater than the risk-free rate of return) *of an asset*, given various realized excess rates of return *of a benchmark index* representing the market.

According to CMT, the excess return of an asset equals its alpha, plus its beta times the excess return of the market (or a market benchmark above a widely accepted risk-free rate of return such as the 90-day U.S. Treasury bill return).

Rearranging the fundamental equation for the excess return of an asset produces the basic equation for the alpha of an asset: the asset's excess return, minus beta times the excess return of the market benchmark. The alpha of an asset is thus determined by its return *and* its beta. Graphically and formulaically, when the excess return of the market benchmark equals zero, whatever excess return of the asset remains is its y-axis intercept, or its alpha. The sample alpha calculation in Figure 3.13 shows that with a risk-free rate of return of 3.5%, an asset with a beta of 1.2 that returned 25% when the market returned 20% has a positive alpha of 1.7%.

Careful consideration of the relationships between alpha, beta, and absolute return can furnish useful perspectives. For example, another asset could have produced the same absolute return of 25%

with: (i) a *lower* beta (for example, 0.9) and a *higher* alpha (+6.65%); or (ii) a *higher* beta (for example, 1.4) and a *lower* alpha (–1.6%). In case (ii) above, plugging in the higher beta of 1.4 and the excess return of 5% into the equation in Figure 3.13 would produce an alpha equal to (25% – 3.5%), or 21.5%, minus 1.4 times (20% – 3.5%), or minus 23.1%, which results in a negative alpha of 1.6%.

Sharpe Ratio

In 1966, the Nobel laureate William F. Sharpe developed a measure to assess the return of an asset (such as a mutual fund, an individual security, or an asset class as a group) relative to its total volatility. Originally called the reward-to-variability ratio, this measure is now more broadly known as the *Sharpe ratio*. In essence, the Sharpe ratio combines two measures, the mean return of an asset and its standard deviation, into a single number.

The Sharpe ratio is calculated by dividing an asset's excess return (also known as its *differential return*) above a risk-free benchmark rate—such as the 90-day U.S. Treasury bill rate—by the standard deviation of the asset's returns:

$$\text{Sharpe Ratio} = \frac{\text{Asset's Return in Excess of Risk} - \text{Free Benchmark Rate}}{\text{Standard Deviation of Asset's Return}}$$

For example, in an environment of 5% 90-day U.S. Treasury bill rates, if an asset generated a return of 30% with a standard deviation of 15%, its Sharpe ratio would be:

$$\text{Sharpe Ratio} = \frac{30\% - 50\%}{15.0\%} = \frac{25\%}{15\%} = 1.67$$

Referring back to Figure 3.2, it is possible to compute the Sharpe ratio for U.S. large company stocks from 1926 through 2006. During this interval, the 90-day U.S. Treasury bill arithmetic mean return was 3.9%, and for U.S. large company stocks, the arithmetic mean return was 12.3% with a standard deviation of 20.1%. Inserting these values into the formula gives a long-term Sharpe ratio of 0.42 for U.S. large company stocks, as shown below:

$$\text{Sharpe Ratio} = \frac{12.3\% - 3.9\%}{20.1\%} = \frac{8.4\%}{20.1\%} = 0.42$$

Whereas alpha measures the excess return of an asset *relative to its beta* (its responsiveness to overall market movements), the Sharpe ratio measures the excess return of an asset *relative to its own standard deviation* of returns. This allows investors to compare on an equal footing and in a reasonably straightforward manner the reward-to-risk ratio of a wide variety of assets. The Sharpe ratio tends to be most useful when it is applied to well-diversified portfolios. Otherwise, the presence of any specific risk in the standard deviation may undermine the comparability of portfolios on the basis of Sharpe ratios.

Investors who are attentive to potential shortfalls with respect to a target return can compute the *Sortino ratio*, formulated by Frank A. Sortino, which measures the expected excess return of an asset divided by its *target semi-variance* rather than its standard deviation. Some investors also use the *Treynor ratio*, which was formulated by Jack L. Treynor and which measures an asset's expected excess return divided by its *beta.* As such, the Treynor ratio measures how much return over the risk-free rate an asset produces per unit of that asset's marketwide, undiversifiable, systematic risk.

Figure 3.14 distinguishes the *Capital Market Line*, or *Investment Opportunity Set*, of a specific set of assets, from the so-called *Security Market Line* of a specific set of assets.

The chief difference between the Capital Market Line and the Security Market Line of a set of assets stems from the measure plotted against return. The Capital Market Line plots the excess return (the return in excess of a Risk-Free Benchmark Rate) versus the standard deviation of the asset, whereas the Security Market Line plots the excess return versus the beta of an asset (its responsiveness to movements in the market index as a whole). In Figure 3.14, the *slope* of the Capital Market Line (the return per unit of standard deviation) is equivalent to the Sharpe ratio of the set of assets, and the *slope* of the Security Market Line (the return per unit of beta) is equivalent to the Treynor ratio of the set of assets. According to the Capital Asset Pricing Model, the expected excess return for an asset with a beta of zero should theoretically be zero. In fact, the y-intercept of the Security Market Line has been statistically observed to have a positive or negative value. The following

F I G U R E   3.14

Capital Market Line Compared to Security Market Line

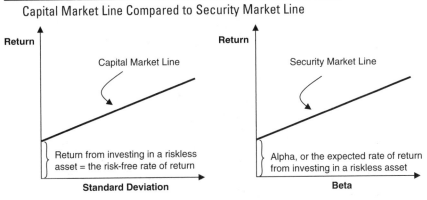

Source: The Author.

section extends the notion of the Capital Market Line or Investment Opportunity Set into the Efficient Frontier.

Efficient Frontier

When the returns from various mixtures (portfolios) of more than two assets are plotted on a graph versus the standard deviations of returns from these portfolios, the results produce a set of portfolios such as the area shown in Figure 3.15.

Figure 3.15 shows that Portfolio B is preferable to Portfolio C, since it generates a *higher expected return* for an equivalent amount of risk. Similarly, Portfolio A is preferable to Portfolio C, since it produces an equivalent expected return for a *lesser degree of risk*. Portfolio C is known as an *inefficient portfolio*, in which extra risk is needlessly assumed without compensation in the form of higher returns or, alternatively, in which higher returns are unnecessarily given up for a specified level of risk.

The collection of portfolios for a given set of investment alternatives which produces the highest level of return for a given degree of risk, or which minimizes the degree of risk for a given level of return, generates a curved line known as the *Efficient Frontier.* As described above, the degree of curvature of the Efficient Frontier is a function of: (i) the less-than-one correlations of the various assets in the portfolios; as well as (ii) the number of separate

F I G U R E   3.15

Efficient Frontier

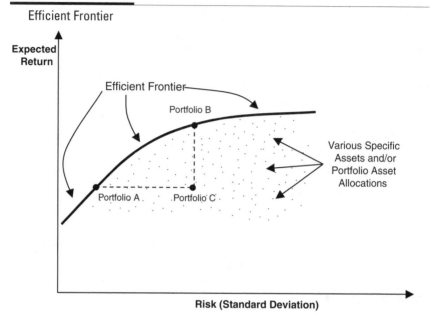

Source: The Author.

asset classes in each portfolio. The Efficient Frontier shows where the most risk efficient portfolios lie for a given collection of assets. Whether an investor prefers Portfolio A rather than Portfolio B *on the Efficient Frontier* is primarily determined by the interplay between the investor's risk tolerance and his or her desires or requirements for increased return. According to the theory of the Capital Asset Pricing Model, investors *should* hold some combination of (i) a mean-variance efficient portfolio along the Efficient Frontier; and (ii) risk-free assets. In practice, investors may or may not hold efficient portfolios, and they may or may not hold some amounts of risk-free assets. As with many other theoretical constructs, even though *theory* requires that investors *should* do something, it does not require that they *actually do so*.

ASSETS' RETURNS AND CORRELATIONS CAVEATS

Several caveats are worth noting concerning historical and projected data about assets' returns and correlations. Historical single-point asset class and security returns covering several years or more are, in fact, *averages* of varying—sometimes widely varying—results experienced in the years constituting the period cited. By the same token, future returns do not possess the degree of certainty or accuracy implied by a single-point projection. A more telling rate of return description about the past or the future should incorporate a *range* of plus or minus returns, and their associated probability, around the single-point projection.

Similar warnings apply to asset class correlation statistics. Correlations measure the tendency of the returns from a given asset class or investment to move in the same *direction* as another asset class or investment, but not the *magnitude* of such movement. Covariance and tracking error data are needed to specify the magnitude of one investment's movement relative to another. Investors must scrutinize correlation data to determine: (i) what holding period they apply to (such as monthly, quarterly, annual, or five-year returns); and (ii) what overall time horizon is described (such as 1960 through 1980, 1926 through 2006, or 1997 through 2006).

Finally, and very importantly, inter-asset or inter-investment correlation data are generally not stable to any significant degree over time, even though many investors and portfolio-optimization programs assume that correlation values are stable. One example of how widely the correlations between two assets can vary through time is set forth in Figure 3.16.

For the 81 years from 1926 through 2006, Figure 3.16 shows the rolling three-year correlations between monthly holding period total returns of large company stocks (as represented by the Standard & Poor's 500 Index) and long-term government bonds (as represented by long-term U.S. Treasury bonds). Over this time frame, the correlation between large company stocks and long-term government bonds fluctuated quite a bit, ranging from a low of –0.51 in March 2003 to a high of +0.65 in October 1992, with a long-term correlation mean of +0.15. From the late 1980s through 2000, the U.S. stocks and bonds represented in the exhibit had *rising correlations*, meaning that their prices showed an increasing tendency to move in the same direction. In contrast, in 2000, U.S. stock-bond correlations began a significant *downward* move, meaning that their prices were increasingly showing a tendency not to move in the same direction. From an asset-allocation perspective,

F I G U R E 3.16

Correlation between Large-Company Stocks and Long-Term Government Bonds

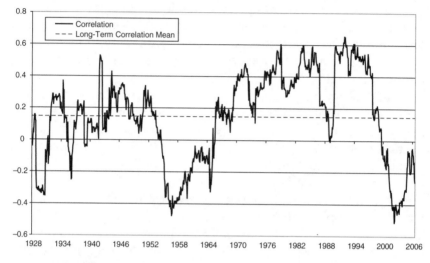

Note: Correlations are rolling three-year correlations of monthly holding period total returns of the S&P 500 Index and the Ibbotson Long-Term U.S. Treasury Bond Index.

Source: Ibbotson Associates, Morningstar, Morgan Stanley Global Wealth Management Asset Allocation Group.

during periods when bonds and stocks have high correlations, bonds tend to have reduced potential for mitigating the risk of an equity portfolio. But when bonds and stocks have low or negative correlations, bonds can play a meaningful role in lowering the risk of an equity portfolio.

ASSET-ALLOCATION OPTIMIZATION MODELS

Asset-allocation optimization refers to the process of identifying portfolios of assets that are projected to generate the highest possible expected return for a given level of risk or, alternatively, to carry the lowest possible degree of risk for a given level of return. The most commonly used optimization technique underlying asset allocation optimization, known as *mean-variance optimization* (MVO), was developed in the early 1950s by the economist Harry Markowitz and was first applied to portfolios of equities.

In essence, this methodology originally sought to blend different groups of stocks, which were not highly correlated with each other, to reduce the overall variance (or its square root, the standard deviation) of a collection of equities. These same ideas were later extended to portfolios of various asset classes. Markowitz effectively showed that for a *single asset*, investors can project and simulate future investment returns by estimating: (i) the asset's mean return; and (ii) its standard deviation around the mean return. For a *group of asset classes*, investors can project and simulate future investment returns by estimating: (i) each asset's mean return; (ii) its standard deviation; and (iii) its correlation with every other asset class in the portfolio.

Portfolio Optimization Methods have been broadly applied to asset groups in part because it is generally easier to estimate returns for *whole classes of assets* than it is for a *single security*. In addition, the range of investable asset classes has expanded over time. Besides traditional equities, fixed-income instruments, and cash, choices now include international developed- and emerging-markets debt and equity investments, commodities, private equity, venture capital, real estate, and newer asset categories and subcategories such as convertible securities, inflation-protected instruments, collateralized futures, securitized debt, hedge funds, and absolute-return strategies such as arbitrage.

How Asset-Allocation Optimization Models Work

Most modern-day asset allocation optimization models are built upon statistical methods and, not least, easy and low-cost access to adequate computing power. At the same time, asset-allocation optimization models assume that: (i) the investor's primary objectives are to maximize return and minimize risk; (ii) standard deviation is a reasonable measure of the risk of an asset; and, especially, (iii) the correlation coefficient of two assets' returns describes the relationship between that pair of assets.

Figure 3.17 shows a schematic diagram of the inner workings of a typical asset-allocation optimization model.

Most asset allocation-optimization models proceed in a relatively straightforward manner, consisting of several steps. First, taking

F I G U R E 3.17

The Inner Workings of an Asset-Allocation Optimization Model

Select Asset Classes for Consideration

Estimate Inputs for Each Asset Class for:
- Return
- Standard Deviation of Return
- Cross-Correlation with Other Asset Classes

Set Appropriate Constraints on Inputs and/or Outputs:
- Maximum Percentages of Total Portfolio
- Minimum Percentages of Total Portfolio
- Specified Target Percentages of Total Portfolio

Review Output:	Portfolios				
Asset Class	**A**	**B**	**C**	**D**	**E**
U.S. Equities	60%	52%	48%	44%	40%
U.S. Fixed-Income	10%	20%	25%	30%	40%
Commodities	5%	5%	5%	5%	5%
Private Equity	20%	15%	10%	8%	0%
Cash	5%	8%	12%	13%	15%
Total	**100%**	**100%**	**100%**	**100%**	**100%**
Expected Return	20.0%	17.3%	15.1%	12.2%	10.0%
Standard Deviation	25.0%	23.2%	18.0%	14.0%	12.0%
Probability of Not Achieving Target Return	20%	22%	25%	28%	30%
Probability of Loss	18%	14%	12%	10%	8%

Perform Sensitivity Analysis by Adjusting:
- Return Assumptions
- Risk Assumptions
- Correlation Assumptions
- Portfolio Percentage Constraints

Source: The Author.

into account the contribution that each asset class makes to the portfolio's expected return, to its risk, and to the correlation of its returns to those of other asset classes, investors identify those assets they are willing to consider. In some cases, the asset-allocation optimization model may not have risk, return, and correlations data for all of the asset classes the investor is contemplating. If so, they can substitute, for purposes of running the model, certain other asset classes' data, with all of the attendant caveats that such substitutions entail.

Second, inputs are estimated for the return, standard deviation (a measure of uncertainty of the return), and cross-correlation for each asset class under consideration. Frequently, investors rely heavily on historical data for this step, but many asset-allocation optimization models allow substitution of different forecasted data for these variables. This is particularly valuable when investors expect a significant change in the financial market environment for certain asset classes.

Third, investors impose any necessary constraints on the inputs to, and the output from, the asset-allocation optimization model. These constraints might be specified target percentages. For example, investors might decide to invest: (i) *no more* than 10%; (ii) *no less* than 10%; or, in certain cases, (iii) *no more or less* than 10% of their assets in international equities. In such an instance, the portfolio output of the asset-allocation optimization model would always recommend: (i) a *maximum* of 10%; (ii) a *minimum* of 10%; or (iii) a *fixed* 10% holding in international stocks.

Fourth comes a review of the output of the asset-allocation optimization model. Such models rely on theoretical methods that attempt to optimize the tradeoff between investors' quest for the highest possible return versus their desire for the lowest possible risk. One way to achieve this goal is to increase the weightings of asset classes that have low or, if at all possible, negative correlations with other asset classes in the portfolio, as depicted in Figure 3.18.

Asset-allocation optimization models generally seek to reduce portfolio risk by selecting asset classes with as low or as negative correlations as possible, to reconcile: (i) the financial reality of *higher* returns attainable only by taking on *more* risk; with (ii) the investor's goal of achieving *high* return with *low* risk. The *output* of

The Interplay of Forces in Portfolio Optimization

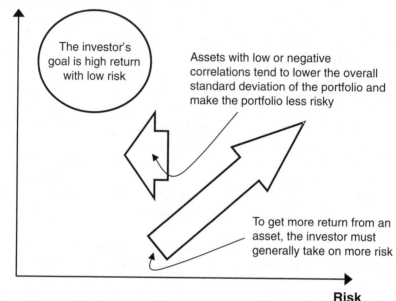

Source: The Author.

many asset-allocation optimization models often is in a format similar to the somewhat exaggerated example shown earlier in Figure 3.17. The output includes several portfolios with varying allocations of the asset classes selected by the investor, taking account of any relevant investor constraints. These portfolios are ranked in order from high return, high risk, to low return, low risk.

In Figure 3.17, commodities have been limited to a maximum of 5 percent in all of the sample portfolios, because this sample optimization model attempts to invest an unrealistically high percentage of the portfolio in the commodities asset class owing to its dissimilar patterns of returns and its projected negative correlations with many other asset classes. Depending on the source of data computation for the model, the output may or may not show: (i) the probability of not achieving a target return specified by the investor; as well as (ii) the probability of experiencing a capital loss in the value of the portfolio as a whole. Plotted together on a risk-return graph, these portfolios represent an Efficient Frontier, given the assets and assumptions that were fed into the model. Investors' risk tolerance, return objectives, and market outlook may influence which portfolio on the Efficient Frontier they prefer at any given time.

Fifth, investors can perform a *sensitivity analysis* by adjusting the model's original assumptions as to expected returns, standard deviations, and correlations, and possibly modifying any of the percentage constraints that they originally placed on the portfolio. One useful by-product of a sensitivity analysis is the determination of how stable the model's proposed efficient allocations are, given slight changes in asset return, risk, and correlation assumptions.

Advantages and Disadvantages of Asset-Allocation Optimization Models

When their underlying estimates and assumptions are sound, up-to-date, internally consistent, and understandable, a significant benefit of asset-allocation optimization models is the rigor, logic, and organization they bring to this aspect of the investment process. An equally important advantage is the attention they direct toward the historical patterns and characteristics of returns, with a resultant deeper understanding of the uncertainties and ranges of outcomes.

By setting minimum and maximum asset class constraints, conducting sensitivity analyses, and periodically reviewing past and projected results, investors can bring quantitative discipline to what has often been a qualitative and subjectivity-prone undertaking. Finally and perhaps most importantly, asset-allocation optimization models may help investors become more comfortable with the benefits of broadened diversification through investment in multiple asset classes over the long term. As part of this activity, asset-allocation optimization models have helped direct global investors' attention to international assets' returns, risk, standard deviation, and the exchange-rate risks involved in trans-national investing. Because currency movements do not provide meaningful extra return, but do increase the overall volatility of an investment, many market participants feel that it is best to eliminate this currency exposure through hedging activity. In fact, a much smaller universe of investors actually devotes the time and expense to establish currency-hedging positions on their non-domestic investments. Investors should not rely too much, or too little, on asset-allocation optimization models. They need to recognize optimization models for what they are—powerful computational engines—and not see them as inspired, all-knowing solutions encompassing great quantities of wisdom and judgment. As robust and mathematically elegant as many asset-allocation optimization models are, they also have several limitations.

First, the quality of the model portfolio outputs is in large part determined by the quality of the inputs. Future expected returns, standard deviations, and correlations can and do vary significantly, and occasionally for long periods of time, from their historical averages. Asset-allocation models assume bell-shaped returns patterns for their underlying assets, whereas assets' returns may very well not follow such patterns. In fact, investors care greatly about, and may be significantly influenced by, returns that occur in the so-called tails of returns distributions, far from the average or mean return figures for these assets.

Second, investors need to keep asset-allocation optimization models in proper perspective, considering them in the context of possible economic and financial scenarios, from deflation and disinflation to various levels of economic growth and price inflation. Investors should also consider their state of mind and realize that their volatility tolerance can undergo substantial changes over time, which can trigger an exasperating and all-too-human tendency to shift in the wrong direction near major turning points.

Third, asset-allocation models sometimes lead investors to believe that asset allocation is a one-time exercise, with only minor tweakings necessary at infrequent intervals. In fact, many successful asset allocations require investors to consider eventual rebalancing of the portfolio. Chapter 4 discusses asset-allocation rebalancing in detail. The rebalancing decision may involve: (i) periodically resetting the portfolio to the original target asset allocation; (ii) allocating assets with some degree of flexibility within a range of minimum and maximum percentages for each asset class; (iii) reallocating assets opportunistically, depending on the outlook for each asset class under consideration; or (iv) adopting a fixed, buy-and-hold asset allocation, with virtually no rebalancing activity undertaken, regardless of the price movements of individual asset classes.

Fourth, computer-driven allocation programs can sometimes suggest extreme allocations to certain asset classes, particularly those deemed to have low or negative cross-correlations with other asset classes. Fifth, not all asset-allocation optimization models take into account the highly important, real-world effects of taxes, transaction costs, and the borrowing or lending of cash and/or securities. Sixth, the outputs of asset-allocation optimization models are sometimes highly sensitive to the mix of inputs, with small changes in the inputs producing large, potentially unstable, and sometimes counterintuitive outputs, such as unreasonable over- or underweightings of asset classes. Finally, an excessive model-based emphasis on asset-class selection may misdirect the investor away from developing or finding skilled resources to select individual investments and/or managers within each asset class.

On balance, the benefits of asset-allocation optimization models appear to outweigh their weaknesses. When using these models as a tool in the asset-allocation process, investors should seek to maximize their strengths—quantitative discipline and insights into asset class characteristics—and minimize their weaknesses—sensitivity to input data and lack of attention to important judgmental factors.

ASSET-ALLOCATION OPTIMIZATION SOFTWARE

Many firms that sell asset-optimization software packages over the Internet have developed tools designed to help investors analyze, create, monitor, and rebalance their asset allocations. These programs evaluate the overall level of portfolio risk and return and create optimal portfolios of assets based on investors' capital-market preferences, tolerances, and constraints. In addition, many, but not all, of these programs can: (i) import data from existing portfolio accounting systems; (ii) have profiling modules to gauge the investor's risk characteristics; and (iii) permit sensitivity analysis through changing assumptions and expectations about the future. Some programs have multiperiod, mean-variance optimizers that can compute an Efficient Frontier through time, and backtesting capabilities to see how asset allocations would have performed using historical data. Further information, product descriptions, and prices are available, among other sources, from: Efficient Solutions, Inc. (*effisols.com*), Frontier Analytics, Inc. (*allocationmaster.com*), Ibbotson Associates, Inc. (*ibbotson.com*), Morningstar, Inc. (*morningstar.com)*, and Vestek Systems, Inc. (*vestek.com*).

CHAPTER 4

ASSET-ALLOCATION REBALANCING

OVERVIEW

This chapter explores the subject of asset-allocation rebalancing, in which investors from time to time reallocate their portfolios to pre-specified target percentages for their holdings of various asset classes. This chapter also considers the advantages, disadvantages, and key decision points in asset-allocation rebalancing, including what to rebalance, when to rebalance, the degree of allowable flexibility in rebalancing, and how to rebalance.

The origins and implications of the main types of asset-allocation overweightings are described and diagrammed here, with reference to the five most commonly encountered asset categories: concentrated positions, liquidity holdings, conventional securities, alternative investments, and personal holdings. *Asset categories* are generally somewhat broader in scope than asset classes and may range beyond capital assets to include: *personal property holdings* such as residences, art, and other valuables; and *concentrated positions* such as ownership interests in a business or a private enterprise, a large block of securities and/or options, extensive real estate holdings, royalties, and patent rights.

The investor's asset-allocation rebalancing decisions and pathways are compared and contrasted when: (i) rebalancing extends only to mainstream asset categories; versus (ii) a broader scope that also includes concentrated positions and/or personal holdings.

A variety of asset-allocation rebalancing methods are then examined in some detail, including: (i) *selling outperforming* assets to *purchase underperforming* assets; (ii) *selling underperforming* assets to *purchase outperforming* assets; and (iii) *not pursuing a formal rebalancing policy*, instead allowing asset-allocation percentages to drift with the fortunes of the markets for each asset class. This chapter then analyzes a two-asset portfolio using actual returns data and several kinds of sensitivity analyses, investigating the effects of varying the initial asset-allocation mix, the portfolio time horizon, and the degree, shape, and slope of assets' returns patterns. The chapter concludes with a discussion of critical factors needed to increase the odds of achieving success in asset-allocation rebalancing.

REBALANCING PRINCIPLES

Asset-allocation rebalancing, also known as portfolio rebalancing, refers to the process of selling a portion of assets and, with the proceeds, buying other assets, usually to align the overall portfolio mix with a specified asset-allocation policy or targeted asset-allocation weightings. Some investors rebalance their asset allocations according to explicitly defined performance, time, or other guidelines; others rebalance purely on an *ad hoc* basis, with no specific plan; and some investors pay little or no attention at all to asset rebalancing activity.

The theory and practice of rebalancing are based on several fundamental assumptions about asset classes and investor behavior. First, investors generally expect assets' investment returns to follow *reversion to the mean* through time. This assumption posits that assets' investment returns do not indefinitely remain at a high level or, alternatively, at a depressed level. At some point, assets that have generated returns *above* their long-term average, or mean, also should produce returns *below* their long-term average, and assets that have yielded returns *below* their long-term average, or mean, also should furnish results *above* their long-term average. Although there are exceptions to this assumption, it has a number of sturdy supporting arguments, ranging from multidecade quantitative analyses of assets' historical returns, to biblical references to alternating seven-year cycles of feast and famine, to such commonly encountered expressions as "trees don't grow to the sky."

Another principle underlying rebalancing stems from the expected merits of diversification theory. Under that theory, an appropriate *diversification* of assets can help investors improve the return on their portfolios relative to a given level of risk. Investors also may be able to reduce the risk relative to a given level of return. In some cases, investors may be able to achieve both of these objectives. For diversification to produce outcomes that approach intended results, the assets in an investor's portfolio should possess appropriate patterns and characteristics of return, risk, and correlation with one another. In brief, rebalancing seeks to improve the overall risk-reward profile of a portfolio by buying judicious amounts of certain assets at low prices and selling them at higher prices, and by selling judicious amounts of other assets at high prices and buying them at lower prices.

Rebalancing also assumes that investors can establish reasonably sensible investment rules and percentages that: (i) properly apply to their own personal circumstances and market outlook; and (ii) can be followed with a sufficient degree of discipline, judgment, and vision. Rebalancing attempts to identify and anticipate the risks and rewards of the intentional or unintentional asset concentration that results from allowing portfolios to migrate from their original weightings as a result of significant and/or prolonged gains or losses in specific asset classes or in specific positions.

ADVANTAGES AND DISADVANTAGES OF REBALANCING

The chief *advantage* of rebalancing stems from an expected increase in the probability of attaining the long-term return goals of specific asset classes and of a given asset allocation. Another important benefit of rebalancing is risk control. The discipline of reallocating assets to targeted percentages of the portfolio can often allow investors to mitigate the financial exposure created by overconcentration of wealth in a small number of assets. Rebalancing can also improve investors' attentiveness, monitoring, and overall involvement with their portfolios.

The main *disadvantage* of rebalancing derives from the danger that an asset allocation ends up being readjusted in a counterproductive manner. Among the ways this can happen are: (i) rebalancing too frequently, introducing an excessive "buy-the-dips" or market-timing mentality that results in high transaction, tax, time, opportunity, and even psychological costs; (ii) focusing on the wrong subject (such as the value-versus-growth decision *within* the equities asset class, rather than thinking about *the appropriate level* of *equities versus fixed-income versus alternative assets*); (iii) some asset classes, asset managers, or specific investments may not revert to the mean within any reasonable time frame (the *purchased* assets suffer semi-permanent or long-lasting damage, and/or some of the *sold* assets may experience extended periods of high valuations); and (iv) the inherent human difficulty involved in leaning against the wind by selling assets that have performed well and risen in price while at the same time purchasing assets that have performed poorly and declined in price.

Some investors may rebalance to readjust the portfolio merely in a general direction; others rebalance when certain assets' valuation measures move above or below historical norms; and still other investors rebalance to specific target percentages. Each of these rebalancing methodologies presupposes that the investor has developed and applied an optimal asset mix that is appropriate to his or her own circumstances and the financial market outlook. In fact, the asset-allocation percentages to which assets are rebalanced may or may not have been financially suitable in the first place.

Decision Points in Asset-Allocation Rebalancing

Investors face a number of important decisions in rebalancing:

- ◆ **What to Rebalance:** Some investors take their entire net worth position into consideration in rebalancing and think about all five of the major asset categories—(i) concentrated positions; (ii) liquidity holdings; (iii) conventional securities;

(iv) alternative investments; and (v) personal holdings. Owing to individual attachment and/or personal reluctance to disturb or part with such assets in the first and fifth of these categories, some investors may decide to *exclude* their personal holdings and/or their concentrated positions from rebalancing. Other asset categories, such as alternative investments, may include relatively illiquid assets such as private equity, venture capital, certain types of real estate, farmland, timberlands, and oil and gas interests. As a consequence of their low turnover and often indivisible nature, many alternative investments, concentrated positions, and/or personal holdings may be taken into account, but not that frequently adjusted. Investors' rebalancing may emphasize: (i) *the macro level* (across broad asset categories and classes); (ii) *the micro level* (across asset subcategories, subclasses, asset managers, or even specific securities or other investments); or (iii) *some combination* of the macro level and the micro level.

♦ **When to Rebalance:** The frequency of rebalancing can range from never, to sporadically, to every few years, to annually or semiannually, and for certain tactically oriented investors, quarterly, monthly, and even weekly. Some investors rebalance according to historical valuation norms or to specified minimum percentage price changes (such as plus or minus 5% or 10%) rather than by the calendar. Characteristics that may influence the price or time to rebalance include, among other factors: (i) the investor's degree of interest, time available, and aptitude for rebalancing; (ii) the absolute size of the portfolio, tax considerations, and transaction costs; (iii) the relative mix and composition of the investor's assets; (iv) the short-, intermediate-, and long-term outlook for returns, risk, correlation, and liquidity within and between each asset class; and (v) whether rebalancing appears to improve the risk-reward results of the portfolio within a reasonable time frame and/or across a partial or complete market cycle.

♦ **Degree of Flexibility in Rebalancing:** Some investors strictly adhere to their planned asset-allocation weightings and their pre-established time and/or percentage-change disciplines, whereas others allow themselves varying degrees of latitude in deciding whether, when, and by how much to rebalance or not rebalance their portfolios. Investors may determine how much or how little flexibility to permit themselves by: (i) their perception and judgment of the degree and duration of specific asset classes' performance and where they are within their respective short- and long-term returns cycles; (ii) internally or externally imposed constraints on the investor; (iii) competing time demands; and (iv) previous positive or negative experiences with any unscheduled or special rebalancing maneuvers.

♦ **How to Rebalance:** Rebalancing may take place through investors' normal buying and selling transactions and/or their designated sources of investment advice. For certain large pools of assets, and when time, efficiency, and cost considerations dictate, investors may utilize futures and other types of derivatives, preset contractual arrangements, and various forms of borrowing and lending capital or securities to effect their desired rebalancing activity.

ORIGINS AND IMPLICATIONS OF ASSET-ALLOCATION OVERWEIGHTING

A fundamental motivation for rebalancing often stems from a significant overweighting in one or a small number of assets, asset classes, or asset categories. Investors' initial asset allocation and ongoing rebalancing usually are focused on broad asset categories such as *liquidity holdings, conventional securities,* and *alternative investments.*

Significant overweightings in asset categories may build up over long periods of time or may occur suddenly after: (i) a financial event, such as the sale of a large block of securities, a merger, an acquisition, refinancing, or an initial public offering; (ii) the deployment of funds into largely undiversified positions in conventional securities, alternative investments, or personal holdings; or (iii) a legal settlement, an inheritance, or the winning of a lottery. Figure 4.1 on pages 101–102 shows the implications of asset allocation overweighting in the five most common asset

F I G U R E   4.1

Origins and Implications of Asset-Allocation Overweighting

Asset-Allocation Overweighting in Concentrated Positions

Representative Examples: Ownership interests in a business; a large block of securities and/or options; extensive real-estate holdings; royalties; and patent rights.

Nature: Concentrated positions are often the engine that built the investor's fortune and/or keeps it going; in many cases, great rewards (often misestimated) have accrued from assuming great risks (also often misestimated); it is frequently a lifetime event to establish or dispose of a concentrated position.

Decisions: At what point and in what a mounts should an investor reduce or add to the concentrated position, during periods of protracted upward or downward price moves, as a result of strong emotional feelings, or due to familial pressure? Whether or not to borrow, hedge, or incur taxable events?

Asset-Allocation Overweighting In Liquidity Holdings

Representative Examples: Cash and cash equivalents, including U.S.Treasury bills, short-term government agency, municipal, corporate, and other money-market instruments; and money-market funds.

Nature: Liquidity often is generated as the result of a specific event, such as an initial public offering, the sale of a concentrated position, retirement, refinancing, inheritance, lottery winnings, a legal settlement, or the disposition of an investment position which has grown to significant size.

Decisions: In what currency or currencies should an investor maintain the liquidity? What are the timing and tax status of income flows, diversification and disposition strategies, and intermediaries?

Asset-Allocation Overweighting In Conventional Securities

Representative Examples: Equities, fixed-income securities, and investment cash, indomestic and international forms.

Nature: Conventional securities canusually be bought and sold in listed or unlisted markets; price quotations are generally available with some degree of frequency and transparency.

Decisions: Should the investor hire asset managers or manage the assets on his or her own? Should the investor own the assets directly or use an intermediary? Should he or she use active or passive investment techniques? What levels and types of fee structures for asset management and custody should the investor consider?

(Continued)

F I G U R E 4.1 (Continued)

Origins and Implications of Asset-Allocation Overweighting

Asset-Allocation Overweighting In Alternative Investments

RepresentativeExamples: Real estate and REITs; private equity, farmland, timberlands, oil and gas interests, venture capital, hedge funds, and funds of funds; precious metals; commodities; and managed futures.

Nature: Alternative investments frequently involve: less liquidity; unconventional frequency, methodology, and transparency of pricing and valuation; extended investment time frames and/or lockup periods; unusual risk/reward profiles; and unpredictable timing of capital inflows and outflows.

Decisions: What are the means and extent of monitoring alternative investments? Whats ourcing and evaluation of asset-management advice in alternative investments should the investor consider?

Asset-Allocation Overweighting In Personal Holdings

RepresentativeExamples: Primary and secondary residences; art, antiques, vintage automobiles, livestock, thoroughbred horses, rare books, jewelry, andother collectibles.

Nature: Personal property tends to accumulate over time, often as a result of the investor'sfamilyties,lifestyle decisions, long-term interests, and collecting passions; the valuation methodologies, pricing transparency, and ease of buying and selling personal holdings may vary from time to time and from asset type to asset type.

Decisions: How much should the investor tie personal assets into, or keep them separate from, other asset categories? What are strategies to insure, borrow against, lend, donate, or bequeath personal holdings?

Source: The Author.

categories—concentrated positions; liquidity holdings; conventional securities; alternative investments; and personal holdings.

For each asset category in Figure 4.1, the large gray circle depicts in highly simplified terms a significant overweighting relative to the other four categories, which are represented by smaller gray circles. An investor may have a significant overweighting in more than one asset category, or the dominant asset category may be composed of more than one asset class or subclasses.

In addition to a range of representative examples for each category, Figure 4.1 describes the nature of these assets and the decisions investors face with an overweighting in them. For example, a concentrated position may be (or have been) the engine that built the investor's fortune and/or keeps it going. In many cases, concentrated positions have generated great *rewards* (which are often misestimated by investors, on the low or the high side) from assuming great *risks* (which are also often misestimated by investors, on the low or the high side). Many times, establishing or disposing of a concentrated position is a highly meaningful lifetime event for an investor.

Investors who own one or more concentrated positions face several important decisions. Of perhaps the greatest consequence are the interrelated decisions of when and in what amounts to reduce or add to the concentrated position, particularly during periods of protracted upward or downward price moves, or as a result of strong emotional feelings or familial pressure. Other momentous decisions revolve around whether to borrow, hedge, or incur taxable events involving the concentrated position.

Asset-Allocation Overweighting Choices and Pathways

Investors with an overweighting in any of the main asset categories may elect to: (i) retain their overweighting in the same asset category; or (ii) direct some or all of the existing overweighting into one or more other asset categories. Figure 4.2 on pages 104–105 contains a somewhat abbreviated illustration of the asset-allocation choices and pathways for investors with an overweighting in: concentrated positions; liquidity holdings; conventional securities; alternative investments; and personal holdings.

In broad terms, investors with an overweighting in one of the asset categories in Figure 4.2 may follow any of several pathways. For example, investors with an existing asset-allocation overweighting in a *concentrated position* may: (i) decide to keep their concentrated position intact, or swap or sell one concentrated position for another concentrated position; (ii) generate liquidity, as a conscious financial market judgment or as an intermediate investment stage on the way to other portfolio allocations; (iii) sell the

F I G U R E 4.2

Asset-Allocation Overweighting Choices and Pathways

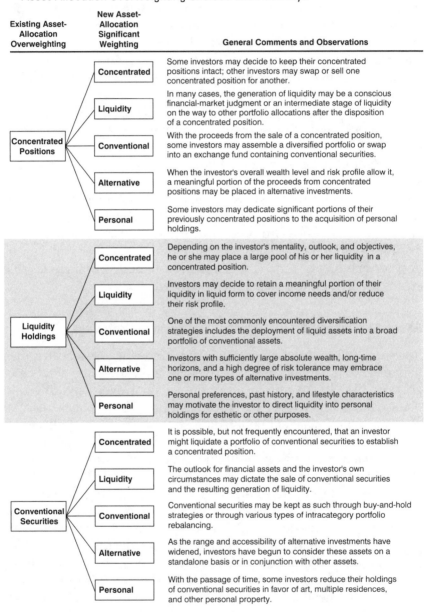

Existing Asset-Allocation Overweighting	New Asset-Allocation Significant Weighting	General Comments and Observations
Concentrated Positions	Concentrated	Some investors may decide to keep their concentrated positions intact; other investors may swap or sell one concentrated position for another.
	Liquidity	In many cases, the generation of liquidity may be a conscious financial-market judgment or an intermediate stage of liquidity on the way to other portfolio allocations after the disposition of a concentrated position.
	Conventional	With the proceeds from the sale of a concentrated position, some investors may assemble a diversified portfolio or swap into an exchange fund containing conventional securities.
	Alternative	When the investor's overall wealth level and risk profile allow it, a meaningful portion of the proceeds from concentrated positions may be placed in alternative investments.
	Personal	Some investors may dedicate significant portions of their previously concentrated positions to the acquisition of personal holdings.
Liquidity Holdings	Concentrated	Depending on the investor's mentality, outlook, and objectives, he or she may place a large pool of his or her liquidity in a concentrated position.
	Liquidity	Investors may decide to retain a meaningful portion of their liquidity in liquid form to cover income needs and/or reduce their risk profile.
	Conventional	One of the most commonly encountered diversification strategies includes the deployment of liquid assets into a broad portfolio of conventional assets.
	Alternative	Investors with sufficiently large absolute wealth, long-time horizons, and a high degree of risk tolerance may embrace one or more types of alternative investments.
	Personal	Personal preferences, past history, and lifestyle characteristics may motivate the investor to direct liquidity into personal holdings for esthetic or other purposes.
Conventional Securities	Concentrated	It is possible, but not frequently encountered, that an investor might liquidate a portfolio of conventional securities to establish a concentrated position.
	Liquidity	The outlook for financial assets and the investor's own circumstances may dictate the sale of conventional securities and the resulting generation of liquidity.
	Conventional	Conventional securities may be kept as such through buy-and-hold strategies or through various types of intracategory portfolio rebalancing.
	Alternative	As the range and accessibility of alternative investments have widened, investors have begun to consider these assets on a standalone basis or in conjunction with other assets.
	Personal	With the passage of time, some investors reduce their holdings of conventional securities in favor of art, multiple residences, and other personal property.

F I G U R E 4.2 **(Continued)**

Asset-Allocation Overweighting Choices and Pathways

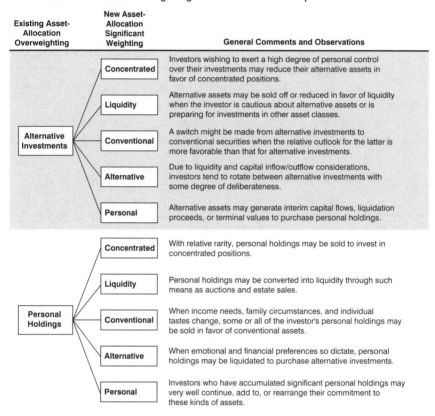

Source: The Author.

concentrated position to assemble a diversified portfolio of conventional securities, or swap the concentrated position into an exchange fund containing conventional securities; (iv) reduce or sell off the concentrated position to invest in alternative investments; or (v) earmark all or some portion of the proceeds of the sale of the concentrated position to acquire personal holdings. In each of these instances, the new asset weighting may itself represent a significant asset-allocation overweighting, or it may be broadly diversified within or across asset categories.

SCOPE OF REBALANCING

Many investors may not consider, or may consciously exclude, their concentrated positions and/or personal holdings from their asset-allocation thinking. These investors thus limit the scope of their rebalancing analysis and activity to their liquidity holdings, conventional securities, and alternative investments. Figure 4.3 sets forth the rebalancing interrelationships among these major asset classes.

The primary drivers of rebalancing among conventional and alternative asset classes—generally grouped into four major

F I G U R E 4.3

Rebalancing Among Conventional and Alternative Asset Classes

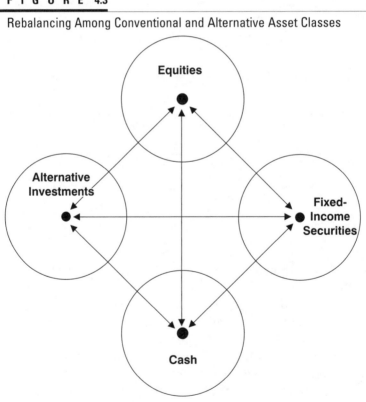

Source: The Author.

classifications, including equities, fixed-income securities, alternative investments, and cash (liquidity)—are: (i) investors' own circumstances, including their overall wealth level, risk tolerance, time horizon, tax status, and liquidity and income needs; (ii) the risk and return outlook for financial markets in general; and (iii) the risk and return outlook, as well as price versus value relationships, for specific investments and investment structures within each asset class. Some investors also take account of their *concentrated positions and personal holdings* in thinking about asset allocation and rebalancing. Figure 4.4 shows these rebalancing interrelationships among the *extended set* of asset categories.

F I G U R E 4.4

Rebalancing Among the Extended Set of Asset Categories

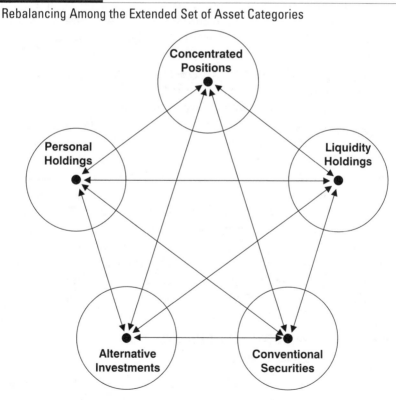

Source: The Author.

The primary drivers of rebalancing among the more extended set of asset categories—including concentrated positions, liquidity holdings, conventional securities, alternative investments, and personal holdings—include: (i) the investor's own circumstances; (ii) the outlook for financial markets; (iii) the outlook for specific investments and structures; (iv) liquidity and price effects of buying or selling concentrated positions and/or significant personal holdings; and (v) family and other qualitative, emotional, and psychological considerations. Generally speaking, when investors factor concentrated positions and personal holdings and, in many cases, alternative investments into their rebalancing, they should consider the relative lack of liquidity of these asset categories and the unconventional frequency, methodology, and transparency of their pricing and valuation.

Particularly during periods of heightened merger, acquisition, initial public offering, and refinancing activity, many investors with concentrated positions may encounter a customary and distinctive pattern of capital flows between asset categories. Figure 4.5 provides a generalized and somewhat simplified diagram of the usual direction and relative magnitude of these capital flows.

A significant portion of capital from the sale or disposition of concentrated positions may tend to flow first into liquidity holdings, and perhaps from there into directly held conventional securities. Less often and extensively, capital may flow: (i) from investors' concentrated positions to liquidity to alternative investments; or (ii) from investors' concentrated positions to liquidity holdings, to conventional securities, to alternative investments. Capital may also sometimes flow toward personal holdings to a somewhat lesser degree than toward other asset categories. As a result, capital may flow at any time in somewhat lesser volumes to personal holdings from any of the other major asset categories—concentrated positions, liquidity holdings, conventional securities, or alternative investments.

SPECIAL CONSIDERATIONS INVOLVING CONCENTRATED POSITIONS

Because they usually represent such a significant portion of investors' aggregate net worth, concentrated positions often

F I G U R E 4.5

Representative Capital Flow Between Asset Categories When Initiated with Concentrated Positions

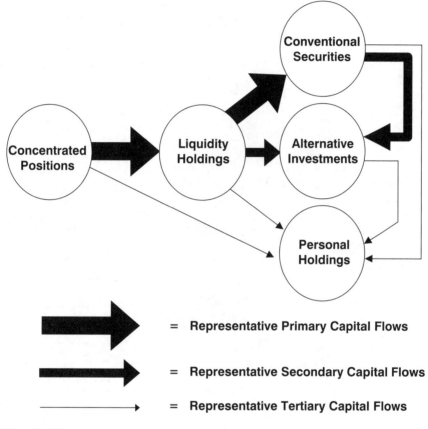

= **Representative Primary Capital Flows**

= **Representative Secondary Capital Flows**

= **Representative Tertiary Capital Flows**

Source: The Author.

deserve special focus and attention. Figure 4.6 sets forth a scenario analysis for six possible outcomes involving various combinations of: (i) a concentrated position; and (ii) a diversified pool of other assets.

On the left side of Figure 4.6, assume the investor owns $110 million of total assets, composed of $100 million in a concentrated position and $10 million in other assets. Data in this analysis are for

F I G U R E   4.6

Concentrated Position (C.P.) Scenario Analysis

Source: The Author.

illustration purposes; investors can divide all the numbers in Figure 4.6 by a factor of 10—in which case the beginning total assets amount to $11 million, made up of $10 million in a concentrated position and $1 million in other assets—or by a factor of 100—in which case the beginning total assets amount to $110,000, consisting of $100,000 in a concentrated position and $10,000 in other assets.

In the example in Figure 4.6, the investor faces two choices: keep the entire concentrated position or sell half of the concentrated position and reinvest the proceeds into a diversified mix of other assets. As a practical matter, the investor faces a much larger number of choices than the two displayed in Figure 4.6, ranging from the percentage of the concentrated position that might be sold off to the diversity of assets to reinvest the proceeds of such sales into.

In some period of time (such as one year), subsequent to the decision whether to dispose of half of the concentrated position, assume: (i) the value of the concentrated position doubles, stays the same, or declines by 50%; and (ii) the value of the other assets increases by 10% in all cases. Figure 4.6 shows three outcomes that could occur *when the investor decides to keep the entire concentrated position.* The most favorable decision results in a total portfolio gain of 91.8%, or $101 million, when the value of the concentrated position doubles. The least favorable result, a loss of 44.5%, or $49 million, occurs when the value of the concentrated position declines by one-half.

However, a somewhat more muted range of outcomes is produced *if the investor elects to sell half of his or her concentrated position* and reinvest the proceeds in a diversified mix of other assets that proceeds to rise 10% in price. The most favorable of the diversification results, a total portfolio gain of 50.9%, or $56 million, takes place when the value of the concentrated position doubles. The least favorable result, a loss of 17.3%, or $19 million, occurs when the value of the concentrated position declines by one-half. Interestingly, the total of the *other assets* alone in each of the outcomes of the 50%-sale-and-diversification decision, $66 million, exceeds the *total* portfolio value, $61 million, of the least favorable outcome of the retain-the-concentrated-position decision.

Investors with concentrated positions should perform a scenario analysis similar to the one in Figure 4.6, perhaps altering such variables as: (i) the percentage amounts by which the concentrated position and/or the other assets rise or fall in price; and (ii) the proportion of the concentrated position that they might liquidate for reinvestment in other assets. Two of the greatest challenges in the construction of a scenario analysis involving concentrated positions include: (i) assigning realistic probabilities to each of the potential outcomes; and (ii) being able to predict investors' true reactions to significant gains or losses in the value of the total portfolio. In many cases, investors may experience the pain of large portfolio losses much more deeply than they derive satisfaction or joy from equivalent monetary gains.

When deciding whether, when, and how much of a concentrated position to sell off and redeploy into other assets, investors should factor in: (i) their absolute wealth level and whether they can meet current and future financial and lifestyle needs at various values of the concentrated position and the total portfolio; (ii) the overall outlook for the concentrated position, for capital markets, and for other assets; (iii) their past experiences with, future plans for, and expectations about the concentrated position; (iv) financial signals and emotional messages occasioned by the disposition of all or part of the concentrated position; (v) the availability, selection, costs, complexity, and efficacy of hedging, monetizing, and leveraging tools and tactics; (vi) investors' skill in assessing probabilities of various outcomes, and realism in gauging their likely future reactions to such outcomes; and (vii) the expected time spans over which anticipated price moves might take place for the concentrated position.

Figure 4.7 shows the risk and reward of the three fully concentrated positions versus the three partially concentrated positions described in Figure 4.6.

Figure 4.7 plots the percentage change in the value of the investor's *total portfolio* as a function of the percentage change in the value of the investor's *concentrated position*. Investors who retain the entire concentrated position in their portfolio experience an overall gain of 91.8% in the portfolio when the value of the entire concentrated position increases by 100%, but such investors will experience an overall loss of 44.5% when the value of the entire concentrated position declines by 50%.

By contrast, investors who sell one-half of the concentrated position and reinvest in diversified other assets that rise in price by 10% experience an overall gain of 50.9% when the value of the remaining concentrated position *increases* by 100%. Such investors

F I G U R E 4.7

Risk and Reward of Fully and Partially Concentrated Position

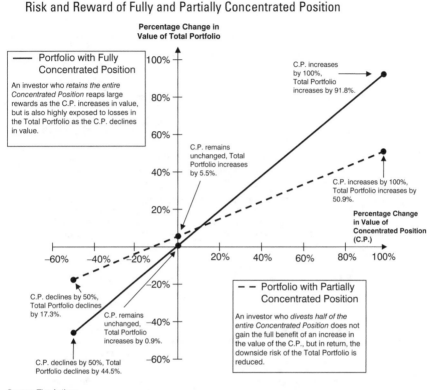

Source: The Author.

suffer a more muted overall loss of 17.3% when the value of the remaining concentrated position *declines* by 50%. Investors who sell one-half of the concentrated position and reinvest in other assets can capture 55% (50.9% divided by 91.8%) of the upside potential of the portfolio with the fully concentrated position. At the same time, such investors limit their exposure to only 39% (17.3% divided by 44.5%) of the downside of the portfolio with the fully concentrated position.

In many cases, the concentrated position's past price history and future price expectations may significantly influence investors' rebalancing or diversification action. For a given concentrated position, Figure 4.8 displays combinations of: (i) rising or falling *past prices* and (ii) expectations of rising or falling *future prices*.

F I G U R E 4.8

Past Price History and Future Price Expectations for Concentrated Positions

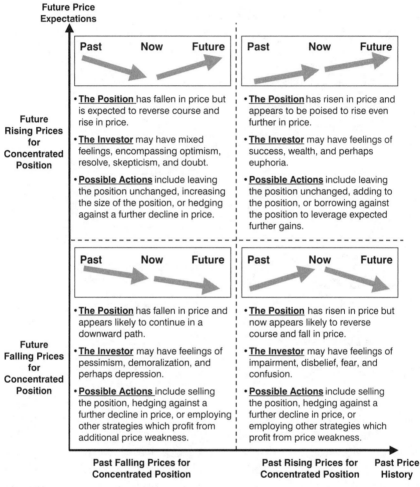

Source: The Author.

One of the chief reasons for leaving a concentrated position intact is the investor's belief that the price of the concentrated asset will go higher in the future. The top two panels in Figure 4.8 present these scenarios. Depending on what happened to the price of the concentrated asset in the past, investors may have feelings of success, wealth, and perhaps euphoria (if past prices have been rising and the outlook is for continued rising prices), or mixed feelings of optimism, resolve, skepticism, and doubt (if past prices have been declining and the outlook is for prices to reverse course and begin to move upward).

In contrast, a primary motivation for selling a meaningful part of a concentrated position may be an expectation that the price will move lower in the future. The bottom two panels in Figure 4.8 present these scenarios. Depending on what happened to the price of the concentrated asset in the past, the investor may have feelings of pessimism, demoralization, and perhaps depression (if past prices have been falling and the outlook is for continued falling prices), or feelings of impairment, fear, disbelief, and confusion (if past prices have been rising and the outlook is for prices to reverse course and begin to move downward).

REBALANCING METHODS

Whether or not investors decide to include concentrated positions and personal holdings in their asset-allocation thinking, it is worthwhile to consider some of the methods that may be employed in rebalancing. With many variations from the basic disciplines, three asset-allocation rebalancing approaches that investors commonly consider are: (i) *selling assets* that have *outperformed*, to *purchase assets* that have *underperformed*; (ii) *selling assets* that have *underperformed*, to *purchase assets* that have *outperformed*; and (iii) *taking no active rebalancing action,* and allowing the asset allocation to drift over time toward higher weightings in the better-performing asset classes.

To graphically and quantitatively examine the results produced by each of these three methods, we must make a number of simplifying assumptions. First, the number of assets is limited to two, Asset Class A and Asset Class B. In practice, the investor's portfolio may contain considerably more than two asset classes and subclasses, potentially complicating the analysis.

Second, we assume that Asset Class A and Asset Class B generally move inversely to each other—when the returns on Asset

Class A are favorable, in many instances the returns on Asset Class B are unfavorable, and vice versa. In fact, asset classes' returns may very well move in the *same* direction, rather than in *opposite* directions, during various intervals of time.

Third, the relative and absolute magnitude, intrayear and year-to-year volatility, direction, and sequencing of returns may in practice vary greatly from the simplified pattern of returns applied uniformly in all three of the examples investigated here. At a deep level, the long-term returns from various methodologies of rebalancing are generally affected by the absolute and relative level of returns generated by each of the asset classes under consideration. Fourth, the *rebalancing interval* may in practice be shorter (such as semiannually, quarterly, or monthly) or longer (such as every two years or every three years) than the annual rebalancing regimen followed here.

Fifth, the investor's *evaluation interval* may vary considerably from the eight years shown here, and the results of various asset-allocation rebalancing methods may rank differently, greatly influenced by the relative stage at which each asset finds itself within its own returns cycle when the books are closed at the end of a given evaluation interval. Sixth, we do not take into consideration the expenses of: transaction costs; annual management, performance, custody, reporting, and consulting fees if applicable; and income and capital gains taxes. Such costs may negatively affect the absolute and relative results of rebalancing.

Selling Outperforming Assets to Purchase Underperforming Assets

Figure 4.9 presents the multiyear results of a rebalancing method that annually sells off a portion of the portfolio's relatively *outperforming* asset and uses the proceeds to purchase an additional quantity of the portfolio's relatively *underperforming* asset, sufficient to rebalance the portfolio to a 50%–50% mix between Asset A and Asset B.

Assuming an initial investment of $100.00 in Asset A and an initial investment of $100.00 in Asset B, a vertical review of the results at the end of year one in Figure 4.9 shows that Asset A and

Rebalancing via Sale of Relatively Outperforming Asset and Purchase of
Relatively Underperforming Asset

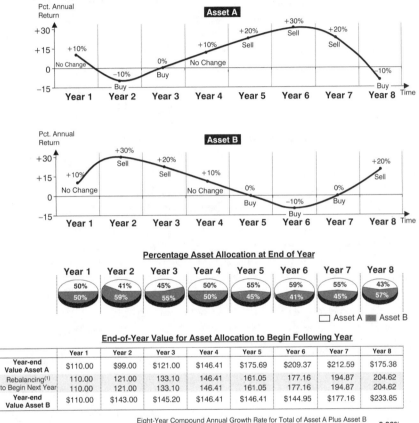

Percentage Asset Allocation at End of Year

End-of-Year Value for Asset Allocation to Begin Following Year

	Year 1	Year 2	Year 3	Year 4	Year 5	Year 6	Year 7	Year 8
Year-end Value Asset A	$110.00	$99.00	$121.00	$146.41	$175.69	$209.37	$212.59	$175.38
Rebalancing[1] to Begin Next Year	110.00	121.00	133.10	146.41	161.05	177.16	194.87	204.62
	110.00	121.00	133.10	146.41	161.05	177.16	194.87	204.62
Year-end Value Asset B	$110.00	$143.00	$145.20	$146.41	$146.41	$144.95	$177.16	$233.85

Eight-Year Compound Annual Growth Rate for Total of Asset A Plus Asset B
(Initial Investment = $200.00; Ending Value = $409.23) = **9.36%**

Note: [1]Rebalancing via 50%–50% allocation between Asset A and Asset B.

Source: The Author.

Asset B each generate a 10% investment return in year one, producing asset values of $110.00 for Asset A and $110.00 for Asset B,
resulting in a 50%–50% asset allocation for Asset A and Asset B at
the end of the first year.

For the $110.00 invested each in Asset A and in Asset B for the
second year, Asset A generates a –10% investment return, resulting

in an end-of-year-two value of $99.00, and Asset B generates a +30% return, resulting in an end-of-year-two value of $143.00. At the end of year two, the pie charts show that Asset A accounts for 41% of the total portfolio (= $99.00/$242.00) and Asset B represents 59% of the total portfolio (= $143.00/$242.00). To rebalance to a 50%–50% weighting to begin year three, one-half of the total port-folio value of $242.00 needs to be allocated each to Asset A and to Asset B. As a result, $22.00 of the outperforming asset, Asset B, is sold, and the resulting $22.00 is invested in Asset A, producing a beginning-of-year-three allocation of $121.00 in Asset A and $121.00 in Asset B.

For the $121.00 invested each in Asset A and in Asset B for the third year, Asset A generates a 0% investment return, resulting in an end-of-year-three value of $121.00, and Asset B generates a +20% return, resulting in an end-of-year-three value of $145.20. At the end of year three, the pie charts show that Asset A accounts for 45% of the total portfolio (= $121.00/$266.20) and Asset B repre-sents 55% of the total portfolio (= $145.20/$266.20). To rebalance to a 50%–50% weighting to begin year four, one-half of the total port-folio value of $266.20 needs to be allocated each to Asset A and to Asset B. As a result, $12.10 of the outperforming asset, Asset B, is sold, and the resulting $12.10 is invested in Asset A, producing a beginning-of-year-four allocation of $133.10 in Asset A and $133.10 in Asset B.

A similar procedure is followed for each of the five years from year four through year eight. At the end of the eight-year period, the portfolio value amounts to $175.38 in Asset A and $233.85 in Asset B, for a total of $409.23, representing a 9.36% compound annual growth rate on the initial investment of $200.00 ($100.00 in Asset A and $100.00 in Asset B).

The year-to-year investment performance of Asset A and Asset B, as traced by their respective graphs in the upper part of Figure 4.9, was achieved by committing additional funds to Asset A in year two, year three, and year eight, immediately after Asset A underper-formed relative to Asset B, and the committing of additional funds to Asset B in year five, year six, and year seven, immediately after Asset B underperformed relative to Asset A. In part, the success of this rebalancing method rests on the assumption that after a period (or series of periods) of investment *underperformance* for Asset A relative to Asset B, or vice versa, the investor is likely to encounter a period (or series of periods) in which Asset A will exhibit investment *outperformance* relative to Asset B, or vice versa. Although reversion-to-the-mean theories may justify such an approach in the long run, over shorter time periods such offsetting cyclicality in the level of investment returns may or may not prove to be the case.

Effects of the Asset Mix Ratio on Rebalancing Results

In the example discussed in Figure 4.9, the asset mix is rebalanced at the end of each year to a 50%–50% percentage allocation to Asset A and to Asset B. To analyze the influence of the asset rebalancing ratio on overall results over eight years, Table 4.1 shows the ending

T A B L E 4.1

Effects of the Asset Mix Ratio on Rebalancing Results

Annual Rebalancing Ratio to Asset A	Asset B	Portfolio Value at End of Eighth Year, Based on $200.00 Initial Investment	Compound Annual Growth Rate	Standard Deviation of Annual Returns	Sharpe Ratio[1]
100%	0%	$366.95	7.88%	13.64%	0.242
90%	10%	$378.58	8.30%	11.08%	0.336
80%	20%	$388.71	8.66%	8.54%	0.478
70%	30%	$397.24	8.96%	6.03%	0.727
60%	40%	$404.10	9.19%	3.60%	1.281
50%	50%	$409.23	9.36%	1.65%	2.899
40%	60%	$412.59	9.47%	2.40%	2.039
30%	70%	$414.13	9.53%	4.69%	1.056
20%	80%	$413.84	9.52%	7.17%	0.689
10%	90%	$411.70	9.44%	9.70%	0.501
0%	100%	$407.72	9.31%	12.25%	0.386

Note: [1]The Sharpe ratio is calculated by subtracting the risk-free rate of 4.58% (the average rate from 1945 through 2006 for the 30-Day U.S. Treasury Bill yield) from the investment's Compound Annual Growth Rate, and dividing the result by the investment's Standard Deviation.

Source: The Author.

portfolio value, compound annual growth rate, standard deviation of annual returns, and Sharpe ratio for 11 different asset rebalancing ratios, applied to the same yearly patterns of returns for Asset A and for Asset B described in Figure 4.9.

Table 4.1 shows that a portfolio consisting *exclusively of Asset A* (equivalent to a 100%–0% Asset A/Asset B rebalancing ratio) generates an eight-year compound annual growth rate of 7.88%, a standard deviation of annual returns of 13.64%, and a Sharpe ratio of 0.242. A portfolio consisting *exclusively of Asset B* (equivalent to a 0%–100% Asset A/Asset B rebalancing ratio) provides an eight-year compound annual growth rate of 9.31%, a standard deviation of annual returns of 12.25%, and a Sharpe ratio of 0.386. Therefore, portfolios that have an annual rebalancing ratio of *greater than 50% directed toward Asset B* generate eight-year compound annual growth rates that are higher than portfolios that have an annual rebalancing ratio of *greater than 50% directed toward Asset A*.

Owing to the annual magnitudes and sequencing of returns generated by Asset A relative to Asset B in Figure 4.9, the optimal portfolio value at the end of the eighth year is generated by a rebalancing mix of 30% for Asset A and 70% for Asset B (shaded in gray). The best asset rebalancing ratio is not the same under all relative patterns of returns for Asset A and for Asset B, and may be different depending on whether the investor is judging according to compound annual rate of growth, standard deviation of annual returns, or the ratio of return per unit of risk (the Sharpe ratio). In fact, the asset rebalancing mix that produces the lowest standard deviation of annual returns, and the highest Sharpe ratio, is a 50%–50% annual rebalancing to Asset A and to Asset B, which yields a standard deviation of annual returns of 1.65% and a Sharpe ratio of 2.899 (also shaded in gray).

Among the *quantitative* factors influencing the optimal rebalancing ratio are: (i) the number of asset classes; (ii) the number of time periods in the investor's time horizon; (iii) the rebalancing frequency; (iv) the direction, magnitude, and sequence of returns for each asset, both on an absolute basis and relative to one another; (v) the correlation of each asset's returns with other assets' returns; and (vi) cost and tax considerations. Among the *qualitative* factors influencing the optimal rebalancing ratio are the investor's: (i) personal characteristics, experience, goals, and objectives; (ii) risk profile, risk tolerance, and risk-management procedures; (iii) time horizon; (iv) annual income needs and spending rules; and (v) preferences, aversions, and externally and internally imposed constraints.

Selling Underperforming Assets to Purchase Outperforming Assets

Figure 4.10 shows the multiyear results of a rebalancing method that annually sells off a sufficient portion of the portfolio's relatively *underperforming* asset to purchase an additional 5% of the portfolio's relatively *outperforming* asset.

Assuming an initial investment of $100.00 in Asset A and an initial investment of $100.00 in Asset B, a vertical review of the results at the end of year one in Figure 4.10 shows that Asset A and Asset B each generate a 10% investment return in year one. This produced asset values of $110.00 for Asset A and $110.00 for Asset B, resulting in a 50%–50% asset allocation for Asset A and Asset B at the end of the first year.

For the $110.00 invested in Asset A for the second year, Asset A generates a –10% investment return, resulting in an end-of-year-two value of $99.00, and Asset B generates a +30% return, resulting in an end-of-year-two value of $143.00. At the end of year two, the pie charts show that Asset A accounts for 41% of the total portfolio ($99.00/$242.00) and Asset B represents 59% of the total portfolio ($143.00/$242.00). To add 5% to the relatively outperforming asset and accordingly rebalance the portfolio to begin year three, 5% of Asset B's end-of-year-two value of $143.00, or $7.15, is sold from Asset A and is added to Asset B. As a result, $91.85 ($99.00 – $7.15) is invested in Asset A and $150.15 ($143.00 + $7.15) is invested in Asset B to begin year three.

For the $91.85 invested in Asset A for the third year, Asset A generates a 0% investment return, resulting in an end-of-year-three value of $91.85, and Asset B generates a +20% return, resulting in an end-of-year-three value of $180.18. At the end of year three, the pie charts show that Asset A accounts for 34% of the total portfolio ($91.85/$272.03) and Asset B represents 66% of the total portfolio

F I G U R E 4.10

Rebalancing via Purchase of Increment 5% of Outperforming Asset and Sale of Underperforming Asset

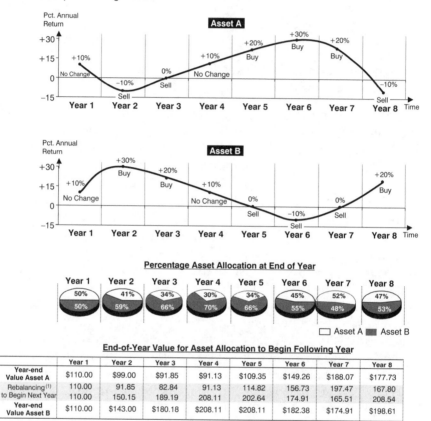

Percentage Asset Allocation at End of Year

Year 1	Year 2	Year 3	Year 4	Year 5	Year 6	Year 7	Year 8
50%	41%	34%	30%	34%	45%	52%	47%
50%	59%	66%	70%	66%	55%	48%	53%

☐ Asset A ■ Asset B

End-of-Year Value for Asset Allocation to Begin Following Year

	Year 1	Year 2	Year 3	Year 4	Year 5	Year 6	Year 7	Year 8
Year-end Value Asset A	$110.00	$99.00	$91.85	$91.13	$109.35	$149.26	$188.07	$177.73
Rebalancing [1] to Begin Next Year	110.00	91.85	82.84	91.13	114.82	156.73	197.47	167.80
	110.00	150.15	189.19	208.11	202.64	174.91	165.51	208.54
Year-end Value Asset B	$110.00	$143.00	$180.18	$208.11	$208.11	$182.38	$174.91	$198.61

Eight-Year Compound Annual Growth Rate for Total of Asset A Plus Asset B
(Initial Investment = $200.00, Ending Value = $376.34) = **8.22%**

Note: [1]Rebalancing via purchase of incremental 5% of relatively outperforming asset and sale of relatively underperforming asset.

Source: The Author.

($180.18/$272.03). To add 5% to the relatively outperforming asset and accordingly rebalance the portfolio to begin year four, 5% of Asset B's end-of-year-three value of $180.18, or $9.01, is sold from Asset A and added to Asset B. As a result, $82.84 ($91.85 − $9.01)

is invested in Asset A and \$189.19 (\$180.18 + \$9.01) is invested in Asset B to begin year four.

A similar procedure is followed for each of the five years from year four through year eight. At the end of the eight-year period, the portfolio value has grown to \$167.80 in Asset A and \$208.54 in Asset B, for a total of \$376.34, representing an 8.22% compound annual growth rate on the initial investment of \$200.00 (\$100.00 in Asset A and \$100.00 in Asset B).

The year-to-year investment performance of Asset A and Asset B, traced by their respective graphs in the upper part of Figure 4.10, shows an investor pursuing a strategy opposite to that employed in Figure 4.9. In Figure 4.10, the investor committed additional funds to Asset B in years two, three, and eight, immediately after *Asset B outperformed relative to Asset A*. The investor committed additional funds to Asset A in years five, six, and seven, immediately after *Asset A outperformed relative to Asset B*. In part, investors who favor this rebalancing method assume that after a period (or series of periods) of investment outperformance for Asset A relative to Asset B, or vice versa, the investor is likely to encounter a period (or series of periods) in which Asset A will continue to exhibit investment outperformance relative to Asset B, or vice versa. Such an approach, akin in some respects to momentum-based investing within certain asset classes, appears to offer attractive results. However, the merits of such an approach must be weighed against the severity, sequencing, and duration of any corrective price behavior that might occur at some point within the investor's portfolio time horizon.

Effects of the Incremental Purchase Percentage on Rebalancing Results

Table 4.2 shows the ending portfolio value, compound annual growth rate, standard deviation of annual returns, and Sharpe ratio for 11 different incremental purchase percentages, applied to the same yearly patterns of returns for Asset A and Asset B that are shown in Figure 4.10.

Table 4.2 demonstrates that selling the portfolio's relatively underperforming asset to purchase an incremental 3% of the

T A B L E 4.2

Effects of Incremental Purchasing Percentage on Rebalancing Results

Incremental Purchase Percentage Added to Previous Year's Outperforming Asset	Portfolio Value at End of Eighth Year, Based on $200.00 Initial Investment	Compound Annual Growth Rate	Standard Deviation of Annual Returns	Sharpe Ratio[1]
3%	$380.79	8.38%	2.74%	1.388
5%	$376.34	8.22%	2.91%	1.252
8%	$369.58	7.98%	3.20%	1.063
10%	$365.07	7.81%	3.43%	0.942
12%	$360.58	7.65%	3.69%	0.833
14%	$356.15	7.48%	4.01%	0.724
16%	$351.81	7.31%	4.39%	0.622
18%	$347.60	7.15%	4.87%	0.528
20%	$343.56	7.00%	5.45%	0.445
22%	$339.73	6.85%	6.17%	0.368
25%	$334.46	6.64%	7.56%	0.273

Note: [1]The Sharpe ratio is calculated by subtracting the risk-free rate of 4.58% (the average rate from 1945 through 2006 for the 30-Day U.S. Treasury Bill yield) from the investment's Compound Annual Growth Rate and dividing the result by the investment's Standard Deviation.

Source: The Author.

portfolio's relatively outperforming asset generates an eight-year compound annual growth rate of 8.38%, a standard deviation of annual returns of 2.74%, and a Sharpe ratio of 1.388 (shaded in gray). Selling the portfolio's relatively underperforming asset to purchase an incremental 25% of the portfolio's relatively outperforming asset produces an eight-year compound annual growth rate of 6.64%, a standard deviation of annual returns of 7.56%, and a Sharpe ratio of 0.273.

Based on the relative performance sequencing of annual returns for Asset A and Asset B, as shown in Figure 4.10, rebalancing portfolios by purchasing the outperforming asset in *smaller* incremental amounts produces higher compound annual growth rates, lower standard deviations of annual returns, and higher Sharpe ratios than rebalancing portfolios annually by purchasing the outperforming asset in *larger* incremental amounts.

ASSET-ALLOCATION DRIFT—NO REBALANCING

Figure 4.11 shows the multiyear results of an asset allocation that is *not* annually rebalanced according to any formal methodology. Instead, after establishing the initial asset-allocation ratio, in this case with a 50% allocation to Asset A and a 50% allocation to Asset B, without rebalancing the portfolio, the respective portfolio percentages of Asset A and Asset B are passively determined by the respective annual investment performance of each asset.

F I G U R E   4.11

Asset-Allocation Drift—No Rebalancing

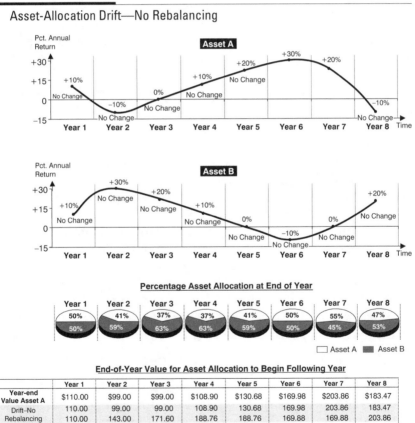

Percentage Asset Allocation at End of Year

	Year 1	Year 2	Year 3	Year 4	Year 5	Year 6	Year 7	Year 8
Asset A	50%	41%	37%	37%	41%	50%	55%	47%
Asset B	50%	59%	63%	63%	59%	50%	45%	53%

□ Asset A ■ Asset B

End-of-Year Value for Asset Allocation to Begin Following Year

	Year 1	Year 2	Year 3	Year 4	Year 5	Year 6	Year 7	Year 8
Year-end Value Asset A	$110.00	$99.00	$99.00	$108.90	$130.68	$169.98	$203.86	$183.47
Drift–No Rebalancing	110.00	99.00	99.00	108.90	130.68	169.98	203.86	183.47
	110.00	143.00	171.60	188.76	188.76	169.88	169.88	203.86
Year-end Value Asset B	$110.00	$143.00	$171.60	$188.76	$188.76	$169.88	$169.88	$203.86

Eight-Year Compound Annual Growth Rate for Total of Asset A Plus Asset B = **8.61%**
(Initial Investment = $200.00, Ending Value = $387.33)

Source: The Author.

With an initial investment of $100.00 in Asset A and an initial investment of $100.00 in Asset B, a vertical review of the results at the end of year one in Figure 4.11 shows that Asset A and Asset B each generate a 10% investment return, producing asset values of $110.00 for Asset A and $110.00 for Asset B and maintaining a 50%–50% asset allocation for Asset A and Asset B.

For the $110.00 invested in Asset A for the second year, Asset A generates a –10% investment return, resulting in an end-of-year-two value of $99.00, and Asset B generates a +30% return, resulting in an end-of-year-two value of $143.00. At the end of year two, the pie charts show that Asset A accounts for 41% of the total portfolio ($99.00/$242.00) and Asset B represents 59% of the total portfolio ($143.00/$242.00).

As no formal rebalancing activity similar to the methods followed in Figures 4.9 and 4.10 takes place in Figure 4.11, the amounts invested in Asset A and in Asset B *at the beginning of year three* are exactly the same amounts of Asset A and of Asset B that the investor owned *at the end of year two*. For the $99.00 invested in Asset A for the third year, Asset A generates a 0% investment return and Asset B generates a +20% return, resulting in an end-of-year-three value of $99.00 for Asset A and $171.60 for Asset B. At the end of year three, the pie charts show that Asset A accounts for 37% of the total portfolio ($99.00/$270.60) and Asset B represents 63% of the total portfolio ($171.60/$270.60).

For each of the five years from year four through eight, a similar process takes place, determining the portfolio's values and the resulting asset-allocation weightings by the investment performance of Asset A and Asset B. At the end of the eight years, the portfolio value has grown to $183.47 in Asset A and $203.86 in Asset B, representing an 8.61% compound annual growth rate on the total initial investment sum of $200.00 ($100.00 in Asset A and $100.00 in Asset B).

The year-to-year investment performance of Asset A and Asset B, traced by the graphs in the upper part of Figure 4.11, shows that the investor is strictly pursuing a buy-and-hold strategy for both assets. In part, the rationale underlying this asset-allocation approach rests on the assumptions that: (i) the investor's efforts and attention would be more appropriately focused on formulating and selecting a long-term asset-allocation ratio than on annual rebalancing, and once such an asset-allocation mix was established, it would be suitable to allow the portfolio's asset allocation to drift from the initial ratio; (ii) the time, attention, and out-of-pocket costs associated with annual rebalancing are not worth the relative gains produced by following formal rebalancing methods; and (iii) the investor may not have the resources, financial insight, or luck to be able to select the rebalancing method most appropriate for a given set of market conditions, asset return patterns, time horizons, and other circumstances. Whether these assumptions hold true is subject to some degree of debate.

REBALANCING SENSITIVITY ANALYSIS

This section analyzes the impact that a number of rebalancing variables can have on the compound annual growth rate, standard derivation of returns, and Sharpe ratio of different rebalancing approaches. Through this process, called *sensitivity analysis*, investors can gain a deeper understanding of the benefits and limitations of rebalancing.

Effects of the Initial Asset-Allocation Mix on Drift-Produced Results

In the drift–no portfolio rebalancing example shown in Figure 4.11, the asset mix drifts according to each position's annual investment results, with no active shifts between Asset A and Asset B. To analyze the influence of the initial asset-allocation ratio on overall investment results during an eight-year horizon, Table 4.3 shows the ending portfolio value, compound annual growth rate, standard deviation of annual returns, and Sharpe ratio for 11 different pre-drift asset allocation percentages, applied to the yearly patterns of returns for Asset A and Asset B described in Figure 4.11.

Table 4.3 demonstrates that allowing the portfolio's asset-allocation mix to drift from an initial investment of 90% in Asset A and 10% in Asset B generates an eight-year compound annual growth rate of 8.03%, a 10.70% standard deviation of annual returns, and a Sharpe ratio of 0.323. Allowing an initial investment

T A B L E 4.3

Effects of the Initial Asset-Allocation Mix on Drift-Produced Results

Initial Asset-Allocation Mix That Is Allowed to Drift		Value at End of Eighth Year, Based on $200 Initial Investment	Compound Annual Growth Rate	Standard Deviation of Annual Returns	Sharpe Ratio[1]
Asset A	Asset B				
100%	0%	$366.95	7.88%	13.64%	0.242
90%	10%	$371.03	8.03%	10.70%	0.323
80%	20%	$375.10	8.18%	7.96%	0.453
70%	30%	$379.18	8.32%	5.45%	0.687
60%	40%	$383.26	8.47%	3.34%	1.165
50%	50%	$387.34	8.61%	2.49%	1.620
40%	60%	$391.41	8.76%	3.67%	1.140
30%	70%	$395.49	8.90%	5.66%	0.764
20%	80%	$399.57	9.04%	7.83%	0.570
10%	90%	$403.64	9.17%	10.03%	0.458
0%	100%	$407.72	9.31%	12.25%	0.386

Note: [1]The Sharpe ratio is calculated by subtracting the risk-free rate of 4.58% (the average rate from 1945 through 2006 for the 30-Day U.S. Treasury Bill yield) from the investment's Compound Annual Growth Rate and dividing the result by the investment's Standard Deviation.

Source: The Author.

of 10% in Asset A and 90% in Asset B produces an eight-year compound annual growth rate of 9.17%, a 10.03% standard deviation of annual returns, and a Sharpe ratio of 0.458.

Portfolios that are allowed to drift from a starting asset allocation that is heavily weighted toward Asset A tend to have lower compound annual growth rates, higher standard deviations of annual returns, and lower Sharpe ratios than portfolios that are allowed to drift from an initial 50-50 allocation in Assets A and B. At the other end of the spectrum, portfolios that are allowed to drift from a starting investment that is heavily weighted toward Asset B tend to have higher compound annual growth rates, higher standard deviations of annual returns, and lower Sharpe ratios than portfolios that are allowed to drift from an initial 50-50 allocation between Assets A and B.

The highest portfolio value, $407.72, representing a 9.31% compound annual growth rate (shaded in gray), is produced by an initial allocation mix that is 0% invested in Asset A and 100% invested in Asset B. The lowest standard deviation of annual returns, 2.49%, and the highest Sharpe ratio, 1.620 (also shaded in gray), are produced by an initial allocation mix that is 50% invested in Asset A and 50% invested in Asset B.

Effects of Portfolio Time Horizon on Rebalancing Results

It is worth repeating that the length of investors' portfolio time horizons can influence the results of rebalancing. The degree of these effects depends on the rebalancing methods and the patterns of the underlying returns on the assets in the investor's portfolio. To analyze the influence of the time horizon on rebalancing, Table 4.4 shows the ending portfolio value, compound annual growth rate, standard deviation of annual returns, and Sharpe ratio for seven different time horizons, applied to the rebalancing methods and patterns of returns for Asset A and for Asset B that are described in: (i) Figure 4.9 (selling *outperforming* assets to purchase *underperforming* assets, in a 70% Asset A to 30% Asset B annual rebalancing ratio and in a 30% Asset A to 70% Asset B annual rebalancing ratio, respectively), and (ii) Figure 4.10 (selling *underperforming* assets to purchase *outperforming* assets, in incremental purchase percentages of 5% and 22%, respectively, of the previous year's outperforming asset).

The part of Table 4.4 on page 130 illustrates how, when the investor's rebalancing method calls for annual rebalancing *through the sale of outperforming assets to purchase underperforming assets to a ratio of 70% in Asset A and 30% in Asset B*, the compound annual growth rate, standard deviation of annual returns, and Sharpe ratio vary from 8.96%, 6.03%, and 0.727, respectively, at the end of the eighth year, to 5.95%, 3.27%, and 0.420, respectively, at the end of the third year. Similarly, when the investor's rebalancing method calls for annual rebalancing to *a ratio of 30% in Asset A and 70% in Asset B*, the compound annual growth rate, standard deviation of annual returns, and Sharpe ratio vary from 9.53%, 4.69%, and 1.056, respectively, at the end of the eighth year, to 13.95%, 3.27%, and 2.866, respectively, at the end of the third year.

T A B L E 4.4

Effects of Portfolio Time Horizon on Rebalancing Results

Selling Outperforming Assets to Purchase Underperforming Assets

Annual Rebalancing Ratio, Asset A–Asset B	Exit Year	Portfolio Value at End of Exit Year Based on $200 Initial Investment	Compound Annual Growth Rate	Standard Deviation of Annual Returns	Sharpe Ratio[1]
70%–30%	8th	$397.24	8.96%	6.03%	0.727
70%–30%	7th	$401.25	10.46%	4.98%	1.181
70%–30%	6th	$351.97	9.88%	5.16%	1.028
70%–30%	5th	$298.28	8.32%	4.08%	0.917
70%–30%	4th	$261.65	6.95%	3.32%	0.715
70%–30%	3rd	$237.86	5.95%	3.27%	0.420
70%–30%	2nd	$224.40	5.92%	4.00%	0.336
30%–70%	8th	$414.13	9.53%	4.69%	1.056
30%–70%	7th	$373.09	9.32%	4.98%	0.952
30%–70%	6th	$351.97	9.88%	5.16%	1.028
30%–70%	5th	$345.07	11.53%	4.08%	1.704
30%–70%	4th	$325.54	12.95%	3.32%	2.522
30%–70%	3rd	$295.94	13.95%	3.27%	2.866
30%–70%	2nd	$259.60	13.93%	4.00%	2.338

Note: [1]The Sharpe ratio is calculated by subtracting the risk–free rate of 4.58% (the average rate from 1945 through 2006 for the 30-Day U.S. Treasury Bill yield) from the investment's Compound Annual Growth Rate, and dividing the result by the investment's Standard Deviation.

Source: The Author.

The highest compound annual growth rate and the highest Sharpe ratio for the 70%–30% Asset A–Asset B annual rebalancing ratio, 10.46% and 1.181, respectively, occur at the end of the seventh year, while the lowest standard deviation of annual returns, 3.2%, occurs at the end of the third year (shaded in gray). The highest compound annual growth rate and the highest Sharpe ratio for the 30%–70% Asset A–Asset B annual rebalancing ratio, 13.95% and 2.866, respectively, occur at the end of the third year, while the lowest standard deviation of annual returns, 3.32%, occurs at the end of the fourth year (shaded in gray).

T A B L E 4.4 (Continued)

Effects of Portfolio Time Horizon on Rebalancing Results

Selling Underperforming Assets to Purchase Outperforming Assets

Annual Rebalancing Ratio, Asset A−Asset B	Exit Year	Portfolio Value at End of Exit Year, Based on $200 Initial Investment	Compound Annual Growth Rate	Standard Deviation of Annual Returns	Sharpe Ratio[1]
5%	8th	$376.34	8.22%	2.91%	1.252
5%	7th	$362.98	8.89%	2.50%	1.725
5%	6th	$331.64	8.79%	2.69%	1.566
5%	5th	$317.46	9.68%	2.03%	2.514
5%	4th	$299.23	10.60%	1.04%	5.791
5%	3rd	$272.03	10.80%	1.14%	5.458
5%	2nd	$242.00	10.00%	0.00%	NM
22%	8th	$339.73	6.85%	6.17%	0.368
22%	7th	$303.19	6.12%	6.28%	0.246
22%	6th	$292.21	6.52%	6.69%	0.290
22%	5th	$309.31	9.11%	4.19%	1.082
22%	4th	$304.58	11.09%	1.91%	3.410
22%	3rd	$276.89	11.45%	2.08%	3.304
22%	2nd	$242.00	10.00%	0.00%	NM

In the other part of Table 4.4 on this page 131, in which the investor annually rebalances *through an incremental purchase of 5% of the outperforming asset*, the compound annual growth rate, standard deviation of annual returns, and Sharpe ratio vary from 8.22%, 2.91%, and 1.252, respectively, at the end of the eighth year, to 10.80%, 1.14%, and 5.458, respectively, at the end of the third year. Similarly, when the investor rebalances by *purchasing an incremental 22% of the outperforming asset*, the compound annual growth rate, standard deviation of annual returns, and Sharpe ratio vary from 6.85%, 6.17%, and 0.368, respectively, at the end of the eighth year, to 11.45%, 2.08%, and 3.304, respectively, at the end of the third year.

The highest compound annual growth rate for the 5% incremental purchase of outperforming assets of 10.80%, occurs at the end of the third year, while the lowest standard deviation of annual returns and the highest Sharpe ratio, 1.14% and 5.791 occur at the end of the fourth year (shaded in gray). Similarly, the highest compound annual growth rate for the 22% incremental purchase of outperforming assets, 11.45%, occurs at the end of the third year, while the lowest standard deviation of returns and the highest Sharpe ratio, 1.91% and 3.4%, occur at the end of the fourth year (also shaded in gray).

Based on the relative patterns and sequencing of annual returns, as well as the rebalancing methods for Asset A and for Asset B, as shown in Figures 4.9 and 4.10, *shorter portfolio time horizons* tend to produce higher compound annual growth rates, lower standard deviations of annual returns, and higher Sharpe ratios than do *longer portfolio time horizons* when one is selling underperforming assets to purchase outperforming assets, or selling outperforming assets to purchase underperforming assets in ratios which favor Asset B over Asset A.

Effects of Returns Patterns on Rebalancing Results

The analyses relating to Figures 4.9 through 4.11 focus primarily on two assets, Asset A and Asset B, whose relative patterns of annual returns trace almost symmetrically offsetting paths through time. These investment-performance curves are here allowed to remain unchanged from Figure 4.10 to Table 4.3 to examine the effects of four factors on the results of rebalancing: (i) the annual rebalancing ratio between Asset A and Asset B that is used to purchase an incremental quantity of the *relatively underperforming* asset; (ii) the incremental percentage employed to commit additional funds to the *relatively outperforming* asset; (iii) the beginning percentage asset mix between Asset A and Asset B, from which the asset allocation is allowed to drift according to each asset's annual investment performance; and (iv) the length of the investor's portfolio time horizon.

Investors should also consider the effects of the *patterns of absolute returns* for Assets A and B on rebalancing results. Figure 4.12 contains a series of 18 simplified investment returns curves, grouped according to: (i) their degree of slope (gradual or extreme);

F I G U R E 4.12

Patterns of Assets' Investment Returns through Time

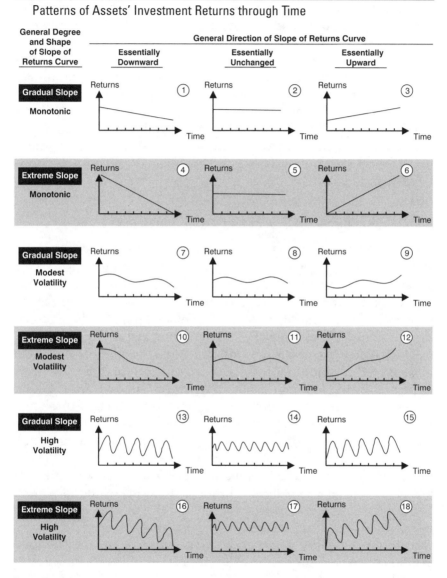

Source: The Author.

(ii) their direction (essentially downward, essentially unchanged, or essentially upward); and (iii) their general shape (generally monotonic, exhibiting generally modest volatility, or exhibiting generally high volatility).

The investment returns curves displayed in Figure 4.12 are principally intended to make the investor aware of the multitude of patterns that assets' investment results can trace through time. Keeping in mind that each asset's returns may entirely or only partially follow any one of the generalized patterns shown in Figure 4.12, it is possible for the investor to conduct a rudimentary two-asset scenario analysis to assess the relative merits of the main rebalancing methods.

Rebalancing between U.S. Equities and Bonds in the 1990s

Actual investment performance data for the years 1997 through 2006, using the Standard & Poor's 500 Composite Index as a proxy for equity returns and the Lehman Brothers Aggregate Index as a proxy for bond returns are shown in Tables 4.5 through 4.9 to gauge the relative merits of several rebalancing methods.

In Table 4.5, assume that the investor begins calendar year 1997 (depicted as year one) with an initial portfolio of $100.00, invested 60% in equities (in the S&P 500 Composite Index) and 40% in bonds (in the Lehman Brothers Aggregate Index). After taking account of the respective investment returns for each of these two indexes at the end of each calendar year, also assume that *the portfolio is rebalanced to 60% equities, 40% bonds* each succeeding year.

For instance, during 1997 (year one) the $60.00 (60% of the initial investment) the investor placed in the equity market generates a 33.4% total return, resulting in an end-of-year value of $80.02. During the same time frame, the $40.00 (40% of the initial investment) that the investor placed in the bond market generates a 9.7% total return, resulting in an end-of-year value of $43.86. The total portfolio thus amounts to $123.88, apportioned as 65% in equities (= $80.02/$123.88) and 35% in bonds (= $43.86/$123.88). To begin the second year at the target asset-allocation ratio of 60% equities and 40% bonds, the investor must sell 5% of the total portfolio, or $5.69, out of equities and reinvest that in bonds. As a result, the investor's portfolio starts out the second year invested $74.33 in equities (rather than $80.02) and $49.55 in bonds (rather than $43.86). This process continues for years 2 through 10 (calendar years 1998 through 2006), resulting in an ending portfolio value of $216.39, which represents a compound annual growth rate of 8.02% and a standard deviation of annual returns of 11.6%.

The "Amount to Be Rebalanced" column at the far right of Table 4.5 illustrates that not inconsequential amounts were taken out of equities in years five, six, seven, eight, and nine in response to the significant investment outperformance of equities relative to bonds in each of those years. In fact, 1997, 1998, and 1999 produced some of the highest five-year investment returns (+33.4%, +28.6%, and +21.0%, respectively) ever experienced by the Standard & Poor's 500 Composite Index. To continue taking money out of equities and redeploying the proceeds into bonds in the face of such favorable outperformance requires significant discipline and perseverance.

However, one of the anticipated benefits of such rebalancing would be less relative exposure to equities if and when equity returns begin to underperform the returns from bonds. The year 2000 (year 4 in Table 4.5) represented just such a year, in which equities (the S&P 500 index) produced a total return of –9.1% and bonds produced a total return of +11.6%. The advantages of rebalancing would be borne out further, to the degree that equities continued relatively to underperform bonds, which, in fact, happened in years 2001 and 2002, when the S&P 500 index declined 11.9% and 22.1%, respectively, again underperforming the Lehman Brothers Aggregate Index for bonds, which rose 8.4% and 10.3%, respectively.

For the same assets and the same time period (the 10 years from 1997 through 2006), Table 4.6 shows what would have happened to the investor's portfolio had it been allowed to drift, with no rebalancing.

In Table 4.6, assume that the investor begins calendar year 1997 (year one) with an initial portfolio of $100.00, initially invested 60% in equities and 40% in bonds. After taking account of the respective investment returns for each of these two indices, at the end of each calendar year also assume that the portfolio is *not rebalanced* to any specific target weighting between equities and bonds.

T A B L E 4.5

Effects of Annual Rebalancing to Target Ratios of 60% Equities, 40% Bonds

Calendar Year	Year	Asset Class	Beginning Value	Percent Return	Ending Value
1997	1	Equities	60.00	33.4%	80.02
		Bonds	40.00	9.7%	43.86
			100.00		123.88
1998	2	Equities	74.33	28.6%	95.57
		Bonds	49.55	8.7%	53.86
			123.88		149.42
1999	3	Equities	89.65	21.0%	108.52
		Bonds	59.77	−0.8%	59.28
			149.42		167.80
2000	4	Equities	100.68	−9.1%	91.52
		Bonds	67.12	11.6%	74.92
			167.80		166.44
2001	5	Equities	99.86	−11.9%	87.99
		Bonds	66.58	8.4%	72.20
			166.44		160.19
2002	6	Equities	96.11	−22.1%	74.87
		Bonds	64.07	10.3%	70.65
			160.19		145.52
2003	7	Equities	87.31	28.7%	112.35
		Bonds	58.21	4.1%	60.60
			145.52		172.95
2004	8	Equities	103.77	10.9%	115.06
		Bonds	69.18	4.3%	72.18
			172.95		187.24
2005	9	Equities	112.35	4.9%	117.86
		Bonds	74.90	2.4%	76.72
			187.24		194.58
2006	10	Equities	116.75	15.8%	135.19
		Bonds	77.83	4.3%	81.20
			194.58		216.39

Compound Annual Growth Rate = 8.02%   3.6577

Standard Deviation of Annual Returns = 11.59%

Note: In the example shown above, actual returns for the years from 1997 through 2006 (years 1 through 10) for the S&P 500 Composite Index and the Lehman Brothers Aggregate Index are used as a proxy for returns from investing in equities and bonds, respectively.

Source: The Author.

Resulting Percentage in Asset Class	Target Percentage Asset Allocation	Target Monetary Asset Allocation	Amount to Be Rebalanced
65%	60%	74.33	(5.69)
35%	40%	49.55	5.69
100%	100%	123.88	
64%	60%	89.65	(5.91)
36%	40%	59.77	5.91
100%	100%	149.42	
65%	60%	100.68	(7.84)
35%	40%	67.12	7.84
100%	100%	167.80	
55%	60%	99.86	8.35
45%	40%	66.58	(8.35)
100%	100%	166.44	
55%	60%	96.11	8.12
45%	40%	64.07	(8.12)
100%	100%	160.19	
51%	60%	87.31	12.44
49%	40%	58.21	(12.44)
100%	100%	145.52	
65%	60%	103.77	(8.58)
35%	40%	69.18	8.58
100%	100%	172.95	
61%	60%	112.35	(2.72)
39%	40%	74.90	2.72
100%	100%	187.24	
61%	60%	116.75	(1.12)
39%	40%	77.83	1.12
100%	100%	194.58	
62%			
38%			
100%			

T A B L E   4.6

Effects of Asset-Allocation Drift (Buy and Hold)

Calendar Year	Year	Asset Class	Beginning Value	Percent Return
1997	1	Equities	60.00	33.4%
		Bonds	40.00	9.7%
			100.00	
1998	2	Equities	80.02	28.6%
		Bonds	43.86	8.7%
			123.88	
1999	3	Equities	102.88	21.0%
		Bonds	47.67	−0.8%
			150.56	
2000	4	Equities	124.53	−9.1%
		Bonds	47.28	11.6%
			171.81	
2001	5	Equities	113.20	−11.9%
		Bonds	52.78	8.4%
			165.98	
2002	6	Equities	99.74	−22.1%
		Bonds	57.23	10.3%
			156.97	
2003	7	Equities	77.70	28.7%
		Bonds	63.10	4.1%
			140.80	
2004	8	Equities	99.98	10.9%
		Bonds	65.69	4.3%
			165.68	
2005	9	Equities	110.86	4.9%
		Bonds	68.54	2.4%
			179.41	
2006	10	Equities	116.31	15.8%
		Bonds	70.21	4.3%
			186.51	

Compound Annual Growth Rate =   7.59%

Standard Deviation of Annual Returns = 12.39%

Note: In the example shown above, actual returns for the years from 1997 through 2006 (years 1 through 10) for the S&P 500 Composite Index and the Lehman Brothers Aggregate Index are used as a proxy for returns from investing in equities and bonds, respectively.

Source: The Author.

Ending Value	Resulting Percentage in Asset Class	Target Percentage Asset Allocation	Target Monetary Asset Allocation	Amount to Be Rebalanced
80.02	65%	Not Applicable Due to Asset-Allocation Drift		
43.86	35%			
123.88	100%			
102.88	68%	Not Applicable Due to Asset-Allocation Drift		
47.67	32%			
150.56	100%			
124.53	72%	Not Applicable Due to Asset-Allocation Drift		
47.28	28%			
171.81	100%			
113.20	68%	Not Applicable Due to Asset-Allocation Drift		
52.78	32%			
165.98	100%			
99.74	64%	Not Applicable Due to Asset-Allocation Drift		
57.23	36%			
156.97	100%			
77.70	55%	Not Applicable Due to Asset-Allocation Drift		
63.10	45%			
140.80	100%			
99.98	60%	Not Applicable Due to Asset-Allocation Drift		
65.69	40%			
165.68	100%			
110.86	62%	Not Applicable Due to Asset-Allocation Drift		
68.54	38%			
179.41	100%			
116.31	62%	Not Applicable Due to Asset-Allocation Drift		
70.21	38%			
186.51	100%			
134.68	65%	Not Applicable Due to Asset-Allocation Drift		
73.25	35%			
207.93	100%			

For instance, during 1997 the $60.00 initial investment in the equity market generates a 33.4% total return, resulting in an end-of-year value of $80.02. At the same time, the $40.00 initial investment in the bond market generates a 9.7% total return, resulting in an end-of-year value of $43.86. The total portfolio thus amounts to $123.88, apportioned 65% in equities (= $80.02/$123.88) and 35% in bonds (= $43.86/$123.88). The investor then begins year 2 (1998) with $80.02 invested in equities and $43.86 invested in bonds. This drift process is allowed to continue for years 2 through 10 (calendar years 1997 through 2006), resulting in an ending portfolio value of $207.93, a compound annual growth rate of 7.59%, and a standard deviation of annual returns of 12.4%.

The "Resulting Percentage in Asset Class" column toward the far right of Table 4.6 indicates that due to their pronounced investment outperformance relative to bonds in years seven through ten, equities began to account for increasing percentages of the total

T A B L E 4.7

Effects of 100% Asset Allocation to Equities

Year	Beginning Value	Percent Return	Ending Value
1	100.00	33.4%	133.36
2	133.36	28.6%	171.47
3	171.47	21.0%	207.55
4	207.55	−9.1%	188.67
5	188.67	−11.9%	166.23
6	166.23	−22.1%	129.50
7	129.50	28.7%	166.64
8	166.64	10.9%	184.77
9	184.77	4.9%	193.85
10	193.85	15.8%	224.46

Compound Annual Growth Rate = 8.42%

Standard Deviation of Annual Returns = 19.14%

Note: In the example above, actual returns for the S&P 500 Composite Index and the Lehman Brothers Aggregate Bond Index are used as a proxy for returns from investing in equities and bonds, respectively.

Source: The Author.

portfolio, returning to 65% at the end of the tenth year after suffering losses in the years 2000 to 2002, reaching a low of 55% in the sixth year. As a result of high returns during the latter half of the 1990s, many investors consciously or unwittingly allowed their asset weightings in equities to drift to levels that may have exceeded their long-term asset-allocation targets and their risk profiles.

Table 4.7 sets forth the results of a portfolio with an asset allocation *invested 100% in equities*, for years 1 through 10 (from 1997 through 2006).

An investor who placed $100.00 entirely in S&P 500 equities at the beginning of 1997 would have seen his or her portfolio grow to $224.46 in value at the end of 2006, producing a 10-year compound annual growth rate of 8.42% and a standard deviation of annual returns of 19.14%.

Table 4.8 presents the results of a portfolio invested 100% in bonds for years 1 through 10 (from 1997 through 2006).

T A B L E   4.8

Effects of 100% Asset Allocation to Bonds

Year	Beginning Value	Percent Return	Ending Value
1	100.00	9.7%	109.65
2	109.65	8.7%	119.18
3	119.18	−0.8%	118.20
4	118.20	11.6%	131.94
5	131.94	8.4%	143.08
6	143.08	10.3%	157.76
7	157.76	4.1%	164.23
8	164.23	4.3%	171.36
9	171.36	2.4%	175.52
10	175.52	4.3%	183.12

Compound Annual Growth Rate = 6.24%

Standard Deviation of Annual Returns = 4.00%

Note: In the example above, actual returns for the S&P 500 Composite Index and the Lehman Brothers Aggregate Bond Index are used as a proxy for returns from investing in equities and bonds, respectively.

Source: The Author.

Investors who placed $100.00 entirely in bonds at the beginning
of 1997 would have seen their portfolio grow to $183.12 in value at
the end of 2006, producing a 10-year compound annual growth rate
of 6.24% and a standard deviation of annual returns of 4.0%.

Table 4.9 brings together the results of the four rebalancing
methods between U.S. equities and bonds in the late 1990s and
early twenty-first century we consider here: (i) annual rebalancing
to target ratios (outlined in Table 4.5, 60% to equities, 40% to
bonds); for comparison purposes, other equities-bonds allocation
ratios are also shown in Table 4.9; (ii) asset-allocation drift, or no
rebalancing strategy (presented in Table 4.6); (iii) an asset allocation
of 100% equities (set forth in Table 4.7); and (iv) an asset allocation
of 100% bonds (described in Table 4.8).

Table 4.9 shows that the highest portfolio value at the end of
the tenth year, based on a $100.00 initial investment, is produced by

T A B L E 4.9

Comparative Analysis of Asset-Allocation Rebalancing Methods[1]

Rebalancing Methods	Portfolio Value at End of Tenth Year, Based on $100 Initial Investment	Compound Annual Growth Rate	Standard Deviation of Annual Returns	Sharpe Ratio[2]
Annual Rebalancing to Target Ratios (Equities: 50%; Bonds: 50%)	$212.25	7.82%	11.2%	0.289
(Equities: 60%; Bonds: 40%)	$216.39	8.02%	11.6%	0.298
(Equities: 70%; Bonds: 30%)	$220.53	8.23%	12.0%	0.304
(Equities: 80%; Bonds: 20%)	$224.67	8.43%	12.5%	0.309
(Equities: 90%; Bonds: 10%)	$228.81	8.63%	12.9%	0.313
Asset-Allocation Drift	$207.93	7.59%	12.4%	0.244
Asset Allocation 100% to Equities	$224.46	8.42%	19.1%	0.201
Asset Allocation 100% to Bonds	$183.12	6.24%	4.0%	0.415

Notes: [1]Actual returns from 1997 through 2006 for the S&P 500 Composite Index and the Lehman Brothers Aggregate Bond Index are used as a proxy for returns from investing in equities and bonds, respectively.

[2]The Sharpe ratio is calculated by subtracting the risk-free rate of 4.58% (the average rate from 1945 through 2006 for the 30-Day U.S. Treasury Bill yield) from the investment's Compound Annual Growth Rate and dividing the result by the investment's Standard Deviation.

Source: The Author.

an asset allocation of 90% to equities and 10% to bonds, which generates a final portfolio value of $228.81 and a compound annual growth rate of 8.63% (shaded in gray). At the same time, these relatively high returns are accompanied by the highest standard deviation of annual returns after the asset allocation of 100% to equities shown in Table 4.9, 12.9%. As a result, the reward-per-unit-of-risk measure, or Sharpe ratio, of the 90% equities and 10% bonds asset allocation is 0.313, above the Sharpe ratios of all of the other annual rebalancing to target ratios methods shown in the table.

The lowest portfolio value at the end of the tenth year is produced by *an asset allocation of 100% to bonds,* which generates a final portfolio value of $183.12 and a compound annual growth rate of 6.24% (shaded in gray). These relatively low returns are accompanied by the lowest standard deviation of annual returns shown in Table 4.9, 4.0%. Owing to the significant decline in equity returns during the 2000–2002 period, the reward-per-unit-of risk measure, or Sharpe ratio, of the 100% equities asset allocation is 0.201, the lowest of any of the rebalancing methods shown in the table.

The asset-allocation *drift—no rebalancing method*—produces a final portfolio value of $207.93, a compound annual growth rate of 7.59%, a 12.4% standard deviation of annual returns, and a Sharpe ratio of 0.244 (shaded in gray). These results are all surpassed by the *annual rebalancing to target ratios method,* when the target rebalancing is to 70% equities or higher. For example, an annual rebalancing to a target ratio of 70% equities, 30% bonds produces a final portfolio value of $220.53, a compound annual growth rate of 8.23%, a standard deviation of annual returns of 12.0%, and a Sharpe ratio of 0.304. From a reward-to-risk standpoint, the highest Sharpe ratio of any of the rebalancing methods shown in Table 4.9 is produced by 100% bonds asset allocation. With a 6.24% compound annual growth rate and a 4% standard deviation of annual returns, the Sharpe ratio of this asset-allocation rebalancing method is 0.415. Because of the fallen Sharpe ratio for equities, as a result of the decline in returns during the 2000–2002 period, the Sharpe ratio for bonds rose relative to equities.

Focusing on the effects of a number of rebalancing methods between U.S. equities and bonds in the 1990s and early twenty-first century can furnish valuable insights into the mechanics, rewards, and risks associated with each strategy. At the same time, investors need to be aware that some of the results and conclusions of such analyses may very well differ under financial circumstances that vary from those prevailing for the Standard & Poor's 500 Composite Index and the Lehman Brothers Aggregate Index from 1997 through 2006.

For example, keep in mind that broad-based, large-capitalization U.S. equities indices such as the Standard & Poor's 500 produced historically high returns for a significant part of 1997–2006, tending to favor rebalancing strategies that in one way or another emphasized S&P 500 equities over bonds. Portfolio time horizons of shorter or longer length, such as 5 years or 15 years, or which include extended intervals in which bonds significantly outperform equities, may rank other rebalancing methods higher than equity-emphasizing rebalancing strategies. Other choices of assets, other choices of indices (such as selecting the Nasdaq Composite Index rather than the S&P 500 as a proxy for equity returns, or using the J.P. Morgan Chase Intermediate-Term Government Bond Index rather than the Lehman Brothers Aggregate Index as a proxy for bond returns), and considering greater numbers of assets may also alter the relative attractiveness of various rebalancing methods. Finally, taxes and other expenses need to be taken into consideration in assessing the merits of any rebalancing activity.

CRITICAL SUCCESS FACTORS IN REBALANCING

Investors may consider several important steps to help them decide whether, when, how, and by what means to rebalance their assets. First, investors should determine the scope of assets they may rebalance. Most often, this determination addresses the question of whether to include concentrated positions, personal holdings, or other asset categories in the investor's rebalancing activity.

Second, the investor should develop a strategic and tactical asset-allocation plan, perhaps embedded within a thoughtfully created, written investment policy statement. In many cases, investors' initial and tactical strategic asset allocation will reflect their personal circumstances, time horizon, risk profile, income needs, market outlook, and goals and objectives. As time passes and investors experience the psychological effects of rising and falling asset values, some may alter their strategic and tactical asset allocations to bring them into closer alignment with their own comfort levels and other new information.

Third, investors may evaluate various rebalancing methods and scenarios in the light of: (i) past intervals of financial history; (ii) a range of expected financial-market conditions, giving particular consideration to various asset classes' valuations relative to long-term levels; and (iii) the potential efficacy of any exceptional rebalancing activity they might undertake.

The ultimate success or failure of rebalancing activity is not only a function of the risk-and-return elements of each asset class, but also of several critical human characteristics. Figure 4.13 lists these critical human characteristics.

Brief elaborations of some of the critical success factors in rebalancing activity are set forth below.

- **Discipline:** Investors need the internal fortitude to stay on course with a rebalancing plan after it has been developed with care and judged to be appropriate to the financial market environment and to the investor's own profile, needs, and destiny.

- **Diligence:** Investors must exercise diligence in monitoring the current and future investment climate and the overall portfolio, each asset class, and specific investments.

- **Discernment:** Investors require sensitive antennae to comprehend: (i) how much of an investment's returns is due to market conditions and how much is due to the skill of a specific asset manager; and (ii) whether an investment's underperformance or outperformance is temporary or likely to endure. Another important and often overlooked element of discernment relates to investors' ability to recognize changes that may occur within themselves.

- **Discovery:** Investors need to search for and remain open to new ideas and new insights about existing and newly introduced assets, investment vehicles, strategies, tactics, and useful information sources.

F I G U R E 4.13

Selected Critical Success Factors in Asset-Allocation Rebalancing Activity

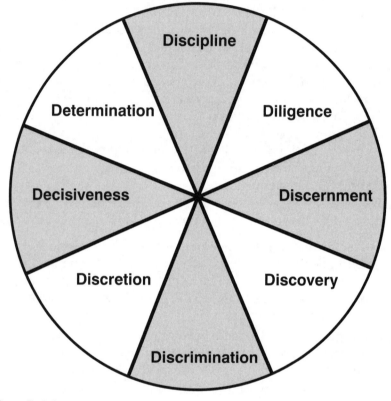

Source: The Author.

- **Discrimination:** Investors need to be able to distinguish actions that *augment* and those that detract from the portfolio's risk-return profile. In addition, investors need to be able to say no to actions and gambits they should avoid.
- **Discretion:** Investors need the ability to listen to a variety of sources, facts, and opinions under a variety of conditions, without letting any one view predominate during the evaluation process. After the evaluation process, investors need to be able to isolate themselves for a time

to an appropriate degree and tune out extraneous and erroneous information.

- **Decisiveness:** After judiciously weighing the arguments in favor of and opposed to a given course of action, investors need to be able to come to a conclusion and take action in an expedient manner.
- **Determination:** Investors should resolve to achieve a balance between flexibility and conviction, neither obstinately holding on to views when the facts have changed or have been incorrectly interpreted nor whimsically abandoning sound views in the face of superficially appealing but specious reasoning.

S E C T I O N

UNDERPINNINGS OF ASSET ALLOCATION

CHAPTER

INDIVIDUAL INVESTOR
BEHAVIOR

OVERVIEW

Although this book is intended for both professional and individual investors, this chapter focuses especially on the investment behavior of individuals, beginning with the factors that affect individual investors' asset-allocation decisions. Next, the chapter describes the evolution of individual investors' asset-allocation focus over the last several decades, showing how individuals have broadened their portfolios from U.S. stocks, bonds, and cash to include international and alternative asset classes and, more recently, to encompass various forms of absolute-return strategies.

The chapter then discusses many primary determinants of individual investors' asset allocation, ranging from wealth-related or balance-sheet factors, to income-related or income-statement factors, to special or off-balance-sheet factors. The chapter also covers asset-allocation tradeoffs that tend to orient individual investors toward lower-risk, lower-return types of assets versus higher-risk, higher-return types of assets.

A number of strategic and tactical principles of asset allocation are reviewed here, followed by a description of individual
investors' behavioral characteristics as they approach asset allocation through varying market conditions. After a review of anticipated versus actual required asset-allocation skills, the chapter
concludes with a discussion of financial insights for individual
investors from market history, the field of behavioral finance, and
the concept of emotional intelligence in investing.

FACTORS AFFECTING INDIVIDUAL INVESTORS' ASSET-ALLOCATION DECISIONS

Individual and professional investors face several critical factors
that affect their asset-allocation decisions. These factors are shown
in Figure 5.1.

As Figure 5.1 illustrates, the factors affecting individual
investors' asset-allocation decisions can influence one another and
can be grouped into three broad categories. Each of these broad categories affects individual investors' behavior, and they collectively
correspond to the detailed Asset-Allocation Worksheets contained
in Chapter 9. These factors include:

- **Investor Profile:** (i) the ultimate length of the time horizon for the portfolio as a whole; and (ii) the degree of
  volatility or value impairment the investor can
  withstand, in the aggregate and for specific investment
  categories.

- **Investment Outlook:** (i) the degree of patience and
  conviction that the investor can maintain in the face of
  significant under- or outperformance by the portfolio
  as a whole or by selected asset classes; and (ii) the
  investor's confidence level in the specific return, risk,
  and correlation projections on which asset-allocation
  decisions are based.

- **Investment Universe:** (i) the desired extent of principal
  protection versus purchasing-power protection; and
  (ii) of the role and amount of core and non-core asset
  classes in the portfolio.

F I G U R E   5.1

F I G U R E   5.1

Factors Affecting Individual Investors' Asset-Allocation Decisions

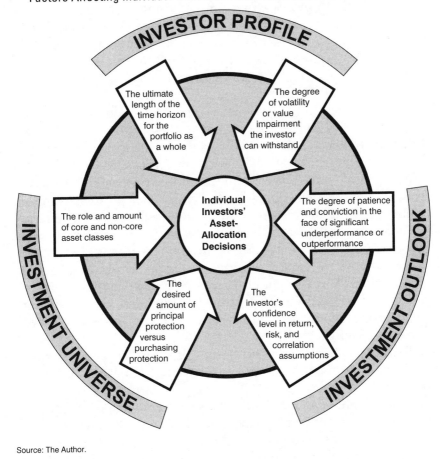

Source: The Author.

THE EVOLUTION OF INDIVIDUAL INVESTORS' ASSET-ALLOCATION ACTIVITY

During the final few decades of the twentieth century, investors' behavior evolved, and that has affected how individual investors deploy funds. Emerging from the 1950s, 1960s, and 1970s and entering into the 1980s, many individual investors were beginning to gain exposure to the concepts and concrete details of asset allocation, and as part of this process, they embraced a variety of investment strategies, including large-, mid-, and small-capitalization equities, value and growth styles, and international equities, both in developed and in emerging markets. For many individual investors, bonds were included primarily as a means of achieving asset diversification. Investment turnover tended to be low, as individual investors pursued buy-and-hold strategies and gauged their performance in relative terms compared with a limited number of benchmarks. Individual investors often accessed equities and other financial assets through mutual funds.

In the 1980s and 1990s, many investors responded to changes within the financial market environment by focusing less on fixed-income securities, international equities, mid- and small-capitalization equities, and value-based investment approaches, favoring instead large-capitalization, growth-based U.S. equity investments. To an increasing degree, investors sought out equity-like alternative asset classes such as private equity, venture capital, real estate, and certain types of hedge funds. Investment turnover tended to increase, compared with portfolio turnover levels of a decade earlier, as investors began to trade more actively in search of momentum-based investment strategies intended to produce high absolute returns rather than relative returns. Investors placed increased emphasis on the construction and selection of, and comparison with, market benchmarks. Partly for tax reasons, partly to reduce investment costs, and partly to try to capture the alluring investment performance of selected equity industry groups, individual companies, and the initial public offering market, individual investors also increasingly focused on the direct ownership of equities as well as owning them through mutual funds.

By the late 1990s, the net effect of these shifting patterns tended to reduce some investors' opinions of the value and efficacy of asset allocation. The merits of asset diversification, risk control, and long-horizon investing were downgraded in the thinking of many investors, in favor of high-performance, annual capital growth as the overriding objective. Beginning in early 2000, these trends were reversed to varying degrees by the precipitous drop in the Nasdaq Composite Index, in many Internet, telecommunications, and technology stocks, and in a number of other sectors. Nasdaq experienced peak-to-trough price declines of more than

70%, and of more than 90% for several high-flying dot-com, telecom, and high-technology shares. Many investors began to embrace (or re-embrace) the principles and practicalities of asset allocation because of U.S. Treasury bonds' and certain hedge funds' positive returns, and back-to-back total-return *declines* of 9.1% in 2000, 11.9% in 2001, and 22.1% in 2002 for the Standard & Poor's 500 and similar broad indices.

The three main phases in the evolution of individual investors' asset-allocation activity, together with the representative asset allocations associated with these phases, are shown in Figure 5.2.

Traditionally, most U.S. private investors tended to deploy their portfolios according to overall perceived-wisdom guidelines reflecting the investment ethos of the age. In the 1930s, one version of these guidelines specified 60% in U.S. domestic bonds and 40% in U.S. stocks. The top part of Figure 5.2 shows a representative version of this standard asset mix, which prevailed for quite some time in the 1950s and 1960s and which generally recommended 60% in U.S. stocks, 30% in U.S. bonds, and 10% in cash.

Beginning in the middle to late 1980s, inspired by the activities of certain professional investors, a smaller proportion of individual investors began to shift some of their assets into venture capital, real estate, private equity (including LBOs and oil and gas investments), and international developed and emerging markets equity and debt securities. A representative portfolio including this expanded range of asset classes is depicted in the middle part of Figure 5.2.

In the third phase of this evolution, individual investors have increased their exposure—generally through domestic or offshore hedge funds or other partnership structures, or as separately managed accounts—to a variety of alternative-investment instruments, including so-called market-neutral or absolute-return strategies. In the *equity* realm, absolute-return strategies include warrant and convertible arbitrage, hedged closed-end fund and cross-ownership arbitrage, synthetic-security arbitrage, and other techniques involving derivative instruments. In the *fixed-income* world, absolute-return strategies include various forms of bond arbitrage, involving futures, swap arrangements, credit risk and yield-curve

F I G U R E   5.2

Representative Asset-Allocation Trends for Individual and Professional Investors

1950s, 1960s, and 1970s: Cash, Stocks, and Bonds

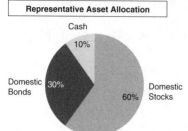

In the decades of the 1950s, 1960s, and 1970s, many U.S. professional and individual investors' portfolios were traditionally invested in domestic stocks, bonds, and cash, with a targeted asset allocation invested 60% in stocks, 30% in bonds, and 10% in cash over time.

1980s and 1990s: Inclusion of Non-Domestic Securities and Alternative Investments

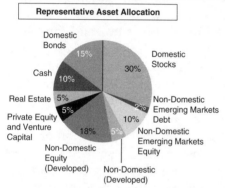

Beginning in the mid- to late 1980s, some professional and a smaller proportion of individual investors began to shift a portion of their assets into private equity, venture capital, real estate, real assets, and non-domestic developed and emerging markets equity and debt securities.

1990s and post-2000: Inclusion of Managed Futures Funds, Hedge Funds and Funds of Funds, and Inflation-Indexed Securities

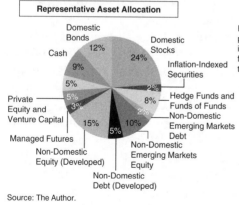

In the 1990s and continuing in the post-2000 era, professional and individual investors began to include managed futures funds, hedge funds and funds of funds, and inflation-indexed securities in their portfolios.

Source: The Author.

shape mispricings, and embedded and explicit options features. The lower part of Figure 5.2 shows a representative portfolio including these newly defined asset classes.

PRIMARY DETERMINANTS OF INDIVIDUAL INVESTORS' ASSET ALLOCATION

Investors' history, current situation, and expectations for the future will shape the *degree of emphasis* they place on the asset-allocation tradeoffs in Figure 5.3.

In very general terms, the asset-allocation tradeoffs in Figure 5.3 may cause potential investors to purchase one broad type of assets versus another. Circumstances or characteristics that tend to move the investor toward *lower-risk, lower-return* assets include: (i) a short-term time frame; (ii) a preference for a diversified asset-allocation strategy; (iii) a desire to spend investment returns currently; (iv) a preference for investment returns in the form of income; (v) a bias toward predictable returns; (vi) an orientation toward liquid investments; and (vii) a need for immediate access to capital. Circumstances or characteristics that tend to move investors toward *higher-risk, higher-return* assets include: (i) a long-term time horizon; (ii) an investment strategy emphasizing concentration in a limited number of assets; (iii) a desire to postpone spending investment returns; (iv) a preference for returns in the form of capital gains; (v) a tolerance for unpredictable patterns of returns; (vi) a willingness to invest in illiquid investments; and (vii) an ability to subject their capital to lockup periods of varying lengths.

In developing an approach to asset selection, individual investors need to assess the primary determinants of asset allocation carefully. Many of these determinants are set forth in Figure 5.4 and can be grouped under a few broad rubrics, analogous in some sense to the investor's own highly individualized set of: (i) income statement factors; (ii) balance sheet factors; and (iii) off-balance sheet factors.

Figure 5.4 briefly describes income-statement, balance-sheet, and off-balance-sheet factors relating to asset allocation.

Asset-Allocation Tradeoffs

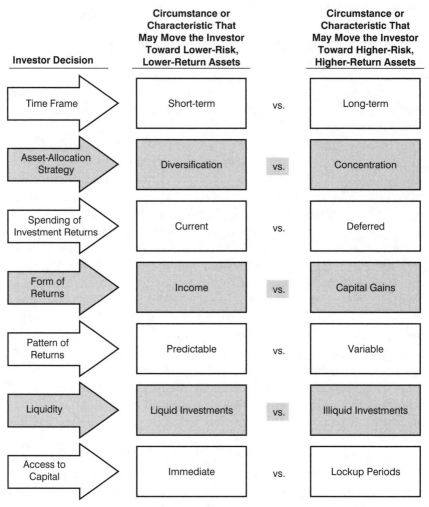

Investor Decision	Circumstance or Characteristic That May Move the Investor Toward Lower-Risk, Lower-Return Assets		Circumstance or Characteristic That May Move the Investor Toward Higher-Risk, Higher-Return Assets
Time Frame	Short-term	vs.	Long-term
Asset-Allocation Strategy	Diversification	vs.	Concentration
Spending of Investment Returns	Current	vs.	Deferred
Form of Returns	Income	vs.	Capital Gains
Pattern of Returns	Predictable	vs.	Variable
Liquidity	Liquid Investments	vs.	Illiquid Investments
Access to Capital	Immediate	vs.	Lockup Periods

Source: The Author.

Income-Statement Factors

+ **Tolerance for Bearing Risk or Loss:** An investor's ability to withstand losses in a given investment position or asset class is influenced by the severity of the loss in percentage

Primary Determinants of Individual Investors' Asset Allocation

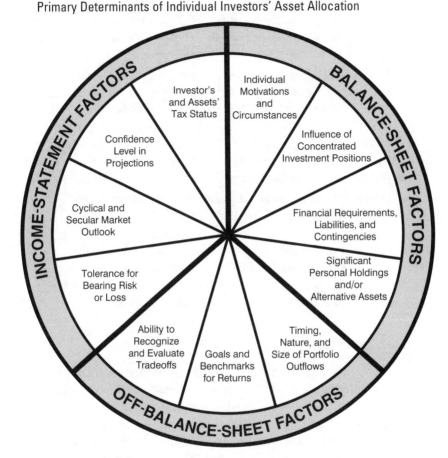

Source: The Author.

and absolute terms, the duration of the loss, whether it is realized or unrealized, expected future price action, the price behavior of other investment instruments, general economic conditions, and, not least, the investor's emotional, financial, and psychological profile.

- **Cyclical and Secular Market Outlook:** A highly important influence on strategic and tactical asset allocation is the investor's qualitatively and quantitatively driven sense of

where specific markets are going, how long they will take
to reach their price targets, and the pattern of expected
price movements, including: (i) stair-step; (ii) continuous;
(iii) highly volatile; or (iv) an extended period of stability
followed by a sharp upward or downward move.

◆ **Confidence Level in Projections:** One of the great separa-
tors of highly successful investors (or asset allocators)
from less fortunate ones is the tradeoff between conviction
and flexibility. Investors who know they are right tend to
have the courage of their convictions; investors who
discover flaws in their assumptions or thinking must have
the flexibility to face facts and reverse course if necessary.

◆ **Investor's and Assets' Tax Status:** The individual
investor's tax status, including: (i) federal, state, local, and
cross-border taxes; (ii) income, capital gains, and estate
taxes; and (iii) current and future tax brackets, brings a
crucial set of variables to bear in structuring an optimal
allocation of assets, as does the tax treatment of all the
capital and income flows from each investment.

Balance Sheet Factors

◆ **Individual Motivations and Circumstances:** Individual
investors should reflect on the ultimate goals and objectives of the assets being allocated. For whose benefit are
they investing in the assets? What do these assets mean in
the context of the beneficiaries' other circumstances? In
what blocks of time does the investor reckon? What
planned commitments and unforeseen developments
should be allowed for?

◆ **Influence of Concentrated Investment Positions:** Asset
allocation for individual investors should take account of
large existing or contractually expected investment positions, capital flows, options, and restricted securities. At
the same time, objectivity and rigorous analysis are
required to weigh the merits and costs of retaining concentrated investment positions versus diversification of all
or a portion of these positions into other asset classes.

♦ **Financial Requirements, Liabilities, and Contingencies:**
Investors' planned annual expenditure levels, margin
debt, mortgages, and other liabilities affect asset-allocation
decision making because the certainty of such outlays
may often lead to the selection of asset classes and investments that have predictable payment streams to meet
these obligations.

♦ **Significant Personal Holdings and/or Alternative Assets:**
Many individual investors have a considerable portion of
their overall wealth tied up in asset categories that are not
included in conventional asset-allocation frameworks. As
described in Figures 4.1 and 4.2 (see pages 101 and 104),
such assets include: (i) royalty streams from media-related,
oil, gas, forestry, and mining interests; (ii) art, collectibles,
antiques, and jewelry; and (iii) ownership positions in
family businesses, undeveloped land, and other real
property.

Off-Balance-Sheet Factors

♦ **Timing, Nature, and Size of Portfolio Outflows:** When
and in what form capital is to be returned to the ultimate
beneficiaries of the portfolio can cause meaningful
differences in asset allocation.

♦ **Goals and Benchmarks for Returns:** Individual investors'
universe of goals that they intend their investment activity
to achieve, and the relative importance assigned to each,
will determine their asset allocation. These goals include
safety of principal, protection of purchasing power, and
specified levels of annual pretax or after-tax returns.
Prudence and realism are essential in the selection of an
appropriate absolute benchmark, or the construction of a
blended benchmark against which results will be measured.

♦ **Ability to Recognize and Evaluate Tradeoffs:** A substantial
portion of the entire asset-allocation process hinges on
skill at recognizing and judging a series of financial factors.
How important is one set of factors compared with
another? For any given tradeoff, how much of the costs

and benefits of one variable must be foregone to obtain a more favorable cost-benefit profile in another variable? Several of the most frequently encountered asset-allocation tradeoffs are listed in Figure 5.3.

STRATEGIC AND TACTICAL PRINCIPLES

Strategic and Tactical Principles of Asset-Allocation and Investment Strategy

When possible, investors should think about, create, collect, and regularly refer to *strategic and tactical principles of asset allocation and investment strategy*. Such principles may serve as: (i) rules and reminders of sound investing; (ii) general guidelines and operating procedures; (iii) words of counsel and advice; and (iv) touchstones to test possible actions during times of overconfidence or self-doubt.

Although strategic principles may differ from tactical principles, in many cases they may overlap with and reinforce each other in the practical worlds of financial markets and investing. The word "strategic" comes from the Greek word *strategos*, which refers to a general officer who is in command of an army. Strategic, or strategy-related, principles encompass the large-scale, overall direction and purpose of asset allocation and investment activity. As such, strategic principles may have a powerful influence on the ultimate successes or failures of investing. Strategic principles seek to address such issues as: (i) how investors should approach, deploy, over- or underweight, avoid, and rebalance broad asset classes, asset managers, and specific investments; (ii) how to think about investing and the aptness of different approaches to various kinds of investments; (iii) behaviors and investment gambits to be pursued or avoided; and (iv) investment maneuvers and actions to consider under diverse financial scenarios and contingencies.

The word "tactical" also has Greek origins, descending from the verb *tattein*, meaning "to arrange or place in order." Tactical principles usually intend to describe all the individual activities and micro-executed actions that, summed together, seek to implement a strategy. Because tactical principles involve carrying out investors' intentions on a day-to-day basis in the financial arena, they too can significantly determine the destiny of a portfolio of assets. Tactical principles seek to address such issues as: (i) how the investor should carry out the nuts-and-bolts, practical details of structuring portfolios and selecting and rejecting specific investments; (ii) the technical aspects of purchasing, selling, evaluating, monitoring, or measuring the returns, volatilities, and correlations of specific investments and specific asset managers; (iii) operating instructions for the execution of portfolio maneuvers; and (iv) prescriptions for what is considered to be efficacious investment activity and proscriptions against what is considered to be unsuitable investment activity.

Strategic and tactical principles can and should be coordinated with each other to constructively affect the overall portfolio. The development of strategic and tactical principles helps formalize and focus investors' thinking, enables the communication of these principles to others across time and distance, and fosters reflective thinking and advance planning that may help prevent hasty decisions.

At the same time, pondering, developing, or adopting a set of strategic and tactical principles does not eliminate the potential for making investment mistakes, sometimes even severe mistakes. The strategic and tactical principles discussed here are by no means all-encompassing or applicable in all financial circumstances. Investors may wish to treat these principles as a subset of a larger body of strategic and tactical guidance. As they do so, investors will want to accept, revise, or reject certain principles. Investors who have read or written a set of strategic and tactical principles of asset allocation and investment strategy need constantly to keep in mind that having such guidelines written down, stored in their computers, or kept in their minds should not engender a false sense of security. Considering such precepts is not the same as applying these principles in action.

The application of strategic and tactical principles to asset allocation and investment strategy thus takes on significant importance. Recognizing that not every investor is the same, each investor's inventories, uses, and applications of strategic and tactical principles vary from those of his or her fellow investor. What works best for a long-term, buy-and-hold investor may not have equal applicability to a short-term, opportunistic investor. Taxes and other personal considerations may cause investors to emphasize certain types of principles and de-emphasize others. Finally, what works best in one set of multiyear financial market conditions may not work well in another environment.

The development of strategic and tactical principles may sometimes form a part of the process of self-analysis, financial planning, and portfolio construction, for which worksheets are provided in Chapter 9. Strategic and tactical principles are generally assembled and adapted over time from: (i) reading; (ii) conversations with persons possessing investment and financial insight; and (iii) examination of other investors' successful and unsuccessful investment experiences. Some of these principles may be expressed in the investor's own words, and some portion of these principles, perhaps even a substantial portion, may be collected from the observations of other investors.

After gathering a collection of strategic and tactical investment principles, investors may: (i) review them at some intervals of time, think about them, and assess their relevance and applicability in light of changing financial conditions and the investor's own circumstances; (ii) add to them, revise them, or discard them, as appropriate; (iii) refer to them in times of crisis, turbulence, or heightened uncertainty; and/or (iv) share them with associates, colleagues, investment advisors, and other counterparties to foster useful discussion.

Representative Strategic Principles

Investors can find in Figure 5.5 sample representative *strategic* principles of asset-allocation and investment strategy, described more fully below.

- ◆ **Asset Selection:** Investors should seek to identify assets with value or growth potential, reasonable prices, and realistic expectations for realizing value or achieving future growth. Investors generally should avoid assets whose future price movements depend highly on elevated expectations going even higher.
- ◆ **Asset Disposition:** It is usually not a good idea to sell a sound investment because of market noise, whim, or

F I G U R E   5.5

Representative Strategic Principles of Asset Allocation and Investment Strategy

Source: The Author.

psychology. The most appropriate time to sell something is when there is no longer a fundamental reason to own it.

- **Asset Fortification:** Investors should select investments and seek to build sound, safe financial havens and mental constructs that can effectively serve as a locus of refuge in times of market fear, panic, and uncertainty.

- **Asset Appropriateness:** Investors should give thought to what kind of investor they are. Some investors are *buy-and-hold* investors, some are *buy-to-sell* investors, some are *buy-to-exploit-temporary-mispricings* investors, a few who engage in short-selling activity are *sell-to-buy* investors, and many investors represent a *blend* of one or more of these types. Investors should select strategies that fit their own mentality, personality, approach to asset management, short-term and long-term market outlook, and personal circumstances.

- **Asset Quality:** Investors should focus on first-class investments that can weather stormy conditions, including asset classes, specific funds, specific structures, and specific securities that can emerge stronger on the other side of crisis conditions. In difficult market phases, investors should try to look for investments that are as egregiously undervalued as other investments had been overvalued in bull markets. Investors should attempt to buy great assets when no one else wants them, colloquially referred to as "Rembrandts in the Rubble."

- **Asset Time Horizon:** For some appropriate portion of the portfolio, investors should seek to be long-term collectors, not short-term dealers. Where possible, investors should hold on to quality investments and allow their returns to compound tax and transaction-cost free over time. For many subsectors of the equity investment realm, the probability of achieving positive returns has been directly related to the length of the holding period.

- **Asset Manager Selection:** Investors should attempt to find asset managers whose returns are positive and uncorrelated, whose risk profile is low, and whose processes are disciplined and understandable.

- **Asset Scenario Analysis:** Investors should think about potential economic, financial, social, and political scenarios and their likely effects on asset prices. The process of scenario analysis is discussed in Chapter 8. If possible, investors should discuss these scenarios with other investors who possess sound investment judgment. It may be helpful to formulate a financial contingency plan showing actions that would be taken, and the asset allocations that would be implemented, under varying scenarios and market conditions. Where applicable, investors should quantify the risks of using leverage under circumstances of maximum stress.

During his highly successful, several-decades career in the investment and business realm, Warren Edward Buffett has consistently expressed his strategic principles of asset allocation and investing in an articulate and noteworthy way. It is worthwhile to reflect upon the clarity, pragmatism, and effectiveness of many of his strategic principles, representative among them being: "When evaluating the potential of an equity investment, the investor should approach the transaction as if he or she were buying into a private business. Key evaluative criteria include: (i) the economic prospects of the business; (ii) the people in charge of running it; and (iii) the price to be paid."

Representative Tactical Principles

Investors can locate in Figure 5.6 several sample representative *tactical* principles of asset-allocation and investment strategy, described more fully below.

F I G U R E   5.6

Representative Tactical Principles of Asset Allocation and Investment Strategy

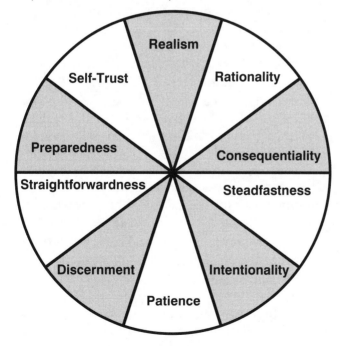

Source: The Author.

- **Realism:** It helps to recognize that a significant proportion of all investment decisions may very well end up being wrong; as a result, it is necessary to maintain a detached, dispassionate, and skeptical view of every investment idea until results prove otherwise.

- **Rationality:** During periods of financial panic or extreme turbulence, it is usually better not to make momentous decisions. Investors should resist the urge to act in haste, because hasty decisions often turn out unfavorably.

- **Consequentiality:** Success in investing is not so much a function of being right versus being wrong as it is a function of how investors behave in the face of being right or being wrong. This principle is discussed in Figure 5.8 on page 179, which addresses anticipated versus required asset-allocation skills.

- **Steadfastness:** Times may change, but time-honored principles endure. Wise methods should not be discarded merely because they are temporarily out of favor or because they have been applied for a long time. Traditional valuation criteria may very well retain their validity, especially near points of extreme over- or undervaluation, just when the consensus wants to ignore or discard those very principles.

- **Intentionality:** When necessary, investors should possess a sufficient degree of will to take action. It helps to keep in mind that although activity merely for the sake of activity may produce unfavorable results, so too may an inappropriate degree of inactivity or neglect. Investors should strive to have an ongoing intentional impact on the direction of the portfolio, regardless of how frequently they make actual changes to the portfolio.

- **Patience:** Investors should seek to take advantage of time and not let time take advantage of them. Similarly, investors should seek to take advantage of change and not let change take advantage of them.

- **Discernment:** Investors should devote sufficient time and resources to selecting an asset mix that feels right over an appropriate time frame and stick with it. In such activity, investors should be discriminating and relentlessly selective. Rigorous analysis and sound advice are essential ingredients in the process of thinking about an asset allocation. Investors should manage their expectations regarding appropriate levels of asset return and risk.

♦ **Straightforwardness:** Especially in turbulent markets, investors should conduct themselves so that when they are wrong, they do not pay too high a price. Investors should address problem investments in a forthright manner, deal with them, and, where fitting, sell the investments and move on.

♦ **Preparedness:** Investors should constantly think about whether and to what degree reserves should be set aside to take advantage of crisis prices. Investors should make lists, do their homework, be disciplined, and follow an approach that is consistent with their own psyche, financial circumstances, and risk profile.

♦ **Self-Trust:** Among other sources of information and counsel, investors should listen to their heads and their hearts. They should carefully take account of and decide whether to trust their instincts. Investors should seek to understand and govern their emotions. They should stay true to sound principles, letting reason have its fair say in investment policy.

John Maynard Keynes (1883–1946), one of the twentieth century's most influential economists, wrote prolifically about the theory and operations of economies and financial markets, including the role of mass psychology in assessing the valuation of virtually any kind of asset. One of his observations almost timelessly applies to tactical principles of asset allocation and investing: "A conventional valuation which is established as the outcome of mass psychology of a larger number of ignorant individuals is liable to change violently as the result of a sudden fluctuation of opinion, since there will be no strong roots of conviction to hold it steady."

Getty Museum Collection Principles

The J. Paul Getty Museum, located in Brentwood and Malibu, California, was founded in 1953 and considerably enlarged in 1982 thanks to Jean Paul Getty, an oil magnate and art collector who lived from 1892 to 1976. As of year end 2006, the endowment of the Getty Museum amounted to $5.6 billion, *excluding* the value of its land, buildings, and collections. As stewards of a relatively new, yet relatively well endowed, participant in the art world, the trustees of the J. Paul Getty Trust and Museum have developed a statement of collection principles to guide them in the acquisition of art.

The 1984 Report to the Trustees of the J. Paul Getty Trust and Museum, as contained in *The J. Paul Getty Museum and Its Collections: A Museum for the New Century*, by John Walsh and Deborah Gribbon, spells out the collection principles of the Getty Museum. This concise, cogent, and comprehensible statement of collection principles is intended to inspire and inform investors seeking direction in the definition and formulation of strategic and tactical principles of asset allocation and investing:

- **Get the Greatest and Rarest Objects.** If nothing is more important to a museum than its collection, nothing is more important to its collection than the great object that gives measure to the rest. There are not many such works left, but it should be our top priority to secure them.

- **Have Principles, but Seize the Unexpected Chance.** The Getty has neither the ancient tradition nor the financial restrictions of America's older museums, such as the Metropolitan Museum of Art, the Boston Museum of Fine Arts, or the Frick Collection. Our youth and our resources give us the ability to respond imaginatively to opportunity that rigid preconceived notions may defeat.

- **Build on Strength.** We should not be afraid of specialization, but exploit its advantages. When we have a chance to form the best collection of a certain type, and it is logically connected to our mission, we should take it at the expense, if necessary, of a well-rounded profile for our holdings. Better to do a limited number of things very well, be prepared to accept limits, and concentrate our resources on achieving greatness in a restricted number of fields.

◆ **Fill Gaps, but Only with Superior Examples.** Once we are in a field, the desire to cover it more and more fully is inevitable. Here, patience and discipline are in order, since the goal of quality is more important than the goal of art-historical coverage.

◆ **Collect Collections.** Our greatest advantage is that we can make great leaps in strengthening our collections, and even annex new territories from time to time. We need both energy and vision to locate these opportunities.

INDIVIDUAL INVESTOR BEHAVIORAL CHARACTERISTICS

Because psychology and human emotion play such an important role in investor behavior, it is worthwhile to explore how the nature, behavior, hopes, and fears of individual investors equip them well and/or poorly for asset allocation. Much has been made of the competitive disadvantage of individual investors in a global financial marketplace dominated by institutions and other professional investors. Many investors feel that institutional and professional investors may be able to outperform individuals due to superior access to investment research, corporate management, trading channels, quantitative tools, and, not least, one another.

At the same time, individual investors have several factors working in their favor. First, as owners or as employees, many individuals are deeply grounded in knowledge of the business world—they may be familiar with cycles of crops, of energy costs, of final-product prices; they tend to think of companies as groups of people, as employees, suppliers, and customers, rather than as abstractions; and they often possess an innate sense of corporate welfare and values as a result of having to meet a payroll, compete and attempt to defend or expand market share, and maintain the viability of their own enterprise.

Second, individual investors are usually not answerable to artificial quarterly or annual demarcations of time, or to the dictates of committee-based thinking. If individual investors so desire, they can withdraw from an asset class altogether or, alternatively, ride through the vicissitudes of markets and leave valuable core long-term holdings undisturbed.

Third, individual investors are eminently capable—although not all individuals display these traits in the investment realm—of distance, objectivity, perspective, perception, independence, and clear thinking. Partly because their own funds are at stake, individual investors tend to experience the pain of financial losses more deeply than they experience the pleasure of financial gains. For some, this can clarify thinking; for others, it can cloud reason.

Fourth, individual investors often have essentially as much access as institutions and professional investors to the great financial leveler: sound judgment. In the asset-allocation and investment selection process, the characteristic in shortest supply is not intelligence, data, or technology resources. It is judgment. Because individual and professional investors may equally be gifted with, or bereft of, good judgment, individual investors must assess candidly whether they have good judgment. If not, individuals should leave no stone unturned in the quest to find a person possessed of good judgment who can provide asset-allocation and investment advice.

A powerful testament to the force, effect, and success of a disciplined investment strategy by individual investors was demonstrated in the world of art on November 10, 1997, when Christie's auctioned the collection of Victor and Sally Ganz for $206.5 million. At the time, this was the record for a single-owner sale of art, surpassing the 1989 sale by Sotheby's of impressionist and modern paintings belonging to John Dorrance, Jr., for $123.4 million.

The Ganzes' holdings generated extraordinarily high returns that are difficult to achieve in any asset class. But in the process, they left a legacy of valuable lessons for any serious investor. The Ganzes had passion and commitment to collecting art; they concentrated and focused their efforts in a defined sphere; they came to know their field in great depth; they bought with care, reflection, and analysis; and they exercised patience, letting time and longevity work for them. Mr. Ganz made his first acquisition, Pablo Picasso's oil painting *Dream*, in 1941 for $7,000, and it was sold at auction for $48.4 million. Over its 56-year holding period, this painting generated a compound annual return of 17.1% before commissions and expenses,[1] an astoundingly high growth rate over such a long time. He and his wife bought another Picasso, *Woman Seated in an*

Armchair (Eva), in 1967 for $200,000; it was auctioned 30 years later for $24.7 million, producing an equally uncommon and lofty compound annual return of 17.4% before commissions and expenses.[1]

Individual investors exhibit certain behavior, often unwittingly, that can influence the realization of their investment goals. Fourteen of these behavioral characteristics are listed in Figure 5.7.

Since many of the traits shown in Figure 5.7 derive from deep-seated human impulses, the main way to control and/or alter them is to recognize their potential existence. Some of the explanations below explaining these characteristics may contradict each other, yet the same investor may encounter them simultaneously.

+ **Misestimate Time Horizons:** Many individual investors *underestimate* their time horizon, specifying a 3- or 5-year investment time horizon and intending to invest with a short-term orientation, when in fact the time frame turns out to be 15 to 20 years or more. In contrast, many other individuals *overestimate* their time horizon, expecting to invest in certain asset classes for 10 to 20 years or longer and then making wholesale shifts within a year of establishing their portfolios.

+ **Attach Too Much Significance to Short-Term Results:** The benefits of dampening volatility and reducing risk through asset class diversification, which are usually gained at the cost of lower overall interim returns than the best-performing asset classes, should be assessed over a sufficiently long period of time.

+ **Overemphasize Volatility Risk versus Purchasing-Power Risk:** Particularly when the individual investor's horizon extends to 10 years or more, inflation can erode purchasing power in asset classes that maintain their nominal value. Figure 1.5 on page 18 discusses the ratio of remaining purchasing power to the investor's original purchasing power for various inflation rates and investment time horizons.

---

[1] *After* deduction of the auction house's commission, which is 15% of the first $50,000 and 10% of the remainder, the compound annual growth rate for *Dream* was 16.9%, and for *Eva* it was 17.0%, before any annual expenses for insurance and other carrying costs, which were not disclosed.

Individual Investor Behavioral Characteristics

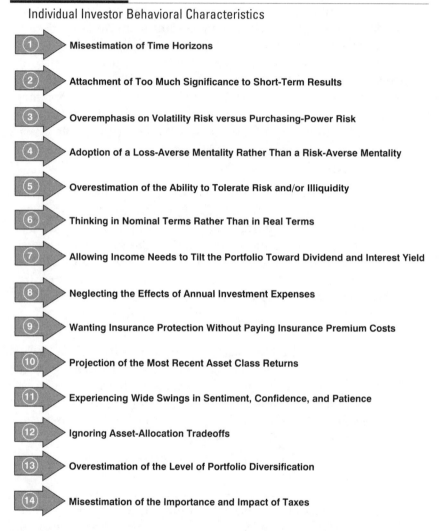

1 Misestimation of Time Horizons

2 Attachment of Too Much Significance to Short-Term Results

3 Overemphasis on Volatility Risk versus Purchasing-Power Risk

4 Adoption of a Loss-Averse Mentality Rather Than a Risk-Averse Mentality

5 Overestimation of the Ability to Tolerate Risk and/or Illiquidity

6 Thinking in Nominal Terms Rather Than in Real Terms

7 Allowing Income Needs to Tilt the Portfolio Toward Dividend and Interest Yield

8 Neglecting the Effects of Annual Investment Expenses

9 Wanting Insurance Protection Without Paying Insurance Premium Costs

10 Projection of the Most Recent Asset Class Returns

11 Experiencing Wide Swings in Sentiment, Confidence, and Patience

12 Ignoring Asset-Allocation Tradeoffs

13 Overestimation of the Level of Portfolio Diversification

14 Misestimation of the Importance and Impact of Taxes

Source: The Author.

Investors need to factor the risks of deflation as well as inflation into their asset-allocation strategy.

♦ **Adopt a Loss-Averse Mentality Rather Than a Risk-Averse Mentality:** Due to an antipathy toward losing money, many individual investors prefer to earn a "smooth" return of 10% (with low or no losses) over a series of market cycles, rather than a "bumpy" return of 15% (with occasional periods of testing, sometimes severe, in down years). Many investors are not willing to experience the intermediate-term volatility usually associated with attempting to achieve higher annual rates of return.

♦ **Overestimate the Ability to Tolerate Risk and/or Illiquidity:** In glaring contradiction to their loss-averse nature, a number of individual investors commonly forecast their loss-withstanding threshold at a much higher level than the profound distress they feel when they actually experience such losses—realized or unrealized.

♦ **Think in Nominal Terms Rather Than in Real Terms:** Assuming no change in interest rates and a 3% inflation rate, a private investor who places $1 million in tax-exempt bonds, and spends the interest income each year, would have only $633,251 in *real* purchasing power remaining at the end of 15 years, even though the $1 million value of the bond remains whole in *nominal* terms when the bonds are redeemed at final maturity.

♦ **Allow Income Needs to Tilt the Portfolio Toward Dividend and Interest Yield Rather than Total Return:** Wealth creation is a product of the compounding of capital over an appropriate time span. Individual investors with high current-income needs should look at the *total return* from an asset-allocation mix, not merely the *current yield level*.

♦ **Neglect the Effects of Annual Investment Expenses:** Individual investors need to be aware of the compounding effects of annual investment expenses. As Table 5.1 shows in the circled data point, during a 15-year holding period with 8% compound returns, annual investment expenses (such as custody fees and transactions costs) of 1.5% effectively reduce the investor's total pretax capital appreciation by 27.6%.

♦ **Want Insurance Protection Without Facing the Premium Costs of Such Protection:** Private investors need to recognize, and be willing to pay for (in the form of dampened overall returns on the upside and the downside), asset classes for defensive, hedging, or insurance purposes.

T A B L E   5.1

Reduction in Pretax Capital Appreciation Due to Annual Expenses

Investment Holding Period	Annual Expenses of 1.0%		Annual Expenses of 1.5%		Annual Expenses of 2.0%	
	Effective Reduction from an 8% to a 7% Return	Effective Reduction from a 15% to a 14% Return	Effective Reduction from an 8% to a 6.5% Return	Effective Reduction from a 15% to a 13.5% Return	Effective Reduction from an 8% to a 6% Return	Effective Reduction from a 15% to a 13% Return
5 years	−14.1%	−8.5%	−21.1%	−12.6%	−27.9%	−16.7%
10 years	−16.6%	−11.1%	−24.3%	−16.3%	−31.8%	−21.4%
15 years	−19.1%	−14.0%	−27.6%	−20.4%	−35.7%	−26.4%
20 years	−21.6%	−17.1%	−31.1%	−24.6%	−39.7%	−31.5%

Source: The Author.

- ◆ **Project the Most Recent Asset Class Returns and Measure Against the Best-Performing Benchmarks:** Particularly after a series of successful (or unsuccessful) years of investment returns, individuals tend to expect such performance to continue indefinitely. At the same time, individual investors frequently want returns that match or exceed the top-performing indices or asset classes. In part, these desires, and the relative outperformance of the S&P 500 index versus a substantial majority of equity mutual funds from 1995 through 1999, helped fuel the dramatic expansion of assets in stock index funds, from $2.1 billion in 1987 to $690.3 billion at the end of 2006.[2] Similarly, exchange-traded funds (ETFs), first created in 1993, replicate popular indices from Dow Jones, Standard & Poor's, MSCI Barra, Frank Russell, and other country, market, and industry sector benchmarks. As of the end of 2006, ETFs totaled more than $455 billion in assets.[3]

---

[2] "Barclay's Quarterly Competitive Analysis Report: Index Funds," Financial Research Corporation.
[3] Morgan Stanley Research.

- **Experience Wide Swings in Sentiment, Confidence, and Patience:** Individuals tend at times to exhibit wide swings in emotions, from euphoria to panic. Investors should be aware of this human proclivity and attempt to resist getting caught up in extreme market moods. Over time, successful asset-allocation and investment strategy come from the ability to distinguish cyclical swings from secular movements and act accordingly.

- **Ignore Asset-Allocation Tradeoffs:** Paying heed to the types of asset-allocation tradeoffs depicted in Figure 5.3 on page 158, individual investors should recognize the virtual impossibility of finding an asset class that simultaneously meets all the desired criteria: (i) deep liquidity; (ii) stable, guaranteed principal values; (iii) high current yields; and (iv) a rate of capital growth that consistently and substantially outperforms inflation, taxes, and the popular benchmark indices.

- **Overestimate the Level of Portfolio Diversification:** Although a high proportion of individual investors are aware of the benefits of diversification, many individuals allow their portfolios to become underdiversified due to inertia, home-country bias, overconfidence, familiarity with one's own company, market price effects, and/or high correlations of returns across certain industry groups and asset classes. This phenomenon was analyzed in a December 2001 National Bureau of Economic Research Working Paper by William N. Goetzmann and Alok Kumar, locatable at *www.nber.org*.

- **Misestimate the Importance and Impact of Taxes:** Investors sometimes let tax considerations play too large a role in their thinking about whether and when to sell a specific asset. At the same time, investors often underestimate the effects of turnover, income received, capital gains and losses, and other taxable events on the long-term after-tax returns from portfolio holdings. Tax considerations are discussed in conjunction with the worksheets in Chapter 9.

Anticipated versus Actual Required Asset-Allocation Skills

Taking into account the strengths, weaknesses, and resources of individual investors, as well as some of their behavioral tendencies described in this chapter, it is possible to formulate some conclusions about the requisite skills for successful asset allocation over time.

To achieve success in asset allocation, individual investors might expect to need and draw upon an approximately equal weighting of skills between: (i) selecting asset classes; (ii) monitoring asset classes; (iii) acting with conviction on high- and low-performing asset classes; and (iv) rebalancing asset classes (the process of rebalancing is discussed in Chapter 4). Figure 5.8 shows that some skills are more important than others.

The pie chart in the top half of Figure 5.8 depicts a roughly equal weighting in each of the four anticipated required asset-allocation skills. In other words, many investors expect that success in asset allocation follows from having and developing approximately the same amounts of skill and expertise in all four sets of skills.

In many cases, two of these skills tend to have an especially large influence on achieving success, as the bottom pie chart in Figure 5.8 illustrates. To a large degree, investors' overall success may stem from their ability to: (i) select the right asset classes; and then (ii) act with conviction with regard to the asset classes that they judge to be long-term winners and losers.

To be sure, monitoring asset classes and rebalancing asset classes are important to the success of the investor's asset-allocation activity. Paraphrasing a widely repeated statement by the investor George Soros, successful asset allocation is often not so much a question of *how many times* the investor is right or wrong, but *how emphatically he or she responds* in consequence of being right or wrong. If investors choose well, and act upon these decisions with conviction, they can increase the odds of achieving success in asset allocation.

FINANCIAL LESSONS FROM MARKET HISTORY

During the late 1990s, many investors intensely debated such topics as: (i) the relevance and applicability of the old versus the new paradigm in the U.S. and global economy; (ii) the proper level of the Equity Risk Premium in the capital markets; and (iii) the

F I G U R E   5.8

Anticipated versus Actual Required Asset-Allocation Skills Weighting

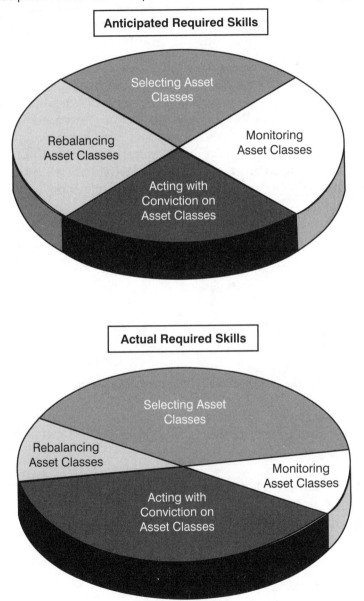

Source: The Author.

effects of the Internet on commerce, financing, and investing. As markets may approach extreme levels of over- or undervaluation from time to time, a number of enduring financial lessons from market history are important to remember, as outlined in Figure 5.9 and described in the following paragraphs.

- ◆ **Lesson 1: Market Trends Do Not Continue Forever.** No matter how euphoric or demoralized financial price trends may seem, at some point, conditions change, and the markets veer in a decidedly new direction, governed by the basic laws and principles of economics, science, statistics, psychology, and compound interest. Perhaps without intending to, in *Henry VI Part 2*, William Shakespeare sums up the cyclical nature of financial trends:

> Thus sometimes hath the brightest day a cloud,
> And after summer evermore succeeds
> Barren winter with his wrathful, nipping cold;
> So cares and joys abound, as seasons fleet.

F I G U R E   5.9

Financial Lessons from Market History

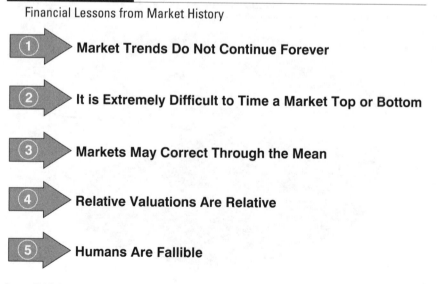

1. Market Trends Do Not Continue Forever

2. It is Extremely Difficult to Time a Market Top or Bottom

3. Markets May Correct Through the Mean

4. Relative Valuations Are Relative

5. Humans Are Fallible

Source: The Author.

- **Lesson 2: It Is Extremely Difficult to Time a Market Top or Bottom.** The financial arena is littered with the reputations of investors and market strategists who at a particular juncture in time concluded that a major turning point had been reached and bet all or a substantial portion of their fortune and credibility on that outcome. Even though the countervailing forces build up on an oscillating pendulum, no matter how high that pendulum reaches, it is just as important to understand the strength and duration of the forces that set the pendulum in motion. The pendulum's path may endure yet longer before eventually reversing. So too with financial market conditions.

- **Lesson 3: Markets May Correct Through the Mean.** During a sustained market upswing or downswing, one of the most discredited principles of asset allocation is that of *reversion to the mean*. This phrase asserts that over time the returns of a given asset class tend to gravitate toward the long-term average for that asset category. When investors have been experiencing some years of abnormally high or low returns, they begin to believe that those returns probably will not return to the long-term mean returns for that asset class. They also generally lose sight of the fact that those long-term average returns imply that the asset will at some point produce returns as far (and sometimes as often) *below* the mean as *above* the mean.

- **Lesson 4: Relative Valuations Are Relative.** Investors may, for instance, purchase an asset because of its attractive valuation relative to some other asset (e.g., the purchase of U.S. technology shares or pharmaceutical shares because their price-earnings ratios appear historically attractive relative to the price-earnings ratio of a broad benchmark such as the S&P 500 index). They should not forget the fact that if *absolute* valuations decline, *relative* valuations may (or may not) improve even as they experience a loss in capital values.

- **Lesson 5: Humans Are Fallible.** In economists' parlance, one of the assertions of *prospect theory* is that individuals ascribe *too low a probability to likely results* and *too high a* *probability to unlikely results.* This tendency is described in the discussion of non-linear probability weighting associated with Figure 5.11 on page 186.

As markets move for a long time in one direction, investors may very well find themselves *overestimating* the likelihood that the markets will continue indefinitely to move in the original direction while *underestimating* (or ignoring altogether) the likelihood that the markets may at some stage reverse course and move against the prevailing market trend. Such behavior is also discussed in the description of extrapolation associated with Figure 5.11.

Over many centuries, perhaps even millennia, of recorded history, several aspects of human reasoning, character, and behavior remain unchanged as they relate to financial affairs. Individual investors are driven by, among other factors, fear, confidence, greed, hindsight, uncertainty, hopes, dreams, regret, and attraction to grandiose schemes. Similarly, individual investors are influenced by, among other factors, self-doubt, despair, self-recrimination, envy, and pangs of conscience. Individual investors act out of noble motives, too. In the following sections, we will subject many of these behavioral traits and patterns to further scrutiny.

INSIGHTS FROM BEHAVIORAL FINANCE

During the past few decades, numerous economists have begun to draw upon the field of psychology to improve their understanding of individual investors' systematic biases, decision-making processes, and emotional influences, and how these forces affect investor behavior and financial markets. These behavioral finance researchers have sought to improve upon the strictly rational decision-making and efficient-markets models of mainstream economics by describing how deeply ingrained human instincts and reflexes can cause individual (and many professional) investors to act in ways that often appear to be erroneous, inconsistent, or even irrational.

Through exposure to the hypotheses and ideas of behavioral finance, investors may be able to: (i) recognize and anticipate the causes and effects of individual financial error, thereby avoiding costly investment mistakes; (ii) be aware of humans' financial information-processing fallibilities and the degree to which individuals rely on intuition; and (iii) gain an appreciation for the types of forces that may cause bubbles, crashes, the disappearance of liquidity, volatility spikes, or market price movements to extreme levels of over- or undervaluation (producing so-called fat tails in the probability distribution of investment returns).

Figure 5.10 places the study of behavioral finance and behavioral economics in context. The *top part* of Figure 5.10 shows that the study of behavioral finance and behavioral economics lies at the intersection of the disciplines of economics and finance and the disciplines of psychology and anthropology. The *middle part* of Figure 5.10 shows that decision making according to the theories of economics and finance is greatly influenced by: (i) the notions of rational expectations; and (ii) expected utility maximization. *Rational expectations* is a highly mathematical theory developed by Robert Lucas, winner of the 1995 Nobel Prize in Economic Sciences. His theory posits that economic agents behave according to their own clear best interests, incorporating in the best way possible important information they have about influences such as the government's announced economic policies. *Expected utility maximization* posits that economic agents seek to obtain the highest possible level of satisfaction from their economic activity.

Decision making according to the theories of psychology and anthropology, and thus behavioral economics and behavioral finance, is influenced by such factors as perceptions, beliefs, emotions, preferences, intuitions, judgments, instinct, probability, uncertainty, and the individual's mental states and processes. Some specialists in behavioral finance have hypothesized that the degree of behavioral factors' influence on individual investors increases with the degree of perceived complexity in a given financial environment. The *bottom part* of Figure 5.10 shows this approximate relationship.

Although investors of all types generally conduct themselves in a rational and reasonably predictable manner much of the time, a more complete picture of investor behavior needs also to take account of their potential biases and irrational tendencies. Many of these foibles are subtle, unacknowledged, or even counterintuitive, and some investors may be more prone than others to erroneous patterns of thinking and acting in the financial realm. Partly driven by their deep-seated dispositions toward action or inaction, or by their ingrained pessimistic or optimistic natures, quite a few

F I G U R E   5.10

Selected Behavioral Traits and Patterns of Individual Investors

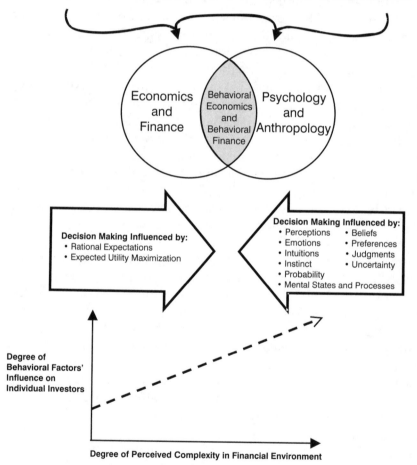

Human Beings':
- Survival instincts
- Search for and use of patterns in daily life
- Quest for security, identity, mastery, and sense of control
- Desire for satisfaction, comfort, pleasure, and success

Source: The Author.

investors may persist in following flawed pathways even after becoming aware of their unintentional mistakes. At a more profound level, these characteristics may be distant atavisms of humans' survival instincts, of their search for and use of patterns in daily life, of their quest for security, identity, mastery, and sense of control, and of their desire for satisfaction, comfort, pleasure, and success. By being able to recognize specific behavioral traits and patterns, and the types of situations in which they may occur, investors may gain a better understanding of investment operations to pursue or avoid. Some of these behavioral traits and patterns are discussed in the following section.

Behavioral Traits and Patterns of Individual Investors

Notions about investor behavior are continuing to evolve as economists, psychologists, investment strategists, and investors devote attention and inquiry to this sphere of thought. The behavioral traits and patterns of individual investors described here: (i) are by no means all-encompassing and should be considered in light of the practical aspects of individual investor behavior discussed earlier in this chapter and outlined in Figure 5.7; (ii) are closely intertwined with conceptions of risk, examined in Chapter 3; (iii) in many cases are closely connected with one another, yet are slightly but importantly differentiated from one another; as such, they may not fit neatly into one of the three main categories used here for classification purposes; and (iv) may very well apply equally to professional investors, who personally possess all of the strengths and eccentricities of individuals.

Broadly speaking, the behavioral traits and patterns of individual investors may be classified according to their involvement with and effects on the investor's *thinking, action,* and *reflection.* Some of these commonly encountered characteristics are set forth in Figure 5.11, grouped together to represent the inter-relatedness and intricacy of the human mind.

Thinking
Investors approach asset allocation and investing, specific investment proposals, and the overall outlook for financial markets with

F I G U R E　5.11

Selected Behavioral Traits and Patterns of Individual Investors

Behavioral Traits and Patterns Related to Thinking
Behavioral Traits and Patterns Related to Action
Behavioral Traits and Patterns Related to Reflection

Source: The Author.

a range of conscious and unconscious judgments, beliefs, and biases. Several of these preferences, aversions, predispositions, leanings, and preconceptions are briefly described below.

- ◆ **Overconfidence:** Many investors have a tendency to overrate their investment acumen, the probability and/or precision of their forecasts, the likely values of future outcomes, and the dependability and worth of their financial decisions.

• **Heroics:** Investors may overestimate their skills at asset allocation and investment selection, with a proclivity to remember, focus on, and attribute to themselves any investment successes, while assigning the blame for failures to others or to bad luck. Another term for this disposition is *self-attribution bias*.

• **Optimism:** A significant proportion of investors view the financial landscape through rose-colored lenses, disproportionately magnifying their abilities, the likelihood of positive consequences, and the degree of control they think they exert over their own financial destiny. Simultaneously, they downplay the odds of unsuccessful results and the degree to which chance can affect investment outcomes.

• **Illusion of Control:** Investors often approach the financial markets under the misleading impression that they can exert a fair degree of control over the way things will turn out; in some ways, this illusion of control motivates investors to assume risks they otherwise would decline to bear. Loyalty to a company, industry, region, or country may lead investors to pursue investment actions for non-financial reasons.

• **Framing:** The concept of framing posits that the way an investment choice or problem is described or positioned can influence investors' decision-making processes.

• **Narrow Framing:** Some investors allow a narrowly defined issue (such as the price performance of a single investment or an inappropriately short time frame) or an incremental change in their financial circumstances to excessively affect the broad outlines of their investment thinking.

• **Anchoring:** Many investors let themselves become unduly fixated on a specific price, or a defined price range, for an asset as a target or reference point in the determination of their buying and selling decisions.

- **Categorization:** Driven by habit, impatience, expediency, or inertia, investors often quickly and sometimes erroneously assign securities, asset classes, investment maneuvers, or financial market conditions into familiar categories.

- **Stereotyping:** Especially during periods of extreme exuberance or pessimism in asset prices, investors may hold highly simplified, tendentious, standardized, and immoderate positive or negative views of specific securities, corporate managements, central authority figures, economic projections, or investment managers.

- **Representativeness:** Some investors may swiftly jump to a conclusion about a given investment or set of investments to the degree that it or they resemble or are representative of other conditions with which they happen to be more familiar.

- **Extrapolation:** Through various periods of market history, investors have tended to extrapolate trends into the future, believing that asset prices that have been generally rising will continue to rise, or that asset prices that have been generally falling will continue to fall. In general, investors may give more weight to long-enduring price movements than to shorter-lived price movements.

- **Mental Accounting:** Rather than taking a holistic and aggregate view of risk and reward relationships encompassing their entire portfolio, many investors compartmentalize their asset management worries and decisions into separate and distinct subsections that may in fact contradict one another or the general objectives of their overall portfolio. Investors may thus adopt more aggressive or more conservative investment policies for separate groupings of assets, such as retirement accounts, educational savings accounts, or accounts set up to purchase a home or found a business.

- **Overweighting the Recent Past:** Partly due to the receding and obscuring nature of memory, investors often give greater weight to events and market movements that have occurred in the recent past than to those which have taken place at more remote times.

♦ **Mistaken Causality:** Investors sometimes recognize or infer a cause-and-effect relationship between: (i) specific events or sets of circumstances; and (ii) asset price movements, when in fact such outcomes are random episodes.

♦ **Conservatism:** After making up their minds about a set of circumstances, many investors may be inclined to resist changing their views, in many cases even when confronted with relevant and contradictory facts.

♦ **Blinders:** Investors may pursue inflexible channels of reasoning or behavior so rigidly that they become virtually oblivious to a significant change in the fundamentals, valuation, or psychological/technical/liquidity forces affecting an asset.

♦ **Perception of Chance and Risk:** Many investors seem to prefer investment opportunities that offer a *reasonably attainable* return, even at the partial expense of lowering *potentially large* returns. Some investors may also view the degree of risk in an investment opportunity in isolation, without taking account of the likely risk-reward profile of future investment opportunity patterns.

♦ **Risk Compensation:** When investors begin to view risk-prone investment activities as less dangerous than is actually the case, they may wittingly or unwittingly allow themselves to expand the risk envelope of their investment behavior, in fact increasing rather than decreasing their overall risk profile. Another form of risk compensation sometimes leads investors to pursue highly risky investment gambits in an attempt to recoup previous losses.

♦ **Ambiguity Aversion:** Investors may sometimes shun ambiguous, vague, or highly indeterminate investment opportunities, preferring instead investments about which they feel a greater degree of familiarity, clarity, or explicitness. Recognizing the unquantifiable yet sometimes meaningful costs associated with second-guessing, worrying, and tinkering, some investors may implicitly assign a

value to comfort and simplicity in their asset-allocation
and investing activity.

+ **Extremism:** Exceeding the bounds of moderation and
sensible judgment, a number of investors may view
unlikely yet possible outcomes as impossible, while simultaneously viewing *likely yet undetermined* outcomes as certain.

Action

Investors may pursue a wide range of tactics and strategies in their
asset-allocation and investment activity. In so doing, they may exhibit
several discernible but not always easily recognizable patterns of
investment behavior, described briefly in the following points:

+ **Herd Instinct:** Quite a few investors prefer the apparent
comfort of investing along with mass opinion and consensus
thinking. Such herd behavior may positively reinforce an
investor when successful results ensue while providing some
degree of solace for unsuccessful outcomes. Some investors
may focus on their relative standing within a group more
than their absolute well-being outside the group.

+ **Loss Aversion:** As a consequence of their tendency to feel
the pain of losses to a greater degree than the pleasure of
an equivalent amount of gains, investors have a distinct
aversion to facing up to or experiencing losses. This causes
many investors to freeze in the face of declining prices. In
a related practice, some investors devote more activity and
attention to avoiding losses than to pursuing gains.

+ **Avoidance:** Investors may inappropriately postpone or
delay taking action for many reasons, ranging from
inertia, to indecision, to an inability or unwillingness to
face facts with resolve.

+ **Idealization:** Particularly during periods of favorable
market conditions, investors may place an undue amount
of faith in and overly exalt broad asset classes and
subclasses, regions, currencies, investment styles, investment managers, specific companies and/or corporate
executives, investment commentators, regulators, and
authoritative bodies.

- **Non-Linear Probability Weighting:** Perhaps in contradiction to the thinking patterns described earlier as extremism, some investors may significantly overestimate the chances of a very low-probability outcome while significantly underestimating the likelihood of a significant- to high-probability outcome.

- **Disposition Effect:** Investors may be more prone to dispose of assets that have appreciated relative to their initial purchase prices than they are to sell assets that have declined relative to their initial purchase prices. Such action is the opposite of "selling the losers and letting the winners run," a time-honored dictum for long-term success in investing.

- **House Money Effect:** Investors may also allow their initial purchase prices for an asset to serve as a so-called *reference point*; they usually view losses associated with asset price declines from profitable levels that are still considerably above the initial purchase prices with less alarm and concern than equivalent monetary losses from levels that are near or already below their original purchase prices. Stated another way, because they can say to themselves and to others that they are still ahead on their investment, investors may be more willing to experience losses that actually subtract from prior gains that still leave them with an overall profit versus their original cost basis.

Reflection

In looking back on the results and implications of their behavior, investors may experience significant mood swings between elation and despondency. Throughout recorded history, one of the ever-present themes of the dramatic canon relates to the mental states that humans manufacture and encounter as a consequence of their thoughts and actions. Some of these worries and exuberances affecting investors are described below.

- **Regret:** Investors may regret the unfavorable outcome of actions they have taken (sometimes known as a regret of *commission*); similarly, they may regret missing out on the favorable outcome of actions they have not taken (sometimes known as a regret of *omission*). In many instances, investors may feel the pain arising from something they did—a regret of commission—more intensely, and thus regret it more, than they experience the pain from something they failed to do—a regret of omission.

+ **Denial:** Because investors dislike admitting and being confronted by their mistakes, they may deny or block out information that reminds them of their erroneous actions and/or thought patterns.

+ **Hindsight Bias:** Looking in the rearview mirror, a great many investors tend to magnify and embellish their predictive abilities, raising their recollected odds that a given outcome would occur in those cases where it did take place, or lowering their after-the-fact assessment of the odds that a given outcome would occur in those cases where it did not take place.

+ **Rationalization:** Rather than addressing causes rooted in their own behavior, investors may attempt in a wide range of situations to make plausible excuses for actions they have taken that led to unfavorable results.

+ **Selective Memory:** Some investors are prone to recall only those positive and/or negative elements of previous conditions, events, and circumstances that are consistent with their current understanding of the past.

+ **Projection of Blame:** Whether or not they were at fault, investors may assign the blame for erroneous or unprofitable asset-allocation and investment strategy decisions to other parties, ranging from proximate sources such as investment advisors to more distant sources such as financial commentators in the mass media.

+ **Splitting or Withdrawal:** Unfavorable financial outcomes may precipitate strong responses of distancing or withdrawal on the part of some investors as they resolve never again to pursue the activities that resulted in such outcomes.

Knowing about behavioral traits and patterns related to thinking, action, and reflection can help investors be mindful of the potential biases, tendencies, and human shortcomings in their asset-allocation and investment activity. At the same time, it is important for investors to recognize that: (i) investing is often fraught with uncertainty and with the distinct possibility of unsuccessful results; (ii) especially for unpracticed investors, it is difficult to assess probabilities, predict outcomes, and accurately forecast the financial effects of such outcomes; and (iii) by their very nature, behavioral mistakes are not so easy to avoid. Self-awareness and a robust, flexible, and wide-ranging intellectual framework are two powerful instruments that can help guide investors in suitable directions.

Information Sources About Behavioral Finance

An abundance of books, special studies, periodicals, scholars, and organizations provide useful information about behavioral finance and behavioral economics. Among the relevant and thought-provoking books are: (i) *Judgment Under Uncertainty: Heuristics and Biases*, edited by Amos Tversky, Daniel Kahneman, and Paul Slovic; (ii) *Advances in Behavioral Finance*, edited by Richard H. Thaler; (iii) *The Winner's Curse*, by Richard H. Thaler; (iv) *Happiness and Economics: How the Economy and Institutions Affect Human Well-Being*, by Bruno S. Frey and Alois Stutzer; and (v) *Fooled by Randomness: The Hidden Role of Chance in the Markets and in Life*, by Nassim Taleb.

Pragmatic understanding of many of the macro forces affecting individual investors' psychology, patterns of risk-taking asset allocation, and net-worth drivers can be found in a number of special studies, most of which are updated and reissued from time to time. These reports include: (i) *The Future of Money Management in America*, by Sanford C. Bernstein & Company, since 2000 a part of Alliance Capital Management; (ii) *AIMR Conference Proceedings on Investment Counseling for Private Clients*, issued in November 1998; (iii) *Household Sector Focus*, published at regular intervals by the U.S. Economics Team at Credit Suisse; and (iv) *World Wealth Report*, produced annually by Capgemini U.S. in association with Merrill Lynch.

Specialized inquiry and research on behavioral finance and economics can be found in the periodicals listed in Table 5.2.

T A B L E 5.2

Selected Periodicals in Behavioral Finance and Behavioral Economics

Periodical	Web Site
Cognitive Psychology	academicpress.com
Journal of Economic Behavior and Organization	elsevier.com
Journal of Financial Engineering	iafe.org
Journal of Economics Perspectives	aeaweb.org/jep
Journal of Psychology and Financial Markets	psychologyandmarkets.org
Journal of Risk and Uncertainty	springerlink.com
Quarterly Journal of Economics	mitpressjournals.org

Source: The Author.

Table 5.3 lists several representative scholars in the fields of behavioral finance and behavioral economics.

Investors can access a compilation of many of these scholars' books, articles, monographs, and other writings through the Web sites listed in Table 5.3.

Several organizations carry out research and consulting activity in the field of behavioral finance and behavioral economics, and a number of these firms are shown in Table 5.4.

The output of the organizations listed in Table 5.4 often represents a highly useful bridge between currents of thought in the academic establishment and areas of inquiry within the financial community.

Emotional Intelligence in Asset Allocation and Investing

In 1994, the psychologist and journalist Daniel Goleman wrote a highly popular book, *Emotional Intelligence*, followed later by *Working with Emotional Intelligence*, with ramifications for individuals seeking to achieve success in asset allocation and investing. Paraphrasing the author, emotional intelligence is the capacity to empathize, judge, relate, be simpatico, and exercise other emotional skills crucial for someone to be truly integrated and successful. Emotional intelligence means being able to: (i) rein in emotional impulses; (ii) read the innermost feelings of others, and (iii) handle

T A B L E   5.3

Representative Scholars in Behavioral Finance and Behavioral Economics

Scholar	Educational Institution	Web Site
Shlomo Benartzi	University of California at Los Angeles	anderson.ucla.edu
Nicholas C. Barberis	Yale School of Management	msb.yale.edu
Gary S. Becker	University of Chicago	home.uchicago.edu/~gbecker
Stephen J. Brown	New York University Stern School of Business	stern.nyu.edu/~sbrown
Simon Gervais	Duke University Fuqua School of Business	duke.edu/~sgervais
William N. Goetzmann	Yale School of Management	viking.som.yale.edu
Roger G. Ibbotson	Yale School of Management	mba.yale.edu
Daniel Kahneman	Princeton University	princeton.edu
Josef Lakonishok	University of Illinois	business.uiuc.edu
Terrance Odean	University of California at Berkeley	faculty.haas.berkeley.edu/odean
William R. Reichenstein	Baylor University	finance.baylor.edu/reichenstein
Hersh Shefrin	Santa Clara University	lsb.scu.edu
Robert J. Shiller	Yale University	econ.yale.edu/~shiller
Jeremy J. Siegel	The Wharton School of the University of Pennsylvania	finance.wharton.upenn.edu
Paul Slovic	University of Oregon	uoregon.edu
Meir Statman	Santa Clara University	lsb.scu.edu
Lawrence H. Summers	Harvard University	harvard.edu
Richard Thaler	University of Chicago Graduate School of Business	chicagogsb.edu
Amos Tversky	Stanford University	stanford.edu
Richard J. Zeckhauser	Harvard University, J.F. Kennedy School of Government	ksghome.harvard.edu/ ~Rzeckhauser

Source: The Author.

relationships smoothly, as Aristotle put it, the rare skill "to be angry with the right person, to the right degree, at the right time, for the right purpose, and in the right way." This is not easy, and quite a few investors and the people they rely on manage to get it all wrong.

T A B L E 5.4

Selected Organizations in Behavioral Finance and Behavioral Economics

Organization	Location	Web Site
Decision Research	Eugene, OR	decisionresearch.org
Financial Psychology Corporation	North Miami, FL	financialpsychology.com
National Association of Personal Financial Advisors	Arlington Heights, IL	napfa.org
National Bureau of Economic Research	Cambridge, MA	nber.com
Psychology of Money Consultants	Los Angeles, CA	psychologyofmoney.com
Spectrem Group	Chicago, IL	spectrem.com

Source: The Author.

Investors who possess a certain level of emotional intelligence may be able to discern and reduce the mistakes of intuitive reasoning, understand and relate to themselves, sense the behavioral characteristics and moods of the financial environment, and make sense of the activities of other participants in the investment marketplace. As described in *Emotional Intelligence*, some of the fundamentals and ingredients of emotional intelligence are depicted in Figure 5.12.

Some of the *fundamentals* of emotional intelligence are summarized below:

- **Self-Awareness:** Having self-knowledge of the investor's own feelings, and using the investor's intuitive sense to make decisions the investor can live with happily.
- **Management of Feelings:** Controlling impulses, soothing anxiety, or having anger that is appropriate.
- **Motivation:** Maintaining and replenishing zeal, persistence, and optimism in the face of setbacks.
- **Empathy:** Reading and responding to unspoken feelings in others and oneself.
- **Social Skill:** Handling emotional reactions in others, interacting smoothly, and managing relationships effectively.

F I G U R E   5.12

Selected Behavioral Traits and Patterns of Individual Investors

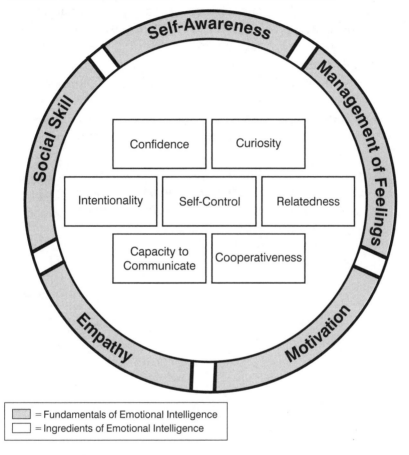

Source: The Author.

Some of the *ingredients* of emotional intelligence are summarized below:

◆ **Confidence:** A sense of control and mastery of investors'
being, behavior, and world; the sense that they are more
likely than not to succeed at what they undertake, and
that others will be helpful in the process.

- **Curiosity:** The sense that finding out about things is positive and leads to satisfaction.
- **Intentionality:** The wish and capacity to have an impact, and to act upon that with persistence. Intentionality is related to a sense of competence, of being effective.
- **Self-Control:** The ability to modulate and control investors' actions in age-appropriate ways; a sense of inner control.
- **Relatedness:** The ability to engage with others based on the sense of being understood by and understanding others.
- **Capacity to Communicate:** The wish and ability to verbally exchange ideas, feelings, and concepts with others. This is related to a sense of trust in others and positive feelings about engaging others.
- **Cooperativeness:** The ability to balance the investors' own needs with those of others in group activity.

S E C T I O N 4

ASSET CLASS CHARACTERISTICS

CHAPTER 6

DISTINGUISHING QUALITIES OF ASSET CLASSES

OVERVIEW

An essential skill in asset allocation is the ability to understand the inherent qualities of each asset class, the circumstances in which specific asset classes should be emphasized or de-emphasized, and how various kinds of assets fit together in a portfolio. After considering the differences between capital assets, consumable or tradable assets, and store-of-value assets, this chapter presents selected measures for evaluating asset classes and asset managers. These criteria focus on factors such as returns, risk, and correlations, as well as other fundamental, valuation, operational, technical, and psychological considerations.

The chapter then examines the roles and influences of the significant participants within each asset class, including suppliers of capital, intermediaries, and users of capital. A comprehensive survey of the major asset classes and subasset classes is then introduced, which leads to a detailed treatment of the rationale for investment and the risks and concerns associated with each of 16 asset classes in broad groupings within the equity, fixed-income, alternative assets, and cash instruments categories.

Appropriate asset class weightings in various phases of capital-market cycles are then discussed, followed by a survey of several kinds of assets, which under certain conditions may behave like other assets. The chapter concludes with an examination of the range of asset-allocation and asset-protection strategies that investors can employ at varying levels of financial, economic, and systemic stress.

ASSET SUPERCATEGORIES

The word "asset" traces its origins to the word *asez*, a sixteenth-century Anglo-French and Old French term meaning "enough," and, as such, refers to useful and desirable resources, items of ownership, or qualities that have exchange value or that may be convertible into money. Much of the great diversity of tangible and financial asset types may be grouped into three supercategories: capital assets, consumable or tradable assets, and store of value assets, as shown in Figure 6.1.

Capital assets, such as publicly traded and privately held equities, fixed-income securities, and real estate, earn their long-term value primarily by the capitalization of cash flows from current and projected dividend, interest, and terminal-value payments. Following this same valuation methodology, some economists classify the potential lifetime earning power of an individual as a form of capital asset known as *human capital*.

Consumable or tradable assets, including energy products, grains and other soft commodities, base metals, and livestock, are valued primarily by the classical forces of supply and demand, which in turn are influenced by the assets' intrinsic value or their value in manufacturing or consumption.

Store of value assets, encompassing art and antiques, currencies, jewelry, precious metals, and other valuables, accrue value primarily by investor psychology and preferences, or what a buyer is willing to pay for the asset at a given point in time.

F I G U R E   6.1

Asset Supercategories

Asset Supercategory	Representative Examples	Valuation Determinants
Capital Assets	Equities Fixed-Income Securities Real Estate	Valuations are determined primarily by the capitalization of cash flows from current and projected dividend, interest, and terminal value payments
Consumable or Tradable Assets	Energy Products Grains and Softs Base Metals Livestock	Valuations are determined primarily by the classical forces of supply and demand
Store of Value Assets	Art and Antiques Currencies Jewelry Precious Metals	Valuations are determined primarily by investor psychology and preferences

Source: The Author, and "What Is an Asset Class Anyway?" by Robert J. Greer, *Journal of Portfolio Management*, Winter 1997.

Some assets, such as consumer durable goods and households' equity in non-corporate businesses (in the form of sole proprietorships or partnership interests), may not fit neatly into one of these asset supercategories. Other assets, such as gold, raw land, and various forms of real estate, may in fact overlap more than one of the asset supercategories. Being aware of the distinctions between the primary value drivers in each asset grouping and the occasional tendency for markets to misclassify assets (for example, when market conditions sometimes treat equities as consumable assets, or other times as store-of-value assets) can help investors establish a strategic asset-allocation framework to implement tactical asset-allocation decisions and select specific investments.

EVALUATING ASSET CLASSES

In many respects, asset allocation resembles the architectural and design aspects of investing, in which the architect (the investor) chooses various building materials (asset classes) based on considerations of the building site, prevailing tastes and conventions, cost, safety, and other factors (such as the financial market outlook and investor preferences). Just as the architect may choose certain types of wood, stone, tile, steel, aluminum, glass, or other construction elements for their intrinsic qualities and how they may be combined to achieve important design and engineering goals, the investor may select certain asset classes on the basis of their specific characteristics and how the best elements of these characteristics may emerge when used individually and/or in combination.

Investors evaluate asset classes on the basis of: (i) projections of how the asset may change in value and how it tends to perform under normal circumstances as well as during extreme economic and financial conditions, such as high inflation or deflation; (ii) the various forms of risk and the probabilities of loss associated with the asset; (iii) how the asset contributes to overall portfolio risk and return, affects other assets, and is affected by other assets in a portfolio context; and (iv) when and under what scenarios the asset may exhibit abnormal behavior. Figure 6.2 sets forth a number of criteria for evaluating asset classes.

Among the evaluation criteria for asset classes are: (i) general considerations, including the degree of efficiency of the asset class, and its responsiveness and sensitivity to external and internal forces; (ii) the essential nature and inherent financial and non-financial characteristics; (iii) the degree to which investor psychology affects the asset class; (iv) historical and projected returns patterns; (v) risk measures and potential risk-control mechanisms; (vi) correlations with other asset classes over various time periods and in different market conditions; (vii) valuation methodologies and ranges; (viii) the potential for investors to generate alpha (returns in excess of benchmark returns for the asset class); and (ix) operational and technical factors associated with investing in the asset class.

For reasons of convenience, access to specialized professional expertise, and cost-effectiveness, many investors may decide to

F I G U R E 6.2

Selected Criteria for Evaluating Asset Classes

General Considerations	Essential Nature	Psychological Aspects
• Responsiveness to periods of high inflation, moderate inflation, price stability, disinflation, and severe deflation • Sensitivity to short- and long-term economic forces • Means and degree of difficulty of obtaining basic and updating information • Availability of analytical concepts, tools, and models • Degree of simplicity and understandability • Size, differentiation, and definability as an asset class • Range, diversity, and completeness of asset class subcategories and investment choices • Ease and utility in portfolio rebalancing activity	• Liquidity, market efficiency, convenience, transparency, normal investment amounts, and divisibility • Tax status and tax efficiency • International influences and forms of the asset • Resemblances to other asset classes • Scope of potential gain versus potential loss • Consistency and effectiveness of combining with other asset classes • Forms of conservative, moderate, and aggressive participation • Data quality, longevity, and potential data biases • Existence and depth of related derivatives markets	• Availability of and potential rewards to contrarian strategies • Pathways and patterns of reaction to external shocks, internal crises, supply/demand imbalances, and ownership distribution shifts • Clarity of signals that the asset may be entering into or emerging from market distress • Susceptibility to and prior episodes of extreme over- or undervaluation • Time and conditions needed for sentiment to shift • Issuer and investor ownership, gross flows, and net flows profile
Return	**Risk**	**Correlation**
• Form, relative importance, and predictability of return components • Compound rates of return over selected time periods • Normal and abnormal patterns of returns • Applicability of buy-to-hold versus buy-to-sell strategies • Forecastability and predictability of returns • Historical and projected nominal and real returns • Cyclical and secular patterns of returns • Chief influences on returns • Range of return enhancement tools and strategies	• Size and degree of variation in historical and expected risk premium versus risk-free assets • Standard deviations of returns during various types of financial market environments • Forms of and degree of exposure to risk • Actual and implied volatility levels • Degree of stability in risk characteristics • Beta or systematic risk within a global market setting • Sensitivity of returns to changes in interest rates • Range of risk reduction tools and strategies	• Diversification characteristics (such as low or negative correlations) within and across asset classes • Degree of independence in returns versus the returns of other asset classes • Consistency of correlations of monthly, quarterly, yearly, and multi-year returns over various portfolio time horizons • Influences on correlations under various financial market conditions • Explicit and implicit linkages with other asset classes • Range of correlation-lowering tools and strategies
Valuation	**Alpha Generation Potential**	**Operational/Technical Element**
• Range and robustness of valuation inputs • Frequency and reliability of valuation methodologies • Measures of intrinsic value • Appropriateness of transaction-, appraisal-, or liquidation-based pricing • Range of historical and projected valuations • Forms and degree of evolution in valuation standards • Key drivers of value creation and destruction	• Availability and efficacy of strategic and tactical maneuvers to generate excess returns • Role, cost, and dispersion of results of intermediaries • Means and degree of difficulty of investing passively (using benchmark indices), actively on one's own, or actively through intermediaries • Means of obtaining and sustaining legitimate incremental performance • Opportunities for discovering and exploiting mispricings and market anomalies	• Costs of transactions, settlement, ownership, and reporting • Forms and frequency of hedging, leverage, and shorting activity • Adequacy, representativeness, and investability of benchmark indices • Scope of and access to Internet-based research and trading resources • Potential ability for the asset to match up with and satisfy projected nominal and real liabilities

Source: The Author.

engage an asset manager. For asset classes such as equities, fixed-income securities, and cash instruments, investors may access full-time asset managers through open-end and closed-end mutual funds, unit trusts, and separate account managers. For many alternative asset classes, such as U.S. and non-U.S. real estate, commodities, private equity and venture capital, and investment strategies such as hedge funds, investors may access asset management talent through various kinds of onshore and offshore partnerships and other structures. To help investors determine the scope of risks associated with a specific firm and its strategies, as well as the likelihood of future results measuring up to indicated outcomes, Figure 6.3 sets forth a number of criteria for evaluating asset managers.

Among the evaluation criteria for asset managers are: (i) general considerations concerning the size, history, experience, and culture of the asset manager; (ii) the manager's investment philosophy and approach within his or her sphere of asset-management activity; (iii) the nature, robustness, and degree of utilization of internal and external resources; (iv) the sources, consistency, and quantification of investment performance; (v) how the asset manager anticipates and deals with risk; (vi) the degree to which the manager's results correlate with those of peers within the same asset class and with other asset classes; (vii) the forms, level, incentives, and fee calculation methodologies associated with utilizing the asset manager; (viii) the manager's tax sensitivity and aftertax-to-pretax returns competency; and (ix) operational and technical elements associated with dealing with the asset manager.

PARTICIPANTS WITHIN ASSET CLASSES

In most asset classes, certain kinds of investors supply capital, either directly or through intermediaries, to certain investment destinations for that capital. In analyzing the outlook for an asset class, it is important to be mindful of the specific roles, relationships between, and influences on the suppliers, agents, and users of investment capital. These associations are depicted in Figure 6.4.

The investor population that supplies capital to any given asset class is shown on the left-hand side of Figure 6.4 and can be

F I G U R E 6.3

Selected Criteria for Evaluating Asset Managers

General Considerations	Philosophy and Approach	Resource Utilization
• The existence of explicit and implicit guidelines to foster ethical investment practices and to manage conflicts • Appropriateness of current and future amounts of assets under management relative to target markets and position sizes • Sources, degree, relevance, and sustainability of competitive advantage • Asset management experience, proficiency, and reliability; structure of investment vehicles; and conflict resolution procedures • Degree of proactivity in influencing the direction of underlying investments • Proximity to idea and deal flow • Minimum and/or maximum amounts that can be invested with the manager	• Definition, articulation, understandability, soundness, and practical application of investment philosophy • Percentage and absolute amount of manager capital participation in their own investment vehicles • Transparency and efficacy of investment identification, ranking, selection, and rebalancing processes • Degree of focus, discipline, and variability in approach • Complementarity with other investments and strategies • Forms and record-keeping of decision-making activity • Potential for tailoring approach to respond to investor-specific goals and directives	• Sources, evolution, strengths, and limitations of quantitative and qualitative inputs, modeling, research, scenario analysis, and sensitivity analysis • Professional and support staff interviewing, hiring, training, evaluation, compensation, and development practices • Organizational design, culture, morale, spirit, adaptation, and perpetuation patterns
Investment Performance	**Risk Management**	**Correlations**
• Prior performance record and sources of significant gains and losses • Compliance with auditing and reporting standards of appropriate oversight bodies • Consistency across investors of investment returns • Pricing, sources, trading practices, and valuation methodologies • Benchmarks used for comparing performance results, and degree of tracking versus benchmarks • Potential and actual means for achieving alpha (excess returns) • Persistence of returns in varying environments	• Mechanisms and procedures for identifying, monitoring, hedging, and diversifying risk exposures • Degree of variability and pattern of investment results • Explicit limitations on risk concentration • Maximum drawdown, number of months in drawdown, and months to recovery under varying conditions • Upside and downside capture ratios • Uses of leverage, short-selling, and derivatives • Measures for anticipating and protecting against adverse scenarios	• Absolute amount and degree of variation in correlations of returns with other similar managers, with asset class benchmarks, and with other asset classes • Behavior of returns versus other assets' and managers' returns over varying time periods and in varying economic and financial conditions • Effectiveness of manager style as a balancing and diversifying agent within a portfolio
Fees and Expenses	**Tax Considerations**	**Operational/Technical Elements**
• Asset management fee structure and means of aligning the interests of managers and investors • Initial and deferred sales charges, marketing fees, wrap fees, and redemption fees • Aggregation procedures, hurdle rates, high water mark structures, breakpoints, and the degree of negotiability of fees • Ability to oversee selected assets "below the line" on a non-fee basis • Forms and amount of multi-layer fee arrangements in fund of fund structures	• Legal structure (such as partnership, mutual fund, LLC, or separately managed account) • Influences on and level of turnover of investments • Tax- and gains-realization efficiency • Ability to adapt investment strategies to take account of significant gain or loss events outside the portfolio or in other asset classes • Attentiveness to loss-harvesting techniques, returns of capital, interest and dividend flows, wash-sale rules, portfolio turnover, tax lot accounting, charitable contribution and exchange fund strategies, and deferred tax liability considerations	• Format and comprehensibility of subscription documents, offering memoranda, tax and regulatory filings, and investor reports • Capital liquidity, lockup, custody, and withdrawal terms • Forms, frequency, and substance of interaction with existing and potential investors • Degree of investor contact, input to, and control over manager decisions • Prior and current litigation, official investigations, arbitration proceedings, or judicial rulings involving the asset manager • Kinds and amounts of insurance coverage

Source: The Author.

F I G U R E 6.4

Representative Participants within Asset Classes

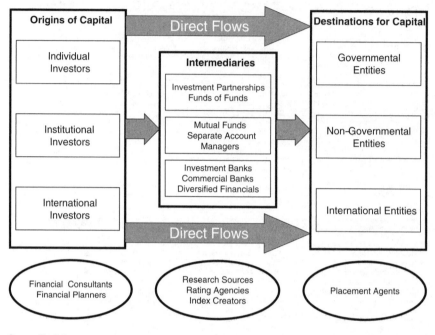

Source: The Author.

divided broadly into individual investors, institutional investors, and international investors. The long-term or short-term entry or withdrawal of any of these investors may lead to significant changes in valuations and investment returns within specific asset classes. The destinations for capital, shown on the right-hand side of Figure 6.4, may be broadly grouped into governmental entities, non-governmental entities, and international entities. For *capital assets* such as equities, fixed-income securities, cash instruments, and many forms of private equity and venture capital, these destination entities tend to be *issuers of securities*. For *consumable or tradable assets*, and *store of value assets* such as commodities, real estate, art, currencies, or precious metals, these destination entities tend to be the assets themselves. The entry or withdrawal of important destinations for capital within an asset class can profoundly affect valuations and investment returns within specific asset classes.

The middle part of Figure 6.4 shows several types of intermediaries that may gather funds from suppliers of capital and invest them in issuers' securities or directly in certain assets. These agents include: (i) investment partnerships (such as hedge funds or private equity, real estate, venture capital, or commodities partnerships) and funds of funds formed to diversify assets and gain access to selected asset managers; (ii) closed-end and open-end mutual funds and separate account managers; and (iii) financial institutions such as investment banks, commercial banks, and diversified financial firms. The entry or withdrawal of major intermediaries for capital to and from an asset class can meaningfully influence valuations and investment returns.

Across the bottom section of Figure 6.4 is a partial selection of important contributors to the capital-investment process within specific asset classes. These participants include: (i) financial consultants and financial planners, who generally help investors select destinations for capital and intermediaries; (ii) research sources, rating agencies, and benchmark index creators, who help capital suppliers assess and measure the performance of various kinds of assets; and (iii) placement agents, who help raise investment capital for intermediaries and/or for destinations for capital. Shifts in opinion, emphasis, or appraisal activity by any of these entities can considerably redirect capital flows to and from asset classes, with important implications for these assets' valuations and investment returns.

ASSET CLASSES AND SUBASSET CLASSES

Within the four major categories of assets—equities, fixed-income securities, alternative assets, and cash instruments—a number of asset classes and subasset classes are available for investment. Many of these asset classes and subasset classes are listed in Figure 6.5.

Figure 6.5 depicts 18 distinct asset classes within the gray boxes, including: (i) U.S. equity, non-U.S. equity, and emerging-markets equity; (ii) U.S. fixed-income, high-yield fixed-income, non-U.S. fixed-income, emerging-markets debt, and convertible securities; (iii) private equity and venture capital, commodities,

F I G U R E 6.5

Selected Asset Classes and Asset Class Subcategories

Equity	**Fixed Income**	**Alternative Investments**	**Cash**

U.S. Equity

Large Capitalization
Mid Capitalization
Small Capitalization
Micro Capitalization
Growth
Value
Core
Preferred Stock
Master Limited Partnerships
Swaps, Options, and Futures

Non-U.S. Equity

Canada
EAFE (Europe, Australasia, and Far East)
Europe
Developed Asia
Japan
U.K.
Swaps, Options, and Futures

Emerging-Markets Equity

Asia ex Japan
Emerging Europe
Middle East
Africa
Latin America
Frontier Markets
Swaps, Options, and Futures

U.S. Fixed Income

U.S. Treasury
Agency
Corporate
Municipal
Mortgage-Backed
Asset-Backed
Guaranteed Investment Contracts
Swaps, Options, and Futures
Credit Default Swaps

High Yield

Upper/Middle Tier
Lower Tier
Non-U.S.

Non-U.S. Fixed Income

Canada
EAFE (Europe, Australasia, and Far East)
Europe
Developed Asia
Japan
U.K.
Interest Rate Swaps
Currency Swaps
Swaps, Options, and Futures
Credit Default Swaps

Emerging-Markets Debt

Africa
Asia ex Japan
Emerging Europe
Latin America
Middle East
Frontier Markets

Convertible Securities

U.S.
Non-U.S.

Private Equity and Venture Capital

Private Equity
Venture Capital
Non-U.S.
Funds of Funds

Commodities

Options and Futures
Collateralized Futures
Physicals
Non-U.S.

Real Estate

Apartment
Commercial
Residential
Office/Industrial
Farmland
REITS
International
Retail/Hotel
Non-U.S.

Hedge Funds

Event-Driven and Merger Arbitrage
Fixed Income
Equity Non-Directional
Convertible and Equity Arbitrage
Variable Bias
Long Bias
Discretionary Trading
Systematic Trading
Funds of Funds

Precious Metals and Gold

Bars and Bullion
Coins and Medals
Gold Shares
Jewelry
Other Precious Metals
Swaps, Options, and Futures

Inflation-Indexed Securities

U.S.
Non-U.S.

Managed Futures

Commodity Trading Advisors
Funds of Funds

Art

U.S. Cash/ Cash Equivalents

Physical and Electronic Holdings
Bank Balances
U.S. Treasury Bills
Agency Notes
Municipal Notes
Bankers Acceptances
Certificates of Deposit
Repurchase Agreements
Money Market Funds
Ultra-Short Bonds Funds
Stable Value Funds
Non-U.S. Instruments

Non-U.S. Cash/ Cash Equivalents

real estate, hedge funds, precious metals and gold, inflation-indexed securities, managed futures, and art; and (iv) U.S. cash instruments and non-U.S. cash instruments. There is no unanimity of opinion as to what determines whether an asset type merits consideration as a separate asset class, yet some of the defining principles may include: sufficient trading volume and amounts outstanding, distinctive functions, features, and degrees of responsiveness to economic and financial forces, the existence of indices for tracking changes in capital values and income generation, and the perceptions of investors and other market participants.

Several caveats are worth noting when one is looking at Figure 6.5. First, not all tangible and financial asset classes and sub-asset classes are identified. For example, human capital is not listed as an asset, and various important subgroupings within the art asset class and other asset classes are not shown. Second, some capital-market participants may prefer to list convertible securities as a form of equity and inflation-indexed securities as a cash-like asset. Third, due to their size, investor base, and individualized patterns of returns, standard deviations, and correlations, some groupings of assets shown in Figure 6.5 as subasset classes are considered distinct asset classes in their own right. Such asset groupings include, but are not limited to, Japanese equity, European equity, Japanese fixed-income, and European fixed-income. Fourth, Figure 6.5 does not list a number of fund structures, including closed-end and open-end mutual funds, index funds, exchange-traded funds, and derivative instruments, including futures, forwards, options, swap agreements, and other constructs, even though they may offer direct and indirect means of isolating and participating in the risk, return, and correlation attributes of the asset classes upon which they are based.

ASSET CLASS DESCRIPTIONS

Investors can make rational asset-allocation and investment strategy decisions by understanding the characteristics of each major asset class. Figure 6.6 groups 18 major asset classes into four broad categories: equity, fixed-income securities, alternative investments, and cash.

For each major asset class, Figure 6.6 summarizes five of the main reasons to include that asset in a portfolio, and five of the main risks or concerns associated with the asset. The summary points in Figure 6.6 are distilled from the detailed asset class descriptions contained in Figures 6.7 through 6.23. For example, the top row of Figure 6.6 summarizes five key reasons to consider

F I G U R E 6.6

Summary of Asset Class Characteristics

Equity		
	Rationale for Investment	**Risks and Concerns**
U.S. Equity Figure 6.11	• Ownership claims • Potentially high long-term returns • Some inflation protection • Sector/style selection • Economic participation	• High standard deviations • Underperformance in deflation • Long-term cycles of return • Dividend reinvestment • Unstable correlations
Non-U.S. Equity Figure 6.12	• Diversified exposure • Potentially favorable correlations • Expanded opportunity set • Different dynamics • Exploitable inefficiencies	• High standard deviations • Unstable correlations • Investment costs • Currency risks • Claims enforceability
Emerging-Markets Equity Figure 6.13	• Growth opportunity • Alpha potential • Potentially attractive returns • Potentially favorable correlations • Global integration	• High standard deviations • Exposure to capital flows • Liquidity, regulation, infrastructure • Ownership costs • Political/geopolitical concerns

Fixed-Income Securities		
	Rationale for Investment	**Risks and Concerns**
U.S. Fixed-Income Figure 6.14	• Low standard deviations • Usually higher-than-cash returns • Portfolio diversifier • Usually senior financial claims • Liquidity	• Capital risk in rising interest rates • Prepayment risk • Unstable correlations • Inflation risk • Pricing/trading challenges
High-Yield Fixed Income Figure 6.15	• Potentially high returns • Low standard deviations • Alpha potential • Capital structure position • Market inefficiencies	• Non-senior credit risk • Economic dependence • Potential market dislocations • Trading liquidity • Selected structural features
Non-U.S. Fixed Income Figure 6.16	• Expanded opportunity set • Predictable cash flows • Alpha potential • Usually low standard deviations • Generally favorable correlations	• Currency risk • Cross-border risk • Sometimes unstable correlations • Bond-inherent risks • Higher costs
Emerging-Markets Fixed Income Figure 6.17	• Economic potential • Potentially high returns • Usually low correlations • Global integration • Market inefficiencies	• Behavior during crises • High volatility • Market liquidity • Exposure to capital flows • Political/geopolitical concerns
Convertibles Figure 6.10	• Equity-debt hybrid • Principal repayment terms • Yield advantage vs. common • Competitive returns • Structural features	• Embedded options • Subordinate credit • Yields generally below bonds • Capped upside potential • Market imbalances

Alternative Investments		
	Rationale for Investment	**Risks and Concerns**
Real Estate Figure 6.23	• Inflation hedge • Usually low standard deviations • Generally low correlations • Defensive characteristics • Opportunity for alpha potential	• Transactions costs • Risks during disinflation/deflation • Ownership costs • Feast/famine returns • Asset heterogeneity
Commodities Figure 6.9	• Diversification characteristics • Intrinsic utility • Inflation hedge • Supply-demand influences • Low correlations	• Returns volatility • Economic exposure • Technical activity • Behaviors during deflation • Generally low long-term returns
Gold Figure 6.18	• Rarity/beauty • Inelastic supply • Protection/refuge • Purchasing power maintenance • Usually negative correlations	• Yield disadvantage • Governmental sales/intervention • Mean reversion • Market structure • Valuation methods
Private Equity/Venture Capital Figure 6.22	• Potentially high returns • Usually moderate correlations • Opportunity for alpha potential • Specialized focus • Connectivity/control	• Capital entry/exit terms • High minimums • High standard deviations • High costs • Returns measurement
Managed Futures Funds Figure 6.21	• Usually moderate returns • Usually low correlations • Generally low standard deviations • Broad opportunity set • Behavior during turmoil	• Underperformance in low volatility • Reliance on quantitative approach • Trend-following systems • Expenses • Tax considerations
Hedge Funds/Fund of Funds Figure 6.19	• Access to special talent • Usually low standard deviations • Broad opportunity set • Generally low correlations • Opportunity for alpha potential	• Alpha erosion • Returns measurement issues • Generally high fees • Returns biases and patterns • May be tax inefficient
Inflation-Indexed Securities Figure 6.20	• Inflation hedge • Low correlations • Low volatility • Risk reduction • Portfolio diversifier	• Tax treatment • Real rate risk • Bond proximity • Disadvantageous in deflation • Sometimes complicated features
Art Figure 6.7	• Aesthetic enjoyment • Intrinsic beauty • Compound returns • Store of value • Generally low correlations	• Illiquid market • Psychological influences • Price volatility • Ownership costs • Indivisibility
Cash		
	Rationale for Investment	**Risks and Concerns**
U.S. Cash/Cash Equivalents Figure 6.8	• Usually low price risk • Generally low correlations • Usually low volatility • Liquidity and access • Deflation protection	• Generally low long-term returns • Reinvestment risk • Purchasing power risk • Potential credit exposure • Costs and attention
Non-U.S. Cash/Cash Equivalents	• Usually low price risk • Currency exposure • Generally low correlations • Usually low volatility • Deflation protections	• Generally low long-term returns • Currency exposure • Reinvestment risk • Potential credit exposure • Costs and attention

investing in U.S. equity: (i) ownership claims on assets and earnings; (ii) the potential for high long-term returns; (iii) some inflation protection; (iv) sector/style diversification selection; and (v) economic participation. Five key risks associated with investing in U.S. equity include: (i) high standard deviations of returns;

F I G U R E   6.7

Asset Class Description for Art

Characteristics
Description:
For secular and sacred motivations during the 10,000 years since cave paintings were limned in Lascaux, France, and in Altamira, Spain, human beings have reified and preserved their interior inspirations and the observable world in many art forms. Although it is difficult to universally, precisely, or unchangingly delineate the border between art and non-art, some exceptional objects have been able to set themselves apart by virtue of their technical mastery, visual empathy, or aesthetic fluency as worthy of artistic admiration in broad or narrow spheres of opinion.
Choices:
The field of art is very broad and, among other categories, includes: (i) American and European impressionist, modern, contemporary, and nineteenth-century paintings; (ii) European Old Master paintings; (iii) sculpture of various periods; (iv) antiquities; (v) drawings and prints; (vi) photography; (vii) Asian, Indian, Persian, Islamic, African, Latin American, Native American, and American folk art; (vii) categories of decorative arts such as furniture and other antiques, silver, jewelry, porcelain, and precious and semiprecious stones; and (ix) collectibles such as rare coins, medals, stamps, banknotes, books, armor, toys, weapons, manuscripts, wine, classic automobiles, sports trading cards, and other memorabilia.

Mei/Moses Fine Art Index

Time Period	No. Yrs.	Total Return CAGR	Std. Dev.	Correlation of Annual Returns with				
				U.S. Equity	U.S. F.I.	Non-U.S. Equity	Cash	CPI Infl.
1970–1979	10	11.2%	26.4%	0.09	NA	0.12	−0.01	−0.25
1970–1989	20	16.7%	24.1%	0.18	NA	0.18	−0.04	−0.09
1970–1999	30	11.2%	23.8%	0.07	NA	0.17	0.14	0.11
1980–1989	10	22.5%	21.7%	0.17	−0.48	0.14	−0.34	0.29
1980–1999	20	11.2%	23.1%	0.07	−0.10	0.20	0.20	0.37
1990–1999	10	1.0%	20.0%	0.02	−0.01	−0.12	0.07	0.07
1997–2006	10	9.3%	12.2%	0.21	−0.44	0.62	−0.07	0.26
2000–2006	7	11.5%	10.2%	0.85	−0.56	0.79	0.17	0.13

Mei/Moses Fine Art Index
Annual Returns

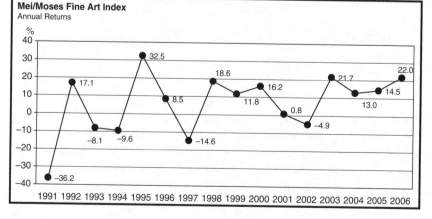

Source: The Author.

Rationale for Investment	Risks and Concerns
• Although some works of art have been purchased in search of short- or long-term financial gain, and others have been acquired in settlement of debts incurred or patronage arrangements for shelter, food, medical care, or other services, many individual pieces or renowned collections have been assembled to furnish a high degree of aesthetic enjoyment and personal pleasure to their owner. For centuries, important non-monetary reasons for purchasing art have included such elusive, indefinable, and subjective motivations as passion, splendor, taste, curiosity, attraction, affinity, cultivation, status, prestige, power, connoisseurship, and delight. • In many instances, art is esteemed for its intrinsic beauty and worth, its reflection of the maker's skill and creativity, and its ability to call forth ineffable an emotional response on the part of the viewer. • As a whole over meaningful holding periods, certain categories of art have sufficiently appreciated in value and thus generated compound annual rates of growth that have outperformed inflation and bond returns and, in many cases, have been competitive with long-term equity performance. A number of individual artworks have generated extraordinary multidecade compound returns, without any need for coupon or dividend reinvestment by the owner. • Despite the physical fragility, sequesterability, and delicacy of certain forms of art, in the minds of many investors art is viewed as a refuge or long-term store of value due to its permanence, portability, rarity, and irreplaceability. • Because art prices are considered to respond at different times, to different degrees, and to different sets of influences than the forces affecting the prices of many other asset classes, preliminary data indicate that artworks may be able to play a role in portfolio diversification because art tends to have low correlations of returns with equities and negative correlations with bonds and cash instruments.	• Artworks may be relatively illiquid and difficult to purchase or sell within specified time and price parameters, partly because of: (i) the heterogeneity of individual artworks; (ii) the seasonality and infrequency of transactions; (iii) a narrow degree of transparency about the price history of comparable objects; (iv) high transactions costs and bid-offer spreads; (v) the occasional use of special financial arrangements between buyers, sellers, and intermediaries; and (vi) an annual global turnover equal to considerably less than one day's U.S. equity trading volume. • Determined by the forces of supply and demand without a robust and commonly accepted valuation framework involving interim cash flows and other factors, prices and values in the art world may be subject to economic and geopolitical perceptions, herd instinct, bidding frenzy, fashion, image dissemination, innuendo, lack of interest, psychology, publicity, exhibition history, image, selectivity, whim, fickleness, and the possible suspicion of retouching or forgery. • Although the Internet has increased the quantity and accessibility of information about art prices, the global art market can exhibit significant price volatility subject to: (i) the sudden entry or exit of auction houses, dealers, galleries, museums, and corporate or individual collectors affected by the rapid creation or destruction of wealth; (ii) taxes or restrictions on the import or export of artworks; and (iii) major programs of donation, acquisition, or deaccessioning activity. • Instead of producing a flow of income, the ownership of treasured and often virtually irreplaceable works of art may involve some degree of out-of-pocket costs for storage, climate control, and insurance against such risks as theft, vandalism, fire, natural disasters, or other calamities. • The indivisibility and high prices of many art objects tends to severely limit the ability to purchase or dispose of a fractional share of a work of art.

Information Sources: "Collecting" Section in Weekend editions of the *Financial Times* (*ft.com*); Mei Moses Family of Fine Art Index (*artasanasset.com*); *Forbes Collector's Guide* (*forbes.com*); Christie's International (*christies.com*); Sotheby's Holdings Inc. (*sothebys.com*); Phillips de Pury & Company (*phillipsdepury.com*); *Best Bids: The Insider's Guide to Buying at Auction*, by Dana Micucci; *The History of Art*, by H.W. Janson; *Portrait of Dr. Gachet*, by Cynthia Saltzman; Antiques Council (*antiquescouncil.com*); Appraisers Association of America (*appraisersassoc.org*); Art & Auction (*artandauction.com*); College Art Association (*collegeart.org*); ARTnews (*artnewsonline.com*); Haughton International Art and Antique Fairs (*haughton.com*); Art Market Research (*artmarketresearch.com*); Tefaf Maastricht Art Fair (*tefaf.com*); Clarion Arts (*olympia-antiques.co.uk*); Kusin & Company (*kusin.com*); *Leonard's Annual Price Index of Art Auctions*, by Susan Theran; Rapaport Diamond Report (*diamonds.net*); Art Price (*artprice.com*); and Art Sales Index (*art-sales-index.com*).

F I G U R E 6.8

Asset Class Description for U.S. Cash Equivalents

Characteristics

Description:

Cash and cash equivalents encompass a wide spectrum of generally liquid assets: (i) usually with less than one year's original or remaining maturity; (ii) whose returns tend to track inflation to some degree; and (iii) some of which can be purchased or sold in a relatively prompt fashion to effect payments or to be reinvested. The investment returns on sovereign cash instruments are frequently considered to be a proxy for the risk-free rate of return within their respective countries. While cash as an asset class may tend to be ignored or underemphasized by some investors during periods of persistently rising prices for goods and services and/or for financial assets, cash may function as a critically important defensive asset class in periods of declining prices for goods and services or negative investment returns in other asset classes.

Choices:

Cash may include: (i) physical and/or electronic holdings of banknotes, coins, bills, call money, and Fed Funds; (ii) money market funds or money market mutual funds; (iii) stable value funds and ultra-short bond funds; (iv) commingled portfolios sometimes known as cash-management or enhanced cash funds; (v) bank balances, passbook accounts, statement accounts, credit union accounts, bank deposits, sweep accounts, and certificates of deposit; and (vi) U.S. Treasury bills and federal agency securities, short-term municipal obligations, repurchase agreements, bankers acceptances, floating rate instruments, some medium-term notes, and commercial paper. Many countries outside the U.S. also have local currency-and/or U.S. dollar-denominated money markets with a variety of investable cash instruments. Cash equivalents may be differentiated as to their credit quality, maturity, taxability, and interest payment and calculation methodology. So-called negative cash may include reverse repurchase and securities lending agreements and borrowing via the Fed Funds market and/or securitized margin facilities.

Citigroup U.S. Treasury Bills (90-Day) Index

				Correlation of Annual Returns with				
Time Period	No. Yrs.	Total Return CAGR	Std. Dev.	U.S. Equity	U.S. F.I.	High Yield	Real Estate	CPI Infl.
1970–1979	10	6.4%	2.1%	−0.26	NA	NA	NA	0.87
1970–1989	20	7.8%	2.8%	−0.03	NA	NA	NA	0.43
1970–1999	30	6.9%	2.8%	−0.10	NA	NA	NA	0.58
1980–1989	10	9.2%	2.9%	−0.25	0.01	NA	0.14	0.69
1980–1999	20	7.1%	3.0%	−0.11	0.27	NA	0.11	0.74
1990–1999	10	5.1%	1.3%	0.08	0.32	−0.18	−0.25	0.61
1997–2006	10	3.7%	1.8%	0.14	0.27	−0.53	−0.28	−0.10
2000–2006	7	3.1%	1.9%	−0.29	0.42	−0.60	0.03	0.24

Rationale for Investment	Risks and Concerns
• Generally low nominal capital price fluctuation risk makes cash a safe haven in periods of negative financial returns. • Cash usually has: (i) low average correlation of returns with U.S. and international equity asset classes; (ii) modest correlations with fixed-income, real estate, and hedge fund asset classes; and (iii) negative correlations with commodities and emerging-market equity asset classes. • The standard deviation of returns on cash instruments tends to be very low. • Convenience, liquidity, and ease of access make cash an advantageous asset class in which to invest funds in anticipation of projected financial obligations or in consideration of future investment opportunities. • Benchmark indices such as the 30- or 90-day U.S. Treasury bill rate and the 1- or 3-month London (or European) Interbank Offered Rate (Libor or Euribor) may outperform other financial asset classes in disinflationary or deflationary economic and financial environments.	• Nominal and real rates of return on cash investments over time generally tend to be below the expected nominal and real returns for most other asset classes. • Reinvestment risk may occur whenever cash principal must be rolled over into new cash instruments at uncertain future rates of return. • Purchasing-power risk usually takes place when the real value of cash holdings is eroded during inflationary eras. • Cash instruments may span a broad degree of credit risk and carry varying degrees of federal, private, or structural protection against loss of principal due to credit downgrades, interest rate risk, duration risk, or other risks. • Asset management expenses, transaction charges, early redemption fees, and other expenses can significantly reduce the modest average returns from cash investments; in many cases, substantial amounts of time and attention must be devoted to the management and reinvestment of cash assets.

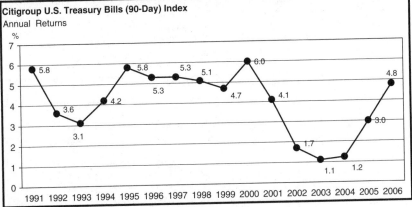

Citigroup U.S. Treasury Bills (90-Day) Index
Annual Returns

Source: The Author.
Information Sources: U.S. Treasury (*treasurydirect.gov*); Bankrate (*bankrate.com*); Securities Industry and Financial Markets Association (*investinginbonds.com*); iMoneyNet (*imoneynet.com*); Money Fund Report (*imoneynet.com*); Financial Research Corporation (*frcnet.com*); Lipper (*lipperweb.com*); Morningstar, Inc. (*morningstar.com*); The Handbook of Fixed Income Securities, Seventh Edition, ed. by Frank J. Fabozzi; Fidelity Money Market Fund (*fidelity.com*); Vanguard Prime Money Market Fund (*vanguard.com*); and Schwab Money Market Fund (*schwab.com*).

F I G U R E 6.9

Asset Class Description for Commodities

Characteristics
Description:
One broad grouping of commodities is characterized by its relatively fixed supply and low degree of perishability. These commodities include: (i) energy (such as crude oil, heating oil, natural gasoline, and unleaded gasoline); (ii) base metals (such as copper, aluminum, lead, nickel, zinc, and tin); and (iii) precious metals (such as gold, silver, platinum, palladium, and rhodium). Another grouping of commodities may be characterized as perishable, consumable, and affected by weather. These commodities include: (i) grains (such as corn, soybeans, and wheat); (ii) softs (such as coffee, sugar, cocoa, orange juice, and cotton); and (iii) livestock (such as live cattle, feeder cattle, and lean hogs). Spot market indices also track the prices of basic materials such as scrap metals; selected textiles and fibers, fats, oils and foodstuffs; and raw industrials.
Choices:
Certain commodities may be bought or sold in physical form, with returns determined by the commodity's upward or downward price movements less any applicable storage, financing, insurance, and other costs. Some investors gain exposure to commodities through collateralized commodity futures, whose returns are determined by: (i) the price performance of the underlying commodity; (ii) the return derived from the continuous rolling of near-term commodity contracts into more deferred lower-priced contracts (in backwardation) or higher-priced contracts (in contango); and (iii) the interest earned from the investment of any excess margin collateral used to secure the overall unleveraged futures position. So-called Commodity Trading Advisors (CTAs) employ highly leveraged, trend-focused, high-turnover trading strategies in commodity futures markets and in financial futures involving currencies, interest rates, and stock indices. Commodity-linked bonds tie the overall returns of such instruments to commodity price movements.

Commodity Research Bureau Total Return Index[1]

Time Period	No. Yrs.	Total Return CAGR	Std. Dev.	Correlation of Annual Returns with				
				U.S. Equity	Non-U.S. Equity	U.S. F.I.	High Yield	CPI Infl.
1982–1986	5	4.8%	11.0%	−0.28	0.16	0.46	NA	−0.67
1982–1991	10	4.0%	9.2%	−0.17	0.33	0.15	NA	−0.41
1982–2001	20	2.5%	10.5%	−0.01	0.24	0.10	NA	0.11
1990–1999	10	0.7%	9.7%	−0.06	0.06	−0.21	0.08	0.04
1990–2004	15	2.8%	11.3%	−0.12	0.14	−0.13	0.02	0.13
1997–2006	10	3.2%	14.0%	−0.26	0.00	−0.11	0.07	0.69
2000–2006	7	7.1%	13.2%	0.03	0.20	−0.06	−0.11	0.65

[1]Data for the Commodity Research Bureau Total Return Index are available beginning in 1982.

Rationale for Investment	Risks and Concerns
• Because they tend to respond to *long-term* forces of mean reversal and *short-term* forces of supply and demand, commodities may exhibit some degree of price volatility but tend to lower the overall volatility of a portfolio by functioning as a diversifying, countercyclical asset relative to most other asset classes. • In their original form and/or after some form of processing, commodities offer intrinsic utility to fulfill basic human needs. • Commodities have value independent of the monetary units in which they are denominated, and thus may serve as an effective hedge against inflation, often preceding upward moves in consumer price indices by 9 to 12 months. • Commodities returns generally: (i) have negative correlations with U.S. equity, bonds, cash, high-yield bonds, real estate, and emerging-markets debt and equity; and (ii) have modestly positive correlations with non-U.S. equity and bonds, hedge funds, private equity, and inflation-indexed bonds. • Due to the fact that different kinds of commodities tend to be subject to different kinds of economic influences, they may have low correlations with each other.	• To varying degrees, many commodities-based investment strategies may involve (i) leverage in the form of futures; and/or (ii) commission-, turnover-and fee-intensive investment vehicles, many of which tend to be tax-inefficient. • Commodities price trends may often reflect a magnified degree of exposure to upward or downward movements in the global economy. • Commodities borrowing and lending activity may exacerbate supply-demand imbalances and exaggerate price movements. • Although producer prices, consumer prices, and commodity futures prices tend to move upward together during periods of accelerating inflation, they do not necessarily move together during periods of disinflation. • Commodities are sometimes viewed as illiquid, volatile assets that exhibit intense and somewhat transient price movements in response to economic or other developments.

Commodity Research Bureau Total Return Index
Annual Returns

Source: The Author.

Information Sources: *Commodities Research Bureau Commodity Yearbook* (*crbtrader.com*); *All About Commodities: From Inside Out*, by Thomas A. McCafferty and Russell R. Wasendorf; *Futures 101: An Introduction to Commodity Trading*, by Richard E. Waldron; Commodities Research Bureau Total Return Index and Spot Index (*crbtrader.com*); Goldman Sachs Commodity Index, Energy Index, and Industrial Metals Index (*gs.com*); Dow Jones-AIG Commodity Index (*djindexes.com*); *Barron's* "Commodities Corner" column and Key Commodity Indexes table in the "Market Lab" Section (*barrons.com*); CPM Marketing Group (*cpm.com*); MSCI Non-Ferrous Metals and Energy Sources Subindexes (*mscibarra.com*); CME Group (*cmegroup.com*); New York Mercantile Exchange, Inc. (*nymex.com*); and *The Economist* Commodity-Price Index (*economist.com*).

F I G U R E 6.10

Asset Class Description for Convertible Securities

Characteristics

Description:

Convertible securities generally refer to coupon-bearing bonds (or dividend-bearing preferred stock) that can be converted at the investor's option into a specified number of shares of common stock of a specific U.S., non-U.S., or emerging-markets issuing company for a certain time period fixed by the issuer at the time of issuance. The *bond equivalent* value of a convertible bond (if it had been issued without a conversion feature) is known as its *investment value.* The *stock equivalent* value of a convertible bond (known as its *conversion value*) can be calculated by multiplying the common stock price times the number of shares into which the bond is convertible. The *conversion premium* expresses the percentage amount by which the market price of a convertible bond (or a convertible preferred stock) exceeds its conversion value, and the *breakeven* time represents the number of years necessary for the greater current income provided by the convertible security versus any dividend yield on its underlying common stock to equal the conversion premium.

Choices:

Investment grade and non-investment grade convertible securities may be issued in underwritten domestic or international public offerings, or as SEC Rule 144A offerings to certain qualified institutional buyers. Among other structures, they may be issued: (i) with coupons at par, with zero coupons, or as original-issue discount bonds; (ii) with features allowing the investor to put the securities back to the company under certain conditions; (iii) with terms allowing the issuer to call the bonds for repayment prior to maturity; (iv) with coupon, conversion rate, or maturity reset features; (v) with detachable warrants; (vi) with provisions for mandatory conversion or exchangeability into the shares of another company; and (vii) as one of a variety of equity-linked securities customized to specific legal structures and risk parameters.

Merrill Lynch All Convertible All Quality Bond Index[1]								
				Correlation of Annual Returns with				
Time Period	No. Yrs.	Total Return CAGR	Std. Dev.	U.S. Equity	U.S. F.I.	High Yield	Real Estate	Cash
1988–1992	5	13.7%	14.5%	0.67	0.46	0.91	0.98	−0.59
1988–1997	10	13.8%	12.5%	0.73	0.64	0.87	0.81	−0.24
1988–2002	15	10.3%	15.6%	0.77	0.09	0.66	0.25	0.06
1990–1999	10	15.9%	14.9%	0.63	0.26	0.63	0.44	−0.27
1990–2004	15	11.0%	16.1%	0.80	0.04	0.71	0.30	−0.08
1997–2006	10	8.5%	16.0%	0.80	−0.69	0.55	−0.02	−0.02
2000–2006	7	3.2%	13.4%	0.95	−0.73	0.95	0.76	−0.48
[1]Data for the Merrill Lynch All Convertible All Quality Bond Index are available beginning in 1988.								

Rationale for Investment	Risks and Concerns
• Due to their equity-like characteristics, convertible securities allow investors to participate in upward movements in the price of the underlying common stock, while at the same time, due to their coupon payments and other bond-like characteristics, convertibles usually provide some degree of capital protection should the underlying common stock move downward in price.	• A significant percentage of convertible securities have embedded call option features that allow the issuer to call the issue if the common stock price exceeds the conversion price; the valuation of such issuer calls, and possibly, investor put options, is not always straightforward and requires some degree of familiarity with stock-option volatility and other aspects of options-valuation methodology.
• Convertibles may offer a relatively higher degree of principal safety as a result of: (i) their explicit maturity date; and (ii) their priority claim on a corporation's assets relative to the residual claims of common stockholders.	• Frequently structured as subordinated securities, convertibles may rank ahead of common stockholders but behind such categories of senior creditors as bank lenders and senior debtholders.
• Convertible securities may provide a higher current yield than the dividend rate on the underlying common shares.	• Because of their conversion privilege, convertible bonds and convertible preferred shares usually trade at yields that are lower than otherwise equivalent non-convertible bonds and non-convertible preferred shares of the same issuer.
• In most financial environments, convertible securities generate compound annual returns that are competitive with the returns on equities, while exhibiting standard deviations of returns which tend to be 20 to 40% lower than the standard deviations of equity returns.	• Some portion of the upside potential of convertible securities may be dampened relative to the return on the underlying equity, depending on the amount of conversion premium in the convertible security.
• Convertible securities generally exhibit very high correlations of returns with equities, modest correlations of returns with bonds, and low or negative correlations with cash instruments.	• Because of periodic concentrations of issuing, hedging, leveraging, and investing activity by companies and investors, the convertible securities market may be prone to rapid expansion and contraction and supply-demand imbalances of varying duration and intensity.

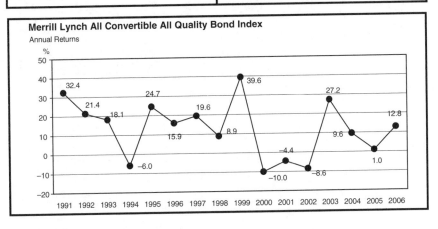

Merrill Lynch All Convertible All Quality Bond Index
Annual Returns

Source: The Author.

Information Sources: *Convertible Securities*, by John P. Calamos; Credit Suisse Convertible Bond Index (*credit-suisse.com*); Credit Suisse Convertible Preferred Index (*credit-suisse.com*); UBS Convertible Bond Index Family (*ubs.com*); Merrill Lynch All Convertible All Quality Index (*ml.com*); Merrill Lynch Global ex-U.S. Convertibles Index (*ml.com*); Convertbond (*convertbond.com*); Fidelity Convertible Mutual Fund (*fidelity.com*); Putnam Convertible Mutual Fund (*putnamfunds.com*); and Calamos Convertible Mutual Fund (*calamos.com*).

F I G U R E 6.11

Asset Class Description for U.S. Equity

Characteristics
Description:
U.S. equity, through ownership of shares in publicly traded enterprises, offers the opportunity to participate in the commercial and financial fortunes of American businesses, their profits and dividends, potential growth in their tangible book value, and the possible buildup of any relevant intangible property. In theoretical terms, a share of equity is generally considered to be worth the sum of future cash flows in the form of any dividend payments and an eventual terminal value, discounted back at some appropriate rate of interest to a net present value. U.S. equity prices and returns are influenced by a combination of forces, including: (i) fundamentals in the form of company developments; (ii) valuations, in the form of the multiple of cash flows, earnings, sales, and book value which investors are willing to assign to the company; and (iii) psychology, in the form of investors' views of the macro- and micro-economic factors likely to affect share prices. Stated another way, equity returns are a function of: (i) dividends, earnings, and the price-earnings multiples that investors are willing to pay for earnings; and (ii) the psychologically and valuation-driven equity risk premium versus certain low-risk bonds.
Choices:
U.S. equity is available in a wide variety of choices and formats, including: (i) by company size (large-capitalization, mid-capitalization, small-capitalization, and micro-capitalization); (ii) by industry group or Global Industry Classification Standard (such as healthcare or finance); (iii) by style classification (such as value, growth, balanced, socially responsible, income-oriented, or core); (iv) by investment vehicle (such as index funds, exchange-traded funds, sector funds, closed- and open-end mutual funds, investment partnerships, or separate account management); (v) by related type (such as preferred stocks, master limited partnerships, or structured notes); and (vi) by derivative instruments (such as warrants and options on companies and indices, futures on indices, and single stock futures (SSFs)).

Standard and Poor's 500 Index

				Correlation of Annual Returns with				
Time Period	No. Yrs.	Total Return CAGR	Std. Dev.	Non-U.S. Equity	U.S. F.I.	High Yield	Hedge Funds	Cash
1970–1979	10	5.9%	19.2%	0.67	NA	NA	NA	−0.26
1970–1989	20	11.6%	16.8%	0.58	NA	NA	NA	−0.03
1970–1999	30	13.7%	16.0%	0.48	NA	NA	NA	−0.10
1980–1989	10	17.6%	12.7%	0.36	0.29	NA	NA	−0.25
1980–1999	20	17.9%	13.1%	0.33	0.36	NA	NA	−0.11
1990–1999	10	18.2%	14.1%	0.40	0.52	0.50	0.13	0.08
1997–2006	10	8.4%	19.1%	0.78	−0.39	0.54	0.63	0.14
2000–2006	7	1.1%	17.7%	0.96	−0.79	0.81	0.98	−0.29

Standard and Poor's 500 Index
Annual Returns

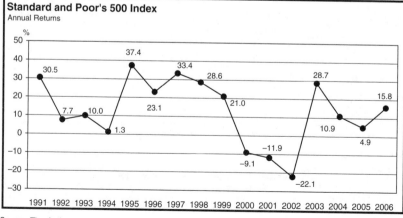

Source: The Author

Rationale for Investment	Risks and Concerns
• As residual ownership claims to the real assets of companies after obligations to debt holders have been satisfied, U.S. equity provides exposure to: (i) human potential, endeavor, and achievement within the American and global economic system; (ii) the opportunity to invest in profit-making activity and effectively compound these results through reinvesting a portion of the returns therefrom in profitable projects and ventures; and (iii) some degree of long-term purchasing power protection during eras of generally rising prices for goods and services.	• Driven in part by the price swings experienced in alternating phases of bull market euphoria and bear market demoralization, the share price volatility for individual companies and the standard deviation of returns for the U.S. equity market as a whole tend to be considerably higher than the standard deviation of returns for U.S. high-grade bonds, cash instruments, and several other asset classes.
• Partially as compensation for taking on exposure to higher-risk assets during certain meaningfully long periods in the 20th century, U.S. equity shareholders have tended to earn real returns in such time frames substantially above the returns on lower-risk assets such as cash and high-grade U.S. debt securities. This so-called historical excess return of stocks versus bonds can vary widely from the expected equity risk premium between expected stock returns and actual stock returns.	• U.S. equity returns tend to be low or negative in deflationary environments. In bankruptcy or liquidation proceedings, equity shareholders may be wiped out or suffer considerable dilution in their ownership stake since stocks represent a secondary claim on the resources of a company after the payment of debt obligations. Due to easy data bias, survivorship bias, and/or success bias in index construction, certain U.S. equity benchmarks may markedly overstate the long-term returns from stock ownership.
• With a number of important exceptions in certain financial environments and market subsectors, the U.S. equity realm may be characterized as a large, diverse, relatively liquid marketplace with divisible assets, reasonable information flow, and established regulatory mechanisms.	• In contrast to conventional wisdom, U.S. equity returns can be low for long periods of time. From 1900–1950, U.S. equity returns were lower, and the standard deviation of returns higher, than in the 1950–2000 time frame, and there have been several 20-year periods in the 20th century when stocks have underperformed bonds. Corporate earnings growth tends not to persist across decades; the rate of GDP growth per capita in a given decade is not necessarily associated with that decade's stock price movement; and a subsequent decade's equity returns tend to be negatively correlated with the prior decade's returns. Just as multiyear P/E expansion and/or increasing corporate returns on equity can boost U.S. equity returns, contracting P/E ratios and/or declining corporate returns on equity can depress U.S. equity returns.
• At different stages and for varying lengths of time, the U.S. equity market offers the opportunity to add value alternatively through: (i) active portfolio management versus passive index-based investing (driven by dispersion of industry and company returns); (ii) large companies versus small companies (driven by perceived growth opportunities, access to capital, barriers to entry, pricing power, and exposure to global and national forces); and (iii) value versus growth stock selection (driven by current and historical price/book, price/earnings, price/sales, and dividend yield relationships).	
• U.S. equity investments offer a means of participating in economic advancement and technological innovation, tending to generate advantageous returns in periods of: (i) rising per-share earnings resulting from GDP, labor force, and GDP-per-capita growth, productivity gains, and profitability enhancements; (ii) some degree of pricing power and/or an absence of extreme movements in the general price index; (iii) expanding price-earnings ratios associated with favorable interest rate movements and investment flows; and (iv) increasing dividends resulting from higher profits and appropriate payout ratios.	• As the investment time horizon is lengthened, U.S. equity dividends, and particularly dividend reinvestment, play a crucially important role in the generation of returns from equity ownership. Between 1900 and 2000, a $1.00 initial investment in U.S. equity would have grown to $198 without dividend reinvestment (a 5.4% compound return), and to $16,797 with dividend reinvestment (a 10.1% compound return).
	• U.S. equity correlations of returns with other asset classes may be relatively unstable over time: (i) versus non-U.S. equity, tending to increase during global equity bubble phases and during financial market turbulence; and ii) versus U.S. high-grade bonds, migrating from modestly negative in the 1930s to modestly positive (early 1950s), to modestly negative (early 1960s), to moderately positive (1980s and 1990s), before declining again (in the late 1990s and early 2000s).

Information Sources: *Irrational Exuberance*, by Robert J. Shiller; *Stocks for the Long Run*, by Jeremy J. Siegel; *The Intelligent Investor*, by Benjamin Graham; *Triumph of the Optimists*, by Elroy Dimson, Paul Marsh, and Mike Staunton; "The Trader" column in the Market Week Section of *Barron's* (*barrons.com*); *Financial Analysts Journal* (*cfainstitute.org*); Center for Financial Research and Analysis (*cfraonline.com*); Morningstar, Inc. (*morningstar.com*); The No Load Fund Investor (*sheldonjacobs.com*); CFA Institute (*cfainstitute.org*); One Chicago (*onechicago.com*); Vanguard 500 Index Fund (*vanguard.com*); Fidelity Magellan Fund (*fidelity.com*); Gateway Fund (*gatewayfund.com*); ShareBuilder (*sharebuilder.com*); Dow Jones Industrial, Transportation, and Utility Indices (*dowjones.com*); Standard & Poor's 500, 400, and 600 Indices (*standardandpoors.com*); Morgan Stanley Capital International U.S. Equity Index (*mscibarra.com*); Russell 1000, 2000, and 300 indices (*russell.com*); Wilshire 5000 Index (*wilshire.com*); and "Mutual Funds Monthly Review" section of the *Wall Street Journal* (*wsj.com*).

F I G U R E 6.12

Asset Class Description for Non-U.S. Equity

Characteristics
Description: For centuries, significant wealth has been created, and destroyed, as a result of making direct or portfolio investments outside of domestic borders. Non-U.S. equity refers to portfolio investment in non-U.S. developed countries, including Canada, the United Kingdom, the European Union, Switzerland, Scandinavia, Japan, New Zealand, and Australia. Representing approximately one-half of the world's total stock market capitalization, non-U.S. equity encompasses a wide range of historical experiences with share ownership, equity market sizes, industry and company diversity, international competitiveness, economic and political structures, monetary, currency and fiscal policies, price inflation and deflation, episodes of international conflict and cooperation, and varying degrees of country- and company-specific sensitivity to global output, trade, and investment cycles.
Choices: In a diverse manner across specific countries and regions, non-U.S. equity offers exposure to large-, mid-, and small-capitalization companies in the information technology, financial, telecommunications, healthcare, consumer, energy, utilities, materials, and industrial sectors. Specific non-U.S. equity markets may be accessed through investments in specific companies, index funds, open- and closed-end mutual funds, exchange-traded funds (ETFs), options and index futures, swaps, index participation funds, structured notes, convertible bonds, certain hedge funds, and other instruments.

MSCI EAFE Index

				Correlation of Annual Returns with				
Time Period	No. Yrs.	Total Return CAGR	Std. Dev.	U.S. Equity	U.S. F.I.	Non-U.S. F.I.	EM Equity	Cash
1970–1979	10	8.8%	22.5%	0.67	NA	NA	NA	−0.18
1970–1989	20	15.2%	23.3%	0.58	NA	NA	NA	−0.24
1970–1999	30	12.4%	21.6%	0.48	NA	NA	NA	−0.14
1980–1989	10	22.0%	23.4%	0.36	0.00	NA	NA	−0.68
1980–1999	20	14.3%	21.4%	0.33	0.09	NA	NA	−0.16
1990–1999	10	7.0%	16.9%	0.40	−0.07	0.06	0.56	−0.54
1997–2006	10	7.7%	20.8%	0.78	−0.74	0.37	0.71	−0.24
2000–2006	7	4.4%	23.7%	0.96	−0.84	0.46	0.91	−0.42

MSCI EAFE Index

Annual Returns

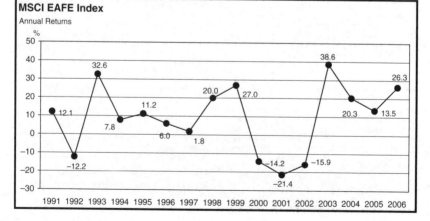

Source: The Author.

Rationale for Investment	Risks and Concerns
• Non-U.S. equity provides exposure to different natural and geographical circumstances, historical and cultural influences, and cycles than those encountered in U.S. equity markets, among them: (i) demographic, social, educational, and net immigration trends; (ii) output per inhabitant and the share of services, industry, and exports in GDP; (iii) household savings rates, equity ownership, and gross fixed capital formation; (iv) labor practices, the relative share of employment in the total population, employment growth, and worker productivity; (v) energy self-sufficiency, financial system strength, pension structures, commercial and entrepreneurial instincts, and receptivity to innovation; and (vi) central government indebtedness, the current account balance of payments, and foreign exchange reserves. • In part, *cross-nation* diversification within an industry generally reduces risk more effectively than *cross-industry* diversification within a country. Therefore, foreign equity ownership has tended over time to lower overall portfolio volatility while generating returns that as a group are highly competitive with U.S. equities; correlations of returns tend to be considerably lower for foreign equity than for U.S. equity with U.S. bonds, high-yield bonds, and private equity. • As markets and economies converge and expand, non-U.S. equity offers a considerably expanded investment opportunity set, particularly within the banking, insurance, pharmaceutical, energy, utilities, electronics, and consumer discretionary industries, as well as in the mid- and small-cap sectors. • Because they are often subject to differing earnings dynamics, interest rates, fiscal policies, deregulation trends, restructuring activity, privatization mores, locally influenced valuation benchmarks and accounting practices, and their own reactions to local and global psychological influences, certain non-U.S. equity markets may exhibit intervals of attractiveness or unattractiveness that are out of cycle with or opposite to those in the U.S. • With an abundance of underresearched companies, varying degrees of investor familiarity, the adoption of International Accounting Standards, and evolving information practices, foreign equity may present numerous opportunities to discover and exploit inefficiencies and increase alpha (excess return).	• In response to unsynchronized patterns of revenue and earnings growth, differing levels of return on equity, and other factors, non-U.S. equity markets individually tend to have standard deviations of returns that are considerably higher, and collectively tend to have standard deviations that are somewhat higher, than the standard deviations of U.S. equity returns. • Evidence has been adduced that non-U.S. equity returns tend to have modest-to-low correlations with U.S. equity returns, particularly in the value sectors and during relatively stable market conditions. However, in times of worldwide equity market volatility, non-U.S. equity versus U.S. equity returns correlations tend to rise, sometimes significantly, thereby vitiating their intended diversification benefits. It has been postulated that non-U.S. equity to U.S. equity correlations are trending upward over time due to the effects of cross-listing of shares, globalization, the Internet, cross-border M&A and technology flows, and greater consistency of economic, monetary, fiscal, currency, trade, accounting, and management policies. • Even with increasing harmonization of trading, settlement, issuance, regulation, and disclosure standards in most developed countries, investment in non-U.S. equity markets may incur high tax, transaction, custody, and reporting costs, travel and information-gathering expenses, and unanticipated barriers to capital flows in times of emergency or crisis. • Attention needs to be paid to the positive and negative currency effects of non-U.S. equity investing and the costs and benefits of investing abroad on a hedged basis or an unhedged basis (in the latter case *profiting from upward* movements in the value of the foreign currency, or *suffering losses* from *downward* movements in the value of the foreign currency). Among other factors, currency exchange rates are influenced by: economic growth, labor market flexibility, and productivity differentials; interest rate, inflation, and purchasing power differentials; portfolio and direct investment flows; central bank monetary and currency management skills; policies of competing nations and/or currency blocs; balance of trade, net transfers, and net investment income effects; and regime stability. • Inspired by inertia and perhaps a historical awareness of the difficulty of enforcing overseas claims in periods of armed conflict, social upheaval, or capital controls, the persistence of home country bias in many time periods and sectors of the investment realm may lead to a heightened degree of self-blame or recrimination by others during and following periods of non-U.S. equity underperformance.

Information Sources: *Triumph of the Optimists: 101 Years of Global Investment Returns*, by Elroy Dimson, Paul Marsh, and Mike Staunton; MSCI Europe, Australasia, and Far East (EAFE) Index (*mscibarra.com*); Fidelity Diversified International Fund (*fidelity.com*); Morgan Stanley International Equity Fund (*morganstanley.com*); Merrill Lynch Global Allocation Fund (*ml.com*), Goldman Sachs International Equity Fund (*gs.com*); ING International Value Fund (*ingfunds.com*); Putnam International Voyager Fund A (*putnaminv.com*); InterSec Research (*intersecresearch.com*); Strategic Insight (*sionline.com*); Vanguard Total International Portfolio (*vanguard.com*); Thomson Financial (*thomson.com*); Reuters (*reuters.com*); Corporate Information (*corporateinformation.com*); Global Investor (*globalinvestor.com*); J.P. Morgan Chase (jpmorgan.com); and the "European Trader" and "Asian Trader" columns in the Market Week section of *Barron's* (*barrons.com*).

F I G U R E 6.13

Asset Class Description for Emerging-Markets Equity

Characteristics

Description:

Representing over 60% of the world's peoples in predominantly youthfully populated countries, some of which are endowed with important natural resources and many of which have evolving social, political, and economic infrastructures and low levels of per-capita income, consumption, and Gross Domestic Product, emerging-markets equity offers exposure to a heterogeneous array of cultures, history, and future potential in industries and companies in Asia, Latin America, Africa and the Middle East, and Eastern Europe. Assuming that growth rates in population and output reasonably track the projections of the United Nations and other global and regional development organizations, emerging-market countries are expected to account for a meaningfully rising share of aggregate headcount and output on planet earth in coming decades.

Choices:

Emerging-equity markets can be grouped in a number of ways and span the gamut from: (i) countries which have living standards that are rapidly converging with or virtually indistinguishable from those of developed nations, to countries which face seemingly intractable health, climate, education, ecological, governance, or other challenges; (ii) high-population countries such as China, India, Brazil, Pakistan, and Nigeria, to low-population lands such as Peru, Chile, and the Czech Republic; and (iii) energy-producing countries such as Mexico, Russia, Indonesia, Venezuela, and Malaysia, to countries completely bereft of indigenous energy sources such as Korea. In view of the developing state of the credit and capital systems in many emerging-market countries, equity demarcations sometimes overlap within these investment destinations to also encompass emerging-markets straight and convertible debt, real estate, direct investment, private equity, and venture capital.

MSCI Emerging Markets Free Gross Index[1]

				Correlation of Annual Returns with				
Time Period	No. Yrs.	Total Return CAGR	Std. Dev.	U.S. Equity	U.S. F.I.	Non-U.S. Equity	EM Debt	High Yield
1988–1992	5	29.8%	32.3%	0.99	0.75	0.81	NA	0.48
1988–1997	10	18.2%	34.3%	0.17	0.36	0.65	NA	0.42
1988–2002	15	10.0%	36.0%	0.34	0.03	0.62	NA	0.46
1990–1999	10	11.0%	36.8%	−0.02	0.00	0.56	NA	0.52
1990–2004	15	8.9%	34.7%	0.31	−0.16	0.68	NA	0.64
1997–2006	10	9.4%	33.8%	0.33	−0.93	0.71	0.65	0.52
2000–2006	7	12.2%	29.8%	0.87	−0.92	0.91	0.42	0.82

[1]Data for the MSCI Emerging Markets Free Gross Index are available beginning in 1988.

MSCI Emerging Markets Free Gross Index

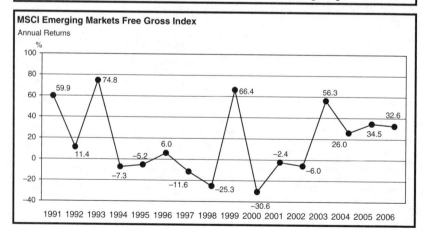

Source: The Author.

Rationale for Investment	Risks and Concerns
• Owing to some combination of historically high savings and investment levels, natural resources, low-cost production capabilities, increasingly skilled and/or educated local work forces, expanding middle classes and internal consumption activity, improving regulatory frameworks, and downward-trending inflation levels and interest rates, equities in certain emerging-market countries may provide exposure to economic growth that may be somewhat independent of developed countries' economic cycles. Given a low base, this economic growth may translate into earnings growth of significant magnitude.	• Emerging-markets economies and their public companies may be recurringly exposed in a magnified way to: (i) trends in global economic and lending activity, protectionism, inventory swings, and information technology cycles; (ii) the commercial health and currency policies of large competing nations; and (iii) boom-and-bust patterns in balances of payments, local liquidity, bank credit, industrial capacity, property investment, and prices received for and levels of commodity or raw materials exports; and (iv) declining living standards or falling trends in output per unit of input.
• As a relatively under-researched and inefficient asset class, emerging-markets equity may offer significant opportunity to add alpha (excess return versus a risk-free rate) through bottom-up company analysis and security selection, sector choice, and country and regional allocation.	• A number of emerging-markets countries may face precarious geopolitical realities and a constrained set of local investment opportunities, or have underdeveloped, unenlightened, or dysfunctional social, fiscal, anti-corruption, capital investment and repatriation, monetary, industrial, judicial, legislative, administrative, law enforcement, environmental, or independent media policies, outmoded communications, transport, and other services infrastructures, unfair or unsafe labor practices, poor means of conflict resolution, and uneven enforcement of accounting, investor protection, and corporate-governance standards.
• In part due to the expected returns premiums associated with their riskier and more volatile returns patterns relative to more mature equity markets, over appropriate time frames and with wide dispersions of returns across different countries, emerging-markets equity may be able to generate annual real returns which meaningfully outstrip the returns on U.S. and non-U.S. equity.	
• Emerging-markets equity has generally had medium correlations of returns with U.S. and non-U.S. equity, emerging-markets debt, hedge funds, and high-yield bonds, low correlations of returns with private equity, and negative correlations of returns with commodities, real estate, U.S. and non-U.S. bonds, and cash.	• Emerging-equity markets may be characterized by high trading, settlement, and custodial costs, relatively illiquid markets and unconventional capital markets practices, ad hoc changes in allowable foreign percentage ownership, short selling, and other restrictions, and persistent or occasional instances of currency instability.
• In essence, emerging-markets equity is a means of gaining direct exposure to the widening aspirations of hundreds of millions of people, including: (i) greater engagement with the developed world through freer cross-border flows of goods, services, people, ideas, technology, and capital; (ii) increased local consumption, intraregional cooperation, and currency convertibility; (iii) reform, restructuring, and/or adaptation of economic, political, financial, and pension systems; and (iv) more rational investment and allocation of financial and human capital to improve growth rates, profitability, and the sharing of profit with non-local equity investors.	• As a result of alternating phases of massive enthusiasm in which prices are bid up to unrealistic levels, followed by massive disenchantment in which prices are driven to extremely cheap valuations, emerging-market equities as an asset class and on a country- and company-specific basis tend to exhibit high standard deviations of returns that may be two to four times more volatile than equities in developed markets.
	• Consisting of foreign direct investment and merger and acquisition activity, loans from banks and official institutions, and debt and equity portfolio investments by mutual funds, hedge funds, pension funds, and individual investors, net short- and long-term flows of capital into and out of emerging-market countries can contribute to or result from financial crises such as those experienced in Mexico (1994), Southeast Asia (1997), Russia (1998), Brazil (1999), and Argentina (2001).

Information Sources: *Financial Times* Country Surveys (*ft.com*), Worldly Investor (*worldlyinvestor.com*), JPMorgan Chase (jpmorgan.com), Fund Research (*emergingportfolio.com*), Economic and Financial Indicators Section of *The Economist* (*theeconomist.com*), ISI Emerging Markets (*securities.com*), "Asian Trader" column in the Market Week section of *Barron's* (*barrons.com*), Stocksmart (*stocksmart.com*), *This China is Different*, by Stephen S. Roach, Standard & Poor's/IFCI Index (*standardandpoors.com*), MSCI Indices for Emerging Markets in Asia; Latin America; and Europe, Middle East, and Africa (*mscibarra.com*), Dreyfus Emerging Markets Fund (*dreyfus.com*), Morgan Stanley Emerging Markets Fund (*morganstanley.com*); Goldman Sachs Emerging Markets Equity (*gs.com*); Oppenheimer Developing Markets Fund A (*oppenheimerfunds.com*), T. Rowe Price International Emerging Markets Stock Fund A (*troweprice.com*); and *Mobius on Emerging Markets*, by J. Mark Mobius.

F I G U R E 6.14

Asset Class Description for U.S. Fixed-Income

Characteristics
Description: As an important asset class with more than $14 trillion in par value amount outstanding at the start of the new millennium, U.S. fixed-income securities represent promises to make money-denominated payments from issuers to investors, typically in the form of a series of coupons and a principal repayment sum due at final maturity. U.S. Treasury notes and bonds are a key segment of the U.S. fixed-income markets and generally establish benchmark interest rates off of which most other debt securities are priced. The total return on U.S. fixed-income securities tends to be a function of: (i) coupon payments; (ii) the reinvestment of coupon flows; (iii) any capital gains or losses realized over the investor's holding period; (iv) the effects of net defaults, if applicable; plus or minus (v) the impact of any hedging activity. Among the chief influences on U.S. fixed-income securities returns are fiscal, monetary, and currency policies, the outlook for economic activity, inflation or deflation in the general price level, asset shifts, issuance volume, portfolio flows, and the shape of the yield curve. **Choices:** The U.S. fixed-income universe is characterized by a wide variety of: (i) maturities, ranging from just over 1 year to 10-, 20-, 30-year, and perpetual-maturity issues; (ii) coupon configurations, including fixed, floating, stripped, and zero coupons; (iii) degrees of seniority, subordination, and credit quality; (iv) special features, such as put or call provisions, sinking funds, maintenance and replacement funds, collateral or escrow backing guarantees, and insurance; (v) packaging formats, such as closed-end and open-end mutual funds, unit trusts, guaranteed investment contracts, pass-through issues, mortgage- and asset-backed securities, structured notes, collateralized obligations, exchange-traded funds, and bond custody receipts; (vi) derivative instruments, including listed and unlisted options, futures, other derivatives, and swaps; (vii) issuer types, including U.S. Treasury, agency, municipal (as general obligation bonds or revenue bonds) and corporate (in sectors such as utility, transportation, industrial, and banks/finance companies); and (viii) investment approaches, including buy-and-hold, swapping, barbell, laddering, using leverage, and duration- and convexity-based strategies.

Lehman Brothers U.S. Aggregate Bond Index[1]

				Correlation of Annual Returns with				
Time Period	No. Yrs.	Total Return CAGR	Std. Dev.	U.S. Equity	Non-U.S. F.I.	High Yield	CPI Infl.	Cash
1976–1980	5	4.8%	6.0%	0.32	NA	NA	−0.69	−0.74
1976–1990	15	10.3%	8.8%	0.40	NA	NA	−0.61	−0.01
1976–2000	25	9.3%	8.0%	0.37	NA	NA	−0.34	0.14
1980–1989	10	12.4%	9.3%	0.29	NA	NA	−0.50	0.01
1980–1999	20	10.1%	8.3%	0.36	NA	NA	−0.19	0.27
1990–1999	10	7.7%	6.6%	0.52	0.66	0.60	0.02	0.32
1997–2006	10	6.2%	4.0%	−0.39	0.14	−0.29	−0.22	0.27
2000–2006	7	6.5%	3.6%	−0.79	−0.07	−0.58	0.03	0.42

[1]Data for the Lehman Brothers U.S. Aggregate Bond Index are available beginning in 1976.

Lehman Brother U.S. Aggregate Bond Index
Annual

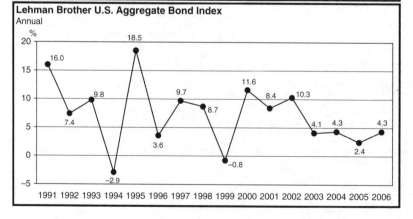

Source: The Author.

Rationale for Investment	Risks and Concerns
• Because they usually offer stable nominal flows of income and relatively predictable payoffs, U.S. fixed-income securities may be useful in matching and/or immunizing known projected liabilities, and tend to exhibit standard deviations of returns that are approximately one-half the standard deviations of returns on U.S. and foreign equity, high-yield bonds, commodities, real estate, and hedge funds, and approximately one-third the standard deviations of returns on private equity and emerging-markets debt and equity.	• For long periods of time on two occasions during the 20th century (once for approximately 20 years and once for approximately 35 years), U.S. fixed-income securities have generated relatively low nominal and real returns. Even though the correlations of returns on various types of high-grade U.S. bonds have generally been high on an intersector basis due to their somewhat homogeneous nature, correlations between the returns on U.S. fixed-income securities and U.S. equities have tended to be somewhat unstable, ranging from –0.02 from 1926 through 1969, to +0.23 from 1970 through 1980, to +0.58 from 1981 through 1998.
• As a result of the so-called bond *maturity premium* which results from investing in long-term bonds rather than short-term instruments of less than one year's maturity, over sufficiently long periods of time U.S. fixed-income securities tend to generate higher *nominal* returns than cash assets (5.1% versus 4.1% from 1900 through 2000) and higher *real* returns than cash assets (2.1% versus 1.0% from 1900 through 2000).	• Many U.S. fixed-income securities are subject to special risks specific to bonds, including: (i) *market risk* (a decline in capital values due to rising interest rates, with longer-maturity and/or lower coupon issues affected most heavily); (ii) *credit risk* (due to the possibility of a rating downgrade, corporate action, or default); (iii) *reinvestment risk* (the possibility that interest or principal payments may have to be reinvested at lower-than-expected yields); or (iv) *prepayment risk* (which happens when bonds are called early or mortgage-related issues are prepaid early).
• Due to their tendency to exhibit negative correlations of returns during episodes of unanticipated stock-market decline, extended eras of poor economic performance, unsatisfactory or privative corporate profitability, and persistently low or negative equity market results, U.S. fixed-income securities may act as an efficacious diversifier and dampen portfolio instability. U.S. domestic bonds generally have low or negative correlations of returns with the returns on non-U.S. equity, emerging-markets equity, private equity, commodities and real estate, and modestly positive correlations with the returns on non-U.S. bonds and certain hedge fund strategies.	• Because bonds' yields and prices are driven by: (i) changes in the real rate of interest; and (ii) changes in inflation expectations, both of which are manifested in the level and degree of positive, flat, or negative slope to the yield curve, bonds can exhibit substantial year-to-year volatility in returns.
• As essentially preferential, senior-to-equity claims on assets and revenues within an issuer's financial structure, U.S. fixed-income securities may function as: (i) a disaster reserve; (ii) a capital-protection tool; and/or (iii) an income generator to sustain or withstand intervals of meaningful price weakness in other asset classes.	• Because their payments are denominated in nominal rather than real monetary units, U.S. fixed-income securities are subject to inflation risk. During highly inflationary periods, bonds may lose a significant portion of their purchasing power. In *nominal* and *real* terms, respectively, U.S. bonds generated annual returns of 2.6% and –2.1% from 1900 through 1919, 5.5% and 6.9% from 1920 through 1940, 2.0% and –2.5% from 1945 through 1981, and 12.6% and 8.9% from 1982 through 2000.
• Many sectors of the U.S. fixed-income market are relatively homogeneous, large in size, well-researched, and efficiently priced, allowing returns to be determined by investors' decisions about the degree to which they wish their bond holdings to be exposed to: (i) changes in basic core rates; and (ii) changes in spreads versus basic core rates.	• Although their relative efficiency increases the difficulty of earning alpha (excess return) in many sectors of the U.S. fixed-income universe, a number of other fixed-income sectors are characterized by a low degree of pricing accuracy and transparency, wide bid-ask spreads, and periodic impairments in trading liquidity.

Information Sources: *The Handbook of Fixed Income Securities,* Seventh Edition, ed. by Frank J. Fabozzi; *Triumph of the Optimists: 101 Years of Global Investment Returns,* by Elroy Dimson, Paul Marsh, and Mike Staunton; *Bond Markets: Analysis and Strategies,* ed. by Frank J. Fabozzi; *Grant's Interest Rate Observer* (*grantspub.com*); Gimme Credit (*gimmecredit.com*); *The Bank Credit Analyst* (*bankcreditanalyst.com*); Bloomberg, LLC (*bloomberg.com*); Securities Industry and Financial Markets Association (*sifma.org*); Online bond trading firms (*shop4bonds.com, tradebonds.com*); Municipal Securities Rulemaking Board (*msrb.org*); Morningstar, Inc. (*morningstar.com*); Interactive Data Fixed Income Analytics (*interactivedata-fia.com*); ICAP (*icap.com*); DPC Data (*dpcdata.com*); Citigroup Yield Book Software (*yieldbook.com*); Bond Resources (*bondresources.com*); PIMCO (*pimco.com*); Barclays Global Investors Exchange-Traded Bond Funds (*barclays.com*); Vanguard Short-Term Corporate Fund (*vanguard.com*); Vanguard Long-Term Tax-Exempt Fund (*vanguard.com*); Morgan Stanley U.S. Government Securities Trust (*morganstanleyindividual.com*); Market Axess (*marketaxess.com*); MFS Multimarket Income Trust (*mfs.com*); "Current Yield" Column in Barron's (*barrons.com*); and U.S. Treasury (*treasurydirect.gov*).

F I G U R E   6.15

Asset Class Description for High-Yield Fixed-Income

Characteristics

Description:
High-yield bonds involve varying degrees of investment risk or elements of speculation, and as such, are ranked below investment grade as defined by the principal securities rating agencies (below BBB-minus by Standard & Poor's, or below Baa3 by Moody's). Beginning in the late 1970s and early 1980s, high-yield bonds: (i) have been used for acquisition and leveraged buyout financing, growth capital, or to refinance existing debt; (ii) generally have original maturities of 7–12 years; and in many cases, (iii) are callable 3 to 5 years after issuance. Consisting variously of strengthening, stable, and weakening credits, the high-yield bond market is highly heterogeneous by industry sector and by issuer, and may be tiered into higher-end credits (bonds rated BB or Ba), more speculative issues (bonds rated B or B), and securities in varying degrees of distress (bonds rated CCC through D, or Caa through C).

Choices:
In addition to their commonly encountered cash-pay, fixed-rate format, high-yield bonds have been structured with a variety of innovative features, some of which have gained wide acceptance and some of which have had only a limited number of examples. High-yield bonds have been issued: (i) with split coupons; step-up coupons, or zero coupons; (ii) with increasing rate, deferred-pay, or payment-in-kind coupons; (iii) with accompanying warrants or stock units; or (iv) with coupon reset features and extendible or retractable maturity dates. Default swaps, a type of credit derivative, are insurance contracts between two counterparties protecting against credit risk. Numerous mutual funds have been formed to invest in high-yield securities, several of which focus on investing in senior, secured-floating rate bank loans extended to non-investment grade borrowers.

High Yield (Credit Suisse Upper/Middle Tier) Index[1]

				Correlation of Annual Returns with				
Time Period	No. Yrs.	Total Return CAGR	Std. Dev.	U.S. Equity	U.S. F.I.	Hedge Funds	Real Estate	Cash
1987–1991	5	10.3%	19.4%	0.58	0.46	NA	0.92	−0.71
1987–1996	10	11.5%	14.1%	0.52	0.48	NA	0.79	−0.35
1987–2001	15	8.7%	12.6%	0.46	0.40	NA	0.62	−0.25
1990–1999	10	11.1%	14.2%	0.48	0.60	0.66	0.81	−0.18
1990–2004	15	10.1%	13.3%	0.57	0.35	0.68	0.67	−0.25
1997–2006	10	7.1%	9.2%	0.51	−0.30	0.41	0.59	−0.55
2000–2006	7	7.8%	10.5%	0.80	−0.59	0.80	0.61	−0.61

[1]Data for the High Yield (Credit Suisse Upper/MiddleTier) Index are available beginning in 1987.

High Yield (Credit Suisse Upper/Middle Tier) Index
Annual Returns

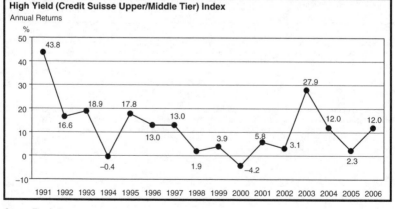

Source: The Author

Rationale for Investment	Risks and Concerns
• Owing in part to their high positive yield spreads versus U.S. Treasury bonds and other investment-grade credits, during appropriate phases of economic and financial market cycles, high-yield bonds may generate returns that are higher than conventional bonds and competitive with equities. • Although their volatility can be quite high during generalized or high-yield-specific episodes of financial market turbulence, during longer time intervals, diversified portfolios of middle- and upper-tier high-yield bonds tend to have standard deviations of returns that are meaningfully lower than those for equities. • As a somewhat less efficient, less broadly analyzed asset class, high-yield bonds offer opportunities to capture excess return (alpha) through bottom-up analysis focusing on creditworthiness-affecting factors such as capital structure and leverage, cash flow and liquidity, indenture covenants and asset quality, competition and corporate earning power, credit availability and rollover risk, and management ability and growth prospects. • Whether secured or unsecured, senior or subordinated, in the event of default, high-yield bonds may have higher recovery rates and priority ranking over other capital categories such as common equity and preferred stock, effectively offering advantaged positioning as the company's capital structure undergoes reorganization. • Sometimes coinciding with or immediately succeeding years of cyclically high-bond default rates, high-yield bonds may deliver high absolute returns during periods of aggressive monetary easing and steepening positive yield-curve slopes.	• Particularly for certain industries and companies at varying stages of the economic and credit market cycle, high-yield bonds may face significant impairment in value as a result of credit deterioration, commercial pressure from better-financed competitors, event risk (generally involving additional senior indebtedness to effect an acquisition), or default (5.9% of high-yield bonds outstanding defaulted in 2000, and 10.3% in 2001). • Due to a relatively concentrated and opportunistically minded population of issuers and investors, and the emergence of credit derivatives which allow traders to short corporate debt, high-yield bonds may experience feast-or-famine new-issue volume and significant intrayear or year-to-year swings in prices and yields, followed by extensive periods of relative quiet. • Consisting primarily of: (i) current yield-driven and portfolio image-conscious high-yield-bond mutual funds subject to erratic cash flows; (ii) nondedicated professional investors seeking to exploit perceived transient investment opportunities or forced by their charters to sell securities when ratings are reduced to below investment grade; and (iii) some number of individual investors, the high-yield bond investor base tends to create momentum-driven markets that may experience sympathy selling or dislocations for non-economic reasons. • Especially during unfavorable financial-market conditions and/or times of contraction for the commercial and investment banking industry, the high-yield bond market may suffer a meaningful decline in trading liquidity, wide bid-asked spreads, and a fair degree of difficulty to liquidate or establish positions at reasonable prices. • A number of high-yield bond structures relating to callability, clawback terms, and other indenture provisions may be arcane, difficult to model under various economic scenarios, and ignored or poorly understood by issuers, investors, and intermediaries, leading to unforeseen and possibly unfavorable consequences.

Information Sources: *High Yield Bonds: Market Structure, Valuation, and Portfolio Strategies,* ed. by Theodore M. Barnhill; T. Rowe Price High Yield Bond Fund (*troweprice.com*); Vanguard High Yield Corporate Bond Fund (*vanguard.com*); Van Kampen Senior Income Trust (*vankampen.com*); Credit Suisse Monthly High Yield Index (*credit-suisse.com*); Lehman Brothers High Yield Index (*lehman.com*); Merrill Lynch High Yield Index (*ml.com*); and Citigroup High Yield Index (*citigroup.com*).

F I G U R E 6.16

Asset Class Description for Non-U.S. Fixed-Income

Characteristics
Description: With more than $17 trillion of par value in bonds and notes outstanding as of early 2000, the non-U.S. fixed-income universe represents a large and diverse asset class spread across many countries, currencies, sectors, quality ratings, maturities, structures, and issue types, including sovereign, supranational, corporate, and other securities. Non-U.S. fixed-income instruments include: (i) *domestic indigenous bonds,* issued by local issuers and traded in the currency and according to the regulations of local securities markets; (ii) *eurobonds,* issued and traded in bearer form on a pan-national basis outside the jurisdiction of any single country; (iii) *foreign bonds,* issued by non-local borrowers in the currency and under the regulations of a specific foreign country; and (iv) *global bonds,* which are issued and traded simultaneously in the Eurobond and one or more foreign bond markets. Several types of foreign bonds include Yankee bonds (U.S.-pay bonds issued in the U.S. market and registered with the SEC), *Bulldog bonds* (issued in the United Kingdom market), and *Samurai bonds* (issued in the Japanese market).
Choices: The non-U.S. fixed-income markets may be accessed through: (i) outright purchase of fixed-coupon and floating-rate notes, bonds, certificates, and depository receipts, or through closed-end and open-end mutual funds, hedge funds, unit trusts, and exchange-traded funds; (ii) the interest rate and currency swap markets; (iii) derivative instruments such as options, futures, and warrants; and (iv) various forms of leverage, repurchase agreements, and special structures. Details about Brady bonds and other emerging-markets issues are contained in the Asset Class Description for emerging-markets debt.

J.P. Morgan Global ex-U.S. Bond Index[1]

				Correlation of Annual Returns with				
Time Period	No. Yrs.	Total Return CAGR	Std. Dev.	U.S. Equity	U.S. F.I.	EM Debt	EM Equity	High Yield
1986–1990	5	18.9%	13.2%	−0.22	−0.19	NA	NA	NA
1986–1995	10	15.0%	11.1%	0.15	0.26	NA	NA	NA
1986–2000	15	10.6%	12.1%	0.10	0.33	NA	NA	NA
1990–1999	10	8.5%	9.3%	0.11	0.66	NA	−0.11	0.19
1990–2004	15	8.1%	9.2%	0.30	0.38	NA	0.17	0.36
1997–2006	10	3.9%	10.6%	0.21	0.14	−0.14	−0.03	0.45
2000–2006	7	4.4%	10.5%	0.39	−0.07	0.60	0.38	0.72

[1]Data for the J.P. Morgan Global ex–U.S. Bond Index are available beginning in 1986.

J.P. Morgan Global ex-U.S. Bond Index

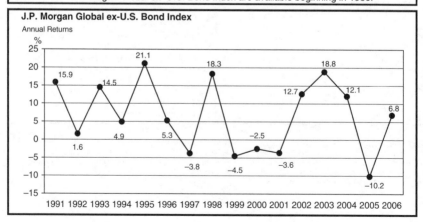

Source: The Author.

Rationale for Investment	Risks and Concerns
• Responding to local as well as global monetary, fiscal, and currency policies, economic and inflation cycles, institutional forces and political developments, debt service, balance of payments, and foreign currency reserves conditions, non-U.S. fixed-income securities offer an expanded opportunity set of bond investment opportunities to protect against deflation or financial accidents. For example, during the decade of the 1990s, Japanese bonds returned 5.4% per annum in yen terms during a period when Japanese equities declined by over 75%.	• During the 20th century, the world experienced four different exchange rate regimes, during the last of which—floating exchange rates—the U.S. dollar experienced several major upward and downward cycles; as a result, the assumption of foreign currency exposure through non-U.S. fixed-income securities offers the possibility of significantly *enhanced* returns when foreign currencies *appreciate* against the U.S. dollar, but also significantly *reduced* returns when foreign currencies *depreciate* against the U.S. dollar. Due to the effects of various powerful counterbalancing forces in foreign exchange markets, it is alleged that unhedged non-U.S. fixed-income returns should be roughly equal to hedged non-U.S. fixed-income returns *over the long term;* however, *in the short run,* it is difficult to accurately forecast exchange rate movements due to: (i) the effects of official intervention; (ii) portfolio and direct investment flows; (iii) money supply, interest rate, economic growth, productivity, and inflation differentials; (iv) technological innovation and labor-force flexibility; and (v) political and geopolitical developments.
• With their returns a function of coupon income, coupon reinvestment, capital value changes, default rates, and currency gains or losses, non-U.S. fixed-income securities provide a relatively predictable series of scheduled coupon and final maturity payments and tend to generate long-term nominal returns in excess of those available on short-term instruments.	
• Offering the potential to discover inefficiencies in international capital markets and to capture alpha (excess return) though active portfolio management, non-U.S. fixed-income securities may enhance returns and reduce risk: (i) in the short run, on an opportunistic basis (with the optimal scenario featuring declining indigenous foreign interest rates and an appreciating currency versus the investor's base currency); or (ii) in the long run, independent of whether the foreign currency is owned on a hedged or unhedged basis.	• Investing outside of national borders may ultimately rescue, or wipe out, portfolio values. While the 20th century began and ended in an atmosphere of globalization and reduced barriers to the free flow of goods, people, and capital, several lengthy periods in the intervening years were marked by embargos, high tariffs, competitive currency devaluations, armed conflict, hyperinflation, debt repudiation, or economic depression, resulting in severe losses for investors in certain non-U.S. bond issues.
• *When expressed in unhedged foreign-currency terms,* many non-U.S. bond markets may reduce the volatility of overall portfolio returns because they exhibit lower standard deviations of returns than the standard deviations of returns of U.S. bond markets. (Due to the added volatility contributed by foreign currency fluctuations, *when expressed in U.S. dollar terms,* non-U.S. fixed-income securities exhibit higher standard deviations of returns than those of U.S. fixed-income securities.)	• As individual capital markets around the world have become more integrated through gains in computing, broadcasting and communications technology, the Internet, financial innovation, and convergence in economic, fiscal, monetary, exchange rate, and inflation policies, the correlations of returns between non-U.S. and U.S. fixed-income securities may exhibit a tendency to rise over time and reduce their portfolio diversification benefits.
• Due in part to the influence of unhedged currency movements, the correlations of returns are low between non-U.S. fixed-income securities and U.S. equity, emerging-markets equity, private equity, high-yield bonds, real estate, and cash, and moderately high between international fixed-income securities and U.S. fixed-income securities and hedge funds. (Hedging the foreign currency risk in international fixed-income securities trends to *increase* their correlations of returns with the returns of U.S. bonds and those of several other asset classes.)	• Non-U.S. fixed-income securities are subject to many of the same bond-inherent risks as U.S. fixed-income securities, including market risk, default or credit risk, reinvestment risk, prepayment risk, and systemic risk.
	• Investing in non-U.S. fixed-income securities may involve lower trading liquidity and higher costs for functions such as: (i) information gathering, research, monitoring, valuation, custody, and reporting; (ii) custody, transfer, and settlement; (iii) transactions in local securities and foreign exchange markets; (iv) withholding taxes and other duties; and (v) hedging expenses.

Information Sources: *Triumph of the Optimists: 101 Years of Global Investment Returns,* by Elroy Dimson, Paul Marsh, and Mike Staunton; *The Handbook of Fixed Income Securities,* ed. by Frank J. Fabozzi; Organization for Economic Co-operation and Development (*oecd.org*); Bank for International Settlements (*bis.org*); Bank of Japan (*boj.or.jp/en*); European Central Bank (*ecb.int*); Payden Global Fixed Income Fund (*payden.com*); FFTW-Worldwide Core Fund (*fftw.com*); Citigroup Analytics Yield Book (*yieldbook.com*); Bloomberg LLC (*bloomberg.com*); Citigroup World Government Bond Index (*citigroup.com*); J.P. Morgan Global Government Bond Index (*jpmorgan.com*); InterSec Research Non-North American Bond Index (*intersecresearch.com*); PIMCO Global Bond Fund (*pimco.com*), UBS Global Bonds (*ubs.com*), Morgan Stanley Global Bond Fund (*morganstanley.com*); and Credit Suisse (*credit-suisse.com*).

F I G U R E   6.17

Asset Class Description for Emerging-Markets Fixed Income

Characteristics
Description: Emerging-markets debt describes a broad range of fixed-income instruments issued primarily by sovereign borrowers, but also by quasi-sovereign and/or corporate entities, in middle- or low-income developing countries most often located in Latin America (such as Argentina, Brazil, Ecuador, Mexico, and Venezuela), Eastern Europe (such as Bulgaria, the Czech Republic, Hungary, Poland, Ukraine, and Russia), Asia (such as Indonesia, Malaysia, the Philippines, and Thailand), the Middle East (such as Jordan, Israel, and Turkey), and Africa (such as Egypt, the Ivory Coast, Nigeria, and South Africa). Emerging-markets debt instruments include Eurobonds, Brady bonds, global bonds, tradable bank loans, local bonds, and a variety of other security types, and in some cases, their associated derivatives. Emerging-markets debt is most often denominated in external currencies, such as the U.S. dollar, the euro, or the Japanese yen. Emerging market local instruments are denominated in the indigenous local currency of the borrower. The emerging-market debt universe is composed of both fixed and floating rate sovereign bonds. The asset class was in effect created by the implementation of the Brady Plan in 1989–1990 when the U.S. Treasury helped to re-engineer defaulted commercial bank loans into performing bonds. Many of these initial "Brady" bonds were secured by U.S. Treasury collateral, but more recently issued emerging market debt instruments generally do not have the collateral backing the bonds. By 1998, all major Brady restructurings had been completed, signaling the transformation from an unsecuritized bank loan market to a bond market. **Choices:** Emerging-market sovereign *external bonds* generally refer to the hard currency denominated government bonds issued by emerging market countries. External instruments are issued in the U.S. or European markets and are subject to U.S. or U.K. regulations and laws. Sovereign external debt instruments include collateralized and uncollateralized Brady bonds, global bonds, Eurobonds, and bank loans. Emerging-market sovereign *local bonds* are generally issued in a domestic market and purchased by local investors. As such, they are generally subject to U.S. and/or U.K. regulations and denominated in the local currency. Emerging-market *corporate bonds* generally refer to the external debt of corporations located in an emerging country. Emerging-market corporate issues are issued in international markets and are primarily purchased by international investors. They are generally subject to U.S. and/or U.K. regulations and in most cases, are denominated in U.S. dollars or euros. Emerging-markets debt investments may also be accessed through open-end and closed-end mutual funds and a variety of derivative instruments including the swaps market.

J.P. Morgan Emerging Markets Bond Index Plus[1]

				Correlation of Annual Returns with				
Time Period	No. Yrs.	Total Return CAGR	Std. Dev.	U.S. Equity	EM Equity	U.S. F.I.	Non-U.S. F.I.	High Yield
1994–1998	5	6.7%	25.4%	0.54	0.73	0.43	−0.05	0.90
1994–2003	10	11.4%	19.1%	0.31	0.49	0.17	0.04	0.57
1994–2006	13	11.4%	16.5%	0.31	0.43	0.18	0.04	0.55
1997–2001	5	6.9%	15.7%	−0.04	0.61	−0.47	−0.81	0.03
1997–2006	10	11.0%	12.3%	0.06	0.65	−0.43	−0.14	0.41
2002–2006	5	15.2%	7.6%	0.48	0.56	−0.04	0.58	0.83
2000–2006	7	12.9%	8.7%	0.54	0.42	−0.18	0.60	0.55

[1]Data for the J.P. Morgan Emerging Markets Bond Index Plus are available beginning in 1994.

J.P. Morgan Emerging Markets Bond Index Plus

Annual Returns

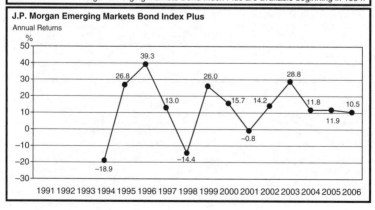

Source: The Author.

Rationale for Investment	Risks and Concerns
• Many emerging-market countries have sizeable and growing populations, access to abundant natural resources, and/or a low-cost labor pool; by several measures of economic performance, a substantial number of emerging-market countries also appear to offer potential for continued gains in national output, per-capita income, and more competitive and diversified external trade, considerably enhancing their capacity to issue, usefully deploy the proceeds from, and service their debt obligations. • When considered on a multiyear basis, emerging-markets debt has generated total annual returns, primarily driven by high coupon income, that have matched or considerably exceeded the returns on emerging-markets equity as well as the returns on many other fixed-income asset classes such as U.S. investment-grade and high-yield corporate bonds. • As an asset class that tends to respond to country-specific as well as global credit and economic influences, emerging-markets debt has generally low correlations of returns with high-grade U.S. and non-U.S. debt, high correlations of returns with emerging-markets equity, and moderately high correlations of returns with U.S. equity, non-U.S. equity, and high-yield debt. In many but not all periods, correlations of returns for the debt of specific emerging-markets countries tends to be low versus the debt of many other emerging-markets countries. • With occasional reversals, investors appear to be exhibiting greater recognition of and increased confidence in emerging-markets debt as a result of an apparent long-term trend toward reform in many emerging-markets countries. Among other policies, such measures include improved fiscal discipline and responsiveness, financial-market liberalization, deregulation and privatization, more flexible exchange rate adjustment and external borrowing initiatives, closer integration with the global economy, increased receptivity to external practices, technology, and currents of thought, and higher levels of communication and disclosure. • Emerging-markets debt may offer the opportunity to generate excess returns (alpha) resulting from event-driven market inefficiencies and exploitable investment opportunities identified through the astute assessment of sovereign political and financial conditions, yield spreads compared with other fixed-income instruments, and the maturity, collateral, guarantee, and other terms of specific issues.	• In part due to weak points in their banking, currency, or economic systems, still-evolving political processes, and significant social challenges, some emerging-market countries—such as Mexico in 1994, several Southeast Asian nations in 1997, Russia in 1998, Brazil in 1999, and Argentina in 2001—may face a financial crisis involving severe price declines in their debt obligations, enforced exchanges of their securities on unfavorable terms for investors, or outright default. Emerging-market debt securities have tended to suffer because of a lack of clear and broadly accepted procedures for coordinating the interests of multilateral lending institutions, debtors, and creditors. • Emerging-market countries are rarely able to exert a high degree of influence and control over their own fortunes; economic cycles in the developed world tend to have an exaggerated impact on the capital inflows, pricing power, export performance, employment levels, total domestic output, and financial asset prices of emerging-market countries. • Driven by wide swings in investor risk-avoidance and risk-preference preceding, during, and following stressful financial episodes for single countries, or for several countries simultaneously (financial "contagion"), emerging-market debt can exhibit high volatility or standard deviation of returns that average over twice the standard deviation of returns for U.S. and non-U.S. debt and approximately 15-30% greater than the standard deviation of returns for U.S. and non-U.S. equity. • An organized market for the issuance, trading, price discovery, valuation, settlement, and custody of emerging-markets debt began to take shape only beginning in the late 1980s and early 1990s and as a result, the liquidity of certain country-specific, region-specific, or asset class-specific issues of emerging-markets debt can be lacking precisely at those times when it is most needed. • Owing to a high concentration of issuers, intermediaries, and investors in emerging-markets debt, prices can be unduly influenced by such factors as; (i) dealers' positions, activity, and market views; (ii) issuers' bond repurchase programs; and (iii) the entry or exit of hedge funds, local and nonlocal individual investors, opportunistic crossover investors from other sectors of the debt markets; and dedicated entities who focus on the emerging-markets debt asset class.

Information Sources: Institute of International Finance (*iif.com*); Economic and Financial Indicators Section of *The Economist* (*economist.com*); J.P. Morgan Emerging Markets Bond Index (*jpmorgan.com*); J.P. Morgan EMBI-Plus Index (*jpmorgan.com*); *Mobius on Emerging Markets*, by J. Mark Mobius; GMO Emerging Country Debt (*gmo.com*); SEI International Emerging Markets (*seic.com*);*Handbook of Emerging Fixed Income and Currency Markets*, ed. By Frank J. Fabozzi and Alberto Franco; PIMCO Emerging Markets Bond Fund (*pimco.com*); Merrill Lynch Emerging Markets Debt Fund (*ml.com*); and Morgan Stanley Emerging Markets Debt Fund (*morganstanley.com*).

F I G U R E 6.18

Asset Class Description for Gold

Characteristics

Description:

Gold is a precious yellow metallic element, not subject to oxidation or corrosion, with 79 protons in its nucleus and an atomic weight of 196.967. One troy ounce of gold equals 1.0941 avoirdupois ounces. The first gold coins are believed to have been minted approximately 2,700 years ago, and since then, gold has for varying lengths of time functioned alongside or instead of various other forms of currency as a medium of exchange, store of value, and unit of account. For example, throughout its 1,100-year history, the Byzantine Empire, with Constantinople as its capital, maintained a monetary economy based on gold. Its gold coin, weighing approximately 4.5 grams and called the *bezant* (also known as the *solidus*, or *nomisma*) circulated freely within and outside the Byzantine Empire for 645 years, from 324 to 969 A.D.

Choices:

Gold can be purchased and sold in a variety of forms, including: (i) recently minted legal tender and commemorative coins; (ii) previously issued coins and medals of numismatic value; (iii) gold bars and bullion; (iv) shares of gold mining companies; (v) gold futures and options; (vi) gold trust receipts, structured notes, and gold-backed bonds; (vii) gold jewelry and objects of art; and in a related but different category, (viii) other precious metals such as silver, platinum, palladium, and rhodium. How and where gold is owned are often determined by the investor's motivations, fears, amounts to invest, objectives, and personal circumstances.

Handy & Harman Spot Gold Price Index

Time Period	No. Yrs.	Total Return CAGR	Std. Dev.	U.S. Equity	Non-U.S. Equity	U.S. F.I.	Real Estate	CPI Infl.
				Correlation of Annual Returns with
1970–1979	10	29.1%	44.9%	−0.38	−0.31	NA	NA	0.70
1970–1989	20	12.3%	38.3%	−0.32	−0.19	NA	NA	0.52
1970–1999	30	6.8%	33.0%	−0.34	−0.06	NA	NA	0.56
1980–1989	10	−2.4%	19.0%	0.45	0.48	0.21	−0.06	−0.15
1980–1999	20	−2.8%	14.8%	0.15	0.47	0.15	−0.10	−0.06
1990–1999	10	−3.2%	10.0%	−0.33	0.50	−0.06	−0.22	0.13
1997–2006	10	5.6%	15.0%	−0.30	0.28	−0.34	0.17	0.24
2000–2006	7	11.9%	12.2%	0.30	0.48	−0.47	−0.08	−0.23

Information Sources: The World Gold Council (*gold.org*); Gold Fields Mineral Services Annual Gold Survey (*gfms.co.uk*); Gold Eagle Gold Research Center (*gold-eagle.com*); American Numismatist Association (*ana.org*); U.S. Mint (*usmint.gov*); The American Institute for Economic Research (*aier.org/*); *The Golden Constant,* by Roy Jastram; FTSE Gold Mines Index (*ft.com*); Goldman Sachs Precious Metals Subindex (*gs.com*); Handy & Harman Precious Metals (*1-800-24-karat*); MSCI International Goldmines Subindex (*mscibarra.com*); Philadelphia Stock Exchange XAU Index of Gold and Silver Mining Stocks (*phlx.com*); and Toronto Stock Exchange Gold and Precious Metals Index (*tsx.com*).

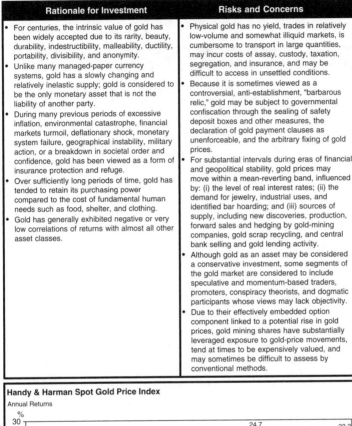

Rationale for Investment	Risks and Concerns
• For centuries, the intrinsic value of gold has been widely accepted due to its rarity, beauty, durability, indestructibility, malleability, ductility, portability, divisibility, and anonymity. • Unlike many managed-paper currency systems, gold has a slowly changing and relatively inelastic supply; gold is considered to be the only monetary asset that is not the liability of another party. • During many previous periods of excessive inflation, environmental catastrophe, financial markets turmoil, deflationary shock, monetary system failure, geographical instability, military action, or a breakdown in societal order and confidence, gold has been viewed as a form of insurance protection and refuge. • Over sufficiently long periods of time, gold has tended to retain its purchasing power compared to the cost of fundamental human needs such as food, shelter, and clothing. • Gold has generally exhibited negative or very low correlations of returns with almost all other asset classes.	• Physical gold has no yield, trades in relatively low-volume and somewhat illiquid markets, is cumbersome to transport in large quantities, may incur costs of assay, custody, taxation, segregation, and insurance, and may be difficult to access in unsettled conditions. • Because it is sometimes viewed as a controversial, anti-establishment, "barbarous relic," gold may be subject to governmental confiscation through the sealing of safety deposit boxes and other measures, the declaration of gold payment clauses as unenforceable, and the arbitrary fixing of gold prices. • For substantial intervals during eras of financial and geopolitical stability, gold prices may move within a mean-reverting band, influenced by: (i) the level of real interest rates; (ii) the demand for jewelry, industrial uses, and identified bar hoarding; and (iii) sources of supply, including new discoveries, production, forward sales and hedging by gold-mining companies, gold scrap recycling, and central bank selling and gold lending activity. • Although gold as an asset may be considered a conservative investment, some segments of the gold market are considered to include speculative and momentum-based traders, promoters, conspiracy theorists, and dogmatic participants whose views may lack objectivity. • Due to their effectively embedded option component linked to a potential rise in gold prices, gold mining shares have substantially leveraged exposure to gold-price movements, tend at times to be expensively valued, and may sometimes be difficult to assess by conventional methods.

Handy & Harman Spot Gold Price Index

Annual Returns

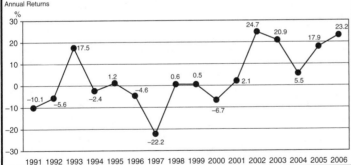

Source: The Author.

F I G U R E   6.19

Asset Class Description for Hedge Funds

Characteristics

Description:
Strictly speaking, hedge funds are not an asset class *per se*, but a form of privately organized, pooled investment vehicle which seeks to achieve consistently positive absolute returns independent of financial conditions, typically through the use of a wide potential range of nontraditional and traditional directional and non-directional strategies, including: (i) long, short, arbitrage, and hedging in niche or mainstream market sectors; (ii) leverage and derivative instruments; and (iii) opportunistic and dynamic trading activity, or patient, workout-intensive investing. Among the principal categories of hedge funds are: (i) *event-driven funds* (focusing on areas such as merger arbitrage, distressed securities, and reorganization or bankruptcy situations); (ii) *relative-value funds* (focusing on areas such as convertible arbitrage, fixed-income arbitrage, or statistical arbitrage); (iii) *market-neutral funds* (focusing on offsetting long and short positions to avoid any directional bet on the market); (iv) *long-short funds* (focusing on maximizing the impact of security selection and varying the proportion of long and short positions to achieve a targeted degree of market exposure); and (v) *global macro funds* (focusing on directional moves in stocks, bonds, currencies, commodities, other asset classes, and their associated derivatives). Some market participants use the term *absolute-return strategies* to describe many of the main forms of hedge fund investing.

Choices:
Hedge funds can be accessed through a variety of structures, including limited partnerships, limited liability companies, privately offered registered investment companies, closed-end registered hedge funds, long-short and merger arbitrage mutual funds, mirror funds, master/feeder structures, offshore insurance companies and tax-deferred insurance policies, passive foreign investment companies (PFICs), controlled foreign companies (CFCs), collateralized fund obligations (CFOs), hedge fund incubators or collectives, funds of funds, fund of fund warrants, and hedge fund structured notes.

HFRI Fund Weighted Composite Hedge Fund Index[1]

Time Period	No. Yrs.	Total Return CAGR	Std. Dev.	Correlation of Annual Returns with				
				U.S. Equity	High Yield	U.S. F.I.	Non-U.S. F.I.	Cash
1990–1994	5	18.2%	13.4%	0.82	0.90	0.75	0.32	−0.40
1990–1999	10	18.3%	11.3%	0.32	0.71	0.25	−0.16	−0.33
1990–2004	15	14.4%	11.4%	0.62	0.70	0.10	0.04	0.05
1994–1998	5	12.9%	9.2%	0.57	0.96	0.52	−0.09	0.76
1994–2003	10	12.0%	10.8%	0.69	0.55	−0.17	−0.08	0.18
1997–2006	10	10.6%	9.6%	0.63	0.42	−0.73	−0.24	0.08
2000–2006	7	8.2%	6.7%	0.98	0.81	−0.73	0.32	−0.21

[1]Data for the HFRI Fund Weighted Composite Hedge Fund Index are available beginning in 1990.

HFRI Fund Weighted Composite Hedge Fund Index
Annual Returns

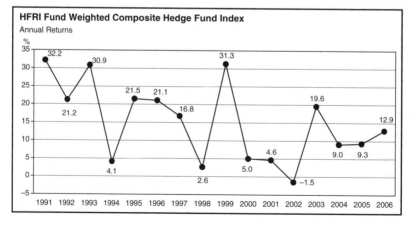

Source: The Author.

Rationale for Investment	Risks and Concerns
• Partly because they are able to attract and reward talented and motivated money managers who focus on special opportunities within the investment world, hedge funds offer attractive, possibly superior risk-adjusted returns and some degree of intended capital protection relative to active managers and passive benchmarks in traditional asset classes, irrespective of the state of the financial markets. • Reflecting greater year-to-year consistency in investment performance, hedge funds' returns tend to have standard deviations of returns which are approximately the same as those of U.S.and non-U.S. bonds, and one-half to two-thirds as high as the standard deviations of returns of U.S.and non-U.S. equity. Because of the typically offsetting patterns of returns resulting from combinations of hedge funds, the standard deviations of returns for hedge fund funds of funds tend to be one-half to one-third those of individual hedge funds. • Due to their organizational nimbleness, skill, knowledge, insight, specialization, lackofconstraints, and an ability to go short, employ margin, and use derivatives and non-linear strategies, hedge funds often face abroader opportunity set that allows them to identify and take advantage of investment opportunities not exploitable by most other investment entities. • Owing to the fact that a given hedge fund's returns derive in large part from the skill of one or a few managers locating and acting up on specific mispricings in the financial markets, individual hedge funds may exhibit low-to-modestly-high correlations of return swith U.S.and non-U.S.equity, typically low correlations of returns withe merging-markets equity and private equity, and generally low correlations of returns with U.S.and non-U.S.bonds.The generally low correlations of returns *among various types* of hedge funds suggests that acombination of several hedge funds may significantly reduce the volatility and maximum draw downs of an investment portfolio. • As a result of their emphasis on generating returns from market inefficiencies,anomalies, dislocations, complex situations, and special analytics, hedge funds as a whole tend to have low systematic (overall market) risk exposure and the opportunity to produce high alpha (excessreturns), with a high idiosyncratic component and dispersions of returns between first- and third-quartile performers that are higher than those for active asset managers in most other categories of U.S. and non-U.S. equity and debt securities.	• Although the process of researching hedge fund scan be time consuming and expensive, in view of the significant number of new entrants, extracare, caution, and due diligence are crucially important in view of: (i) the devastating losses and hedge fund closures during the bear markets of 1969–1970 and 1973–1974; (ii) several highly publicized cases in the post-1998 period of fund collapse caused by manager incompetence, major style deviation, fraudulent misrepresentation of returns and investment strategies, or the improper use of leverage or derivatives; (iii) the occasional unsustainability of returns in response to large new capital inflows; (iv) the misevaluation and mismanagement of market price, correlation, term structure, nonlinearity, and volatility risk, counterparty credit risk, and funding and asset liquidity risk; (v) disproportionately large exposure to highly volatile positions or sectors; and (vi) eccentric manager risk, organizational immaturity, and/or high professional staff turnover. • Analyzing, understanding, and comparing the investment performance of hedge funds with benchmarks, each other, and other asset classes can be difficult due to: (i) the relatively brief historical records, non-normal distribution of returns, unstandardized and voluntary reporting methods, and lack of strategy transparency of certain managers and fund subcategories; (ii) uncertainty as to whether a specific fund is actually open to new investors; (iii) the high degree of heterogeneity among different hedge fund strategies and among individual hedge funds within a specific strategy; (iv) the possibility of survivorship bias, selection bias, backfill bias, age bias, size bias, and serial correlation (stale pricing) bias;(v) a tendency for some funds to overestimate the value of illiquid positions and underestimate the degree of exposure to significant adverse financial-market developments. • Investment in hedge funds typically involves high annual management fees and performance fees, lengthy lockup periods, and stringent capital investment and withdrawal conditions. • Diversification within the hedge fund universe may be necessary because of: (i) position concentration and/or high leverage within specificfunds; (ii) fluctuating fund investment opportunities in certain subsectors due to lower market volatility, narrower deal spreads, and reduced transaction activity; (iii) the tendency of some strategiestoproducehighlyepisodicreturnswhile others may generate more consistent patterns of returns. • Due to the high trading velocity and short-term gains generation tendency of many hedge funds, the reduction from their pre-tax to their after-tax returns can be quite substantial, in the process generating significant tax liabilities for their limited partners.

Information Sources: *Investing in Hedge Funds*, by Joseph G. Nicholas; *Hedge Fund Handbook*, by Stefano Lavinio; *Evaluating and Implementing Hedge Fund Strategies*, ed. by Ronald A. Lake; *The Prudent Investor's Guide to Hedge Funds*, by James P. Owen; *The Handbook of Alternative Investment Strategies*, ed. By Thomas Schneeweiss and Joseph Pescatore; *When Genius Failed: The Rise and Fall of Long-Term Capital Management,* by Roger Lowenstein; Credit Suisse/Tremont Index (*hedgeindex.com*); Hennessee Hedge Fund Advisory Group Index (*hennesseegroup.com*); MSCI Hedge Fund Index (*mscibarra.com*); Standard & Poor's Hedge Fund Index (*spglobal.com*); Greenwich Fund Advisors International Index (*greenwichai.com*); Zurich Capital Markets Index (*zcmgroup.com*); Managed Funds Association (*mfainfo.org*); Hedge Fund Center (*hedgefundcenter.com*); Lipper Hedge World Markets (*hedgeworld.com*); Hedge Fund Research Inc. Equity Hedge Index (*hfr.com*); Tremont Capital Management (*tremont.com*); Hedge Fund Association (*thehfa.org*); Cambridge Associates, LLC. (*cambridgeassociates.com*); Cerulli Associates (*cerulli.com*); Robeco Boston Partners Long-Short Equity Fund (*robecoinvest.com*); The Arbitrage Fund (*thearbfund.com*); The Merger Fund (Westchester Capital Management); "Sound Practices for Hedge Fund Managers," by Caxton Corporation, Kingdon Capital Management, Moore Capital Management, Soros Fund Management, and Tudor Investment Corporation; and "The Search for Alpha Continues," by Alexander M. Ineichen (*usbw.com*).

F I G U R E   6.20

Asset Class Description for Inflation-Indexed Securities

Characteristics

Description:

Inflation-indexed securities refer to bonds whose principal and/or coupon payments are adjusted with the general level of prices as measured by a commonly accepted price index. In January 1997, the U.S. Treasury began auctioning capital-indexed bonds, known alternatively as Treasury Inflation Protection Securities (TIPS) or Treasury Inflation-Indexed Securities (TIIS). Originally issued with maturities of 5, 10, and 30 years, TIPS pay semiannual fixed real coupons multiplied by a principal amount that is adjusted upward monthly by an accretion amount paid to the investor at maturity and determined with a 3-month time lag by the non-seasonally adjusted Consumer Price Index for All Urban Consumers (CPI-U). TIPS are noncallable securities and have fairly long durations relative to their maturities because a significant portion of the total return is in the form of the inflation-adjusted principal amount paid at final maturity. Any interim price deflation accruals are deducted from inflation accruals; in the arguably tumultuous and highly unlikely event of cumulative deflation over the life of a TIPS security, its principal amount is guaranteed to be repaid by the U.S. Treasury at its original face value.

Choices:

In addition to TIPS, other *capital-indexed bonds* (and in a more limited number of cases, *interest-only indexed bonds* and *indexed-annuity bonds*) have been issued on a limited basis in a variety of maturities and structures by federal agencies, corporations, and municipalities, and sometimes in meaningful quantities by non-U.S. issuers in more than 20 foreign-capital markets. Several inflation-protection mutual funds seek to add value in excess of annual management fees through sector, issuer, and maturity selection and other tactics aimed at benefiting from supply-demand imbalances, seasonal factors, yield-curve movements, and changing inflation expectations. Some investors monitor the

equivalent maturity, preferring TIPS if the actual inflation rate is expected to be *above* the breakeven spread, and conventional U.S. Treasury bonds if the actual inflation rate is expected to be *below* the breakeven spread. Subject to annual per-person limitations on new purchases, Series I inflation-indexed accrual security U.S. savings bonds have a number of TIPS-like features.

Lehman Brothers TIPS Index/Bridgewater Index[1]

				Correlation of Annual Returns with				
Time Period	No. Yrs.	Total Return CAGR	Std. Dev.	U.S. Equity	U.S. F.I.	High Yield	Cash	CPI Infl.
1970–1979	10	11.8%	4.5%	−0.60	NA	NA	0.70	0.89
1970–1989	20	10.6%	4.0%	−0.35	NA	NA	0.25	0.75
1970–1999	30	9.2%	4.3%	−0.34	NA	NA	0.42	0.77
1980–1989	10	9.3%	3.2%	0.43	0.39	NA	0.38	0.47
1980–1999	20	7.9%	3.6%	0.10	0.55	NA	0.51	0.56
1990–1999	10	6.4%	3.4%	−0.15	0.64	0.25	0.33	0.60
1997–2006	10	6.2%	4.5%	−0.63	0.52	−0.11	−0.36	0.22
2000–2006	7	7.6%	4.6%	−0.46	0.75	−0.18	−0.12	−0.01

[1]Bridgewater stimulated TIPS data used for 1970 to February 1997; Lehman Brothers TIPS Index used after February 1997.

Information Sources: *Handbook of Inflation Indexed Bonds*, ed. by John Brynjolfsson and Frank J. Fabozzi; Series I U.S. Savings Bonds (*savingsbonds.gov*); BondHelp (*bondhelp.com*); U.S. Savings Bond Consultant (*savingsbonds.com*); Bloomberg ILB <Go> for a listing of government, municipal, and corporate inflation-indexed bonds (*bloomberg.com*); Barclays Inflation-Linked Bonds Total Return Index (*barclays.com*); Lehman Brothers Inflation-Linked Index (*lehman.com*); Citigroup Inflation-Linked Securities Index (*citigroup.com*); American Century Inflation-Adjusted Fund (*americancentury.com*); Brown Brothers Harriman Inflation-Indexed Securities Fund (*bbh.com*); Fidelity Inflation-Protected Bond Fund (*fidelity.com*); PIMCO Real Return Bond Fund (*pimco.com*); and Vanguard Inflation-Protected Securities Fund (*vanguard.com*).

Rationale for Investment	Risks and Concerns
• TIPS offer an effective hedge against inflation through a reliable stream of real income payments and adjustments to principal that can keep pace with the price increases in a market basket of consumer-oriented goods and services. • Due to their high degree of correlation with unanticipated inflation episodes over the course of multidecade economic and financial cycles, TIPS have exhibited very low or meaningfully negative correlations of 1- to 10-year returns with U.S. and non-U.S. equities, similar-duration conventional U.S. bonds, and alternative asset classes, and moderate to high correlations of 1- to 10-year returns with cash instruments. • Because of the relative stability of *real* interest rates, which are approximately one-half as volatile as *nominal* interest rates, TIPS generally behave as low-volatility assets, with standard deviations of annual returns that tend to be one-fourth to one-fifth those of equities and similar-duration bonds. • Owing to their low standard deviations of annual returns, their low or negative correlations of 1- to 10-year returns with most asset classes, and their frequently favorable real-yield comparisons versus the real yields of conventional bonds, TIPS may reduce the overall long-term risk level of a portfolio of assets. • As a result of their different degree of price responsiveness compared to other asset classes in varying financial environments, and their positive return characteristics in periods of stable-to-falling real interest rates coupled with rising inflation, in appropriate circumstances, TIPS can serve as an effective diversifying substitute for conventional bond-like asset classes, in some cases allowing potentially greater emphasis on equity-like and/or alternative asset classes.	• For taxable investors, the semiannual real interest payments on TIPS are taxed each year as ordinary income; even though the monthly inflation adjustments to principal are not received until the final maturity of the bond; the amount of this "phantom income" is also fully taxable each year. In sufficiently high tax brackets and at moderately high CPI inflation rates, TIPS tend to generate negative current cash flow. As a result, taxable investors may need to hold TIPS in tax-deferred accounts and/or to consider instead *tax-exempt* inflation protection securities (TEIPS). • Depending upon the duration of the TIPS and the magnitude of the real interest rate rise, higher real interest rates may cause capital losses on TIPS. The level of real interest rates is generally influenced by fluctuations in capital supply-demand factors such as real economic growth rates, federal budget and/or balance of payments surpluses or deficits, and monetary policy. • For a series of holding periods of one year or less, TIPS may lose some of their beneficial diversification features due to moderate to high correlations of returns with conventional bonds caused by short-term common movements in real and nominal yields, flight-to-quality effects, and other factors. • During periods of declining inflation expectations, falling inflation rates, or outright deflation, TIPS tend to underperform conventional bonds of the same maturity or duration. • TIPS possess certain potentially complicating features associated with: (i) their post-1997 status as a relatively new, untested, not widely understood, and somewhat lower liquidity instrument having wider bid-asked trading spreads; (ii) the behavior of, and interaction among, expected inflation, inflation risk premiums, nominal interest rates, and real interest rates; (iii) the risk that a decline in the external purchasing power of the U.S. dollar may exceed its domestic adjustment for inflation; and (iv) the efficacy of various index contingencies available to the U.S. Treasury in the event that the applicable Consumer Price Index is discontinued or fundamentally altered in a manner materially adverse to TIPS investors.

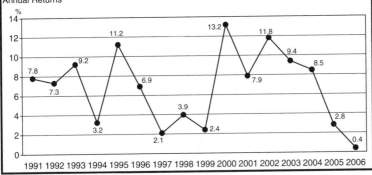

Lehman Brothers TIPS Index/Bridgewater Index

Annual Returns

Source: The Author.

F I G U R E 6.21

Asset Class Description for Managed Futures Funds

Characteristics

Description:

Futures contracts are standardized contracts that require the delivery or the acceptance of an underlying commodity or financial instrument at a specific price on a stipulated future date. A futures contract obligates the buyer to purchase the underlying commodity or instrument, and the seller to sell it, unless the contract is sold, transferred, or closed out prior to the established settlement date. Futures contracts involve a form of inherent leverage through the posting of initial, variation, and maintenance margin, which is a performance guarantee that the contract will be honored. Because futures prices are driven by and derived from the behavior of the underlying commodity or financial instrument, futures are considered derivative instruments. Originally, the futures market focused on grains and agricultural commodities. Futures contracts provided farmers, ranchers, distributors, and others in the commodities markets with an efficient mechanism to help manage and hedge against the price volatility often experienced in agricultural markets. As time passed, the risk management benefits of the futures markets became apparent to other sectors of the economy, and beginning in the late 1970s and early 1980s, the futures industry introduced contracts which created new futures products and markets for metals, energy, interest rates, currencies, and other financial instruments. During the late 1970s, a number of Commodity Trading Advisors (CTAs) were established, inaugurating the managed futures industry. In the latter two decades of the twentieth century and on into the twenty-first, the managed futures industry has exhibited rapid growth, and as of the end of 2006, it was estimated that futures trading advisors had over $170 billion under management globally.

Choice:

Commodity Trading Advisors (CTAs) are investment managers who use the global futures, options, and related markets as an investment medium to manage their clients' assets. The principal means of implementation of managed futures funds include: (i) financial futures; (ii) commodity futures; (iii) forwards and cash instruments; (iv) options, swaps, and swaptions; and (v) physical commodities. Many domestic and international corporations, financial institutions, trading firms, and securities broker-dealers are active participants in the managed futures marketplace. Hedgers rely on the futures markets to obtain protection against rising or falling prices, while speculators and traders seek to profit from trading and investment strategies in the futures markets. The determinants of investment success in managed futures funds are: (i) manager selection; (ii) manager trading skill; (iii) manager model construction; (iv) manager use of leverage; and (v) risk control systems and behavior. The Commodity Futures Trading Commission (CFTC), created by Congress in 1974, is responsible for regulating futures trading and markets. The mission of the CFTC is to protect market users and the public from fraud, manipulation, and abusive practices related to the sale of commodity and financial futures and options, and to foster open, competitive, and financially sound futures and option markets.

Barclay CTA (Commodity Trading Advisors) Index[1]

Time Period	No. Yrs.	Total Return CAGR	Std. Dev.	Correlation of Annual Returns with				
				U.S. Equity	Non-U.S Equity	U.S. F.I.	High Yield	CPI Infl.
1980–1984	5	26.1%	21.2%	0.61	0.58	−0.58	NA	0.88
1980–1989	10	23.2%	20.7%	0.00	−0.04	−0.56	NA	0.64
1980–1994	15	17.4%	19.4%	0.11	0.13	−0.25	NA	0.70
1980–1999	20	14.9%	17.6%	−0.01	0.11	−0.12	NA	0.71
1990–1999	10	7.1%	7.2%	0.02	−0.34	0.51	−0.19	0.51
1990–2004	15	6.9%	6.3%	−0.35	−0.27	0.32	−0.38	0.86
1997–2006	10	5.5%	4.5%	−0.02	−0.24	0.71	0.17	−0.25
2000–2006	7	5.5%	4.2%	−0.22	−0.10	0.50	0.06	0.00

[1]Data for the Barclay CTA (Commodity Trading Advisors) Index are available beginning in 1990.

Information Sources: Center for International Securities and Derivatives Markets (CISDM) (*cisdm.org*); Chicago Board of Trade (*cbot.com*); Commodity Futures Trading Commission (*cftc.gov*); Eurex Futures and Options Exchange (*eurexchange.com*); Futures Industry Association (futuresindustry.org); International Traders Research (*managedfutures.com*); Managed Futures Association (*mfainfo.org*); National Futures Association (*nfa.futures.org*); Barclay Trading Group (*barclaygrp.com*); *How the Futures Markets Work*, by Jacob Bernstein; *Managed Futures: An Investor's Guide*, by Beverly Chandler; *Fundamentals of Futures and Options Markets*, by John C. Hull; *Commodity Futures and Options* by George Kleinman; *A Complete Guide to the Futures Markets: Fundamental Analysis, Technical Analysis, Trading, Spreads, and Options* by Jack Schwager; and *Barclay Managed Funds Report*, published quarterly by the Barclay Group.

Rationale for Investment

- Because of their generally low correlations of returns with many other conventional and alternative asset classes (including hedge funds), managed futures and Managed Futures Funds have tended to offer diversification opportunities that may have the potential to lower the standard deviation of returns and improve the risk-reward profile of an investment portfolio.
- Managed futures and Managed Futures Funds have the potential to generate attractive returns and may be positioned to perform well in various economic and financial market scenarios.
- On several occasions during periods of substantial turmoil or stress in financial markets, investment returns for managed futures have been favorable.
- Managed futures advisors may utilize futures contracts traded on many global exchanges involving typically 75-100 underlying assets or indices, including equity indices, financial instruments, agricultural products, precious and nonferrous metals, currencies, and energy products, offering potential trading and investment opportunities across a broad spectrum of assets and markets.
- As a heavily quantitatively and computer-driven strategy, managed futures trading systems seek to identify and profit from price, volume, volatility, and covariance trends across multiple time zones and in multiple markets. One differentiating factor among Managed Futures Funds is the degree to which a fund's strategy utilizes discretionary trading as substitutes for, or overlays of, the fund's underlying model and trading algorithms.
- Managed Futures: (i) offer the opportunity to establish with equal facility long and short positions; (ii) often employ stop-loss, trend-following, and/or mean-reverting trading disciplines; (iii) can incorporate leverage and interest income derivatives by means of margin and cash balances; and (iv) provide participation in a broad range of underlying markets.

Risks and Concerns

- Substantial risks may be associated with investing, hedging, and speculating in Managed Futures Funds, including: (i) the possibility for an investor to lose all or a substantial portion of his or her investment capital; (ii) a limited ability to readily redeem partnership interests or units in a Managed Futures Fund; (iii) no established secondary market for Managed Futures Fund partnership interests or units; and (iv) the possibility for Managed Futures Funds' high fees and expenses to potentially vitiate or negate portfolio profits or gains.
- According to the NASD, "managed futures are complicated and risky investment instruments that may be unsuitable for many investors. Commodity futures and financial futures trading itself is speculative, potentially volatile, and involves a high degree of leverage. Because managed futures investing is not well understood by mainstream individual investors, it is crucial that securities broker-dealer firms meet their suitability and disclosure obligations when recommending these products."
- In certain sideways-trending, choppy, directionless market conditions in some or many of their underlying instruments, Managed Futures Funds' returns patterns may be characterized by capital losses (drawdowns) and/or by high volatility, which may not be appropriate for all investors.
- Correlations of returns for Managed Futures Funds with the returns on other asset classes may: (i) vary over time; (ii) change significantly during periods of increased market volatility; and/or (iii) be substantially affected by managers' varying usage of leverage, derivatives, and short selling strategies and techniques.
- Given the fact that many Managed Futures Funds' trading strategies tend to rely on: (i) trend following; (ii) momentum-based investment approaches; (iii) pattern recognition; (iv) stop-loss position unwinding; and (v) hedging disciplines, they may or may not be applied by their managers with an appropriately successful degree of discipline and insight under certain kinds of capital markets conditions and futures trading environments.

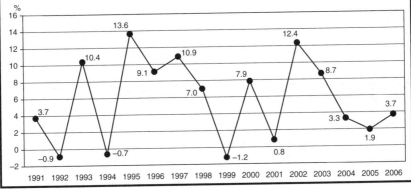

Barclay CTA (Commodity Trading Advisors) Index

Annual Returns

Source: The Author.

F I G U R E 6.22

Asset Class Description for Private Equity

Characteristics
Description:
The term private equity describes a broad spectrum of investment activity, generally grouped into two major categories: venture capital and leveraged buyouts (LBOs), which are distinguished from each other primarily in terms of the typical size of the equity investment, the technological riskiness or stage of maturity of the investee company, and the amount and role of debt in the transaction. *Venture capital* involves early-stage investing in the equity of privately owned companies with high potential for future growth and may encompass (i) angel, incubation, seed, or early-stage financings; (ii) startup, product prototype, or expansion-round financings; (iii) mezzanine or structured financings utilizing debt securities with equity-like features; and/or (iv) bridge-stage financings for companies expecting to go public within some known time frame. *Leveraged buyouts* involve taking a 100% or a significant controlling stake in more mature, existing businesses and may include management buyouts (MBOs), workouts, or turnaround situations involving reasonably stable businesses that may be experiencing financial or operating distress. Through their knowledge, experience, contacts, management selection skills, and proactive involvement, private equity investors in the sometimes overlapping venture capital and LBO fields seek to add value through: (i) identifying attractive opportunities; (ii) evaluating, structuring, or restructuring financial transactions; (iii) strategically and tactically influencing the structure, health, survival, growth, and profitability of their investee companies; and (iv) exiting their investments on favorable time and price terms.
Choices:
While a not inconsiderable proportion of private-equity investments are made directly by corporate, institutional, and individual investors, a substantial majority of private equity is managed by the general partners of investment partnerships, with most of the capital supplied by limited partners. Such partnerships may have a broad mandate, or they may be differentiated as to the stage, industry, region, or size of the intended investment activity. Private equity may be accessed through one or more individual investments or partnerships, through funds of funds, through closed-end funds, through co-investment opportunities, and through entities focusing on developed international or emerging markets. Other vehicles for private-equity investment include: (i) PIPE financings (private investment in public equity) which involve a private placement of public stock usually at a discount to the prevailing market price and often with other structural features; and, with appropriate consents and approvals, (ii) the purchase of partnership interests in the secondary market from exiting limited partners.

Venture Economics All Private Equity Fund Index

				Correlation of Annual Returns with				
Time Period	No. Yrs.	Total Return CAGR	Std. Dev.	U.S. Equity	U.S. F.I.	Non-U.S. Equity	Hedge Funds	Cash
1970–1979	10	19.8%	54.1%	0.85	NA	0.78	NA	−0.17
1970–1989	20	16.4%	42.5%	0.67	NA	0.40	NA	−0.12
1970–1999	30	20.6%	42.5%	0.57	NA	0.39	NA	−0.17
1980–1989	10	13.0%	27.2%	0.61	−0.15	−0.01	NA	0.17
1980–1999	20	21.1%	36.7%	0.40	−0.28	0.14	NA	−0.17
1990–1999	10	29.6%	43.7%	0.30	−0.30	0.54	0.48	−0.18
1997–2006	10	20.8%	46.9%	0.42	−0.66	0.47	0.83	0.27
2000–2006	7	8.2%	17.6%	0.66	−0.48	0.68	0.61	0.10

Venture Economics All Private Equity Fund Index

Annual Returns

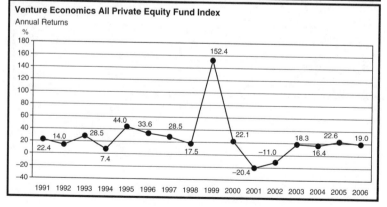

Source: The Author.

Rationale for Investment	Risks and Concerns
• When gauged over several market cycles, private equity has tended to generate relatively high compound annual growth rates in nominal and real returns, in many instances substantially exceeding the returns of publicly traded U.S. and non-U.S. equity. Private-equity returns are usually similar, if not equivalent, to the returns accruing to the entrepreneurial drive which underpins and rewards corporate risk-taking and advancement and that offers significant upside potential returns in robust bull market environments.	• Private-equity investments may be characterized by: (i) irregular inflows and outflows of cash, stemming from the periodic unscheduled drawdowns of investors ' funds until their total capital commitment is reached, and from the uncertain timing and form (money versus stock distributions) of capital disbursements; and (ii) low liquidity, with typical partnership terms of 7 to 10 years or more, lack of standardization in lockup and withdrawal conditions, and difficulty in transferring investments freely.
• Because private equity often involves concentrated investing in highly firm-specific rather than financial market-specific technologies, ideas, products, people, or business management acumen and restructuring activity, the correlation of returns between private equity and most other asset classes is usually low in the case of U.S., non-U.S., and emerging-markets equity, cash, hedge funds, high-yield bonds, commodities, and real estate, and often is modestly negative in the case of U.S. and non-U.S. bonds. As a result, private equity may be considered an effective diversifying asset within an overall portfolio.	• Unusual or potentially unfavorable elements of investing through private-equity partnerships include: (i) the wide degree of investment latitude ceded to the general partner and any applicable oversight, conflict-resolution, or general partner replacement conditions; (ii) high minimum capital commitments, management fees on undrawn capital contributions, and penalties if limited partners decide not to continue their capital commitments; and (iii) the typical dependency of high expected returns on one or two highly successful investments, in the absence of which actual returns may be reduced by as much as 40–50%.
• Through what is effectively an investment in a businessperson's and/or a general partner's judgment skills—of strategic positioning, of competitive advantage, of innovation, of valuations, of people—private equity offers top quartile entities the opportunity to exploit unique or unusual situations and earn significant excess return (alpha) from inflection points, market inefficiencies, and pricing anomalies.	• Influenced by feast-or-famine swings in returns, capital raised and deployed, investee industries, number of investments, focus on new-versus-existing investments, investor expectations, clawback provisions, valuations, competitive bidding scenarios, deal pricing, financing availability, leverage employed, and exit opportunities, private-equity returns can be highly volatile over time, producing standard deviations of returns considerably in excess of those for publicly traded U.S. and non-U.S. equity.
• Private equity tends to focus on investment in sectors experiencing fundamental change or a capital shortage and may reward the application of specialized industry and operating expertise, in venture capital in areas such as biotechnology, computer software storage and services, optics, content management, and other technology-intensive fields, and in leveraged buyouts in industries such as consumer products and other stable cash-flow industries.	• The costs of private-equity investing are not insubstantial, typically consisting of 1 –2% of capital committed plus a 20% carry, or participation in profits earned; in addition, private-equity investors may incur burdensome legal, due diligence, informational, tax, negotiation, accounting, consulting, monitoring, and administrative expenses.
• In view of the fact that the investor or the investor's general partner can have a more direct degree of closeness to, connectivity with, involvement in, and potential control over investee companies, private equity may allow for a tighter alignment of corporate and personal incentives, more timely replacement of underperforming managers or assets, or strategic coordination with other existing business and investment interests.	• It is difficult to compare the returns from one "vintage year" partnership formation period to another, because of: (i) inherent difficulties in verifying and interpreting internal rates of return (IRRs) as a measure of performance; (ii) the possible influence of survivorship bias and selection bias on reported results; and (iii) understated volatility and delayed or inaccurate recognition of the true worth of investments stemming from the use of historical book values, relatively infrequent appraisals, and assumed liquidation values rather than publicly tradable prices.

Information Sources: National Venture Capital Association (*nvca.org*); European Venture Capital Association (*evca.com*); Private Equity Central (*privateequitycentral.net*); Buyouts Newsletter (*buyoutsnews.com*); *The Venture Capital Journal* (*vcjnews.com*); Deloitte & Touche Quarterly Venture Capital Survey (*deloitte.com*); PricewaterhouseCoopers MoneyTree Venture Capital Survey (*pwcmoneytree.com*); NYPPEX (*offroadcapital.com*); Sagient Research Systems, Inc. (*sagientresearch.com*); *The Money of Invention*, by Paul A. Gompers and Joshua Lerner; *Angel Investing: Matching Startup Funds with Startup Companies*, by Robert J. Robinson and Mark van Osnabrugge; Kleiner Perkins Caufield & Byers (*kpcb.com*); Kohlberg Kravis Roberts & Co. (*kkr.com*); Blackstone Group (*blackstone.com*); Welsh Carson Anderson & Stowe (*welshcarson.com*); The Carlyle Group (*thecarlylegroup.com*); 3i (*3i.com*); Cambridge Associates U.S. Private Equity Index (*cambridgeassociates.com*); VentureOne (*ventureone.com*); and Venture Law Group (*venlaw.com*).

F I G U R E 6.23

Asset Class Description for Real Estate

Characteristics

Description:

In its broadest sense, real estate refers to tangible property such as lands, buildings, oil and mineral rights, or crops that give its owner the right of possession, enjoyment, lease/rental to another party, and disposal. Real estate may be distinguished from moveable possessions and personal property such as automobiles and livestock and encompasses a large, fragmented, diverse group of property types, geographic locations, direct and non-direct ownership structures, and financial characteristics ranging from highly predictable income-producing properties to speculative assets whose return is purely a function of changes in capital value. Three related and sometimes imprecise methodologies for valuing real estate include: (i) the predictability, amount, growth, and financial engineering potential of the cash flow a property can generate, and the multiple that buyers are willing to pay for this cash flow (this method is known as the Net Present Value approach); (ii) reviewing prices for comparable property types; and (iii) the cap rate, defined as a property's net operating income before debt service and depreciation, divided by its purchase price. Two important legislative acts affecting real estate include: (ii) the Real Estate Investment Trust Act of 1960, intended to foster public share ownership of real estate, and (ii) the Tax Reform Act of 1986, which eliminated most real estate tax shelters.

Choices:

Public securities markets exposure to real estate and other real assets is available through direct or mutual fund investment in: (i) REITs dedicated to the apartment, office/industrial, hotel, retail, and other sectors in the U.S., Europe, and Asia; (ii) non-REIT real estate operating companies; (iii) equities with significant real-estate assets, in the hotels, gaming, and healthcare industries; and (iv) real estate-related companies such as homebuilders, construction firms, and title insurers. The *non-public markets* for U.S. and non-U.S. real estate and other real assets are many times larger than the public markets and include leveraged or unleveraged exposure to: (i) owner-occupied residential homes, second homes, single-family rental properties, and smaller commercial assets; (ii) outright ownership of real estate properties, participation in real estate opportunity funds, core funds, and other types of funds that focus on underperforming assets, or co-investment with partnership sponsors; and (iii) farmland, forestry and timber, and oil and gas properties.

NAREIT (Real Estate Investment Trusts) Index[1]

Time Period	No. Yrs.	Total Return CAGR	Std. Dev.	U.S. Equity	U.S. F.I.	Non-U.S. Equity	Hedge Funds	TIPS
				correlation				
1972–1981	10	11.8%	21.2%	0.74	NA	0.43	NA	−0.39
1972–1991	20	12.9%	18.0%	0.70	NA	0.38	NA	−0.34
1972–2001	30	12.5%	16.9%	0.45	NA	0.20	NA	−0.07
1980–1989	10	15.6%	10.0%	0.51	0.32	0.16	NA	0.00
1980–1999	20	12.4%	15.0%	0.39	0.32	0.18	NA	0.17
1990–1999	10	9.2%	18.9%	0.37	0.30	0.12	0.55	0.17
1997–2006	10	14.5%	17.9%	0.01	−0.03	0.14	0.12	0.20
2000–2006	7	22.3%	12.9%	0.83	−0.39	0.73	0.81	−0.19

The header row also includes a spanning header **Correlation of Annual Returns with** over the U.S. Equity, U.S. F.I., Non-U.S. Equity, Hedge Funds, and TIPS columns.

[1]Data for the NAREIT (Real Estate Investment Trusts) Index are available beginning in 1990.

Information Sources: *Investing in Real Estate,* Fifth Edition, by Andrew James McLean and Gary W. Eldred; Green Street Advisors (*greenstreetadvisors.com*); "The Ground Floor," Real Estate Column in *Barron's* (*barrons.com*); Pension Real Estate Association (*prea.org*); SNL Securities Real Estate (*snl.com*); Fidelity Real Estate Investment (*fidelity.com*); Cohen & Steers Realty Shares (*cohenandsteers.com*); Vanguard REIT Index (*vanguard.com*); National Association of Real Estate Investment Trusts Equity Index (*nareit.com*); NCREIF Commercial Property Index (*ncreif.com*); GPR European Property Index (*gpr.nl*); GPR Asian Property (*gpr.nl*); Topix Real Estate Index (*spglobal.com*); Dow Jones Equity REIT Index (*djindexes.com*); REIS Inc. (*reis.com*); MSCI U.S. Equity REIT Index (*mscibarra*); and Morgan Stanley Real Estate Fund (*morganstanley.com*).

Rationale for Investment	Risks and Concerns
• Due to their relatively straightforward pattern of income generation, several segments of the real-estate asset class possess important defensive characteristics. The opportunity for cash flows to increase over time may also allow real estate to prosper in favorable economic and demographic environments. REIT returns tend to exceed bond returns and at times are competitive with equity returns.	• Real estate may not be a good investment in disinflationary or deflationary global, national, or local economic environments. Although operating income from property tends to lag changes in the economy due to the nature of lease terms, during highly adverse times lessors may cut back on their space commitments, possibly reducing or skipping their real-estate rental payments without declaring default on their other outstanding debt.
• Due partly to the fact that their returns are largely driven by asset-specific supply and demand influences, real-estate assets have low correlations of returns with U.S. and developed non-U.S. equity, and slightly negative correlations of returns with U.S. and non-U.S. bonds, high-yield bonds, and emerging-markets equity; they thus may act as an effective diversifier within a portfolio. The heterogeneity of real estate types and locations also allows diversification within and across real-estate sectors.	• In response to cycles of expansion and contraction, shifting supply-demand conditions, interest rate movements, borrowing and lending practices, capital gluts and capital vacuums, real estate may at times be subject to feast-or-famine prices and returns, with substantial divergences between: (i) property prices and replacement values; and (ii) (for REITs) share prices and per-share net asset values.
• As a tangible, visible, and possibly aesthetically pleasing asset whose supply is reasonably fixed or which may not be readily expandable due to zoning laws, development restrictions, or land management and conservation policies, and whose income-generating ability and/or capital values respond to such forces as employment trends, immigration, new household formation, and long-term inflation, many forms of real estate may function as a hedge against rises in the general price level.	• Many real estate assets are not divisible and are characterized by illiquidity, high transactions costs, lengthy time periods to effect the sale or purchase of a property, and significant price discounts associated with distressed sales.
• Owing in part to the relative infrequency and subjectivity of the appraisal process for many property types, the standard deviation of real-estate returns is generally lower than the standard deviation of equity returns, and for REITs, may be higher than the standard deviation of bond returns.	• Certain real-estate properties and forms of ownership may be expensive and/or complicated to locate, research, value, finance, maintain, manage, lease out, pay taxes on, recapitalize, improve, transfer, and calculate returns and identify sound exit strategies for.
• Because it is a relatively inefficient market, real estate offers the opportunity for skilled participants to identify and capture value through understanding the structure and potential of specific properties, financial and operating expertise, market knowledge, and access to relationships.	• Due to the single-asset, single-region, single-type nature of real estate, its virtual immovability, and shifts in the relative popularity of certain property types and locations, real estate may be subject to a number of special considerations, including: (i) bubble-like asset price movements, possibly followed by sharp price declines; (ii) environmental laws and claims relating to the property itself or its building materials; (iii) depreciation, depletion, or obsolescence; (iv) the quality of funds from operations (FFO); (v) localized tax codes, zoning requirements, legal rights, and customs; (vi) exposure to uninsurable losses stemming from acts of God, terrorism, and other risks; (vii) the somewhat shorter lease terms for hotels and apartments than for other properties; and (viii) the generation of Unrelated Business Taxable Income for tax-exempt U.S. investors.

NAREIT (Real Estate Investment Trusts) Index

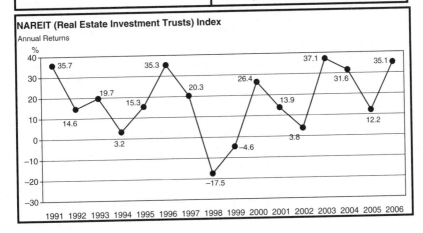

Source: The Author.

(ii) investment underperformance in deflation; (iii) long-term cycles of positive and zero or negative returns; (iv) the need to reinvest dividends to achieve favorable results; and (v) unstable correlations of returns with other asset classes.

Figures 6.7 through 6.23 present 17 of the 18 asset classes' (all except non-U.S. cash/cash equivalents): (i) description; (ii) principal choices open to investors; (iii) chief reasons investors might consider owning them; (iv) risks and concerns associated with owning them; (v) returns, standard deviations, and correlations with other relevant asset classes over selected time periods; (vi) chart of annual returns from 1991 through 2006; and (vii) selected sources of further information.

Investors should base asset-allocation decisions on: (i) how the asset class will perform in various kinds of economic and financial market conditions; (ii) the degree of fluctuation in the asset's returns over time; and (iii) how the asset class behaves relative to the returns and volatility of other asset classes within an overall portfolio. Chapter 7 presents more detailed year-by-year returns and standard deviations data covering the three decades from 1970 through 2006 for the assets described in Figures 6.7 through 6.23.

ASSET CLASS WEIGHTINGS AND USES

Recognizing that long-term average returns are not necessarily accurate predictions of short-term performance, and that short-term returns may deviate substantially from long-term returns, it is nevertheless possible to suggest general guidelines for the weightings of various asset classes during important phases of a complete financial-market cycle. Figure 6.24 shows one version of the relative emphasis investors may place on each of the 18 asset classes at various *cyclical* stages.

The tactical asset class weightings in Figure 6.24 are representative only and do not apply in all financial market circumstances. The cyclical curve displayed in the top part of Figure 6.24 represents general price trends for equity-related assets. During the downward part of the phase shown in the left-hand part of the cycle, defensive and non-equity correlating asset classes are overweighted, with underweighting in U.S., non-U.S., and emerging-markets

Representative Cyclical Tactical Asset Class Weightings

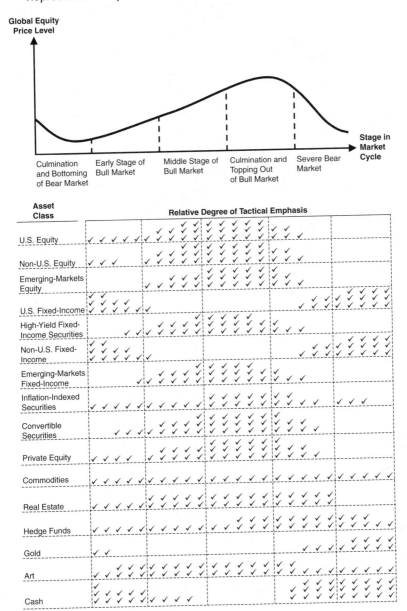

Source: The Author.

equity and equity-like alternative assets. As the equity bear market reaches bottom, begins to turn up, and continues into the early and middle stages of the equity bull market, investors may tactically increase emphasis on all forms of equity and equity-like alternative assets, simultaneously downplaying cash, fixed-income, and fixed-income-like alternative assets.

As the equity market begins to reach a cyclical peak, investors may tactically redirect their portfolio toward defensive asset classes

F I G U R E 6.25

Assets That May Behave Like Other Assets

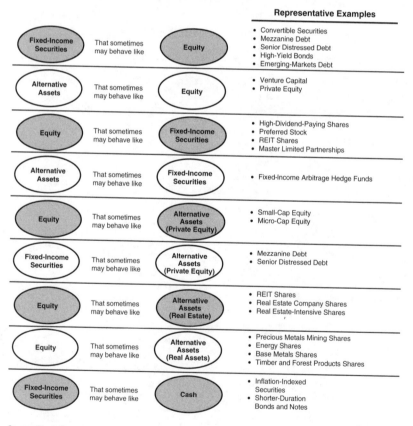

Source: The Author.

such as high-quality fixed-income securities, cash and liquidity instruments, and other types of capital-protection assets and investment strategies. During the trough of an equity bear market, investors can determine the degree and type of allocation to fixed-income instruments based on whether the equity bear market is accompanied by: (i) *rising interest rates* (such as in the U.S. during significant portions of the 1970s), in which case investors should downplay long-duration fixed-income securities and gravitate toward very short-duration instruments; or (ii) *falling interest rates* (such as occurred in Japan during significant portions of the 1990s), in which case, as Figure 6.24 illustrates, investors should emphasize long-duration fixed-income securities and cash instruments.

Certain assets may at times behave like other assets. Figure 6.25 presents nine groupings of these multi-role assets.

The top row of Figure 6.25 lists several types of fixed-income securities that under certain circumstances may display patterns of returns, standard deviations of returns, and correlations of returns that are analogous to those of equity assets. Such fixed-income instruments include convertible securities, mezzanine debt, senior distressed debt, high-yield bonds, and emerging-markets debt. In pursuit of similar flexibility, some investors may employ derivatives and/or various hedging techniques to separate out and recombine the various asset-related return, risk, and correlations factors to which a portfolio may be exposed, thereby disconnecting the factor exposure of a portfolio from the specific selection of assets. While thinking about the roles that specific asset classes can play in a variety of economic and financial market conditions and *asset-allocation strategies*, investors would be wise also to think about, if only for peace of mind and contingency planning purposes, *asset-protection strategies*. Figure 6.26 sets forth a number of possible asset-allocation and asset-protection strategies for different kinds of economic and financial conditions.

During normal economic and financial cycles (in the bottom part of Figure 6.26), asset-allocation strategies are driven primarily by considerations of the investment outlook and investment policy, investor preferences, the characteristics of various asset classes, and other qualitative and quantitative factors. Under such conditions, the systemic elements associated with asset protection are perceived

F I G U R E 6.26

Asset Allocation and Asset Protection Under Varying Circumstances

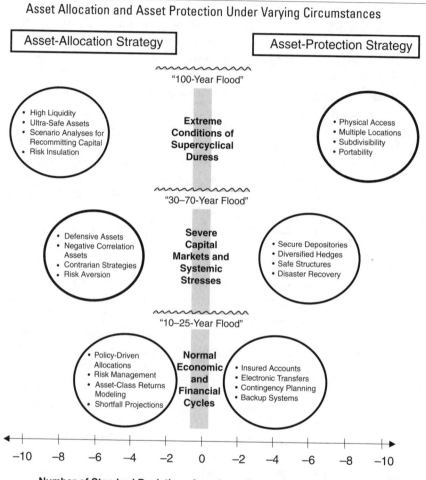

Number of Standard Deviations from Long-Term Average Conditions

Source: The Author.

to function as expected and will generally not be severely tested beyond usual and previously encountered conditions, depicted in Figure 6.26 as a 10- to 25-year flood that might occur between 4 and 10 times in a century.

In anticipation of and during severe and highly unpredictable capital markets and systemic stresses (depicted in the middle part of Figure 6.26), asset-allocation strategies tend to be highly cautious and defensive, emphasizing risk control, risk transfer, negatively correlated assets, and other loss-averting actions. Under such conditions, which might occur as rarely as two to three times per century, asset-protection measures tend to focus on the physical security and financial soundness of asset depositories, diversification of counterparties with whom hedges may have been structured, safe legal and oversight structures, and sound, pretested disaster-recovery procedures and facilities. To prepare for extreme conditions of supercyclical duress (depicted in the top part of Figure 6.26), asset-allocation strategies may contemplate highly remote developments with only a minuscule probability of occurring during the lifetime of an investor. High-liquidity, ultra-safe assets, and risk containment strategies will tend to be emphasized, possibly accompanied by opportunistic plans to recommit capital at seriously dislocated price levels. Under such conditions, which an investor may very well never encounter, asset-protection measures may emphasize physical access to assets at multiple locations, as well as verifiable, subdividable, portable asset types.

CHAPTER 7

ANALYZING ASSETS' RATES OF RETURN

OVERVIEW

Investors would be wise to develop an understanding of the rates of return that generally result from investments in specific asset classes. Despite the fact that past investment performance does not guarantee future results, investors can gain important insights, formulate reasonable expectations, and construct sound and appropriate portfolios through careful study and analysis of assets' rates of return data.

This chapter examines three ways of organizing assets' rates of returns data: (i) by groups of years; (ii) by individual years during the 1970–1979, 1980–1989, 1990–1999, and 2000–2006 time periods; and (iii) by economic environment. Next, the chapter explores the rotating returns leadership among several asset classes during the 1980–2006 period, followed by: (i) a review of U.S. equities industry sector performance from 1990 through 2006; (ii) a historical survey of leading U.S. companies ranked by equity market capitalization at the end of

1925, 1950, 1975, 2000, and the second half 2007; and (iii) a review of the year-by-year price changes of the largest-capitalization U.S. companies from 1991 through the second half of 2007.

Close scrutiny and contemplation of investment returns through time are likely to furnish useful perspective on: (i) prior eras' experiences within and across asset classes; (ii) the best- and worst-performing time periods for specific assets; and (iii) the degree of variability that investment results may display from period to period. Armed with such understanding, investors can maintain balanced views about whether recent years' investment gains or losses are substantially above, below, or in line with previous longer-term experiences. In short, analysis of assets' annual rates of return can help investors distinguish the extraordinary from the normal, and in so doing better manage their hopes and fears.

ORGANIZATION OF RETURNS DATA

Investors can collect and present assets' annual rates of return data in a variety of ways. When looking at such information, investors should think about which organizations constructed the data and how they did so, what time span they cover, and how the methods of organizing these results fit with one another. Figure 7.1 shows three of the methodologies used in this chapter for gathering and displaying assets' annual rates of return data.

Figure 7.1 organizes annual rates of return data *by groups of years* (from 1945 through the present), which allows the investor to gain a sense of the compound-annual investment results that could have been achieved by holding an asset—as represented by its total return performance index—for multiyear time frames. Figure 7.1 also presents data *by individual years* (from 1971 through the present), which lets the investor visually trace specific variations in, and the continuity of, investment results from year to year in sequence; and *by economic environment* (from 1871 through the present), which sheds light on the investment performance of asset classes in phases of economic expansion and contraction of varying length in a multidecade context. The following sections make observations and describe the uses of each of these three methods of organizing assets' returns data.

F I G U R E   7.1

Methods of Organizing Assets' Returns Data

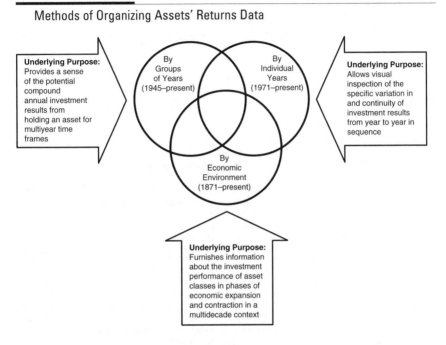

ASSETS' ANNUAL RATES OF RETURN BY GROUPS OF YEARS

By studying assets' annual rates of return *over periods of 10, 20, and 30 years or more*, investors can gain some sense of the historical returns offered by various categories of assets. Table 7.1 contains the compound annual rates of return for 25 asset categories, for recent periods of 10 years, 20 years, 30 years, and modern times (defined here as extending from 1945 through 2006). Single-year rates of return are also shown for these asset categories for 2004, 2005, and 2006.

General Observations and Caveats

Before looking at the interperiod and interasset class returns comparisons in Table 7.1, investors should consider a number of general observations and caveats about these data. First, the returns for modern times and recent 30-, 20-, and 10-year periods represent *compound annual rates of return* for these groups of years and, as

T A B L E 7.1

Assets' Annual Rates of Return by Groups of Years, 1945–2006

Nominal Total Returns in U.S. Dollars Except Where Noted

Index/Source

U.S. Department of Labor Consumer Price Index—All Urban Wage Earners

Equities

U.S. Equities	S&P 500 Index Total Return
U.S. Emerging-Growth Equities	T. Rowe Price New Horizons Fund
U.S. Small-Capitalization Equities	Dimensional Fund Advisors Small Company Fund
EAFE Equities	MSCI Europe, Australasia, and Far East (EAFE) Index
European Equities	MSCI Europe Net Index (Local Currency)
Japanese Equities	MSCI Japan Index
Asian Equities	MSCI Pacific Ex-Japan Gross Index
Emerging-Markets Equities	S&P/IFCI Composite Index[2]

Fixed-Income

Cash	90-Day U.S. Treasury Bills
U.S. Long-Term Treasury Bonds	Ibbotson Associates Long-Term Government Bond Index
U.S. Intermediate-Term Govt. Bonds	Ibbotson Associates Intermediate-Term Bond Index
Corporate Bonds	Ibbotson Associates Long-Term Corporate Bond Index
High-Yield Bonds	Ibbotson Associates High-Yield Corporate Bond Index
Non-U.S. Bonds	Citigroup Non-U.S. 1 + Year Government Bonds Total Return Index
Municipal Bonds	Lehman Brothers 7-Year Municipal Bond Index

Real Estate

Commercial Real Estate	NCREIF Property Index
Real Estate Investment Trusts	NAREIT Real Estate Investment Trusts Index
Residential Housing	National Association of Realtors (Residential Housing)
U.S. Farmland	U.S. Department of Agriculture/NCREIF Farmland Index/Morgan Stanley Research

Commodities and Precious Metals

Collaterized Commodities	Commodity Research Bureau Index All Commodity Futures Total Return Index[3]
Gold	Handy & Harman Spot Gold Price
Silver	Handy & Harman Spot Silver Price

Private Equity, Venture Capital, and Hedge Funds

Private Equity	Cambridge Associates U.S. Private Equity Funds Index
Venture Capital	Cambridge Associates U.S. Venture Funds Index
Hedge Funds	HFRI Fund Weighted Composite Hedge Fund Index

Past performance is not a guarantee of future results.

[1] Modern Times covers the period 1945–2006 for all asset classes, except: emerging-growth (1946–2006); EAFE (1950–2006); commercial real estate (1960–2006); and collateralized commodities (1957–2006).

[2] Emerging-markets equities consist of selected emerging markets for the 1945–1984 period; after 1984, the Standard and Poor's/International Finance Corporation Investable Composite Index is used.

[3] Collateral is considered to be invested in 90-Day U.S. Treasury Bills.

Modern Times (1945–2006)[1]		Recent 30 Years (1977–2006)	Recent 20 Years (1987–2006)	Recent 10 Years (1997–2006)	2004	2005	2006
Annualized Return	Std. Dev.	Annualized Return	Annualized Return	Annualized Return	Total Return	Total Return	Total Return
4.0%	3.5%	4.2%	3.1%	2.4%	3.1%	3.4%	2.6%
11.9%	16.9%	12.5%	11.8%	8.4%	10.9%	4.9%	15.8%
12.8	25.2	14.9	13.7	9.9	19.2	13.2	8.6
14.6	25.3	16.4	13.2	13.5	18.4	5.7	16.2
11.9	25.3	12.2	8.1	7.7	20.3	13.5	26.3
NA	NA	12.2	9.0	7.8	20.9	9.4	33.7
13.0	33.7	9.8	2.8	2.2	15.9	25.5	6.2
NA	NA	11.6	9.8	3.9	29.6	14.8	33.2
13.4	31.7	12.4	15.4	10.5	28.1	35.2	35.1
4.5%	3.0%	6.0%	4.5%	3.6%	1.2%	3.0%	4.8%
5.7	10.2	9.0	8.6	7.8	8.5	7.8	1.2
5.7	6.2	8.0	6.8	5.8	2.2	1.4	3.1
6.0	9.6	9.0	8.6	7.7	8.7	5.9	3.2
7.2	10.8	10.1	8.9	6.5	11.1	2.7	11.9
NA	NA	NA	NA	4.7	12.1	−9.1	7.0
NA	NA	NA	6.2	5.2	3.2	1.7	4.0
8.7%	5.6%	9.8%	8.0%	12.1%	14.5%	20.1%	16.0%
NA	NA	15.7	13.3	14.9	31.6	12.2	35.1
6.9	4.0	6.0	5.2	6.0	8.1	12.2	0.0
9.2	9.1	6.5	8.1	11.4	20.5	33.9	20.6
6.9%	13.1%	6.6%	5.3%	4.7%	12.5%	18.9%	−2.9%
NA	NA	5.3	2.4	5.5	5.5	17.9	23.2
5.6	50.1	3.7	4.5	10.6	14.9	23.2	44.0
NA	NA	NA	14.2%	14.9%	24.4%	27.6%	25.8%
NA	NA	NA	17.5	17.8	15.4	8.0	17.6
NA	NA	NA	NA	10.6	9.0	9.3	12.9

Source: Morgan Stanley Global Wealth Management Asset Allocation Group; the Author; Morgan Stanley Investment Research; MSCI Barra; Frank Russell Companies; Citigroup; National Council of Real Estate Investment Fiduciaries (NCREIF); Dimensional Fund Advisors; Credit Suisse; National Association of Realtors; T. Rowe Price; Standard & Poor's; *The Wall Street Journal*; Lehman Brothers; Goldman Sachs; Thomson Financial; Cambridge Associates; Hedge Funds Research; Ibbotson Associates, Morningstar; DRI; and FactSet.

such, do not display certain individual years' results that may have been considerably higher or considerably lower—including loss years—than the compound annual averages.

Second, in most cases the returns are nominal *total returns*, which means that the asset's annual capital gains or losses are combined with its dividend or interest payments, if applicable. To convert *nominal* returns into *real* returns, investors must *subtract* the rate of price *inflation* from the nominal rate of return, or *add* the rate of price *deflation* to the nominal rate of return. Except where noted, the rates of return in Table 7.1 are expressed in U.S. dollars. This means that if a currency has *appreciated* in value versus the U.S. dollar for the time period shown, the rate of return as expressed in U.S. dollars will be *higher* than the rate of return as expressed in local currency terms. Similarly, if a currency has *depreciated* in value versus the U.S. dollar for the time period shown, the rate of return as expressed in U.S. dollars will be *lower* than the rate of return as expressed in local currency terms.

Third, while historical rates of return may provide rough approximations of the order-of-magnitude returns that investors might expect to earn from investing in these asset classes in the future, these data are by no means a guarantee of future results. To construct an asset allocation that is appropriate to the investor's own investment time horizon, degree of risk tolerance, income needs, liquidity requirements, and other characteristics, the investor must take into account not only the asset's annual rate of return but, equally important, its standard deviation and correlation with other asset classes. To provide broad perspective on the degree of returns variation of asset classes, Table 7.1 shows standard deviations of annual returns for each asset category for the 1945–2006 period. Assets' standard deviations of annual returns for the modern times era (1945–2006) may very well differ from their standard deviations of annual returns for shorter or longer time periods.

Fourth, investors should be aware of the specific construction methodology, the advantages, and the disadvantages of the index or data source selected to represent the investment performance of each asset class. Finally, the quantity and quality of data for some asset classes may not be uniform over time, with significant shortcomings possibly arising in the more distant time periods.

Interperiod and Interasset Class Observations

As a guide to potential uses of "Assets' Annual Rates of Return by Groups of Years" data such as those shown in Table 7.1, several observations are set forth below. First, the annual rate of return generated by ownership of U.S. equities—as embodied in the S&P 500 Composite Index total return—averaged 11.9% per year between 1945 and 2006 (with a 16.9% standard deviation), 8.4% per year from 1997 through 2006, 11.8% per year from 1987 through 2006, and 12.5% per year from 1977 through 2006.

Second, the annual rates of return from ownership of U.S. emerging-growth equities—as measured by the performance of the T. Rowe Price New Horizons Fund—and U.S. small-capitalization equities—as measured by the performance of the Dimensional Fund Advisors Small Company Fund—were considerably higher from 1945 through 2006—at 12.8% per year and 14.6% per year, respectively—than the returns generated by these asset classes from 1997 through 2006, which were 9.9% and 13.5%, respectively.

Third, note the high standard deviations of annual returns during the 1945–2006 time period for: Japanese equities, 33.7%; emerging-markets equities, 31.7%; and silver, 50.1%. By contrast, relatively low standard deviations of returns from 1945 through 2006 were exhibited by: cash, 3.0%; U.S. intermediate-term government bonds, 6.2%; commercial real estate, 5.6%; and residential housing, 4.0%.

Fourth, the returns from 1997 through 2006 sharply diverged from the returns from 1945 through 2006 for: (i) Japanese equities, at 2.2% per year from 1997 through 2006, versus 13.0% per year for modern times; (ii) emerging-markets equities, at 10.5% per year from 1997 through 2006, versus 13.4% per year for modern times; (iii) EAFE equities, at 7.7% per year from 1997 through 2006, versus 11.9% per year for modern times; and (iv) U.S. long-term Treasury bonds, at 7.8% per year from 1997 through 2006, versus 5.7% per year for modern times.

Fifth, the returns from the gold and silver asset classes were significantly greater in 2006, 23.2% and 44.0%, respectively, than they were in 2004, when they were 5.5% and 14.9%, respectively, and than they were in 2005, when they were 17.9% and 23.2%, respectively.

Sixth, during the 1997–2006 period, the returns from holding real estate investment trusts, 14.9% per year, considerably exceeded the returns from holding residential housing, 6.0% per year.

ASSETS' ANNUAL RATES OF RETURN BY INDIVIDUAL YEARS

Careful scrutiny of assets' annual rates of return *on a year-to-year basis* can help investors more deeply understand how asset prices perform over time. Tables 7.2, 7.3, 7.4, and 7.5 contain the year-by-year rates of return from 1970 through 2006 for 44 indices and U.S. inflation, arrayed broadly into asset groups encompassing U.S. equity, non-U.S. equity, U.S. and non-U.S. fixed-income securities, alternative investments, and U.S. cash equivalents.

General Observations and Caveats

Many of the general notes and caveats that were discussed in connection with Table 7.1 also apply to Tables 7.2, 7.3, 7.4, and 7.5. In particular, the percentage annual returns are *nominal total returns expressed in U.S. dollars,* and the investor should be aware of the construction methodology, the advantages, and the disadvantages of the index or data source that is used to represent the investment performance of each type of asset. For the equity indices, the term "gross" denotes total returns inclusive of dividends without any deduction for non-U.S. withholding taxes. The term "net" denotes total returns inclusive of dividends after the deduction of non-U.S. withholding taxes, and "price return" indicates that dividends are not included in the percentage returns data. Finally, the fact that an asset's price index has exhibited a certain type of price performance during a single year or a period of years in the past does not imply that such price behavior will be repeated in the future. In fact, extraordinary price behavior on a one-year or a multiyear basis may in many cases argue for a *reversal* of such behavior, regardless of how strong the case may appear to be for a continuation of prior trends.

Interyear and Interindex Observations for the 2000–2006 Period

Returns data for the entire 2000–2006 period are available for 44 asset categories in Table 7.2. After strong growth in the late 1990s,

U.S. equities in 2000, 2001, and 2002 declined 9.1%, 11.9%, and 22.1%, respectively, as measured by the S&P 500 Index, and 39.3%, 21.1%, and 31.5%, respectively, as measured by the Nasdaq Composite Index.

Mid-capitalization equities, as represented by the Standard & Poor's 400 Mid-Cap Index, outperformed large-capitalization equities, as represented by the Standard & Poor's 500 Index for six consecutive years: 2000 (17.5% to –9.1%), 2001 (–0.6% to –11.9%), 2002 (–14.5% to –22.1%), 2003 (35.6% to 28.7%), 2004 (16.5% to 10.9%), and 2005 (12.6% to 4.9%).

Large-capitalization *value* stocks, as represented by the Russell 1000 Value Index, again outperformed large-capitalization *growth* stocks, as represented by the Russell 1000 Growth Index, for all 7 years from 2000 through 2006, most notably in 2000, when value stocks rose 7.0% while growth stocks declined 22.4%.

In the years from 2000 to 2002, all non-U.S. equity indices declined before rebounding with almost four consecutive years of double-digit returns during the 2003–2006 time period. The MSCI EAFE Net Index increased by 38.6%, 20.3%, 13.5%, and 26.3% from 2003 through 2006, respectively. An investor who invested $1.00 in the MSCI EAFE Net Index on January 1, 2000, would have seen his or her investment grow to a value of $1.36 by the end of 2006. From 2003 through 2006, the MSCI Emerging Global Free Latin America Gross Index produced high positive returns of 73.7%, 39.6%, 50.4%, and 43.5%, respectively. As a result, the value of $1.00 invested on January 1, 2000, grew to $3.47 on December 31, 2006—the highest of any U.S. or non-U.S. equity index.

The Lehman Brothers Aggregate (Taxable) Index produced positive returns for all 7 years with returns exceeding 10% in 2000 (11.6%) and 2002 (10.3%). Emerging markets bonds, as measured by the J.P. Morgan Emerging Markets Bond Index Plus, outperformed, global bonds, as measured by the J.P. Morgan Global Government Bond Index (Traded Unhedged), for five of the seven years shown: 2000, 2003, 2004, 2005, and 2006.

Real estate investment trusts produced the highest returns of any other asset class. An investor who placed $1.00 in the National Association of Real Estate Investment Trusts (NAREIT) Index on January 1, 2000, would have seen his investment grow to $4.08 on

T A B L E 7.2

Assets' Annual Rates of Return, 2000–2006

Value of $1.00 on 12/31/06
(Compounded Annually)

10 Years or Subperiod Shown (2000–2006)				Nominal Total Returns Expressed in U.S. Dollars
Value	CAGR	Std. Dev.	Sharpe Ratio	Asset Class Indices
				U.S. Equity Indices
$1.08	1.1%	17.7%	(0.11)	S&P 500 Index
$1.96	10.1%	15.6%	0.45	S&P 400 Mid-Cap Index
$2.15	11.5%	16.3%	0.52	S&P 600 Small-Cap Index
$0.59	−7.2%	30.5%	(0.34)	NASDAQ Composite (Price Return) Index
$1.70	7.9%	21.3%	0.23	Russell 2000 Index (Smaller Cap of 3000 Index)
$0.70	−4.9%	21.1%	(0.38)	Russell 1000 Growth Index
$1.69	7.8%	15.8%	0.30	Russell 1000 Value Index
$0.98	−0.2%	26.5%	(0.13)	Russell 2000 Growth Index
$2.86	16.2%	17.8%	0.73	Russell 2000 Value Index
$1.14	2.0%	18.4%	(0.06)	Wilshire 5000 Index
				Non-U.S. Equity Indices
$1.20	2.6%	20.8%	(0.02)	MSCI World Free Gross Index
$1.42	5.1%	23.9%	0.08	MSCI World ex-U.S. Gross Index
$1.00	0.0%	18.2%	(0.17)	MSCI U.S. Net Index
$1.36	4.4%	23.7%	0.06	MSCI EAFE Net Index
$1.47	5.6%	24.2%	0.10	MSCI Europe Free Net Index
$0.96	−0.6%	25.7%	(0.15)	MSCI Japan Net Index
$1.54	6.4%	27.7%	0.12	MSCI Far East Free ex-Japan Gross Index
$1.14	1.9%	25.0%	(0.05)	MSCI Pacific (Developed Asia) Net Index
$3.47	19.5%	36.5%	0.45	MSCI Emerging Global Free Latin America Gross Index
$2.24	12.2%	29.8%	0.30	MSCI Emerging Markets Free Gross Index
				U.S. and Non-U.S. Fixed Income Indices
$1.55	6.5%	3.6%	0.94	Lehman Brothers Aggregate (Taxable) Index[1]
$1.46	5.5%	3.1%	0.76	Lehman Brothers 7-Year Municipal Bond Index[2]
$1.71	8.0%	10.3%	0.47	High Yield (Credit Suisse Upper/Middle Tier) Index
$1.50	6.0%	5.9%	0.48	10-Year Treasury Note Index
$1.35	4.4%	10.5%	0.12	Non-U.S. (J.P. Morgan Non-US Bond) Index
$1.51	6.1%	9.0%	0.33	Global (J.P. Morgan Global Government Bond Traded Unhedged) Index
$2.33	12.9%	8.7%	1.12	Emerging Markets Bond Index (J.P. Morgan EMBI+)[3]
$1.25	3.2%	13.4%	0.01	Merrill Lynch All Convertible All Quality Bond Index

2000	2001	2002	2003	2004	2005	2006
−9.1%	−11.9%	−22.1%	28.7%	10.9%	4.9%	15.8%
17.5%	−0.6%	−14.5%	35.6%	16.5%	12.6%	10.3%
11.8%	6.6%	−14.6%	38.8%	22.6%	7.7%	15.1%
−39.3%	−21.1%	−31.5%	50.0%	8.6%	1.4%	9.5%
−3.0%	2.5%	−20.5%	47.3%	18.3%	4.6%	18.4%
−22.4%	−20.4%	−27.9%	29.7%	6.3%	5.3%	9.1%
7.0%	−5.6%	−15.5%	30.0%	16.5%	7.1%	22.3%
−22.4%	−9.2%	−30.3%	48.5%	14.3%	4.2%	13.4%
22.8%	14.0%	−11.4%	46.0%	22.3%	4.7%	23.5%
−10.9%	−11.0%	−20.9%	31.6%	12.5%	6.4%	15.8%
−12.9%	−16.5%	−19.5%	33.8%	15.3%	10.0%	20.7%
−13.2%	−21.2%	−15.5%	40.0%	20.8%	15.0%	26.2%
−12.8%	−12.4%	−23.1%	28.4%	10.1%	5.1%	14.7%
−14.2%	−21.4%	−15.9%	38.6%	20.3%	13.5%	26.3%
−8.4%	−19.9%	−18.4%	38.5%	20.9%	9.4%	33.7%
−28.2%	−29.4%	−10.3%	35.9%	15.9%	25.5%	6.2%
−36.8%	−2.1%	−9.2%	45.0%	17.6%	21.8%	32.2%
−25.8%	−25.4%	−9.3%	38.5%	19.0%	22.6%	12.2%
−14.0%	−0.4%	−22.5%	73.7%	39.6%	50.4%	43.5%
−30.6%	−2.4%	−6.0%	56.3%	26.0%	34.5%	32.6%
11.6%	8.4%	10.3%	4.1%	4.3%	2.4%	4.3%
9.1%	5.2%	10.4%	5.4%	3.2%	1.7%	4.0%
−4.2%	5.8%	3.1%	27.9%	12.0%	2.3%	12.0%
14.5%	4.0%	14.7%	1.3%	4.9%	2.0%	1.4%
−2.5%	−3.6%	12.7%	18.8%	12.1%	−10.2%	6.8%
2.3%	−0.8%	19.4%	14.5%	10.1%	−6.5%	5.9%
15.7%	−0.8%	14.2%	28.8%	11.8%	11.9%	10.5%
−10.0%	−4.4%	−8.6%	27.2%	9.6%	1.0%	12.8%

T A B L E   7.2 (Continued)

Assets' Annual Rates of Return, 2000–2006

Value of $1.00 on 12/31/06
(Compounded Annually)

10 Years or Subperiod Shown (2000–2006)				*Nominal Total Returns Expressed in U.S. Dollars*
Value	CAGR	Std. Dev.	Sharpe Ratio	Asset Class Indices
				Alternative Investments Indices
$4.08	22.3%	12.9%	1.48	NAREIT (Real Estate Investment Trusts) Index
$2.25 ·	12.3%	5.0%	1.82	NCREIF Property (Commercial Real Estate) Index
$1.58	6.8%	3.9%	0.93	National Association of Realtors (Residential Housing) Index
$2.22	12.0%	12.9%	0.69	NCREIF Farmland (U.S. Farmland) Index
$1.99	10.4%	17.4%	0.42	Cambridge Associates U.S. Private Equity Index
$0.78	−3.4%	25.8%	(0.25)	Cambridge Associates U.S. Venture Capital Index
$1.74	8.2%	17.6%	0.29	Venture Economics All Private Equity Fund Index
$1.74	8.2%	6.7%	0.77	HFRI Fund Weighted Composite Hedge Fund Index
$1.53	6.3%	3.9%	0.80	HFRI Fund of Funds Index
$1.62	7.1%	13.2%	0.30	Commodity Research Bureau Total Return Index
$1.45	5.4%	4.2%	0.54	Barclay Commodity Trading Advisors (CTA) Index
$2.20	11.9%	12.2%	0.72	Handy & Harman Spot Gold Price Index
$2.38	13.2%	20.2%	0.50	Handy & Harman Spot Silver Price Index
$1.67	7.6%	4.6%	0.98	Lehman Brothers TIPS Index/Bridgewater Index[4]
$2.14	11.5%	10.2%	0.82	Mei Moses Fine Art Index
				U.S. Cash Equivalent Indices
$1.24	3.1%	1.9%	0.00	Citigroup U.S. Treasury Bill (90-Day) Index
$1.20	2.7%	0.7%	(0.64)	Inflation (CPI-U)

All indices are expressed in total return terms unless noted in the description. "Gross" denotes total returns inclusive of gross dividends; "Net" denotes total returns inclusive of dividends net of foreign withholding taxes; and "Price Return" indicates that dividends are not included in the percentage returns data; "Free" denotes that portion of the relevant underlying market whose securities are freely tradable by international investors.

[1]The Lehman Brothers Aggregate Index represents securities that are U.S. domestic, taxable, and dollar denominated, representing the U.S. investment-grade, fixed-rate bond market. As of June 2007, components of the index included approximately: 38% Mortgage-Backed Securities; 23% U.S. Treasury; 19% Corporate; 14% Government Related; 5% Commercial Mortgage-Backed Securities; and 1% Asset-Backed Securities.

[2]Pre-1990 Municipal Bond data are furnished courtesy of Morgan Stanley Investment Management.

2000	2001	2002	2003	2004	2005	2006
26.4%	13.9%	3.8%	37.1%	31.6%	12.2%	35.1%
12.3%	7.3%	6.8%	9.0%	14.5%	20.1%	16.6%
4.5%	9.6%	6.4%	7.3%	8.1%	12.2%	−0.2%
4.8%	0.9%	−1.8%	9.7%	20.5%	33.9%	20.6%
0.1%	−11.9%	−7.9%	23.2%	24.0%	27.6%	25.8%
29.9%	−38.9%	−31.2%	−1.8%	15.2%	7.9%	17.6%
22.1%	−20.4%	−11.0%	18.3%	16.4%	22.6%	19.0%
5.0%	4.6%	−1.5%	19.6%	9.0%	9.3%	12.9%
4.1%	2.8%	1.0%	11.6%	6.9%	7.5%	10.4%
14.3%	−17.2%	18.4%	11.3%	12.5%	18.9%	−2.9%
7.9%	0.8%	12.4%	8.7%	3.3%	1.7%	3.7%
−6.7%	2.1%	24.7%	20.9%	5.5%	17.9%	23.2%
−14.8%	1.1%	1.6%	26.1%	14.9%	30.2%	44.0%
13.2%	7.9%	11.8%	9.4%	8.5%	2.8%	0.4%
16.2%	0.8%	−4.9%	21.7%	13.0%	14.5%	22.0%
6.0%	4.1%	1.7%	1.1%	1.2%	3.0%	4.8%
3.4%	1.8%	2.7%	1.8%	3.1%	3.4%	2.6%

[3]EMBI+ used 1994 to present; EMBI for prior periods.

[4]The synthetically constructed Bridgewater Strategic Benchmark U.S. TIPS 8-Year Duration Index is used for the January 1970 through February 1997 time period; the Lehman Brothers TIPS Index is used after February 1997.

Source: Morgan Stanley Investment Management; Morgan Stanley Global Wealth Management Asset Allocation Group; the Author.

December 31, 2006. Venture capital, as represented by the Cambridge Associates U.S. Venture Capital Index, was the only alternative investments asset class to produce three consecutive years of negative returns: –38.9% in 2001, –31.2% in 2002, and –1.8% in 2003. The Cambridge Associates U.S. Private Equity Index and the Venture Economics All Private Equity Index both experienced two consecutive years of negative returns: –11.9% and –20.4% in 2001, respectively, and –7.9% and –11.0% in 2002, respectively, before rebounding with four years of strong positive returns. After declining 14.8% in 2000, the Handy and Harman Spot Silver Price Index had four consecutive years of double-digit returns from 2003 through 2006: 26.1%, 14.9%, 30.2%, and 44.0%, respectively.

The Citigroup 90-Day U.S. Treasury Bill Index outperformed inflation, as measured by the Consumer Price Index, in only three of the seven years between 2000 and 2006: 6.0% versus 3.4% in 2000, 4.1% versus 1.8% in 2001, and 4.8% versus 2.6% in 2006.

Interyear and Interindex Observations for the 1990–1999 Period

Returns data for the entire 1990–1999 period are available for 44 asset categories in Table 7.3. One of the most striking series of returns phenomena in Table 7.3 is the price behavior of the Standard & Poor's 500 Index and the Nasdaq Composite Index from 1995 through 1999, when the S&P 500 returned 37.4%, 23.1%, 33.4%, 28.6%, and 21.0%, respectively, and the Nasdaq Composite advanced 39.9%, 22.7%, 21.6%, 39.6%, and 85.6%, respectively. Prior to this extraordinary five-year period of 20%-plus returns, the S&P 500 and the Nasdaq Composite rarely rose by 20% or more for three years in a row, much less for four years or five years.

The year 1997 was the fourth time during the 1990–1999 period (the other years being 1992, 1993, and 1995) that large-capitalization *value* stocks, as represented by the Russell 1000 Value Index, outperformed large-capitalization *growth* stocks, as represented by the Russell 1000 Growth Index.

From 1993 through 1999, European equities, as represented by the Morgan Stanley Capital International (MSCI) Europe Free Net Index, sustained high positive returns, rising 29.3%, 2.3%, 21.6%, 21.1%, 23.8%, 28.5%, and 15.9%, respectively. An investor who invested $1.00 in the MSCI Europe Free Net Index on January 1, 1990, would have seen his or her investment grow to a value of $3.72 by the end of 1999. For an equivalent monetary investment during an equivalent time period, this compares with an ending value of $5.33 for the S&P 500 Index, $0.92 for the MSCI Japan Net Index, $2.67 for the MSCI Far East Free ex-Japan Gross Index, $1.03 for the MSCI Pacific (Developed Asia) Net Index, $5.74 for the MSCI Emerging Latin American Gross Index, and $2.85 for the MSCI Emerging Markets Free Gross Index.

Equity indices in Japan, non-Japan Asia, developed Asia, Latin America, and emerging markets all exhibited negative investment returns for three or more years during the 1990–1999 period. The MSCI Japan Net Index lost 36.1% in 1990, 21.5% in 1992, 15.5% in 1996, and 23.7% in 1997; the MSCI Far East Free ex-Japan Gross Index generated negative returns of 19.0% in 1994, 45.5% in 1997, and 4.8% in 1998; the MSCI Pacific (Developed Asia) Net Index declined 34.4% in 1990, 18.4% in 1992, 8.6% in 1996, and 25.5% in 1997; the MSCI Emerging Global Free Latin America Gross Index had negative returns of 7.8% in 1990, 15.8% in 1995, and 35.3% in 1998; and the MSCI Emerging Markets Free Gross Index declined 10.6% in 1990, 7.3% in 1994, 5.2% in 1995, 11.6% in 1997, and 25.3% in 1998.

In the fixed-income arena, the Lehman Brothers Aggregate (Taxable) Index underperformed the Credit Suisse Upper/Middle Tier High Yield Index on a total return basis from 1990 through 1999 in 7 of the 10 years. An investor who placed $1.00 in the Lehman Brothers Aggregate Bond Index on January 1, 1990, would have accumulated a total value of $2.10 as of December 31, 1999, compared to a total value of $2.96 in the Credit Suisse Upper/Middle Tier High Yield Index over the same time period. In part due to total returns of 32.4% in 1991, 21.4% in 1992, 18.1% in 1993, 24.7% in 1995, 15.9% in 1996, 19.6% in 1997, and 39.6% in 1999, a 10-year investor in the Merrill Lynch All Convertible All Quality *Bond* Index would have outperformed all of the other fixed-income indices in Table 7.3 (and, for that matter, he or she would have nearly doubled the performance generated by the MSCI Emerging Markets Free Gross *Equities* Index). An investment of $1.00 in the Merrill Lynch All Convertible All Quality Bond Index on January 1, 1990, would have been worth $4.36 on December 31, 1999.

T A B L E 7.3

Assets' Annual Rates of Return, 1990–1999

Value of $1.00 on 12/31/99
(Compounded Annually)

10 Years or Subperiod Shown (1990–1999)				Nominal Total Returns Expressed in U.S. Dollars
Value	CAGR	Std. Dev.	Sharpe Ratio	Asset Class Indices
				U.S. Equity Indices
$5.33	18.2%	14.1%	0.93	S&P 500 Index
$4.94	17.3%	16.6%	0.74	S&P 400 Mid-Cap Index
$3.17	12.2%	20.2%	0.35	S&P 600 Small-Cap Index
$8.95	24.5%	29.6%	0.66	NASDAQ Composite (Price Return) Index
$3.52	13.4%	18.4%	0.45	Russell 2000 Index (Smaller Cap of 3000 Index)
$6.35	20.3%	17.0%	0.90	Russell 1000 Growth Index
$4.25	15.6%	14.8%	0.71	Russell 1000 Value Index
$3.55	13.5%	21.0%	0.40	Russell 2000 Growth Index
$3.23	12.4%	20.5%	0.36	Russell 2000 Value Index
$5.02	17.5%	14.3%	0.87	Wilshire 5000 Index
				Non-U.S. Equity Indices
$3.06	11.8%	13.9%	0.49	MSCI World Free Gross Index
$2.64	11.4%	13.5%	0.47	MSCI World ex-U.S. Gross Index
$5.28	18.1%	14.4%	0.90	MSCI U.S. Net Index
$1.97	7.0%	16.9%	0.11	MSCI EAFE Net Index
$3.72	14.0%	12.7%	0.71	MSCI Europe Free Net Index
$0.92	−0.9%	28.9%	(0.21)	MSCI Japan Net Index
$2.67	11.5%	44.0%	0.15	MSCI Far East Free ex-Japan Gross Index
$1.03	0.3%	27.9%	(0.17)	MSCI Pacific (Developed Asia) Net Index
$5.74	19.1%	51.8%	0.27	MSCI Emerging Global Free Latin America Gross Index
$2.85	11.0%	36.8%	0.16	MSCI Emerging Markets Free Gross Index
				U.S. and Non-U.S. Fixed Income Indices
$2.10	7.7%	6.6%	0.40	Lehman Brothers Aggregate (Taxable) Index[1]
$1.89	6.6%	5.2%	0.30	Lehman Brothers 7-Year Municipal Bond Index[2]
$2.96	11.5%	14.0%	0.45	High Yield (Credit Suisse Upper/Middle Tier) Index
$1.96	6.9%	10.4%	0.18	10-Year Treasury Note Index
$2.27	8.5%	9.3%	0.37	Non-U.S. (J.P. Morgan Non-US Bond) Index
$2.06	7.5%	7.7%	0.31	Global (J.P. Morgan Global Government Bond Traded Unhedged) Index
$3.74	15.8%	23.1%	0.46	Emerging Markets Bond Index (J.P. Morgan EMBI+)[3]
$4.36	15.9%	14.9%	0.72	Merrill Lynch All Convertible All Quality Bond Index

1990	1991	1992	1993	1994	1995	1996	1997	1998	1999
−3.1%	30.5%	7.7%	10.0%	1.3%	37.4%	23.1%	33.4%	28.6%	21.0%
−5.1%	50.1%	11.9%	13.9%	−3.6%	30.9%	19.2%	32.3%	19.1%	14.7%
−25.4%	45.9%	19.4%	17.6%	−5.7%	30.0%	21.3%	25.6%	−1.3%	12.4%
−17.8%	56.8%	15.5%	14.8%	−3.2%	39.9%	22.7%	21.6%	39.6%	85.6%
−19.5%	46.0%	18.4%	18.9%	−1.8%	28.5%	16.5%	22.4%	−2.6%	21.3%
−0.3%	41.3%	5.0%	2.9%	2.6%	37.2%	23.1%	30.5%	38.7%	33.2%
−8.1%	24.6%	13.6%	18.1%	−2.0%	38.4%	21.6%	35.2%	15.6%	7.4%
−17.4%	51.2%	7.8%	13.4%	−2.4%	31.0%	11.3%	13.0%	1.2%	43.1%
−21.8%	41.7%	29.1%	23.8%	−1.5%	25.8%	21.4%	31.8%	−6.5%	−1.5%
−6.2%	33.4%	9.2%	11.4%	−0.1%	36.5%	22.4%	31.0%	22.9%	22.9%
−16.5%	19.1%	−4.6%	23.2%	5.1%	20.7%	13.5%	16.2%	24.8%	25.2%
	12.4%	−11.9%	32.6%	7.3%	11.8%	6.9%	2.6%	19.1%	28.3%
−3.2%	30.1%	6.4%	9.1%	1.1%	37.1%	23.2%	33.4%	30.1%	21.9%
−23.5%	12.1%	−12.2%	32.6%	7.8%	11.2%	6.0%	1.8%	20.0%	27.0%
−3.9%	13.1%	−4.7%	29.3%	2.3%	21.6%	21.1%	23.8%	28.5%	15.9%
−36.1%	8.9%	−21.5%	25.5%	21.4%	0.7%	−15.5%	−23.7%	5.1%	61.5%
	31.0%	21.8%	103.4%	−19.0%	8.8%	11.1%	−45.5%	−4.8%	62.1%
−34.4%	11.3%	−18.4%	35.7%	12.8%	2.8%	−8.6%	−25.5%	2.4%	57.6%
−7.8%	146.2%	17.0%	52.3%	0.6%	−15.8%	18.9%	31.7%	−35.3%	65.5%
−10.6%	59.9%	11.4%	74.8%	−7.3%	−5.2%	6.0%	−11.6%	−25.3%	66.4%
9.0%	16.0%	7.4%	9.8%	−2.9%	18.5%	3.6%	9.7%	8.7%	−0.8%
7.4%	11.7%	8.1%	10.4%	−2.8%	14.1%	4.4%	7.7%	6.2%	−0.1%
−6.4%	43.8%	16.6%	18.9%	−0.4%	17.8%	13.0%	13.0%	1.9%	3.9%
6.8%	17.2%	6.5%	11.8%	−7.9%	23.7%	0.1%	11.3%	12.9%	−8.4%
15.6%	15.9%	1.6%	14.5%	4.9%	21.1%	5.3%	−3.8%	18.3%	−4.5%
8.6%	15.5%	4.6%	12.3%	1.3%	19.3%	4.4%	1.4%	15.3%	−5.1%
	38.8%	6.9%	44.2%	−18.9%	26.8%	39.3%	13.0%	−14.4%	26.0%
−7.0%	32.4%	21.4%	18.1%	−6.0%	24.7%	15.9%	19.6%	8.9%	39.6%

T A B L E 7.3 (Continued)

Assets' Annual Rates of Return, 1990–1999

Value of $1.00 on 12/31/99
(Compounded Annually)

10 Years or Subperiod Shown (1990–1999)				Nominal Total Returns Expressed in U.S. Dollars
Value	CAGR	Std. Dev.	Sharpe Ratio	Asset Class Indices
				Alternative Investments Indices
$2.40	9.2%	18.9%	0.22	NAREIT (Real Estate Investment Trusts) Index
$1.74	5.7%	7.4%	0.09	NCREIF Property (Commercial Real Estate) Index
$1.49	4.0%	2.7%	(0.38)	National Association of Realtors (Residential Housing) Index
$2.13	7.9%	1.1%	2.53	NCREIF Farmland (U.S. Farmland) Index
$5.66	18.9%	9.4%	1.47	Cambridge Associates U.S. Private Equity Index
$27.14	39.1%	78.8%	0.43	Cambridge Associates U.S. Venture Capital Index
$13.41	29.6%	43.7%	0.56	Venture Economics All Private Equity Fund Index
$5.35	18.3%	11.3%	1.17	HFRI Fund Weighted Composite Hedge Fund Index
$3.27	12.6%	10.5%	0.71	HFRI Fund of Funds Index
$1.08	0.7%	9.7%	(0.45)	Commodity Research Bureau Total Return Index
$1.98	7.1%	7.2%	0.28	Barclay Commodity Trading Advisors (CTA) Index
$0.72	− 3.2%	10.0%	(0.83)	Handy & Harman Spot Gold Price Index
$1.04	0.4%	18.1%	(0.26)	Handy & Harman Spot Silver Price Index
$1.87	6.4%	3.4%	0.40	Lehman Brothers TIPS Index/Bridgewater Index[4]
$1.11	1.0%	20.0%	(0.20)	Mei Moses Fine Art Index
				U.S. Cash Equivalent Indices
$1.64	5.1%	1.3%	0.00	Citigroup U.S. Treasury Bill (90-Day) Index
$1.33	2.9%	1.2%	(1.74)	Inflation (CPI-U)

All indices are expressed in total return terms unless noted in the description. "Gross" denotes total returns inclusive of gross dividends; "Net" denotes total returns inclusive of dividends net of foreign withholding taxes; and "Price Return" indicates that dividends are not included in the percentage returns data; "Free" denotes that portion of the relevant underlying market whose securities are freely tradable by international investors.

[1]The Lehman Brothers Aggregate Index represents securities that are U.S. domestic, taxable, and dollar denominated, representing the U.S. investment-grade, fixed-rate bond market. As of June 2007, components of the index included approximately: 38% Mortgage-Backed Securities; 23% U.S. Treasury; 19% Corporate; 14% Government Related; 5% Commercial Mortgage-Backed Securities; and 1% Asset-Backed Securities.

[2]Pre-1990 Municipal Bond data are furnished courtesy of Morgan Stanley Investment Management.

1990	1991	1992	1993	1994	1995	1996	1997	1998	1999
−15.4%	35.7%	14.6%	19.7%	3.2%	15.3%	35.3%	20.3%	−17.5%	−4.6%
2.3%	−5.6%	−4.3%	1.4%	6.4%	7.5%	10.3%	13.9%	16.3%	11.4%
−1.1%	9.4%	2.4%	4.9%	2.5%	4.2%	4.7%	6.0%	3.7%	4.0%
8.2%	8.9%	6.3%	8.2%	8.7%	8.9%	9.0%	7.7%	7.2%	5.9%
4.7%	9.3%	14.9%	24.8%	11.5%	22.7%	26.8%	29.9%	15.4%	32.8%
2.3%	21.0%	13.6%	19.8%	18.1%	47.8%	42.3%	37.3%	27.5%	271.0%
−5.0%	22.4%	14.0%	28.5%	7.4%	44.0%	33.6%	28.5%	17.5%	152.4%
5.8%	32.2%	21.2%	30.9%	4.1%	21.5%	21.1%	16.8%	2.6%	31.3%
17.5%	14.5%	12.3%	26.3%	−3.5%	11.1%	14.4%	16.2%	−5.1%	26.5%
−4.0%	−4.0%	−3.2%	6.1%	10.2%	8.9%	12.0%	4.4%	−20.5%	2.1%
21.0%	3.7%	−0.9%	10.4%	−0.7%	13.6%	9.1%	10.9%	7.0%	−1.2%
−2.5%	−10.1%	−5.6%	17.5%	−2.4%	1.2%	−4.6%	−22.2%	0.6%	0.5%
−19.3%	−7.9%	−4.7%	38.4%	−4.1%	4.9%	−7.4%	25.8%	−15.1%	6.9%
10.8%	7.8%	7.3%	9.2%	3.2%	11.2%	6.9%	2.1%	3.9%	2.4%
9.5%	−36.2%	17.1%	−8.1%	−9.6%	32.5%	8.5%	−14.6%	18.6%	11.8%
7.9%	5.8%	3.6%	3.1%	4.2%	5.8%	5.3%	5.3%	5.1%	4.7%
6.1%	3.0%	3.0%	2.8%	2.6%	2.6%	3.2%	1.7%	1.6%	2.7%

[3]EMBI+ used 1994 to present; EMBI for prior periods.

[4]The synthetically constructed Bridgewater Strategic Benchmark U.S. TIPS 8-Year Duration Index is used for the January 1970 through February 1997 time period; the Lehman Brothers TIPS Index is used after February 1997.

Source: Morgan Stanley Investment Management; Morgan Stanley Global Wealth Management Asset Allocation Group; the Author.

During the 1990–1999 decade, the National Association of Real Estate Investment Trusts (NAREIT) Index outperformed the NCREIF Commercial Real Estate Property Index, the National Association of Realtors Residential Housing Index, and the NCREIF Farmland Index. In the latter half of the decade, the NAREIT Index generated a return of 35.3% in 1996, followed by 20.3% in 1997, succeeded by back-to-back *loss* years, 17.5% in 1998 and 4.6% in 1999. The Venture Economics All Private Equity Funds Index and the Cambridge Associates U.S. Venture Funds Index exhibited strong investment performance in the 1990–1999 period. Investors who placed $1.00 on January 1, 1990, into the Cambridge Associates U.S. Private Equity Index would have seen their investment increase in value to $5.66 as of December 31, 1999.

The HFRI Fund Weighted Composite Hedge Fund Index witnessed positive returns exceeding 20% in 6 of the 10 years from 1990–1999, rising 32.2% in 1991, 21.2% in 1992, 30.9% in 1993, 21.5% in 1995, 21.1% in 1996, and 31.3% in 1999. The HFRI Fund of Funds Index generated returns greater than 20% in 2 of the 10 years from 1990–1999, increasing by 26.3% in 1993 and 26.5% in 1999, with negative returns in two years, –3.5% in 1994 and –5.1% in 1998. Also within the alternative investments category, the Handy & Harmon Spot Gold Price Index declined in 6 of the 10 years from 1990 through 1999, generating negative returns of 2.5% in 1990, 10.1% in 1991, 5.6% in 1992, 2.4% in 1994, 4.6% in 1996, and 22.2% in 1997. As a consequence, $1.00 placed in this index on January 1, 1990, would have had the lowest value on December 31, 1999, of any of the asset classes shown in Table 7.3—just $0.72.

The returns from investing in the Citigroup U.S. Treasury Bill (90-Day) Index exceeded the U.S. inflation rate as measured by the Consumer Price Index (CPI) in each of the years from 1990 through 2006. A $1.00 investment in 90-Day U.S. Treasury bills on January 1, 1990, would have amounted to $1.64 on December 30, 1999, surpassing the $1.33 earned from investing in a basket of goods and services as tracked by the CPI, as well as the returns from investing in the indices representing several other asset categories, including gold, silver, fine art, commodities, residential housing, developed Asia equities, and Japanese equities.

Interyear and Interindex Observations for the 1980–1989 Decade

Several important observations can be gleaned from the decade from 1980 through 1989, which turned out to be a period of transition from the high-inflation, high-interest rate environment of the late 1970s to the generally more equity-friendly investment environment of the 1990s. Table 7.4 presents returns data for 24 asset categories during the entire 10 years. The Standard & Poor's 400 Mid-Cap Index outperformed the S&P 500 Index five times, in 1982, 1983, 1985, 1988, and 1989. In five years, large-capitalization *growth* stocks, as represented by the Russell 1000 Growth Index, outperformed large-capitalization *value* stocks, as represented by the Russell 1000 Value Index: in 1980 (39.6% to 24.4%), 1982 (20.5% to 20.0%), 1985 (32.9% to 31.5%), 1987 (5.3% to 0.5%), and 1989 (35.9% to 25.2%). In seven years, mid- and small-capitalization *value* stocks (the Russell 2000 Value Index) outperformed mid- and small-capitalization *growth* stocks (the Russell 2000 Growth Index): in 1981 (14.9% to –9.2%), 1982 (28.5% to 21.0%), 1983 (38.6% to 20.1%), 1984 (2.3% to –15.8%), 1986 (7.4% to 3.6%), 1987 (–7.1% to –10.5%), and 1988 (29.5% to 20.4%).

From 1980 to 1989, the MSCI EAFE Net Index outperformed the S&P 500 Index in seven years: 1981 (–2.3% to –4.9%), 1983 (23.7% to 22.6%), 1984 (7.4% to 6.3%), 1985 (56.2% to 31.7%), 1986 (69.4% to 18.7%), 1987 (24.6% to 5.3%), and 1988 (28.3% to 16.6%). The MSCI Japan Net Index experienced six consecutive years of high returns from 1983 through 1988, rising by 24.5%, 16.9%, 43.1%, 99.4%, 43.0%, and 35.4%, respectively, before eking out a very small gain of 1.7% in 1989.

The Lehman Brothers Aggregate (Taxable) Index generated double-digit positive returns in 1982 (32.6%), 1984 (15.2%), 1985 (22.1%), 1986 (15.3%), and 1989 (14.5%). From 1980 through 1989, real estate investment trusts outperformed commercial real estate eight times: in 1980 (24.4% to 18.1%), 1982 (21.6% to 9.4%), 1983 (30.6% to 13.1%), 1984 (20.9% to 13.8%), 1985 (19.1% to 11.2%), 1986 (19.2% to 8.3%), 1988 (13.5% to 9.6%), and 1989 (8.8% to 7.8%). U.S. farmland exhibited negative returns in five years: –3.1% in 1982, –4.9% in 1984, –4.1% in 1985, –16.3% in 1986, and –18.4% in 1987. Venture Capital, as measured by the Cambridge Associates U.S.

T A B L E 7.4

Assets' Annual Rates of Return, 1980–1989

**Value of $1.00 on 12/31/89
(Compounded Annually)**

10 Years or Subperiod Shown (1980–1989)				Nominal Total Returns Expressed in U.S. Dollars
Value	CAGR	Std. Dev.	Sharpe Ratio	Asset Class Indices
				U.S. Equity Indices
$5.04	17.6%	12.7%	0.66	S&P 500 Index
$3.96	18.8%	14.0%	0.68	S&P 400 Mid-Cap Index
				S&P 600 Small-Cap Index
$3.01	11.7%	15.3%	0.16	NASDAQ Composite (Price Return) Index
$3.89	14.5%	16.8%	0.32	Russell 2000 Index (Smaller Cap of 3000 Index)
$4.19	15.4%	16.4%	0.38	Russell 1000 Growth Index
$5.23	18.0%	10.9%	0.81	Russell 1000 Value Index
$2.98	11.5%	21.2%	0.11	Russell 2000 Growth Index
$4.99	17.4%	14.6%	0.56	Russell 2000 Value Index
$4.66	16.6%	13.2%	0.56	Wilshire 5000 Index
				Non-U.S. Equity Indices
				MSCI World Free Gross Index
				MSCI World ex-U.S. Gross Index
$3.33	14.3%	12.4%	0.41	MSCI U.S. Net Index
$7.30	22.0%	23.4%	0.55	MSCI EAFE Net Index
$4.92	17.3%	26.1%	0.31	MSCI Europe Free Net Index
$12.14	28.4%	28.6%	0.67	MSCI Japan Net Index
				MSCI Far East Free ex-Japan Gross Index
$10.12	26.0%	28.1%	0.60	MSCI Pacific (Developed Asia) Net Index
				MSCI Emerging Global Free Latin America Gross Index
				MSCI Emerging Markets Free Gross Index
				U.S. and Non-U.S. Fixed Income Indices
$3.23	12.4%	9.3%	0.35	Lehman Brothers Aggregate (Taxable) Index[1]
$2.21	8.2%	20.1%	(0.05)	Lehman Brothers 7-Year Municipal Bond Index[2]
				High Yield (Credit Suisse Upper/Middle Tier) Index
$3.02	11.7%	12.1%	0.21	10-Year Treasury Note Index
				Non-U.S. (J.P. Morgan Non-US Bond) Index
				Global (J.P. Morgan Global Government Bond Traded Unhedged) Index
				Emerging Markets Bond Index (J.P. Morgan EMBI+)[3]
				Merrill Lynch All Convertible All Quality Bond Index

1980	1981	1982	1983	1984	1985	1986	1987	1988	1989
32.5%	−4.9%	21.5%	22.6%	6.3%	31.7%	18.7%	5.3%	16.6%	31.7%
		22.7%	26.1%	1.2%	35.6%	16.2%	2.0%	20.9%	35.5%
33.9%	−3.2%	18.7%	19.9%	−11.2%	31.4%	7.4%	−5.3%	15.4%	18.3%
38.6%	2.0%	25.0%	29.1%	−7.3%	31.1%	5.7%	8.8%	25.0%	16.3%
39.6%	−11.3%	20.5%	16.0%	−1.0%	32.9%	15.4%	5.3%	11.3%	35.9%
24.4%	1.3%	20.0%	28.3%	10.1%	31.5%	20.0%	0.5%	23.2%	25.2%
52.3%	−9.2%	21.0%	20.1%	−15.8%	31.0%	3.6%	−10.5%	20.4%	20.2%
25.4%	14.9%	28.5%	38.6%	2.3%	31.0%	7.4%	−7.1%	29.5%	12.4%
33.7%	−3.8%	18.7%	23.5%	3.0%	32.6%	16.1%	2.3%	17.9%	29.2%
								23.9%	17.2%
	−5.7%	20.0%	20.4%	4.5%	31.1%	16.3%	2.9%	14.6%	30.0%
22.6%	−2.3%	−1.9%	23.7%	7.4%	56.2%	69.4%	24.6%	28.3%	10.5%
11.9%	−12.5%	4.0%	21.0%	0.6%	78.6%	43.9%	3.7%	15.8%	28.5%
29.7%	15.5%	−0.9%	24.5%	16.9%	43.1%	99.4%	43.0%	35.4%	1.7%
35.7%	7.8%	−6.7%	26.0%	13.1%	39.0%	93.4%	39.7%	35.0%	2.5%
								40.4%	65.0%
2.7%	6.3%	32.6%	8.4%	15.2%	22.1%	15.3%	2.8%	7.9%	14.5%
−17.6%	−15.5%	47.9%	3.3%	8.4%	24.0%	27.3%	−5.1%	11.5%	14.6%
							6.5%	13.7%	0.4%
−0.1%	5.4%	33.5%	2.9%	14.3%	27.3%	19.7%	−3.2%	6.4%	16.4%
						28.1%	36.1%	1.8%	15.6%
							2.2%	6.8%	14.0%
								12.8%	12.5%

T A B L E 7.4 (Continued)

Assets' Annual Rates of Return, 1980–1989

**Value of $1.00 on 12/31/89
(Compounded Annually)**

10 Years or Subperiod Shown (1980–1989)				*Nominal Total Returns Expressed in U.S. Dollars*
Value	**CAGR**	**Std. Dev.**	**Sharpe Ratio**	**Asset Class Indices**
				Alternative Investments Indices
$4.28	15.6%	10.0%	0.64	NAREIT (Real Estate Investment Trusts) Index
$2.98	11.5%	3.7%	0.63	NCREIF Property (Commercial Real Estate) Index
$1.59	4.8%	2.9%	(1.51)	National Association of Realtors (Residential Housing) Index
$0.69	−4.4%	9.3%	(1.46)	NCREIF Farmland (U.S. Farmland) Index
				Cambridge Associates U.S. Private Equity Index
$1.86	7.2%	6.7%	(0.31)	Cambridge Associates U.S. Venture Capital Index
$3.41	13.0%	27.2%	0.14	Venture Economics All Private Equity Fund Index
				HFRI Fund Weighted Composite Hedge Fund Index
				HFRI Fund of Funds Index
$1.61	6.1%	9.2%	(0.33)	Commodity Research Bureau Total Return Index
$4.94	19.4%	16.5%	0.62	Barclay Commodity Trading Advisors (CTA) Index
$0.78	−2.4%	19.0%	(0.61)	Handy & Harman Spot Gold Price Index
$0.19	−15.5%	25.7%	(0.96)	Handy & Harman Spot Silver Price Index
$2.44	9.3%	3.2%	0.04	Lehman Brothers TIPS Index / Bridgewater Index[4]
$7.60	22.5%	21.7%	0.61	Mei Moses Fine Art Index
				U.S. Cash Equivalent Indices
$2.41	9.2%	2.9%	0.00	Citigroup U.S. Treasury Bill (90-Day) Index
$1.64	5.1%	3.2%	(1.28)	Inflation (CPI-U)

All indices are expressed in total return terms unless noted in the description. "Gross" denotes total returns inclusive of gross dividends; "Net" denotes total returns inclusive of dividends net of foreign withholding taxes; and "Price Return" indicates that dividends are not included in the percentage returns data; "Free" denotes that portion of the relevant underlying market whose securities are freely tradable by international investors.

[1]The Lehman Brothers Aggregate Index represents securities that are U.S. domestic, taxable, and dollar denominated, representing the U.S. investment-grade, fixed-rate bond market. As of June 2007, components of the index included approximately: 38% Mortgage-Backed Securities; 23% U.S. Treasury; 19% Corporate; 14% Government Related; 5% Commercial Mortgage-Backed Securities; and 1% Asset-Backed Securities.

[2]Pre-1990 Municipal Bond data are furnished courtesy of Morgan Stanley Investment Management.

1980	1981	1982	1983	1984	1985	1986	1987	1988	1989
24.4%	6.0%	21.6%	30.6%	20.9%	19.1%	19.2%	−3.6%	13.5%	8.8%
18.1%	16.6%	9.4%	13.1%	13.8%	11.2%	8.3%	8.0%	9.6%	7.8%
11.5%	5.7%	1.8%	3.1%	3.1%	4.7%	7.0%	5.7%	3.9%	1.5%
		−3.1%	2.1%	−4.9%	−4.1%	−16.3%	−18.4%	4.7%	7.7%
						1.2%	3.5%	12.7%	10.4%
	18.1%	5.3%	18.1%	−1.2%	2.0%	7.3%	6.7%	3.1%	6.6%
77.4%	−13.1%	27.4%	43.7%	−6.6%	9.0%	0.9%	2.9%	9.3%	4.5%
		12.9%	−9.1%	4.9%	−1.2%	18.7%	16.0%	4.6%	5.1%
	23.9%	16.7%	23.8%	8.7%	25.5%	3.8%	57.3%	21.8%	1.8%
14.5%	−31.9%	13.9%	−16.5%	−19.2%	6.9%	20.4%	21.9%	−5.1%	−9%
−44.1%	−47.3%	32.1%	−17.9%	−28.9%	−8.3%	−7.9%	24.8%	10.1%	−14.0%
13.7%	9.4%	13.2%	3.5%	7.8%	12.4%	6.9%	7.1%	8.7%	11.1%
40.9%	9.8%	−4.3%	11.3%	17.8%	41.5%	−3.9%	43.5%	60.0%	26.5%
11.9%	15.0%	11.3%	8.9%	10.0%	7.8%	6.2%	5.9%	6.8%	8.6%
12.5%	8.9%	3.8%	3.8%	4.0%	3.8%	1.1%	4.4%	4.4%	4.7%

[3]EMBI+ used 1994 to present; EMBI for prior periods.

[4]The synthetically constructed Bridgewater Strategic Benchmark U.S. TIPS 8-Year Duration Index is used for the January 1970 through February 1997 time period; the Lehman Brothers TIPS Index is used after February 1997.

Source: Morgan Stanley Investment Management; Morgan Stanley Global Wealth Management Asset Allocation Group; the Author.

Venture Capital Index, experienced relatively low multiyear performance from 1984 through 1989, with returns of –1.2%, 2.0%, 7.3%, 6.7%, 3.1%, and 6.6%, respectively. Managed Futures Funds, as represented by the Barclay Commodity Trading Advisors (CTA) Index, produced six years of returns exceeding 15%: 23.9% in 1981, 16.7% in 1982, 23.8% in 1983, 25.5% in 1985, 57.3% in 1987, and 21.8% in 1988.

Partially reflecting the winding down of inflationary expectations during the 1980–1989 period, the Handy & Harmon Spot Silver Price experienced negative returns in 8 of 10 years: –44.1% in 1980, –47.3% in 1981, –17.9% in 1983, –28.9% in 1984, –8.3% in 1985, –7.9% in 1986, –10.1% in 1988, and –14.0% in 1989. Art, in the form of the Mei/Moses Fine Art Index, experienced two negative-return years, –4.3% in 1982 and –3.9% in 1986, offset by seven years of returns exceeding 10%: 40.9% in 1980, 11.3% in 1983, 17.8% in 1984, 41.5% in 1985, 43.5% in 1987, 60.0% in 1988, and 25.5% in 1989. In four years at the beginning of the 1980–1989 period, 90-Day U.S. Treasury Bills generated double-digit returns: 11.9% in 1980, 15.0% in 1981, 11.3% in 1982, and 10.0% in 1984.

Interyear and Interindex Observations for the 1970–1979 Decade

Thirteen asset categories in Table 7.5 have returns data covering the entire 10 years. During the 1970s, a number of significant developments occurred, including large increases in energy prices, inflation, and interest rates, which affected assets' rates of return in a variety of ways. In the 1973–1974 bear market, the Standard & Poor's 500 Index declined by 14.7% and 26.5%, respectively. During the same time period, the Nasdaq Index declined by 31.1% and 35.1%, respectively, before price increases of 29.8% in 1975, 12.3% in 1978, and 28.1% in 1979. In 1979, the Small/Mid-Capitalization Russell 2000 Value Index increased 35.4% and the Small/Mid-Capitalization Russell 2000 Growth Index increased 50.8%.

From 1970 through 1979, the MSCI EAFE Net Index rose by more than 20% in four years: 29.6% in 1971, 36.3% in 1972, 35.4% in 1975, and 32.6% in 1978. The MSCI Japan Net Index rose by more than 15% in six of the 1970–1979 years: 53.6% in 1971, 125.8% in

1972, 19.4% in 1975, 25.1% in 1976, 15.4% in 1977, and 52.8% in 1978. Annual returns on real estate investment trusts were negative in two years during the 1970–1979 period: –15.5% in 1973 and –21.4% in 1974. The returns from ownership of residential housing exceeded 9.0% in 6 of the 10 years: 9.2% in 1971, 10.8% in 1974, 9.5% in 1975, 13.3% in 1977, 15.2% in 1978, and 11.0% in 1979. Interrupted by negative-return years of –5.1% in 1970, –24.8% in 1975, and –4.0% in 1976, the Handy & Harmon Spot Gold Price index increased by more than 10% in each of the other seven years: 16.5%, 48.7%, 72.2%, and 66.3% in 1971, 1972, 1973, and 1974, respectively, and 22.4%, 37.0%, and 126.5% in 1977, 1978, and 1979, respectively.

The Mei/Moses Fine Art Index rose by more than 15% in 6 of the 10 years in the 1970–1979 period: 44.5% in 1971, 18.2% in 1972, 46.5% in 1973, 44.0% in 1976, 20.4% in 1978, and 18.8% in 1979. Reflecting increases in the CPI and in many short-term interest rates, the Citigroup 90-Day U.S. Treasury Bill Index returns trended in a generally upward direction for much of the 1970–1979 period, with 6.1%, 9.1%, and 10.3% returns in 1977, 1978, and 1979, respectively.

ASSETS' ANNUAL RATES OF RETURN BY ECONOMIC ENVIRONMENT

Investors can gain valuable perspective on the medium- and long-term attractiveness of the major classes of assets by studying their annual rates of return under varying economic conditions. Table 7.6 reviews the multiyear rates of return for the CPI, equities, bonds, U.S. Treasury bills and commercial paper, housing, farmland, gold, and silver, under four broad economic environments: (i) deflation; (ii) price stability; (iii) disinflation and moderate inflation; and (iv) rapid inflation.

General Observations and Caveats

The data described in Table 7.6 extend over more than 130 years, from 1871 to the beginning of the 21st century. These years have been grouped into economic periods of varying length. Thoughtful historians and economists may agree about the duration and

T A B L E 7.5

Assets' Annual Rates of Return, 1970–1979

**Value of $1.00 on 12/31/79
(Compounded Annually)**

10 Years or Subperiod Shown (1970–1979)				Nominal Total Returns Expressed in U.S. Dollars
Value	CAGR	Std. Dev.	Sharpe Ratio	Asset Class Indices
				U.S. Equity Indices
$1.77	5.9%	19.2%	(0.03)	S&P 500 Index
				S&P 400 Mid-Cap Index
				S&P 600 Small-Cap Index
$1.32	3.6%	25.9%	(0.11)	NASDAQ Composite (Price Return) Index
				Russell 2000 Index (Smaller Cap of 3000 Index)
				Russell 1000 Growth Index
				Russell 1000 Value Index
				Russell 2000 Growth Index
				Russell 2000 Value Index
$1.90	7.4%	22.1%	0.05	Wilshire 5000 Index
				Non-U.S. Equity Indices
				MSCI World Free Gross Index
				MSCI World ex-U.S. Gross Index
				MSCI U.S. Net Index
$2.32	8.8%	22.5%	0.11	MSCI EAFE Net Index
$1.95	6.9%	20.6%	0.02	MSCI Europe Free Net Index
$4.70	16.7%	45.2%	0.23	MSCI Japan Net Index
				MSCI Far East Free ex-Japan Gross Index
$3.74	14.1%	39.0%	0.20	MSCI Pacific (Developed Asia) Net Index
				MSCI Emerging Global Free Latin America Gross Index
				MSCI Emerging Markets Free Gross Index
				U.S. and Non-U.S. Fixed Income Indices
				Lehman Brothers Aggregate (Taxable) Index[1]
$1.67	5.3%	9.6%	(0.11)	Lehman Brothers 7-Year Municipal Bond Index[2]
				High Yield (Credit Suisse Upper/Middle Tier) Index
$1.70	5.4%	6.4%	(0.15)	10-Year Treasury Note Index
				Non-U.S. (J.P. Morgan Non-US Bond) Index
				Global (J.P. Morgan Global Government Bond Traded Unhedged) Index
				Emerging Markets Bond Index (J.P. Morgan EMBI+)[3]
				Merrill Lynch All Convertible All Quality Bond Index

1970	1971	1972	1973	1974	1975	1976	1977	1978	1979
3.9%	14.3%	19.0%	−14.7%	−26.5%	37.2%	23.9%	−7.1%	6.6%	18.6%
		17.2%	−31.1%	−35.1%	29.8%	26.1%	7.3%	12.3%	28.1%
									43.1%
									23.9%
									20.5%
									50.8%
									35.4%
	17.6%	18.0%	−18.5%	−28.4%	38.5%	26.6%	− 2.6%	9.3%	25.6%
−11.7%	29.6%	36.3%	−14.9%	−23.2%	35.4%	2.5%	18.1%	32.6%	4.8%
−10.6%	26.3%	14.4%	−8.8%	−24.1%	41.5%	−7.8%	21.9%	21.9%	12.3%
−12.2%	53.6%	125.8%	−20.5%	−16.1%	19.4%	25.1%	15.4%	52.8%	−12.2%
−12.8%	37.6%	106.4%	− 21.3%	− 21.5%	25.9%	20.9%	13.0%	48.0%	−4.0%
						15.6%	3.0%	1.4%	1.9%
21.1%	12.3%	1.5%	4.3%	− 10.7%	11.6%	15.8%	3.9%	−4.0%	1.0%
16.8%	9.8%	2.8%	3.7%	2.0%	3.6%	16.0%	1.3%	−0.8%	0.7%

T A B L E 7.5 (Continued)

Assets' Annual Rates of Return, 1970–1979

Value of $1.00 on 12/31/79
(Compounded Annually)

10 Years or Subperiod Shown (1970–1979)				Nominal Total Returns Expressed in U.S. Dollars
Value	CAGR	Std. Dev.	Sharpe Ratio	Asset Class Indices
				Alternative Investments Indices
$2.32	11.1%	23.5%	0.20	NAREIT (Real Estate Investment Trusts) Index
				NCREIF Property (Commercial Real Estate) Index
$2.57	9.9%	3.1%	1.14	National Association of Realtors (Residential Housing) Index
				NCREIF Farmland (U.S. Farmland) Index
				Cambridge Associates U.S. Private Equity Index
				Cambridge Associates U.S. Venture Capital Index
$6.10	19.8%	54.1%	0.25	Venture Economics All Private Equity Fund Index
				HFRI Fund Weighted Composite Hedge Fund Index
				HFRI Fund of Funds Index
				Commodity Research Bureau Total Return Index
				Barclay Commodity Trading Advisors (CTA) Index
$12.91	29.1%	44.9%	0.51	Handy & Harman Spot Gold Price Index
$17.04	37.0%	116.3%	0.26	Handy & Harman Spot Silver Price Index
$3.06	11.8%	4.5%	1.21	Lehman Brothers TIPS Index/Bridgewater Index[4]
$2.90	11.2%	26.4%	0.18	Mei Moses Fine Art Index
				U.S. Cash Equivalent Indices
$1.86	6.4%	2.1%	0.00	Citigroup U.S. Treasury Bill (90-Day) Index
$2.03	7.4%	3.4%	0.29	Inflation (CPI-U)

All indices are expressed in total return terms unless noted in the description. "Gross" denotes total returns inclusive of gross dividends; "Net" denotes total returns inclusive of dividends net of foreign withholding taxes; and "Price Return" indicates that dividends are not included in the percentage returns data; "Free" denotes that portion of the relevant underlying market whose securities are freely tradable by international investors.

[1]The Lehman Brothers Aggregate Index represents securities that are U.S. domestic, taxable, and dollar denominated, representing the U.S. investment-grade, fixed-rate bond market. As of June 2007, components of the index included approximately: 38% Mortgage-Backed Securities; 23% U.S. Treasury; 19% Corporate; 14% Government Related; 5% Commercial Mortgage-Backed Securities; and 1% Asset-Backed Securities.

[2]Pre-1990 Municipal Bond data are furnished courtesy of Morgan Stanley Investment Management.

1970	1971	1972	1973	1974	1975	1976	1977	1978	1979
		8.0%	−15.5%	−21.4%	19.3%	47.6%	22.4%	10.3%	35.9%
								16.1%	20.5%
3.6%	9.2%	8.8%	8.9%	10.8%	9.5%	8.9%	13.3%	15.2%	11.0%
−11.9%	54.0%	21.7%	−41.5%	−47.2%	134.3%	60.3%	41.4%	59.4%	41.4%
−5.1%	16.5%	48.7%	72.2%	66.3%	−24.8%	−4.0%	22.4%	37.0%	126.5%
	−15.9%	47.8%	59.8%	34.0%	−4.6%	5.0%	9.1%	27.0%	361.3%
11.4%	7.9%	7.6%	15.4%	20.4%	8.0%	10.1%	8.3%	12.6%	17.6%
−20.5%	44.5%	18.2%	46.5%	−17.2%	−18.9%	44.0%	5.1%	20.4%	18.8%
4.9%	4.0%	5.1%	7.5%	7.2%	5.4%	4.4%	6.1%	9.1%	10.3%
5.6%	3.3%	3.4%	8.7%	12.3%	6.9%	4.9%	6.7%	9.0%	13.3%

[3]EMBI+ used 1994 to present; EMBI for prior periods.

[4]The synthetically constructed Bridgewater Strategic Benchmark U.S. TIPS 8-Year Duration Index is used for the January 1970 through February 1997 time period; the Lehman Brothers TIPS Index is used after February 1997.

Source: Morgan Stanley Investment Management; Morgan Stanley Global Wealth Management Asset Allocation Group; the Author.

T A B L E 7.6

Assets' Annual Rates of Return by Economic Environment, 1871–2000

Nominal Returns in U.S. Dollars Except Where Noted

Era	Characteristic Developments
Deflation: A General Decline in the Overall Price Level (all or part of 38 years)	
1871–1896	The Opening of the West by the Railroads
1892–1895	1893 and 1895 Panics; Industrial Recession/Strikes
1919–1922	Post-WWI Money Supply Contraction
1929–1932	The Great Crash and The Great Depression
	4-Period Average[10]
Price Stability: A Virtually Stable Overall Price Level (all or part of 25 years)	
1896–1900	Spanish-American War Victory
1921–1929	The Roaring Twenties
1934–1940	Emergence from The Great Depression
1952–1955	The Early Eisenhower Years
	4-Period Average[10]
Disinflation/Moderate Inflation: Moderate Rises in Overall Prices (all or part of 63 years)	
1885–1892	Railroads and Robber Baron Era
1899–1915	Boom-Bust Cycles Give Way to Fed Creation
1942–1945	World War II
1951–1965	Countercyclical Fed/Treasury Policies
1982–2000	The Expanding Eighties and Nifty Nineties
	5-Period Average[10]
Rapid Inflation: A Rapid Increase in the Overall Price Level (all or part of 30 years)	
1914–1919	World War I
1945–1947	Post-WWII Release of Pent-Up Demand
1949–1951	Korean War (1950–1953)
1965–1971	Vietnam War Buildup
1971–1981	Monetary Expansion and Higher Energy Prices
	5-Period Average[10]

[1]Consumer Price Index and predecessor measures.
[2]S&P 500 Composite Index Total Return and predecessor measures.
[3]Long-Term Government Bond Index and predecessor measures.
[4]Ibbotson Associates and NY Federal Reserve Commercial Paper Index.
[5]National Association of Realtors.
[6]NCREIF Farmland Index, which also incorporates estimated return data.
[7]Handy & Harman Spot Gold Price.
[8]Handy & Harman Spot Silver Price.
[9]Due to U.S. Government regulation, the official U.S. price of gold did not exhibit a meaningful degree of change

			Cash Equivalents	Real Estate-Related Assets		Precious Metals	
CPI[1]	Equities[2]	Bonds[3]	U.S. T-Bills and CP[4]	Housing[5]	Farmland[6]	Gold[7]	Silver[8]
−1.5%	5.5%	6.4%	5.4%	N/AV	N/AV	(9)	−6.8%
−3.3%	−2.5%	5.1%	4.1%	1.5%	N/AV	(9)	−8.0%
−2.0%	5.0%	4.2%	6.7%	1.0%	−12.1%	(9)	−18.2%
−6.4%	−21.2%	5.0%	3.0%	−3.9%	−12.3%	(9)	−19.8%
−3.3%	−3.3%	5.2%	4.8%	−0.4%	−12.2%		−13.2%
0.3%	26.1%	3.3%	3.3%	0.0%	9.3%	(9)	−1.0%
−1.3%	20.2%	6.4%	5.4%	4.4%	−2.8%	(9)	−3.3%
1.0%	12.2%	6.2%	0.7%	7.2%	3.9%	6.3%	1.0%
0.3%	24.5%	3.5%	1.5%	4.5%	6.5%	(9)	2.1%
0.1%	20.8%	4.9%	2.7%	4.0%	4.2%		−0.3%
0.0%	4.5%	4.4%	5.1%	N/AV	N/AV	(9)	−4.5%
1.3%	8.2%	4.1%	5.3%	5.7%	N/AV	(9)	−0.5%
2.5%	26.1%	4.5%	0.9%	10.0%	18.1%	(9)	3.3%
1.6%	16.5%	2.2%	3.5%	5.5%	6.7%	(9)	3.0%
3.3%	16.9%	12.6%	6.2%	4.1%	2.4%	−2.0%	−3.0%
1.7%	14.4%	5.6%	4.2%	6.3%	9.1%		−0.3%
13.3%	11.6%	2.1%	4.7%	17.5%	14.7%	(9)	15.5%
6.8%	12.3%	2.6%	1.0%	12.2%	18.5%	(9)	8.6%
5.8%	24.8%	0.9%	2.3%	10.2%	21.7%	(9)	20.5%
4.0%	6.4%	6.1%	6.8%	10.3%	12.7%	31.6%	23.7%
8.3%	5.8%	3.8%	8.8%	10.3%	14.6%	28.0%	21.5%
8.3%	12.1%	3.1%	4.7%	12.1%	16.4%	24.8%	18.0%

[10]Multiperiod averages do not double count multi-year overlaps.

N/AV= Complete data are not available.

Numerous asset classes and subclasses are not shown here, including: value and growth equity investment styles; small-, mid-, and large-cap equity demarcations; international equities from developed and/or emerging countries; non-U.S. bonds from developed and/or emerging countries; high-yield bonds; collateralized commodities; private equity; venture capital; inflation-indexed bonds; fine art; hedge funds; and hedge fund funds of funds.

Past performance is not a guarantee of future results.

Source: Morgan Stanley Investment Management; the Author; and the sources cited above in each of the accompanying footnotes.

characterization of some, but not all, of these eras. For virtually all of these asset classes, the quantity and quality of the data, especially prior to the 1950s and particularly before 1900, are subject to some degree of imprecision, survivorship and selection bias, and subjectivity. Even in the modern era, data for asset categories such as housing and farmland may not always have been collected and organized with the same frequency or by the same methods as data for asset categories such as equities and bonds.

In the top portion of Table 7.6, on average during the four deflationary episodes lasting for all or part of 38 years in the 1870–2000 period, the CPI fell 3.3% per year, equities declined 3.3% annually, and housing, farmland, and silver declined 0.4%, 12.2%, and 13.2% per annum, respectively. By contrast, short-term cash instruments and bonds rose an average annual rate of 4.8% and 5.2%, respectively.

One of the chief objectives of examining the investment performance of broad groups of assets in different economic climates is to help investors consider when it might be appropriate to strategically overweight or underweight certain asset classes. Figure 7.2 summarizes general asset weightings in various economic conditions.

Along the horizontal axis of Figure 7.2 are the four major types of economic conditions described in Table 7.6: *deflation*, featuring a general decline in the overall price level; *price stability*, with virtually unchanged levels of overall prices; *disinflation and moderate inflation*, reflecting a moderate increase and perhaps occasionally small declines in the overall price level; and *rapid inflation*, characterized by a rapid increase in the overall price level. Each of these economic conditions may: (i) be caused by different sets of influences; (ii) last for meaningfully different lengths of time; (iii) occur in differing degrees of severity; and (iv) produce a variety of governmental, monetary, and international responses that may affect the depth, degree, and duration of subsequent economic conditions.

Along the vertical axis of Figure 7.2 are six groups of asset classes: cash equivalents, bonds, equities, housing, farmland, and gold and silver. The modern-day range of asset classes encompasses numerous other types and important subgroups of assets, including non-U.S. equities and bonds in developed and emerging markets, convertible securities, high-yield securities,

F I G U R E 7.2

Generalized Asset Class Weightings in Varying Economic Conditions

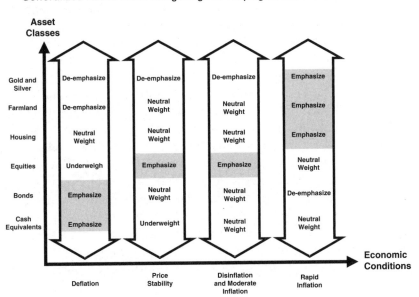

inflation-indexed fixed-income securities, commodities, absolute-return investment strategies via hedge funds and other formats, private equity, venture capital, art, commercial real estate, and managed futures strategies.

For the six highly simplified asset classes displayed in Figure 7.2, the wide vertical arrows represent four strategic mixes of assets that are based on the historical experience from 1871 through 2000. The emphases and de-emphases on assets in Figure 7.2 are highly simplified, gross generalizations in the form of *guidelines*, rather than hard-and-fast rules. The general directives depicted within each arrow do not take into account: (i) potentially significant differences in specific scenarios within each of the four groups of economic conditions; (ii) special ways of hedging or investing in the asset classes shown here or in other kinds of assets; (iii) the investor's own risk profile, market outlook, asset preferences, demographic circumstances, and any mandated diversification or concentration strictures; and (iv) the switching costs, information sources about, liquidity characteristics, available investment vehicles, and other important attributes of specific asset classes.

With these overall cautions in mind, in the *deflation* scenario, successful investment strategies tend to emphasize cash equivalents and bonds; give neutral weight to housing; underweight equities; and de-emphasize farmland and gold and silver. In periods of *price stability,* successful investment strategies have emphasized equities; given neutral weight to bonds, farmland, and housing; underweighted cash equivalents; and de-emphasized gold and silver. In times of *disinflation and moderate inflation,* successful investment strategies have generally resembled the asset allocations applied during eras of price stability. Such asset mixes tend to emphasize equities; give neutral weight to bonds, cash equivalents, housing, and farmland; and de-emphasize gold and silver. By contrast, in periods of *rapid inflation,* successful investment strategies have emphasized tangible asset classes such as gold and silver, farmland, and housing; placed a neutral weight on equities and cash equivalents; and de-emphasized bonds.

Interperiod and Interasset Class Observations

Table 7.6 depicts the U.S. economy as having experienced *deflation* for all or part of 38 years, encompassing four separate periods, as short as 4 years and as long as 26 years. During the four-period average for eras of deflation, the CPI declined an average of 3.3% per year, and equities fell in price by an average of 3.3% per year (actually *rising* an average of 5.0% per year in 1919–1922, and 5.5% per year in 1871–1896, during periods of extended or relatively modest price deflation). Bonds exhibited strong investment performance during deflationary eras, generating total returns of 5.2% per year, whereas farmland declined an average of 12.2% per year, and silver fell an average of 13.2% per year. Housing prices declined an average of 0.4% per year, much less than the decline in farmland prices during deflationary eras.

The U.S. economy exhibited virtual *price stability* for all or part of 25 years, comprising four separate periods from as short as 4 years to as long as 9 years. During the four-period average for eras of price stability, the CPI rose an average of only 0.1% per year. Equities have tended to flourish in times of price stability, generating the highest compound average returns of any asset class and for any economic climate among those shown in Table 7.6: 20.8% per year. Stable price eras have witnessed annual average returns of 4.9% per year for bonds, 4.2% per year for farmland, and 4.0% per year for housing. In such periods, silver declined an average of 0.3% per year.

The U.S. economy witnessed conditions of *disinflation and moderate inflation* for all or part of 63 years, composed of five separate periods lasting from 4 years to 19 years. During the five-period average for eras of disinflation and moderate inflation, the CPI rose by an average of 1.7% per year. Equities, farmland, and housing fared relatively well during disinflation and moderate inflation, rising 14.4% per year, 9.1% per year, and 6.3% per year, respectively. Perhaps surprisingly, bonds generated a total *nominal* return of 5.6% per year during eras of disinflation and moderate inflation, actually outperforming bonds' total *nominal* return of 5.2% per year during deflationary eras. On a real-return basis, however, *after* adjusting for changes in the CPI, bonds' *real* returns in times of disinflation and moderate inflation amounted to 3.9% per year (equal to their 5.6% per year nominal return *minus* the 1.7% per year average CPI for similar eras). This was less than bonds' effective *real* returns of 8.5% during times of deflation (equal to their 5.2% per year *nominal* return *plus* the 3.3% per year *deflation* in the CPI for similar eras).

The U.S. economy experienced conditions of *rapid inflation* for all or part of 30 years, consisting of five separate periods lasting from 3 to 11 years. During the five-period average for eras of rapid inflation, the CPI rose by an average of 8.3% per year. Assets with high returns during eras of rapid inflation include gold, silver, and farmland, which generated total returns of 24.8% per year, 18.0% per year, and 16.4% per year, respectively. In periods of rapid inflation, housing and equities each generated total returns of 12.1% per year, while bonds produced a five-period average of total returns amounting to 3.1% per year.

ROTATING RETURNS LEADERSHIP AMONG ASSET CLASSES

From 1980 through 2006, Figure 7.3 displays a limited number of asset classes and subasset classes considered by an investor whose

F I G U R E 7.3

Rotating Returns Leadership Among Asset Classes

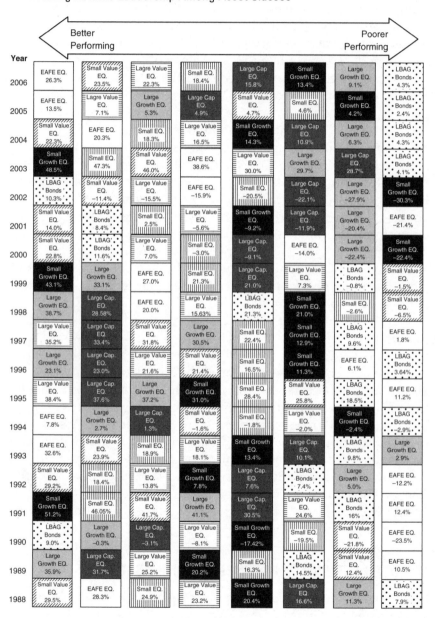

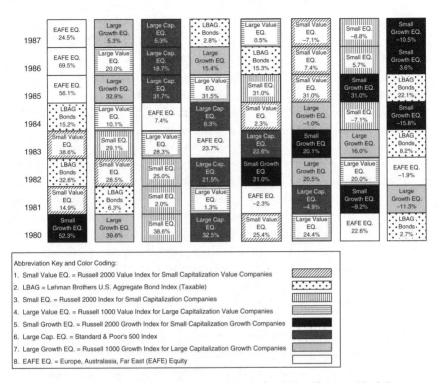

1987	EAFE EQ. 24.5%	Large Growth EQ. 5.3%	Large Cap. EQ. 5.3%	LBAG. Bonds. 2.8%	Large Value EQ. 0.5%	Small Value EQ. -7.1%	Small EQ. -8.8%	Small Growth EQ. -10.5%
1986	EAFE EQ. 69.5%	Large Value EQ. 20.0%	Large Cap. EQ. 18.7%	Large Growth EQ. 15.4%	LBAG Bonds 15.3%	Small Value EQ. 7.4%	Small EQ. 5.7%	Small Growth EQ. 3.6%
1985	EAFE EQ. 56.1%	Large Growth EQ. 32.9%	Large Cap. EQ. 31.7%	Large Value EQ. 31.5%	Small EQ. 31.0%	Small Value EQ. 31.0%	Small Growth EQ. 31.0%	LBAG Bonds, 22.1%,
1984	LBAG Bonds 15.2%	Large Value EQ. 10.1%	EAFE EQ. 7.4%	Large Cap EQ. 6.3%	Small Value EQ. 2.3%	Large Growth EQ. -1.0%	Small EQ. -7.1%	Small Growth EQ. -15.8%
1983	Small Value EQ. 38.6%	Small EQ. 29.1%	Large Value EQ. 28.3%	EAFE EQ. 23.7%	Large Cap. EQ. 22.6%	Small Growth EQ. 20.1%	Large Growth EQ. 16.0%	LBAG. Bonds, 8.2%
1982	LBAG Bonds 32.6%	Small Value EQ. 28.5%	Small EQ. 25.0%	Large Cap. EQ. 21.5%	Small Growth EQ. 21.0%	Large Growth EQ. 20.5%	Large Value EQ. 20.0%	EAFE EQ. -1.9%
1981	Small Value EQ. 14.9%	LBAG Bonds 6.3%	Small EQ. 2.0%	Large Value EQ. 1.3%	EAFE EQ. -2.3%	Large Cap. EQ. -4.9%	Small Growth EQ. -9.2%	Large Growth EQ. -11.3%
1980	Small Growth EQ. 52.3%	Large Growth EQ. 39.6%	Small EQ. 38.6%	Large Cap. EQ. 32.5%	Small Value EQ. 25.4%	Large Value EQ. 24.4%	EAFE EQ. 22.6%	LBAG. Bonds 2.7%

Abbreviation Key and Color Coding:

1. Small Value EQ. = Russell 2000 Value Index for Small Capitalization Value Companies
2. LBAG = Lehman Brothers U.S. Aggregate Bond Index (Taxable)
3. Small EQ. = Russell 2000 Index for Small Capitalization Companies
4. Large Value EQ. = Russell 1000 Value Index for Large Capitalization Value Companies
5. Small Growth EQ. = Russell 2000 Growth Index for Small Capitalization Growth Companies
6. Large Cap. EQ. = Standard & Poor's 500 Index
7. Large Growth EQ. = Russell 1000 Growth Index for Large Capitalization Growth Companies
8. EAFE EQ. = Europe, Australasia, Far East (EAFE) Equity

Source: Frank Russell Companies; MSCI Barra; Lehman Brothers; Standard and Poor's; and the Author.

portfolio might contain: (i) large- and small-capitalization U.S. equity in a growth, value, or combined growth and value investment style; (ii) U.S. taxable bonds; and (iii) non-U.S. developed equity. These asset classes are represented by the following indices: (i) the Standard and Poor's 500 Index, for large-capitalization equity; (ii) the Russell 1000 Growth Index, for large-capitalization growth equity; (iii) the Russell 1000 Value Index, for large-capitalization value equity; (iv) the Russell 2000 Growth Index, for small-capitalization growth equity; (v) the Russell 2000 Value Index, for small-capitalization value equity; (vi) the Russell 2000 Index, for small-capitalization combined growth and value equity; (vii) the Europe, Australasia, and Far East (EAFE) Index, for non-U.S. developed equity; and (viii) the Lehman Brothers Aggregate Bond Index, for taxable U.S. bonds.

Several important asset-allocation implications emerge from careful observation of the performance data in Figure 7.3. First, the six asset classes and subasset classes of the U.S. equity market have often generated widely differing returns. For example, in the years in which *small-capitalization value* equities ranked *first* in investment performance (1981, 1983, 1988, 1992, 2000, 2001, and 2004), *large-capitalization growth* equities ranked much lower—eighth, seventh, seventh, seventh, seventh, seventh, and seventh, respectively. Second, all the asset groups have ranked as the best or second-best performing asset class at least twice and occasionally as many as nine times. Non-U.S. equity ranked first or second nine times, small-capitalization value equity eleven times, large-capitalization growth equity nine times, large-capitalization value equity five times, U.S. taxable bonds seven times, small-capitalization equity four times, and small capitalization growth equity four times. Third, non-U.S. equities were the *best* performing asset class for three years in a row (1985–1987), followed shortly thereafter by four years in a row (1989–1992) in which they were the *poorest* performing among these eight asset groups, followed yet again by two years in a row (1993–1994) in which they were the *best* performing asset class. From 2005–2006, non-U.S. equities were once again the *best* performing asset class.

While deeper analysis of Figure 7.3 can yield many additional comparisons, two additional powerful insights relating to asset allocation stand out. First is the difficulty and costs investors might experience in attempting to shift successfully *each year* (or even every two years) into the best performing asset groups. A sensible investment strategy (which also has the benefit of reducing transaction costs) might therefore involve some healthy diversification and rebalancing activity, leavened with as much perspective as possible on how certain asset groups might be reasonably expected to perform on a multiyear basis. Second, and equally important, is the way asset groups rotate from the worst to the best, or from the best to the worst, of the performance rankings. The cycling of non-U.S. equity from the best-ranked to the worst-ranked, and back again to the best-ranked, has already been cited; of equal note is the fall of large-capitalization growth equities from the top performance ranking in 1989, to second in 1990, fourth in 1991, seventh in

1992, and eighth in 1993, before rebounding to second place in 1994, followed by third place in 1995, first place in 1996, fourth place in 1997, first place in 1998, and second place in 1999, before plunging to seventh place in 2000, 2001, and 2002, sixth in 2003 and back to seventh in 2004, then rebounding back to third in 2005 before falling to seventh for the fifth time in seven years in 2006. This pattern of high-to-low-to-high-to-low investment results is another argument in favor of judicious *tactical* portfolio rebalancing (discussed in Chapter 4), with intensive thought devoted to the investor's *strategic* asset allocation.

EQUITIES INDUSTRY SECTORS BY INDIVIDUAL YEARS

Many of the methods of organizing and analyzing assets' returns data can also be applied *within* a specific asset class. For example, U.S. equity investors may wish to organize *various industry sectors'* rates of returns: (i) *by groups of years* (for example, on a 10-year or 20-year basis); (ii) *by individual years* (for example, for each of the years from 1997 through 2006); and (iii) *by economic environment* (for example, showing investment performance in periods of inflation, price stability, and deflation). To demonstrate the insights that investors can glean through such an intra-asset class approach, Table 7.7 sets forth the total investment return, including dividends plus or minus any change in capital value, for the 10 industry sectors in the Standard & Poor's 500 Composite Index, for each year from 1990 through 2006.

General Observations and Caveats

The number of companies constituting each of the 10 industry sectors in the S&P 500 index as of calendar year 2006 is shown in column 2 on the left side of the lower-most part of Table 7.7, and the number within each industry sector as of the beginning of calendar year 1990 is shown in column 2 on the left side of the two upper parts of the exhibit. A quick visual comparison of the data in these two columns shows the changing nature of the S&P 500 index through time. For example, there were 78 information technology

T A B L E 7.7

S&P 500 Industry Sectors' Annual Rates of Return

		Total Returns (%)							
S&P 500 Industry Sector	1990 No. Cos	1990	1991	1992	1993	1994	1995	1996	1997
Consumer Discretionary	101	−12.2	41.5	19.7	14.6	−8.3	20.3	12.4	34.4
Consumer Staples	45	15.3	41.7	5.3	−3.9	9.8	39.6	25.9	32.9
Energy	28	2.9	6.9	2.3	15.9	3.7	31.0	25.9	25.3
Financials	57	−20.8	49.1	23.3	10.6	−3.5	54.1	35.2	48.2
Health Care	26	17.3	53.7	−16.2	−8.2	13.7	58.0	21.0	43.7
Industrials	101	−7.6	29.5	9.6	18.6	−2.4	39.1	25.1	27.0
Information Technology	35	3.0	9.1	2.9	21.7	19.9	39.4	43.9	28.5
Materials	61	−10.7	25.5	10.3	13.5	5.8	20.0	15.8	8.4
Telecommunication Services	11	−13.9	13.2	16.2	15.1	−4.8	42.3	1.1	41.2
Utilities	35	−0.6	23.9	6.6	13.7	−11.8	32.7	5.7	24.7
S&P 500	**500**	**−3.1**	**30.5**	**7.6**	**10.1**	**1.3**	**37.6**	**23.0**	**33.4**

		Total Returns (%)							
S&P 500 Industry Sector	1990 No. Cos	1998	1999	2000	2001	2002	2003	2004	2005	2006
Consumer Discretionary	101	41.1	25.2	−20.0	2.8	−23.8	37.4	13.2	−6.4	18.6
Consumer Staples	45	15.8	−15.1	16.8	−6.4	−4.3	11.6	8.2	3.6	14.4
Energy	28	0.6	18.7	15.7	−10.4	−11.1	25.6	31.5	31.4	24.2
Financials	57	11.4	4.1	25.7	−9.0	−14.6	31.0	10.9	6.5	19.2
Health Care	26	43.9	−10.7	37.1	−11.9	−18.8	15.1	1.7	6.5	7.5
Industrials	101	10.9	21.5	5.9	−5.7	−26.3	32.2	18.0	2.3	13.3
Information Technology	35	78.1	78.7	−40.9	−25.9	−37.4	47.2	2.6	1.0	8.4
Materials	61	−6.2	25.3	−15.7	3.5	−5.5	38.2	13.2	4.4	18.6
Telecommunication Services	11	52.4	19.1	−38.8	−12.2	−34.1	7.1	19.9	−5.6	36.8
Utilities	35	14.8	−9.2	57.2	−30.4	−30.0	26.3	24.3	16.8	21.0
S&P 500	**500**	**28.6**	**21.0**	**−9.1**	**−11.9**	**−22.1**	**28.7**	**10.9**	**4.9**	**15.8**

		Value of $1.00 on 12/31/2006 (Compounded Annually)		
		10 Years (1997–2006)		
S&P 500 Industry Sector	2006 No. Cos	Value	CAGR %	Std. Dev. %	Sharpe Ratio
Consumer Discretionary	88	$2.57	9.9	23.4	0.42
Consumer Staples	38	$1.95	6.9	13.8	0.50
Energy	31	$3.72	14.0	16.3	0.86
Financials	87	$3.10	12.0	18.7	0.64
Health Care	55	$2.42	9.3	23.2	0.40
Industrials	52	$2.28	8.6	17.1	0.50
Information Technology	78	$1.86	6.4	43.7	0.14
Materials	29	$2.04	7.4	16.1	0.46
Telecommunication Services	10	$1.50	4.2	31.1	0.13
Utilities	32	$2.21	8.2	27.2	0.30
S&P 500	**500**	**$2.24**	**8.4**	**19.1**	**0.44**

Source: The Author, Standard & Poor's, and FactSet.

companies in the S&P 500 index at the end of 2006, compared with 35 information technology companies in the S&P 500 index at the end of 1990. Similarly, as of the end of 2006, there were 87 financial companies in the S&P 500 index, versus 57 such companies at the end of 1990.

The number of companies in each industry in the S&P 500 index, as well as each company's total market capitalization, drives the shifting weights in the industry sector composition of the S&P 500. Shifts in equity market prices and/or S&P 500 index composition policies may cause a specific S&P industry sector to over- or underrepresent its importance in the index and the economy as a whole. For historical perspective, Table 7.8 shows the changing industry sector composition of the S&P 500 index for each year from 1984 through 2006.

As of the end of 2006, Table 7.8 shows that the information technology sector represented 15.1% of the total market capitalization of the S&P 500, down from 29.2% at the end of 1999, and up from 8.6% in 1994. Similarly, the financials sector accounted for 22.3% of the total market capitalization of the S&P 500 at the end of 2006, up from 13.0% at the end of 1999. By contrast, the energy sector represented 9.8% of the year-end 2006 total market capitalization of the S&P 500, essentially unchanged from the prior year and down considerably from 15.3% of the S&P 500 in 1984.

Interyear and Intersector Observations

Referring back to Table 7.7, *from 1997 through 2006*, the S&P 500 generated a compound growth rate of 8.4% per year. As a result, $1.00 invested in the S&P 500 index on January 1, 1997, would have appreciated in value to $2.24 as of December 31, 2006. During the 1997–2006 decade, two S&P industry sectors generated compound annual rates of return in excess of 10%: the energy sector, with a 14.0% compound annual rate of growth, and the financials sector, with a 12.0% compound annual rate of growth (CAGR). An investor who placed $1.00 in the energy and financial sectors on January 1, 1997, would have seen his or her investment increase in value to $3.72, and $3.10, respectively, on December 31, 2006.

T A B L E 7.8

S&P 500 Industry Sector Composition

Percentage of S&P 500 Index Market Capitalization

S&P Industry Sector	1984	1985	1986	1987	1988	1989	1990	1991	1992	1993	1994
Consumer Discretionary	15.0%	15.5%	16.3%	16.0%	16.4%	15.0%	12.8%	14.0%	15.8%	16.4%	14.9%
Consumer Staples	10.2	10.3	10.8	11.0	11.3	11.3	14.0	15.2	14.5	12.5	13.2
Energy	15.3	11.6	11.5	11.6	11.8	12.4	13.4	10.6	9.7	10.0	10.0
Financials	6.4	7.5	7.2	6.1	8.0	8.9	7.5	8.7	10.6	11.2	10.7
Health Care	6.4	6.9	8.0	8.4	8.1	8.4	10.4	12.4	9.9	8.2	9.2
Industrials	13.7	15.0	14.5	15.4	15.0	14.2	13.6	13.2	13.3	13.9	13.0
Information Technology	14.4	13.9	11.2	9.6	8.1	5.9	6.3	5.3	5.1	5.9	8.6
Materials	7.3	7.6	8.0	8.8	8.2	7.8	7.2	6.8	6.9	7.1	7.1
Telecommunication Services	5.3	5.6	6.1	7.5	7.6	9.8	8.7	8.0	8.5	9.1	8.6
Utilities	6.1	6.1	6.4	5.6	5.6	6.3	6.2	5.8	5.6	5.6	4.8
Total	100.0%	100.0%	100.0%	100.0%	100.0%	100.0%	100.0%	100.0%	100.0%	100.0%	100.0%

Percentage of S&P 500 Index Market Capitalization

S&P Industry Sector	1995	1996	1997	1998	1999	2000	2001	2002	2003	2004	2005	2006
Consumer Discretionary	13.0%	11.7%	12.1%	12.5%	12.7%	10.3%	13.1%	13.4%	11.3%	11.9%	10.8%	10.6%
Consumer Staples	12.8	12.7	12.3	11.1	7.2	8.1	8.2	9.5	11.0	10.5	9.5	9.3
Energy	9.1	9.2	8.4	6.3	5.6	6.6	6.3	6.0	5.8	7.2	9.3	9.8
Financials	13.1	15.0	17.2	15.4	13.0	17.3	17.8	20.5	20.6	20.6	21.3	22.3
Health Care	10.8	10.4	11.3	12.3	9.3	14.4	14.4	14.9	13.3	12.7	13.3	12.0
Industrials	12.6	12.7	11.7	10.1	9.9	10.6	11.3	11.5	10.9	11.8	11.3	10.8
Information Technology	9.4	12.4	12.3	17.7	29.2	21.2	17.6	14.3	17.7	16.1	15.1	15.1
Materials	6.1	5.7	4.5	3.1	3.0	2.3	2.6	2.8	3.0	3.1	3.0	3.0
Telecommunication Services	8.5	6.5	6.9	8.4	7.9	5.5	5.5	4.2	3.5	3.3	3.0	3.5
Utilities	4.5	3.7	3.3	3.0	2.2	3.8	3.1	2.9	2.8	2.9	3.4	3.6
Total	100.0%	100.0%	100.0%	100.0%	100.0%	100.0%	100.0%	100.0%	100.0%	100.0%	100.0%	100.0%

Note: These S&P 500 sector histories do not reflect official numbers published by S&P or MSCI and are based on the proprietrary reconstruction by Morgan Stanley Quantitative Strategies; as such, they may be subject to revision.

Source: FactSet; Morgan Stanley Quantitative Strategies, Morgan Stanley Investment Research, and the Author.

Sectors exhibiting the slowest rate of investment performance over the 1997–2006 period were telecommunications services, information technology, and consumer staples. Investors who placed $1.00 in the telecommunications services, information technology, and consumer staples sectors at the beginning of 1997 would have seen their investment grow to a value of $1.50, $1.86, and $1.95, respectively, at the end of 2006.

LEADING COMPANIES BY EQUITY MARKET CAPITALIZATION

Another important degree of perspective on the growth of the U.S. economy and financial markets, and the shifting fortunes of specific companies over time, can be gained from a multidecade observation of the *largest companies* by equity market capitalization. Table 7.9 shows the 10 largest companies according to equity market capitalization at 25-year intervals during the 20th century, at the end of 1925, 1950, 1975, and 2000.

On an aggregate basis, in 1925 the 10 largest U.S. companies were worth $6.9 billion, or 25.38% of the overall U.S equity market capitalization of $27.3 billion. The largest U.S. company was AT&T, with an equity market capitalization of $1.3 billion, equal to 4.82% of the total U.S. equity market. Other industries represented among the top 10 companies included 2 oil companies (Standard Oil of New Jersey and Standard Oil of California), 3 industrial companies (General Electric, United States Steel, and General Motors), one retailing company (F.W. Woolworth), and 3 railroads (the Pennsylvania, the New York Central, and the Southern Pacific).

By 1950, the total U.S. equity market capitalization had risen to $85.7 billion, or 3.13 times the level of 1925. The top 10 companies accounted for 26.52% of the U.S. equity market, with AT&T again the largest company, at $4.3 billion, or 5.04% of the total market. Other companies in the top 10 included 3 industrial companies (General Motors, General Electric, and United States Steel), 2 chemical companies (Du Pont and Union Carbide), 1 retailing company (Sears, Roebuck), and 3 oil companies (Standard Oil of New Jersey, Standard Oil of California, and Texas Company).

With the passage of 25 more years, 1975 witnessed a total U.S. equity market capitalization of $657.4 billion, equal to 7.67 times 1950's total. IBM had displaced AT&T in the top position, with a market capitalization of $33.3 billion, representing 5.06% of the total. Other industries represented in the top 10 included 1 communications company (AT&T), 2 oil companies (Exxon and Texaco), 1 chemical company (Dow Chemical), 1 retailing firm (Sears, Roebuck), 2 industrial companies (General Motors and General Electric), and 2 consumer products companies (Eastman Kodak and Procter & Gamble).

At the end of 2000, the total U.S. equity market capitalization had increased to $11.7 trillion, equal to 17.82 times the level of 1975.

T A B L E   7.9

Leading U.S. Companies by Equity Market Capitalization

1925

1925 Company	Market Capitalization ($MM)	Percent of U.S. Equity Market
AT&T	$1,318	4.82%
Standard Oil (NJ)	952	3.48
General Electric	784	2.87
United States Steel	691	2.53
General Motors	606	2.22
Standard Oil (CA)	589	2.15
F.W. Woolworth	549	2.01
Pennsylvania R.R.	548	2.00
New York Central R.R.	516	1.89
Southern Pacific R.R.	387	1.41
Total for 10 Companies	$6,940	25.38%
Total Equity Market	$27,344	100.00%

1950

1950 Company	Market Capitalization ($MM)	Percent of U.S. Equity Market
AT&T	$4,320	5.04%
General Motors	4,049	4.73
General Electric	3,782	4.41
Du Pont	2,778	3.24
Standard Oil (NJ)	1,587	1.85
Union Carbide	1,425	1.66
Standard Oil (CA)	1,317	1.54
Sears, Roebuck	1,241	1.45
Texas Company	1,132	1.32
United States Steel	1,099	1.28
Total for 10 Companies	$22,730	26.52%
Total Equity Market	$85,709	100.00%

Source: *The New York Times*, December 20, 1999, and the Author.

T A B L E   7.9 (Continued)

Leading U.S. Companies by Equity Market Capitalization

1975

1975 Company	Market Capitalization ($MM)	Percent of U.S. Equity Market
IBM	$33,289	5.06%
AT&T	28,856	4.39
Exxon	19,855	3.02
Eastman Kodak	17,148	2.61
General Motors	16,503	2.51
Sears, Roebuck	10,189	1.55
Dow Chemical	8,491	1.29
General Electric	8,446	1.28
Procter & Gamble	7,341	1.12
Texaco	6,344	0.97
Total for 10 Companies	$156,462	23.80%
Total Equity Market	$657,403	100.00%

2000

2000 Company	Market Capitalization ($MM)	Percent of U.S. Equity Market
General Electric	$476,115	4.06%
Exxon Mobil	302,195	2.58
Cisco Systems	275,017	2.35
Citigroup	256,446	2.19
Wal-Mart Stores	237,203	2.02
Microsoft	230,798	1.97
Intel	202,110	1.73
SBC Communications	161,632	1.38
Coca-Cola	151,415	1.29
IBM	150,822	1.29
Total for 10 Companies	$2,443,753	20.86%
Total Equity Market	$11,715,019	100.00%

(*One year earlier*, as of the end of 1999, the total U.S. equity market capitalization had been $15.1 trillion, with Microsoft's market capitalization equal to $594.7 billion.) With a year-end 2000 market capitalization of $476.1 billion, General Electric represented 4.06% of the total U.S. equity market capitalization—which would have equaled slightly over 72% of the entire U.S. equity market capitalization back in 1975. General Electric ranked among the top 10 companies in 1925, 1950, 1975, and 2000. Other industries represented in the top 10 included 1 oil company (Exxon Mobil, which as Exxon and Standard Oil of New Jersey also made all four of the top 10 lists shown in Table 7.9), 1 retailing company (Wal-Mart Stores), 4 technology companies (Cisco Systems, Microsoft, Intel, and IBM), 1 financial company (Citigroup), 1 communications company (SBC Communications, a descendant of AT&T), and 1 consumer products company (Coca-Cola).

LEADING U.S. COMPANIES' RATES OF RETURN BY INDIVIDUAL YEARS

Investors can learn some of the ways in which the value of companies grows and contracts by tracing the pattern of specific companies' equity price returns on a year-to-year basis through time. Some growth patterns that may emerge include: (i) steady, reasonably consistent growth; (ii) some degree of recurrent cyclicality, such as repeating episodes of two years of price gains followed by two years of price stagnation or decline; or (iii) a long sequence of large yearly price movements, succeeded by a single- or multiyear period of significant price reversal. Investors should expect to encounter a wide variety of annual returns patterns, influenced in part by the overall course of financial market conditions, how well or how poorly the specific company executes, and how positively or how negatively investors as a whole assess prior results and future prospects for a specific company.

For the years 1997 through 2006, Table 7.10 displays the annual percentage price returns, excluding dividends, for the 10 largest U.S. companies, as measured by equity market capitalization at the end of the second quarter in 2007. These companies include, in descending order of total equity market values, Exxon

Mobil, General Electric, Microsoft, AT&T, Citigroup, Bank of America, Wal-Mart Stores, Procter & Gamble, American International Group, and Chevron.

General Observations and Caveats

First, the equity price returns of the leading U.S. companies shown in Table 7.10 reflect the year-end-to-year-end changes in these enterprises' share prices, adjusted for any stock splits. They do not include corporate spinoffs distributed to shareholders, or dividends paid on or reinvested in the common shares. Second, the overall year-end market capitalization of a company is calculated by multiplying the number of shares by the total outstanding number of common share equivalents (including quantities such as the shares underlying convertible securities and shares issuable under warrants and employee stock-option programs). A company's total equity market capitalization can increase or decrease as a result of: (i) an increase or decrease in the company's split-adjusted price per share; and (ii) an increase or decrease in the company's total common share equivalents, through events such as common share offerings, corporate repurchases of shares, or an acquiring company's use of newly issued shares to acquire another company.

Third, future price returns may or may not resemble the price returns of previous years. Consequently, investors should be very wary of drawing overly meaningful conclusions and inferences about companies' share price behavior in times to come from their share price patterns in times gone by.

Interyear and Intercompany Observations

On a 10-year basis, the highest compound annual rate of growth among the leading U.S. companies as measured by equity market capitalization was the 15.0% per year increase registered by Wal-Mart Stores. As a result, $1.00 invested in Wal-Mart Stores on January 1, 1997, would have been worth $4.06 at the end of the year 2006. Over this same time period, the next highest compound annual growth rates were exhibited by Citigroup, Exxon Mobil,

T A B L E 7.10

Leading U.S. Companies' Annual Price Rates of Return

Companies	1997	1998	1999	2000	2001	2002	2003	2004	2005	2006	2Q2007
Exxon Mobil	24.9%	19.5%	10.2%	7.9%	−9.6%	−11.1%	17.3%	25.0%	9.6%	36.4%	9.5%
General Electric	48.4%	39.0%	51.7%	−7.1%	−16.4%	−39.2%	27.2%	17.8%	−4.0%	6.2%	2.9%
Microsoft	56.4%	114.6%	68.4%	−62.8%	52.7%	−22.0%	5.9%	−2.4%	−2.1%	14.2%	−1.3%
AT&T	41.2%	46.4%	−9.1%	−2.1%	−18.0%	−30.8%	−3.8%	−1.2%	−5.0%	46.0%	16.1%
Citigroup	78.1%	−7.8%	68.1%	22.3%	−1.1%	−25.3%	37.9%	−0.7%	0.7%	14.8%	−7.9%
Bank of America	24.4%	−1.1%	−16.5%	−8.6%	37.2%	10.5%	15.6%	16.8%	−1.8%	15.7%	−8.4%
Wal-Mart Stores	73.4%	106.5%	69.8%	−23.1%	8.3%	−12.2%	5.0%	−0.4%	−11.4%	−1.3%	4.2%
Procter & Gamble	48.3%	14.4%	20.0%	−28.4%	0.9%	9.4%	16.2%	10.3%	5.1%	11.0%	−4.8%
American Int Grp	50.7%	33.3%	39.9%	36.7%	−19.4%	−27.1%	14.6%	−0.9%	3.9%	5.0%	−2.3%
Chevron	18.5%	7.7%	4.4%	−2.5%	6.1%	−25.8%	29.9%	21.6%	8.1%	29.5%	14.6%

Value of $1.00 on 12/31/06
(Compounded Annually)
10 Years (1997–2006)

Companies	Value	CAGR	Std Dev.	Sharpe Ratio
Exxon Mobil	$ 3.13	12.1%	15.0%	0.50
General Electric	$ 2.26	8.5%	29.8%	0.13
Microsoft	$ 2.89	11.2%	51.1%	0.13
AT&T	$ 1.38	3.3%	27.8%	−0.05
Citigroup	$ 3.95	14.7%	33.5%	0.30
Bank of America	$ 2.18	8.1%	16.2%	0.22
Wal-Mart Stores	$ 4.06	15.0%	44.6%	0.23
Procter & Gamble	$ 2.41	9.2%	18.9%	0.24
American Int Grp	$ 2.79	10.8%	26.1%	0.24
Chevron	$ 2.26	8.5%	16.6%	0.24

All annual price returns exclude dividend payments and reflect stock splits as follows: Exxon Mobil: 2-for-1 in 1997 and 2000; General Electric: 2-for-1 in 1997 and 3-for-1 in 2000; Microsoft: 2-for-1 in 1998, 1999, and 2003; AT&T: 3-for-2 in 1999 and reverse stock split 1-for-5 in 2002; Citigroup: 3-for-2 in 1997, and 1999, and 4-for-3 in 2000; Bank of America: 2-for-1 in 2004; Wal-Mart Stores: 2-for-1 in 1999; Procter & Gamble: 2-for-1 in 1997 and 2004; American International Group: 3-for-2 in 1997, 1998, and 2000 and 5-for-4 in 1999; Chevron: 2-for-1 in 2004.

Source: FactSet and the Author.

Microsoft, and American International Group, with per-year rates of increase of 14.7%, 12.1%, 11.2%, and 10.8%, respectively. An investor who placed $1.00 into Citigroup, Exxon Mobil, Microsoft, and American International Group on January 1, 1997, would have seen his or her investment increase in value to $3.95, $3.13, $2.89, and $2.79, respectively, as of December 31, 2006. Among the 10 leading market-capitalization companies, General Electric, Chevron, Bank of America, and AT&T had the slowest compound rates of growth in annual return from 1997 through 2006, at 8.5% per year, 8.5% per year, 8.1% per year, and 3.3% per year, respectively. An investment of $1.00 on January 1, 1997, would have grown in worth by the end of the year 2006 to $2.26 in both General Electric and Chevron, $2.18 in Bank of America, and $1.38 in AT&T.

For a firm's equity market capitalization to rank among the top 10 U.S. corporations at the end of 2000, either it had to be of significant size at the beginning of the 1990s and stay large, as did General Electric, Exxon Mobil, Wal-Mart Stores, SBC Communications, Coca-Cola, and IBM, or it had to experience rapid growth in market capitalization, as did Microsoft, Intel, Citigroup, and, especially, Cisco Systems. From 1995 through 1999, General Electric experienced five back-to-back years of very high price appreciation—rising 41.2%, 37.3%, 48.4%, 39.0%, and 51.7%, respectively—before declining 7.1% in 2000 and 16.4% in 2001.

On the whole, the late 1990s and the early twenty-first century were a favorable decade for the share prices of the 10 companies shown in Table 7.10. Out of total of 100 company-years (10 companies times 10 years), prices declined in 36 company-years (excluding the second quarter 2007). Microsoft exhibited the most severe single-year price decline (–62.8% in 2000), followed by General Electric (–39.2% in 2002). Microsoft posted the largest single-year price gain (114.6% in 1998).

In large measure influenced by anticipated and actual energy price movements, Exxon Mobil's share price performance during the 10 years shown displayed 4 consecutive years of appreciation from 1997 through 2000, increasing 24.9%, 19.5%, 10.2%, and 7.9%, respectively. Partly affected by interest rate and credit quality cycles, Citigroup's share price exhibited intermittent periods of advances and declines, rising 78.1% in 1997 before declining 7.8% in 1998 and rising again, by 68.1% in 1999 and 22.3% in 2000. In 2001 and 2002, Citigroup's share price fell –1.1% and –25.3%, respectively, and then increased 37.9% in 2003 before falling –0.7% once again in 2004. Following the decline in 2004, Citigroup experienced share price growth of 0.7% in 2005 and 14.8% in 2006.

During the 1990s, Wal-Mart's share price exhibited three years of sizable share price increases—+73.4 % in 1997, +106.5% in 1998, and +69.8% in 1999, before declining 23.1% in 2000. Wal-Mart's share price continued to rise in 2001 and 2003 (8.3% and 5.0%, respectively), with a significant decline of –12.2% in 2002. Wal-Mart's share price then fell again for three consecutive years from

2004 through 2006, –0.4%, –11.4%, and –1.3%, respectively. Within the technology sector, Microsoft experienced three years in a row of large advances in its share price, gaining 56.4%, 114.6%, and 68.4%, respectively, in years 1997, 1998, and 1999, before its –62.8% share price decline in 2000 (and a 52.7% rebound in 2001). Microsoft's share price continued to rise and fall between 2002 and 2006, with changes of –22.0%, +5.9%, –2.4%, –2.1%, and +14.2%, respectively. American International Group saw a strong rise in share price from 1997 through 2000, 50.7%, 33.3%, 39.9%, and 36.7%, respectively. Chevron saw increases in share prices for four consecutive years from 2003 through 2006, rising 29.9%, 21.6%, 8.1%, and 29.5%, respectively.

Investors should keep in mind that the enterprises listed in Table 7.10 represent the 10 largest companies in the United States at the end of the second quarter of 2007, as gauged by equity market capitalization. As such, their year-to-year equity price returns may very well not reflect the share price performance patterns of other companies. Historical awareness of different patterns of year-to-year equity price performance can: (i) reinforce the virtues of patience, perspective, and astute investment selection; (ii) reveal cyclical and other periodic influences on companies' share price behavior; and (iii) furnish important insights as to the rarity or ordinariness of specific periods in financial history.

SECTION 5

FINANCIAL MARKETS ANALYSIS
AND INVESTMENT INSIGHTS

CHAPTER 8

CONSTRUCTING AN ANALYTICAL FRAMEWORK

OVERVIEW

In the asset-allocation process, investors may be able to reap important benefits, and reduce the impact of suboptimal decisions, when they can simultaneously apply *perspective* (a long-term, macro tool), and *depth of analysis* (a short-term, micro tool). This takes patience, skill, and experience. To this end, investors require an array of tools that can furnish structure and sharpen reflection. When considering each of the major asset classes, investors need a figurative *telescope* to identify: (i) important trends; (ii) the duration of trends; and (iii) the magnitude of the likely effects of these trends. At the same time, investors need a figurative *microscope* to deconstruct and evaluate the essential features of specific investments and investment managers within a given asset class.

This chapter describes a number of analytical tools and techniques, including: (i) *societal analysis*, which looks at the health of a nation's interlinked financial, economic, political, and social conditions; (ii) *market-cycle analysis*, which sheds light on the varying degrees of influence that fundamental, valuation, and psychological factors exert on asset prices in different market phases; (iii) *scenario analysis*, which assigns probabilities to various economic and financial outcomes, links these outcomes to tactical asset-allocation decisions, and considers possible shocks, imbalances, and errors that can interrupt long-term market trends; and (iv) *investor-satisfaction analysis*, which examines the effects of investor actions and market outcomes on investor satisfaction.

This chapter also explores additional analytical constructs such as: (i) *strategy-implementation analysis*, which reviews many of the key decision points in investment-strategy implementation and selected factors influencing each decision; (ii) *comparative-financial analysis*, which demonstrates how to assemble and evaluate critical financial measures for investments within an asset class; (iii) *financial market climate analysis*, which characterizes investors' motives, actions, and expectations in favorable and unfavorable financial climates; and (iv) *phases and cycles in asset allocation*, which gives an account of the engagement, growth, realization, and affirmation stages within an investor's extended financial life.

Investors should marshal as many relevant tools as they can to apply insight, rigor, and fresh thinking to the asset-allocation process. The relative degree of time and emphasis devoted to each of these tools often depends largely on market conditions, the asset classes and investments being considered, and the investor's frame of mind.

SOCIETAL ANALYSIS

Investors should consider the degree of stability, growth, national cohesiveness, and forward thinking in an economy. This line of analysis applies to investing in U.S. and non-U.S. equities, fixed-income securities, and alternative investments, including venture capital, private equity, real estate, and other vehicles such as hedge funds. In general, the soundness and attractiveness of an investment depend vitally on the overall health of a country's society, composed of interdependent financial, economic, political, and social factors, among other features.

Figure 8.1 displays many of these building blocks of the human condition.

Nations, regions, and peoples seek to realize their aspirations in a continuous, upward-moving pattern. But along the way, their dreams often encounter the vagaries of economic and financial cycles, external events, periods of conflict and peace, shifting confidence levels, and altered priorities. Before committing significant amounts of assets to an asset class and/or a specific area of the world, investors would be wise to ask themselves where a nation appears to be heading on a spectrum of constructive or destructive

F I G U R E 8.1

Building Blocks of the Human Condition

Constructive

Financial	Economic	Political	Social
• Free-market solutions • Prudent risk assumption • Healthy growth, price level changes, valuation, and psychology • Declining risk premiums • Capital formation • Portfolio and direct investment flows	• GDP expansion • Rising living standards • Adjustment and reform energy • Integration into regional and world markets • Transparency • Structural reform	• Enlightened leadership • Respect for and support of empowerment • Pluralism, checks and balances • Credible legal and regulatory frameworks • Asset privatization	• Respect for contracts and rights • Access to opportunity • Atmosphere of liberation • Rising expectations and life expectancy • Environmental enhancement • Physical and mental well being

Destructive

Financial	Economic	Political	Social
• Capital destruction • Capital flight • Increasing risk premiums • Forced and voluntary deleveraging and risk aversion • Puncturing of asset bubbles • Government intervention • Exchange controls	• GDP contraction • Reduced consumption, savings, and investment • Monetary hoarding • Commodity-driven deflation • Currency-induced inflation • Isolationism and trade barriers • Declining living standards	• Reduced legitimacy of authority • Leadership turnover • Repressive policies • Nationalist fervor • Oligarchic control • Asset nationalization • Rule by decree	• Rending of traditional order • Backlash against the status quo • Sense of impoverishment • Xenophobia and international confrontation • Denunciation of free markets • Ethnic, social, or religious tensions • Acts of desperation • Negation of contracts and rights • Environmental abuse • Chronic illness, malnutrition, and reduced life expectancy

Source: The Author.

actions. Often, the answers to these questions cannot be based on precise measurement or calculation. Investors can and must, however, try to gain an overall sense of the current and future climate affecting asset allocation and investment activity. For example, in the *financial* realm, investors may wish to reflect on whether a nation is likely to pursue or continue pursuing capital-friendly policies, or whether it is likely to adopt capital-unfriendly policies. Figure 8.1 presents several causes and effects associated with each of these governmental and market tendencies. In the *economic* sphere, investors need to note favorable versus unfavorable developments and policies, and whether the forces behind those policies are outside the system (*exogenous* events) or inside the system (*endogenous* events). In the *political* sector, investors are well advised to ascertain whether a country's policies and politics are keeping pace with, leading, or out of phase with the support and will of a majority of the people. Finally, in the *social* arena, it is important to know to what degree the country is upholding or ignoring the basic rights, responsibilities, and entitlements of the populace.

MARKET-CYCLE ANALYSIS

A critically important cornerstone of the asset-allocation process is the ability to determine: (i) what stage of the market cycle a specific asset class (or subcategory of an asset class) is in; and (ii) the principal forces driving price levels within that stage. The prices of financial assets (such as equities and bonds) and real assets (such as commodities, precious metals, art, and collectibles) typically depend on some varying combination of a trinity of forces: (i) *fundamentals*; (ii) *valuation*; and (iii) *psychological/technical/ liquidity factors.* Figure 8.2 shows a pattern that asset prices generally follow.

Figure 8.2 depicts five major phases that, in simplified form, most assets' prices progress through, subject to reversals, to different degrees of magnitude, and, especially, to differing durations of time. These phases include: (i) a *bottoming*, in which depressed prices generate little or no investor enthusiasm; (ii) an *early-stage recovery*, in which bargain prices begin to convince investors of

F I G U R E 8.2

Factors Influencing Asset Prices in Different Market Phases

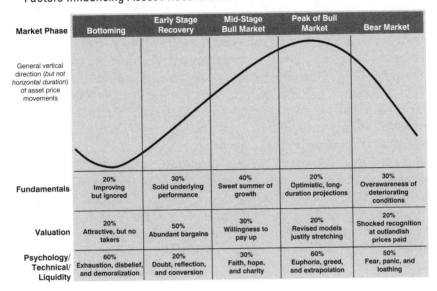

Market Phase	Bottoming	Early Stage Recovery	Mid-Stage Bull Market	Peak of Bull Market	Bear Market
General vertical direction (*but not horizontal duration*) of asset price movements					
Fundamentals	20% Improving but ignored	30% Solid underlying performance	40% Sweet summer of growth	20% Optimistic, long-duration projections	30% Overawareness of deteriorating conditions
Valuation	20% Attractive, but no takers	50% Abundant bargains	30% Willingness to pay up	20% Revised models justify stretching	20% Shocked recognition at outlandish prices paid
Psychology/ Technical/ Liquidity	60% Exhaustion, disbelief, and demoralization	20% Doubt, reflection, and conversion	30% Faith, hope, and charity	60% Euphoria, greed, and extrapolation	50% Fear, panic, and loathing

Note: The percentages indicated above are hypothetical only and reflect the personal views of the Author.

Source: The Author.

their underlying merits; (iii) a *mid-stage bull market*, in which fundamental measures of worth attract greater numbers of investors and/or increasing amounts of investment capital; (iv) a *peak bull market*, in which investors' increasing enthusiasm for the asset class pushes prices to extreme levels; and (v) a *bear market*, in which swelling ranks of investors abandon their enthusiasm for the asset and willingly offer it for sale.

Figure 8.2 also displays the varying degree of importance of the three key driving forces across the five phases experienced in a classical market cycle. *Fundamentals* (characteristics that define the inherent attractiveness, utility, or purpose of the asset) tend to exert only a small influence on price movements at the bottom, and at the top, of a market cycle. Fundamentals generally play a bigger role in determining prices during the middle stage of a bull market, when investors usually exhibit their most rational behavior.

Valuation (which takes into account the pattern, timing, and present worth of an asset's cash flows and terminal value, relative to itself and to other kinds of assets) tends to exert its greatest influence in the early stages of a bull market. During such phases, very attractive values often convert investors from disbelievers to believers. In other phases of a market cycle, values may be more of a lagging than a leading instigator of investor action.

Psychological, technical, and liquidity factors play a very important role in pushing asset prices to extremely elevated or depressed levels at the peaks or troughs of market cycles. Psychological forces (discussed in detail in Chapter 5) span the gamut of human emotion and include mania, greed, euphoria, gullibility, doubt, fear, panic, regret, and even loathing of others and oneself. Technical and liquidity forces encompass the liquidity of an asset, the origins and destinations of investors' funds flows, and the attractiveness or unattractiveness of an asset relative to other assets. Together, psychological, technical, and liquidity factors often dominate fundamental and valuation influences at market extremes.

SCENARIO ANALYSIS

After investors give thought to societal influences and to the prevailing phase and associated forces of the market cycle for an asset class (or subclass), they may profitably devote thought and resources to a hypothetical economic and financial scenario analysis. The chief value of such an analysis derives from: (i) the relative completeness of the range of scenarios, from optimistic to pessimistic; (ii) the rough translation of forecasted economic results into their potential effects on various asset classes; (iii) the assignment of probabilities to each scenario; and (iv) the construction of a tactical asset allocation (usually having a one-year time horizon) appropriate for each investor.

Investors should keep several caveats in mind when constructing and evaluating scenarios and their anticipated effects on financial markets and portfolio construction. Forecasts, and especially their associated probabilities, are purely *predictions*, not actual circumstances. They rarely come to pass in as internally consistent a manner and to the degree that they are projected to happen. Moreover, economic and financial history is filled with many outcomes that were not originally part of the forecasting vernacular, and thus were totally unpredicted.

Table 8.1 contains a matrix analyzing the likely effects of various U.S. economic and financial scenarios.

In Table 8.1, which covers the 12 months from the date of the analysis, *Scenario 1* calls for a period of good real economic growth (+3.5%), accompanied by rising consumer price inflation (+3.5%), and increasing S&P 500 after-tax corporate profits (+18.0%). Such an outcome might be associated with a rising world real GDP (+3.5%). In such circumstances, 10-year U.S. Treasury interest rates are *projected* to end the period at 6.0% and the 30-year U.S. Treasury bond is *projected* to yield 6.5%. The S&P 500 equity index is *projected* to provide a total return (including dividends) of +15.0%, and the 30-year U.S. Treasury bond is *projected* to provide a total return (including coupons) of –20.4%, assuming that long Treasury rates begin the 12-month period at 5.5% before rising to 6.5%.

In this hypothetical example, a probability of 10% is assigned to Scenario 1. Should moderate investors disagree with this probability and instead feel more strongly that Scenario 1 will in fact come to pass, they may adopt a tactical (one-year) asset allocation consisting of 55% equities, 25% bonds (with the maturity and coupon dependent on the degree of the investor's conviction about the interest rate outlook), 10% alternative investments, and 10% in cash equivalent instruments.

At the other end of the spectrum, *Scenario 6* predicts a period of deflation, in which real economic activity contracts by 1.0%, consumer prices fall 2.0%, and S&P 500 after-tax corporate profits decline 15.0%. An outright decline in world GDP of 1.0% might accompany such an environment, with 10-year U.S. Treasury interest rates *projected* to end the period at 3.0% and the 30-year U.S. Treasury bond *projected* to yield 3.5%. As a result, the S&P 500 equity index might provide a total return (including dividends) of –30.0%, and the 30-year U.S. Treasury bond might provide a total return (including coupons) of +56.7%.

This hypothetical Scenario 6 comes with a probability of 5%. Moderate investors who feel more strongly that Scenario 6 will in fact come to pass may adopt a highly defensive tactical (one-year)

T A B L E 8.1

Hypothetical Economic and Financial Scenario Analysis

Economic and Financial Outlook[1]	Scenario 1 Good Growth Rising Inflation	Scenario 2 Some Growth, Some Inflation	Scenario 3 Some Growth, Low Inflation
U.S. Real GDP	+ 3.5%	+ 2.5%	+ 1.5%
CPI Inflation Rate	+ 3.5%	+ 2.2%	+ 1.4%
Overall After-tax U.S. Corporate Profits	+ 10.0%	+ 7.0%	− 5.1%
S&P 500 After-tax Corporate Profits	+ 18.0%	+ 15.0%	+ 8.0%
World Real GDP	+ 3.5%	+ 3.0%	+ 2.0%
Capital Markets			
U.S. Treasury 10-Yr Interest Rates	6.0%	5.4%	5.3%
U.S. Treasury 30-Yr Interest Rates[2]	6.5%	6.0%	5.5%
U.S. Equities Total Return (S&P 500)	+ 15.0%	+ 10.0%	+ 6.0%
U.S. Treasury 30-Yr Total Return[2]	− 20.4%	− 8.2%	+ 5.5%
Probabilities	10%	25%	30%
Moderate Tactical Asset Allocation			
Equities	55%	50%	45%
Bonds (Duration Investor-Dependent)	25%	25%	30%
Alternative Investments[3]	10%	15%	20%
Cash	10%	10%	5%

Economic and Financial Outlook[1]	Scenario 4 Zero Growth, Low Inflation	Scenario 5 Disinflation	Scenario 6 Deflation
U.S. Real GDP	0.0%	0.0%	− 1.0%
CPI Inflation Rate	+ 1.0%	+ 0.5%	− 2.0%
Overall After-tax U.S. Corporate Profits	− 14.0%	− 16.0%	− 20.0%
S&P 500 After-tax Corporate Profits	− 5.0%	− 10.0%	− 15.0%
World Real GDP	+ 2.0%	0.0%	− 1.0%
Capital Markets			
U.S. Treasury 10-Yr Interest Rates	4.5%	4.0%	3.0%
U.S. Treasury 30-Yr Interest Rates[2]	4.8%	4.5%	3.5%
U.S. Equities Total Return (S&P 500)	− 10.0%	− 20.0%	− 30.0%
U.S. Treasury 30-Yr Total Return[2]	+ 20.7%	+ 37.7%	+ 56.7%
Probabilities	20%	10%	5%
Moderate Tactical Asset Allocation			
Equities	35%	30%	25%
Bonds (Duration Investor-Dependent)	35%	45%	50%
Alternative Investments[3]	15%	10%	5%
Cash	15%	15%	20%

Note: [1]The projected outcomes, probabilities, and allocations shown here are hypothetical only and reflect the personal views of the Author.

[2]Long-term (30-year) U.S. Treasury rates are assumed to be 5.5% at the beginning of a projected one-year holding period.

[3]Includes real estate/REITs, commodities and precious metals; private equity and venture capital; inflation-linked securities; hedge funds, and hedge fund funds of funds.

Source: The Author.

asset allocation consisting of 25% equities, 50% bonds (with the maturity and coupon dependent on the degree of the investor's convictions about interest rates), 5% alternative investments, and 20% in cash equivalent instruments.

Scenarios with Potentially Serious Consequences

Investors looking for potential excesses that might foretell major turning points in financial markets should keep in mind that the temporal length and percentage change of an index price, by themselves, are not sufficient to spark a reversal in trend. As a general principle, there are three ways to interrupt a long upward or downward price movement and perhaps send it in a new direction: (i) one or more major *external shocks* to the economic system or prevailing confidence levels; (ii) the buildup and eventual denouement of significant *internal imbalances* within an economy; and/or (iii) monetary, fiscal, trade, or other *policy errors* that harm key sectors of a national, a regional, or the worldwide economy.

Figure 8.3 sets forth a number of scenarios with potentially serious consequences, grouped into the broad categories of External Shocks, Internal Imbalances, and Policy Errors.

The potential scenarios shown in Figure 8.3 are by no means a complete listing of possible developments. However, such a list can help investors reflect in advance on: (i) *anticipated effects* of one or more of these (or other) outcomes on the short-term and long-term price behavior of equities, fixed-income securities, alternative investments, cash, and currencies; and, importantly, (ii) the substance and pathways of *likely responses* to a given scenario by central banks, regulators, governments, investors, and other financial-market participants.

INVESTOR SATISFACTION ANALYSIS

While investors survey the external forces that may affect specific asset classes, the financial markets, and the economy, they should consider and, if possible, approximately quantify how they might

F I G U R E 8.3

Scenarios with Potentially Serious Consequences

External Shocks	Internal Imbalances	Policy Errors
• Debt rescheduling talks are initiated and/or default is declared by a major international borrower. • Non-U.S. investors execute major sales of U.S. dollar denominated financial assets. • A serious terrorist act is perpetrated, involving conventional or unconventional weapons, or possibly biological, chemical, or nuclear agents. • Tensions escalate toward wider armed conflict in troubled regions. • Confrontation spreads between governments and financial markets. • An export battle breaks out between a major economy and countries within its own region. • Operational and/or financial problems at a large securities custodian or payments network prevent the timely clearing and settlement of transactions. • Hackers and virus writers effectively disrupt or disable a significant part of a nation's or the globe's computer-reliant utility, telecommunications, air traffic control, defense, or other infrastructures.	• Large-scale losses are revealed in the lending and/or derivatives markets. • One or more large financial institutions and/or industrial enterprises declares insolvency. • Highly valued equity market sectors experience significant price declines. • Economic growth falls sharply in selected economies. • External debt burdens and/or non-performing financial loans lead to a banking crisis within a major economy.	• Excessive monetary liquidity is injected (or suddenly withdrawn) worldwide, leading to significant asset-price inflation (or deflation), and/or general price level inflation (or deflation). • Major currency instability develops in the yen, euro, U.S. dollar, and/or other currencies. • Governments adopt protectionist policies that restrict the flow of goods, services, and/or capital.

Source: The Author.

respond to the market's affirmation or rejection of their asset-allocation decisions.

For example, investors who expect the price of a specific asset class to rise will need to decide whether to: (i) *buy* the asset; (ii) *hold* the asset, if already owned; or (iii) *sell* the asset. Figure 8.4 presents these decisions in the form of a decision tree.

In the aftermath of the decision to buy, hold, or sell a specific asset, its price may rise, remain about the same, or decline. Each of these outcomes will produce some degree of *utility*—happiness or

FIGURE 8.4

The Influence of Investor Actions and Market Outcomes on Investor Satisfaction

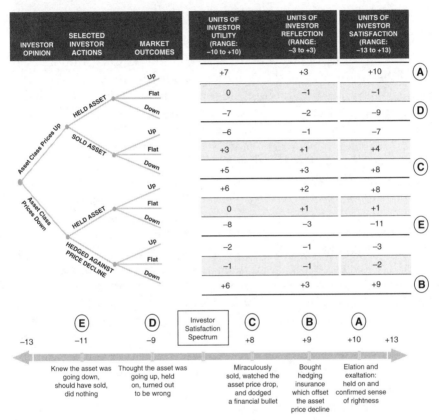

INVESTOR OPINION	SELECTED INVESTOR ACTIONS	MARKET OUTCOMES	UNITS OF INVESTOR UTILITY (RANGE: −10 to +10)	UNITS OF INVESTOR REFLECTION (RANGE: −3 to +3)	UNITS OF INVESTOR SATISFACTION (RANGE: −13 to +13)	
		Up	+7	+3	+10	(A)
	HELD ASSET	Flat	0	−1	−1	
		Down	−7	−2	−9	(D)
		Up	−6	−1	−7	
Asset Class Prices Up	SOLD ASSET	Flat	+3	+1	+4	
		Down	+5	+3	+8	(C)
		Up	+6	+2	+8	
	HELD ASSET	Flat	0	+1	+1	
Asset Class Prices Down		Down	−8	−3	−11	(E)
		Up	−2	−1	−3	
	HEDGED AGAINST PRICE DECLINE	Flat	−1	−1	−2	
		Down	+6	+3	+9	(B)

(E)	(D)	Investor Satisfaction Spectrum	(C)	(B)	(A)	
−13	−11	−9	+8	+9	+10	+13
	Knew the asset was going down, should have sold, did nothing	Thought the asset was going up, held on, turned out to be wrong	Miraculously sold, watched the asset price drop, and dodged a financial bullet	Bought hedging insurance which offset the asset price decline	Elation and exaltation: held on and confirmed sense of rightness	

Note: The numerical values indicated above are hypothetical only and reflect the personal views of the Author.

Source: The Author.

disappointment—on the part of the investor, with some degree of investor *reflection*, causing the entirely human second-guessing of previous actions to follow in its wake. Investor utility combined with investor reflection yields some degree of investor *satisfaction* or *dissatisfaction*, ranging from mild to extreme.

Investors can assign some arbitrary, yet consistent, scale of numerical rating to these potential outcomes to assess the relative effect on their psyches and to rank various results versus other results (even though the scale is numerically based, the units of satisfaction tend to be highly subjective and specific to each investor). For instance, Figure 8.4 shows how *one investor* might react to 12 possible outcomes, which are a function of: (i) the investor's opinion as to the likely future course of asset prices; (ii) the action he or she actually takes, based on that opinion, or in total disregard of it; and (iii) actual market outcomes.

For example, following the top branch in Figure 8.4 (labeled "Asset Class Prices Up," then "Held Asset," and then "Up,"), at each of the three nodes on the decision tree, signifies that: (i) the investor thought the prices of the asset class were going to rise; (ii) the investor held (or purchased) the asset; and in fact; (iii) prices did go up. This sequence of events produced +7 units of *investor utility* (on a subjective scale of +10 units to –10 units). Adding that to +3 units of *investor reflection* (on a subjective scale of +3 units to –3 units) produces +10 units of overall *investor satisfaction* (on a combined potential scale of +13 units to –13 units). Point A on the decision tree at the top of Figure 8.4 and the corresponding point A along the Investor Satisfaction Spectrum at the bottom of the figure indicates: (i) the investor's conviction that prices were going to rise; (ii) his or her holding on to the asset; and (iii) the fact that the actual price rise led, in this instance, to a highly positive set of emotions, including a sense of rightness about investment outcomes, and elation over the investor's own feelings of mastery and financial acumen.

At the opposite end of the Investor Satisfaction Spectrum is the range of feelings brought about by: (i) the investor's belief that the prices of an asset were going to decline; (ii) the investor holding on to the asset rather than selling it; and (iii) prices subsequently experiencing a downturn. For a given investor, this sequence of events produced –8 units of *investor utility*, which, added to –3 units of *investor reflection*, produced –11 units of overall *investor satisfaction*. Point E on the decision tree at the top of Figure 8.4 and the corresponding point E along the Investor Satisfaction Spectrum at the bottom of the figure result from such an outcome. The investor ignored his or her strong feeling that prices were going down, and did not sell the asset. On the Investor

Satisfaction Spectrum, the price decline led to complex and unsatisfactory emotions, such as self-recrimination and the constant playing out of a series of what-if scenarios.

Although the attempt to place numerical values on what are usually variable and highly personalized feelings is imprecise and not scientific, this approach can stimulate and organize the investor's thinking about potential outcomes and their financial and emotional effects, prior to taking investment action.

STRATEGY IMPLEMENTATION ANALYSIS

Throughout the asset-allocation process, investors may be faced with choices about how to implement an investment strategy that is consistent with and reflective of their asset-allocation goals. A series of factors can help investors determine which choice is most appropriate for them. Figure 8.5 presents several of these decision points, and a limited number of the many possibilities available to investors at each decision point.

The choices along the continuum, from left to right in Figure 8.5, start with large-scale issues, such as the *macro asset class selection decision*: whether to invest only in conventional asset classes, or also in alternative asset classes. For simplification purposes, other choices, such as investing only in alternative classes, are not shown at any of the decision points in Figure 8.5. An arc encompassing each decision point denotes the *range* of choices investors face. The right side of the figure lists selected factors that may influence investors to select one branch of the decision tree or another. Figure 8.5 assumes that investors have chosen the conventional asset classes branch, then the equity branch, and then the direct ownership branch of the decision tree. Many of the same decisions and choices displayed in Figure 8.5 apply, with some modification, to other asset classes, such as debt securities or alternative investments. Given the choice of equities in Figure 8.5, a number of more detailed choices present themselves.

The *direct versus pooled ownership decision* may guide investors to own securities directly or via a pooled vehicle such as a mutual fund. Time, cost, and tax considerations will bear on this decision.

F I G U R E 8.5

Decision Points in Investment Strategy Implementation

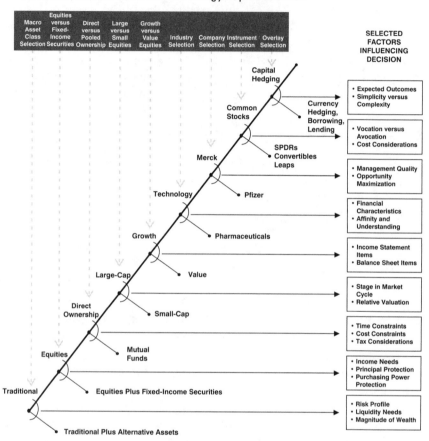

Source: The Author.

Investors who decide to invest in equities need to determine whether *large-capitalization, mid-capitalization*, or *small-capitalization* issues are more appropriate. For simplification purposes, Figure 8.5 does not show mid-capitalization issues. The numerous factors that have a bearing on this decision include: (i) the position of large-cap versus small-cap issues in their respective market cycles;

and (ii) the relative valuation of these two equity groupings, compared with their respective historical valuation ranges and with each other.

Similarly, the *growth equity versus value equity decision* hinges in part on whether the marketplace as a whole is, and/or may likely become, focused primarily on *income-statement items*, such as margins and growth rates in revenues, cash flow, and earnings. Such an environment may indicate a tilt toward *growth equities.* Alternatively, the market as a whole may be, and/or may likely become, focused primarily on *balance-sheet items,* such as cash and other tangible asset levels, debt-to-equity ratios, contingent liabilities, and book values. Such an environment may motivate many investors to favor *value equities.*

Having made a selection between large- and small-cap equities, and between value and growth, investors usually select an industry or industries, and then select one or more than one company in these industries. Cyclical and secular financial and operating characteristics of the industry, as well as the investors' affinity for and understanding of industry dynamics, will influence the *industry choice.* Three important factors influencing *company choice* are: (i) the quality of management; (ii) the attractiveness of the company's business; and (iii) how well the company is taking advantage of its business opportunities.

Once investors decide on industries and companies, they often encounter a number of different ways to invest: common stock, options, futures, warrants, convertible bonds and preferred stock, futures, equity-linked bonds, index-tracking securities, and other instruments. *Which investment instrument* to use depends on: (i) how much time and understanding the investor brings to the process; and (ii) comparative transaction costs. After determining the form of investment, some investors consider the *overlay selection decision.* A portfolio overlay usually shifts the risk-return profile toward either a more conservative or a more aggressive investment stance. The range, form, cost spectrum, and availability of these portfolio overlay tools have expanded considerably in recent years, and include devices for: (i) hedging the capital value of the portfolio or individual positions; (ii) currency hedging; and (iii) borrowing or lending money or securities. Investors' predilection for simplicity versus complexity will influence whether they employ these techniques, and which ones to use.

COMPARATIVE FINANCIAL ANALYSIS

Over time, success in asset allocation and investment strategy depends highly on the investor's skill in evaluating price-versus-value relationships, between and within asset classes, specific investments, and currencies. Based upon this knowledge and acumen, successful investors can identify and purchase superior-performing investments and asset classes. Equally important, they can avoid inferior-performing investments and asset classes.

At its heart, the entire investment-banking and investment-management realm revolves around *assessing the true value of something compared to its price*. Investment research and asset-management disciplines, public and private equities and debt trading, capital markets, and underwriting functions, as well as merger, acquisition, and restructuring and divestiture activity, all hinge upon the cardinal question: Is the value of a given asset greater than, equal to, or less than its price?

Significant effort, and a great many quantitative and qualitative tools and techniques, have been brought to bear on the question of how to determine the value of financial and real assets. Many investors believe that the value of an asset is determined by *what someone will pay* for it at a particular moment in time. Other investors use various *discounted cash flow* (DCF) models and similar constructs that take into account the timing, magnitude, and riskiness of the income streams and terminal price of an asset. Still others rely on market-clearing prices of *comparable assets* that have recently been bought and sold.

Common sense, perceptiveness, honest and rigorous analysis, and good judgment are potentially at the disposal of most investors. With a modest degree of effort, it is possible to assemble relevant data about comparable investments in an identified asset class. Within reason, and when applied with a dose of healthy skepticism, this information can often help identify investments that are substantially overvalued or undervalued.

To demonstrate how to apply this approach, the following paragraphs discuss one asset class, publicly traded equities. Investors can follow a similar approach in a number of other asset classes, ranging from high-grade, high-yield, convertible, inflation-indexed, or emerging-markets debt, to mutual funds, hedge funds, or unit trusts, to various forms of commodities, private equity, oil and gas, venture capital, or real estate investments. Each of these asset classes or subasset classes has certain characteristics that are unique, and thus worthy of special analytical methodologies. At the same time, many of the underlying goals and principles apply broadly across asset classes. These guidelines include: (i) consistency of calculation; (ii) selection of an appropriate analytical time frame; (iii) creativity and soundness in comparing data; (iv) restraint in drawing unrealistic conclusions; and (v) conviction and patience in waiting for prices to come back into line with value.

Within the publicly traded equities asset class, one approach to generating outstanding long-term investment performance has been to identify great businesses, invest in them at reasonable prices, and hold on to them for long periods of time. In this way, the favorable fundamental economics of the company, the power of compound returns, and the relative tax advantages and reduced expenses of a low-turnover approach can generally produce superior investment results, eventually overcoming short-term fluctuations in securities prices.

A critical ingredient in this approach to common stock investing is the ability to identify companies that have: (i) *profitability*—true long-term economic *attractiveness*; (ii) *protection*—the *ability to defend* their money-making characteristics from competitive and/or governmental inroads; and (iii) *plowback*—sufficient *opportunities to reinvest* their retained profits at high rates of return. Effectiveness of this approach also requires investors to select appropriate indications of these traits that can be measured across a number of years and that are reasonably comparable across companies and industries.

Table 8.2 contains profitability, protection, and plowback data for a number of well-known corporations, to illustrate a range of performance results according to each of these three criteria.

T A B L E   8.2

Comparative Financial Measures for Selected U.S. Corporations

| Company | Profitability 2004–2006 Average (%) | | Protection 2004–2006 Average (%) | | Plowback ROE (%) | | |
	Gross Margin	Operating Margin	R&D Margin	SG&A Margin	2000	2003	2006
Boeing	16.4	4.9	4.3	7.1	22.8	9.9	46.7
Dell	18.1	8.3	1.0	8.8	41.1	42.1	68.5
Heinz	36.2	14.8	n/a	21.3	65.8	41.1	35.0
IBM	39.8	12.3	6.3	21.9	29.2	27.3	33.0
Sun Microsystems	41.6	−6.7	16.3	29.0	23.6	−42.1	−12.9
Wyeth	50.4	15.7	14.7	32.7	89.2	32.8	29.2
Procter & Gamble	51.2	19.3	3.3	32.0	34.4	35.4	13.8
Intel	56.2	25.6	14.6	15.2	28.6	14.9	14.0
Google	57.5	28.8	9.5	16.6	n/a	17.5	17.3
Coca Cola	65.3	26.2	n/a	39.1	39.4	34.0	27.9
Estee Lauder	74.3	10.7	1.1	63.1	20.7	18.7	25.7
Microsoft	83.0	32.8	17.2	33.0	22.8	17.3	31.4
Pfizer	84.4	25.4	14.9	32.5	40.4	19.5	21.0

Past performance is not a guarantee of future results.

Definitions:
Gross Margin = Sales less cost of goods sold as a percent of sales.
Operating Margin = Gross margin less SG&A and R&D as a percent of sales.
SG&A Margin = Selling, general, and administrative expense as a percent of sales.
R&D Margin = Research and development costs as a percent of sales.
ROE = Return on equity = Earnings as a percent of book value at the beginning of the year.

Source: Value Line, Inc.; FactSet; and the Author.

Profitability

For each company in Table 8.2, profitability from 2004 through 2006 is measured according to two benchmarks—gross margin and operating margin. *Gross margin* is a company's sales less its cost of goods sold, expressed as a percentage of sales. For example, the 2004–2006 gross margin for Intel averaged 56.2%; for IBM, 39.8%;

and for Estee Lauder, 74.3%. Microsoft's three-year average gross margin was 83.0%, and Boeing's was 16.4%.

The *operating margin* measure generally reflects how well a company can bring its revenue to the bottom line, after deducting: (i) the cost of goods sold; (ii) selling, general, and administrative (SG&A) expenses; and (iii) research and development (R&D) outlays. For example, the 2004–2006 average operating margin of Dell was 8.3%, even though its gross margin was a relatively slender 18.1. By comparison, the three-year average operating margin of IBM was 12.3%, 4 percentage points more than Dell's, while IBM's gross margin was 39.8%, a full 21.7 percentage points more than Dell's. Armed with this information, investors can weigh the relative strategic and tactical advantages and disadvantages of Dell's much lower rate of spending on R&D (1.0% of sales, compared with 6.3% of sales for IBM), as well as its lower selling, general, and administrative expenses (8.8% of 2004–2006 sales for Dell, compared with 21.9% of 2004–2006 sales for IBM).

Protection

Two rough measures of a company's skill at protecting its profitability are: (i) its percentage of sales spent on *R&D*; and (ii) its percentage of sales spent on *selling, general, and administrative* expenditures, which include marketing, promotion, and advertising outlays intended to preserve the company's competitive standing and market share. A high level of R&D and/or a high level of SG&A expenses are in and of themselves no guarantee of a company's success in defending its position. What is most important is the *degree* of *efficacy* of these two expense streams, which in turn reflects management's ability to wisely deploy corporate resources, to conceive and execute a winning strategic vision, and to hire, empower, motivate, and retain talented human resources.

Of the companies shown in Table 8.2, Boeing and Dell spent 4.3% and 1.0%, respectively, of their 2004–2006 sales on R&D, while Pfizer and Microsoft spent 14.9% and 17.2%, respectively. Sun Microsystems spent 16.3%, Intel spent 14.6%, and Wyeth (formerly known as American Home Products) spent 14.7% of their 2004–2006 sales on R&D.

For many companies, the percentage of sales spent on SG&A expenses is a barometer of these firms' ongoing efforts to fortify their competitive position. Such companies may well be investing in marketing, advertising, selling, and promotion expenses to widen and deepen the strategic and tactical defenses around their brand, their sales force, and/or their distribution system. At the same time, however, an overly high absolute percentage of sales spent on SG&A expenses may be an indicator of managerial inefficiency, excessive corporate largesse, and/or an inefficient and bureaucratic infrastructure that impedes rather than fosters competitive innovation and market responsiveness. For this reason, investors and their sources of investing counsel should spare no effort in attempting to deconstruct the SG&A expense category and look at the data in their various component parts.

For example, Table 8.2 shows that Pfizer, Coca-Cola, and Estee Lauder spent 32.5%, 39.1%, and 63.1%, respectively, of their 2004–2006 sales on SG&A expenses. Each of these companies devotes considerable corporate funds and managerial energy to its sales force, its distribution infrastructure, and its advertising and promotion activities, all of which are integral to the protection and renewal of its brands and competitive positioning.

At the other end of the spectrum, Boeing and Dell spent 7.1% and 8.8% of their 2004–2006 sales on SG&A expenses, respectively. Each of these companies has a considerably lower gross margin than Pfizer, Coca-Cola, and Estee Lauder, and thus there is less absolute room in percentage of sales terms to devote to SG&A expenses. In addition, part of Boeing's protection of its competitive position derives from such things as its technological know-how, its purchasing acumen and the management of supplier relations, its servicing network, and its aftermarket support. Dell's defense of its competitive edge stems in part from its sophisticated manufacturing and assembly prowess, its Internet-based sales and marketing strategy, and its inventory and financial-management skills.

A company's defensive strength may, or may not, be associated with a high percentage of its sales spent on R&D and/or SG&A expenses. Investors should consider these expenditures: (i) as a percentage of the overall gross margin *available* for protection activity; (ii) in the context of industry dynamics relating to changing forms of corporate differentiation and competition; (iii) as but two *among several* measures of franchise protection and enhancement; and (iv) in their deconstructed or component form, if more detailed data are available.

Plowback

One characteristic of a business as an attractive investment candidate is the range of opportunities for that company to continue to reinvest its earnings at high rates of return over a long period of time. Among the measures of this *plowback* ability are multiyear trends in the company's *return on equity* (ROE), defined as the company's net earnings after taxes as a percentage of its shareholders' equity, or book value.

Table 8.2 shows that Dell had a 2006 ROE of 68.5% (compared with 41.1% in 2000 and 42.1% in 2003), Heinz had a 2006 ROE of 35.0% (compared with 65.8% in 2000 and 41.1% in 2003), Google had a 2006 ROE of 17.3% (compared with 17.5 in 2003), and Coca-Cola had a 2006 ROE of 27.9% (compared with 39.4% in 2000 and 34.0% in 2003).

Certain caveats should be noted about using a company's ROE as a measure of its profit plowback potential. First, a company's ROE may change over the short or intermediate term due to shifting industry fundamentals over which the company has little or no control. Such factors include interest rates, energy and other commodity prices, the overall level of economic activity, and specific demand trends for the industry(ies) and country(ies) in which the company operates. Investors thus tend to value highly a company's ability to generate high ROE through changing circumstances.

Second, the quality of a company's ROE is only as good as the quality of its accounting policies and financial-management practices. The quality of earnings data may be influenced by: revenue-recognition procedures; customer payment-behavior assumptions; inventory, R&D, and depreciation conventions; assumed and actual pension-plan investment returns; the level of employee stock option compensation; and a host of subjective accounting judgments associated with merger, acquisition, restructuring, and

divestiture activity. The degree of subjectivity in earnings calculations underscores the need to read footnotes to corporate financial
statements and to look behind stated numbers to allow investors to
make consistent multiyear, multicompany comparisons.

Third, ROE computations are influenced by the amount of
financial leverage (the debt-equity mix) a company has on (and
off) its balance sheet. For instance, a company that earns $100
million after taxes, with $500 million in equity and no long-term
debt on its balance sheet, may generate a 20% ROE, while a
similar company that earns $100 million after taxes with $200
million in equity and $300 million in long-term debt may gener-
ate a 50% ROE. In practice, both companies have earned the same
amount of money after taxes in an absolute sense: $100 million.
Whether investors should consider a 20% ROE or a 50% ROE a
valid measure of plowback and whether one result is superior to
the other are functions of: (i) industry operating and financial
characteristics; (ii) corporate policies affecting the generation and
deployment of cash flow; (iii) the nature of the industry and
economic environment in which the company operates; and especially importantly, (iv) investors' views of the risks associated
with corporate leverage.

FINANCIAL MARKET CLIMATE ANALYSIS

Knowing how to recognize, anticipate, and respond to changes *in* the
financial climate (as distinguished from changes *within* a financial
climate) is one of the chief challenges to achieving successful investment results during any meaningful time horizon.

Major climatic shifts in the outlook for financial assets often
call for profound reflection and a reordering of asset-allocation percentages. For example, significant economic expansion in the
United States during the 1950s and 1960s called for an asset allocation that overweighted equities and equity-like assets. By contrast,
the 1970s witnessed rising inflation (accompanied by two significant OPEC-led increases in crude oil prices), rising interest rates, a
14.7% decline in the S&P 500 index in 1973—followed by a 26.5%
decline in 1974—and generally unappealing returns for equities as
an asset class for the better part of 10 years.

Helped by heightened Federal Reserve resolve to bring down inflation beginning in October 1979, a return to multiyear economic and profit growth, and households' increasing allocations of their retirement and investment plans into stocks and equity mutual funds, the 1980s and 1990s again rewarded an emphasis on equities and equity-like assets. In contrast, in Japan during the 1990s, a period of economic retrenchment and general price disinflation, the returns from owning Japanese government bonds were two and one-half times greater than the returns from owning Japanese equities.

After the turn of the 20th century into the 21st century, U.S. and many non-U.S. equity markets exhibited price declines, with the S&P 500 index falling 9.1% in 2000, 11.9% in 2001, and 22.1% in 2002. The relative outperformance of several fixed-income, cash, and alternative asset classes led a number of investors to reflect upon and assess the climate for financial markets and specific asset classes. Long-term factors arguing in favor of a sustained *high commitment* to equities and equity-like assets included: (i) an expected return to economic growth and profitability in the United States and in many other areas of the world; (ii) continued technological progress and generally capitalism-friendly governments; and not least, (iii) reasonably benign prognoses for price changes, liquidity and capital flows, and monetary and fiscal policies.

Long-term factors arguing for a *reduction* in the asset-allocation percentage devoted to equities and equity-like assets included: (i) high historical equity valuation measures (such as price-earnings, price-book value, price-sales, and dividend ratios); (ii) the magnitude, complexity, and pervasiveness of various forms of financial leverage, among them consumer and corporate borrowing, the dramatically expanded use of derivatives, and the proliferation of highly leveraged institutions; and (iii) low U.S. personal savings rates and current-account balance-of-payments deficits at the highest levels in 115 years, depicted in Figure 8.6.

Financial market conditions can powerfully influence not only asset allocation, but also prevailing approaches to investor behavior and investment strategy. For example, in a maturing bull market for equities, cash as an asset class and market timing tend to be denigrated in favor of a virtually fully invested investment

U.S. Current-Account Balance of Payments: 1889–2006

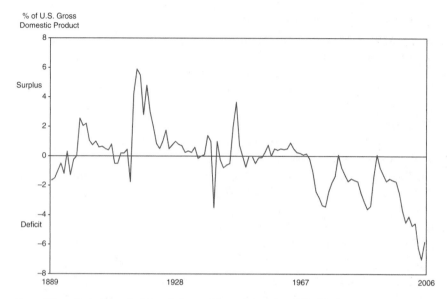

Source: Morgan Stanley Economics Research; Bureau of Economic Analysis; and *Historical Statistics of the United States*

approach and a long-horizon, buy-the-dips mentality toward stocks. Figure 8.7 depicts some of the effects of favorable and unfavorable financial climates on investors' motives, actions, and expectations.

The two pie charts in Figure 8.7 estimate investors' motives in a bull market compared with their motives in a bear market. During a bull market, investors' primary motives revolve around making money; during a bear market, their primary motives shift to avoiding losses.

Figure 8.7 also contrasts some of the common effects of a *favorable* financial market environment on investors' actions and expectations with those of an *unfavorable* financial market environment. In prolonged periods of rising prices for financial assets, investors are willing to entertain a wider range of geographical, asset class, and implementation strategies. Amid heightened expectations and risk assumption, many investors tend to emphasize capital

F I G U R E   8.7

Financial Market Climate Effects on Investors

Favorable Financial Market Climate

Investors' Motives in a Bull Market

Making Money 60%

10%

30% Avoiding Losses

Diversification

Effects on Investors' Actions and Expectations

- Significant amounts of newly created individual wealth
- Wide range of geographical, asset class, and implementation strategies
- Heightened and frequently unrealistic investor expectations
- Investor satisfaction with existing financial intermediaries
- Explicit and implicit assumption of risk
- Equities, equity-like products, and margin borrowing more important in asset allocations
- Increased interest in performance investing and "offensive-style" alternative investment categories and hedge fund strategies
- Proliferation of investment management boutiques, consultants, and third-party capital raisers
- Emphasis on capital appreciation

Unfavorable Financial Market Climate

Investors' Motives in a Bear Market

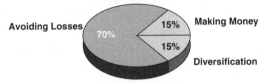

Avoiding Losses 15% Making Money

70%

15%

Diversification

Effects on Investors' Actions and Expectations

- Wealth reduction and less newly created wealth
- Narrow range of geographical, asset class, and implementation strategies
- Investor dissatisfaction with investment performance
- Investor flight to high-quality financial intermediaries
- Emphasis on risk reduction, risk control, and risk management
- Short- and intermediate-term fixed-income securities more important in asset allocations
- Increased interest in "defensive-style" alternative investment categories and hedge fund strategies
- Consolidation/closure of investment management boutiques, consultants, and third-party capital raisers
- Emphasis on capital preservation

Source: The Author.

appreciation, equities and equity-like products, and "offensive-style" alternative investment categories and hedge fund strategies.

In periods of prolonged falling financial asset prices, many investors tend to concentrate on a narrowed range of geographic, asset class, and implementation strategies. Investors primarily focus on capital preservation and mainstream investments of a defensive character, such as short- and intermediate-term fixed-income securities. With restrained expectations and heightened risk awareness, investors tend to emphasize "defensive-style" alternative investment categories and hedge fund strategies.

PHASES AND CYCLES IN ASSET ALLOCATION

Investors face a series of phases and cycles in the structuring, allocation, and investment management of their assets. Figure 8.8 depicts these phases and cycles.

The periods shown along the bottom of Figure 8.8 are not fixed for all investors, but give a representative idea of the time that may be devoted to each major phase of an investor's experience, which may last between 20 years and 40 years. Some investors may devote time and attention to learning asset-allocation and investment-management skills *themselves*, while others may devote resources to learning how to evaluate the asset-allocation and investment-management skills of *third parties acting on their behalf.*

The first phase of the asset-allocation and investment-management process may be called the *engagement phase*, generally lasting two to five years, in which investors *acquire and learn* investment skills. In this phase, investors may find out what investment areas they have an affinity for, while studying and learning from the great body of investment wisdom and knowledge.

The second phase may be termed the *growth phase*, generally lasting 4 to 10 years, in which investors *broaden and deepen* their skills. In this phase, investors may apply an increasing degree of acumen and understanding to asset-allocation and investment-management styles, techniques, and resources.

The third phase may be called the *realization phase*, generally lasting 6 to 15 years, in which investors *leverage and demonstrate mastery* in the investment realm. In this phase, investors may take

F I G U R E 8.8

Phases and Cycles in Asset Allocation and Investment Management

Skills Acquiring	Skills Learning	Skills Deepening	Skills Broadening	Skills Mastery	Skills Leveraging	Skills Renewal	Skills Treasury

Engagement	Growth	Realization	Affirmation

Goals

- Find investment areas you are good at.
- Find investment areas you like.
- Be honest with yourself.
- Develop good investment habits.
- Know your strengths and weaknesses.
- Focus on: price versus value.

Goals

- Pick your investment areas of emphasis.
- Take appropriate risks.
- Understand the risks and rewards of concentration versus diversification.
- Find one, two, or three significant investment ideas each year.
- Focus on: price versus value.

Goals

- Exchange tools and knowledge with others.
- Produce, reap, harvest, and reinvest.
- Concentrate on reaching your fullest human and investment potential.
- Foster positive energy in yourself and others.
- Focus on: price versus value.

Goals

- Learn from all quarters.
- Synthesize, create, advise, and cross-pollinate.
- Teach others to think not merely in one-year increments.
- Focus on: price versus value.

The lengths and slopes of *phases* will vary widely. The mix of required investment skills will vary within phases.	*Cycles* and secular market forces will be powerful and will sometimes augment, sometimes neutralize, each other.	*Phases* often overlap and blend into one another. Pace in one phase may or may not carry over into the next phase.	*Cycles* come in several forms: financial, learning, attitude, and life cycles.

Advice

- Work on valuation skills and study them.
- Set investment goals and write them down.
- Learn from mistakes.
- Be expert in certain investment areas.
- Develop an investment philosophy.
- Find great investors, and learn from them.
- Hone judgment skills.

Advice

- Engage each resource in personal, professional, intellectual, and emotional excellence.
- Expand investment competence along several fronts.
- Stay focused, stay organized.
- Build and maintain reserves of mental and psychological strength.

Advice

- Leverage knowledge, relationships, and wisdom.
- Support, enhance, and encourage your major fonts of investment wisdom.
- Nurture others and yourself.
- Do not let yourself get upset by your own or others' mistakes.

Advice

- Keep learning, growing, and pushing the envelope.
- Stay excited and transmit enthusiasm.
- Reflect on what has gone before and apply it.
- Grow by helping others grow.
- Make your gifts count.

Year 0 / Year 0	2–5 Years	Year 2 / Year 5	Year 2 / Year 5	4–10 Years	Year 6 / Year 15	Year 6 / Year 15	6–15 Years	Year 12 / Year 30	Year 12 / Year 30	8–10 Years	Year 20 / Year 40

Source: The Author.

advantage of the tools, experience, relationships, and know-how that they have built up through a variety of financial environments and their changing personal financial circumstances.

The fourth phase may be termed the *affirmation phase*, generally lasting 8 to 10 years or more, in which investors *renew, draw upon, and extend* their financial understanding and skills storehouse. In this phase, investors may be engaged in an active and fruitful two-way exchange of learning and lore with other investors.

Cycles of market volatility, price advance and decline, and fundamental, valuation, and psychological/technical/liquidity excesses will be woven through each of these four broad phases. In the process of blending cycles and phases, several general principles are worth keeping in mind. The lengths and rates of progress within phases can vary widely. The mix of required asset-allocation and investment-management skills tends to vary within phases. Cyclical and secular market forces can be powerful and can sometimes augment, sometimes offset, each other. Asset-allocation and investment-management phases often overlap and blend into one another. The pace of progress in one phase may or may not carry over into a succeeding phase. Finally, cycles come and go in several forms; these include financial cycles, learning cycles, attitude cycles, and life cycles.

S E C T I O N

TACTICS AND STRATEGIES

CHAPTER 9

ASSET-ALLOCATION MATRICES AND WORKSHEETS

OVERVIEW

As individual investors assume increasing levels of responsibility for their financial and investment decision making, they need practical tools to help bring order and organization to their thinking. Among these tools are a variety of worksheets, questionnaires, profiling forms, risk assessment quizzes, software, and planning analyzers, originating from many sources and all designed to evoke responses from the investor about the present and the future. Some of these worksheets are brief and simple, and others are lengthy and complicated; some are available primarily in hard-copy form through investment counseling and financial planning firms, and many are posted on financial web sites; some are free, and others are available for a fee. Most add value, some far more than others.

This chapter surveys the role of asset-allocation worksheets and matrices, placing these tools in context with several other instruments, including the development of financial goals, a personal financial statement, a financial plan, a summary of the investor's investment philosophy, and an investment-policy statement. Some generalized mentality-, outlook-, and age-based guidelines for asset allocation are then discussed, leading to a review of how various kinds of financial, economic, and personal cycles and market outcomes may affect investors' asset allocation.

After presentation of a matrix that organizes most of the principal asset classes and subasset classes in various regions of the world and according to local and non-local currency denominations, this chapter contains detailed worksheets with questions to help investors determine their asset allocation. Each worksheet addresses 10 key themes: (i) the *profile* of the investor (with 26 questions and commentary); (ii) the *investment outlook* (with 21 questions and commentary); and (iii) the *investment universe* (with 20 questions and commentary). A risk mitigation matrix can help investors recognize, anticipate, and attempt to reduce 15 of the most important investor-, market outlook-, and investor-specific risks associated with asset allocation.

The array of worksheets, guidelines, and matrices described in this chapter can be a powerful tool in helping transform investors' opinions, circumstances, and ideas into a specific asset allocation. At the same time, it is important to keep these tools in proper perspective, neither ignoring important details nor getting excessively bogged down in details. Investors should not address and then put aside these worksheets; instead, they should review them from time to time at various stages in life and in a variety of financial market circumstances.

WORKSHEETS IN THE ASSET-ALLOCATION PROCESS

Worksheets and related tools provide a relatively straightforward way to explore and build on investors' experience, while expanding their knowledge base to make sense out of the vastly expanded resources and financial choices from which to choose. To gain this understanding, asset-allocation worksheets can help investors find out: (i) what personal and external factors are of greatest importance in making asset-allocation and investment-strategy decisions; (ii) how their assets are allocated compared to earlier periods, to broad guidelines, or to appropriate investment benchmarks; and (iii) what returns and values investors expect their preferred asset mix (and other asset mixes) to generate in the future.

Many individual investors' overriding investment goal is to allocate assets and manage spending levels so as not to outlive their assets, i.e., run out of funds. Put another way, during the course of investors' lifetimes, their investment focus may undergo a gradual shift, from an emphasis on building and accumulating wealth to an emphasis on preserving and protecting wealth. Asset-allocation worksheets can help investors anticipate, design, and implement their evolving goals and plans.

The intent of the asset-allocation worksheets and matrices described in this chapter is to help investors develop an accurate and insightful portrayal of: (i) their unique circumstances, tolerance for risk, and personality characteristics; (ii) the short-term and long-term market outlook for financial assets that investors intend to include in their asset allocation; (iii) the features, benefits, and drawbacks of specific instruments within the universe of possible investments; (iv) the different kinds of risk associated with investing and some potential means of mitigating, or potentially minimizing, these risks; and (v) the projected and actual deployment of assets among regions, currencies, and specific asset classes.

These worksheets and matrices highlight the dynamic interplay between the investor, the investment environment, and the array of investment selections. They are intended for use alongside the diverse selection of risk quizzes, profiling questionnaires, and worksheets that are widely available from other sources. Each worksheet or matrix is meant to stimulate comprehensive, independent, objective thinking and guide behavior as investors review and complete these worksheets and any worksheets or questionnaires which may have been accessed elsewhere.

Several important behavioral-finance concepts, described earlier in Chapter 5, hold that many otherwise highly rational individual investors do not always respond in a completely rational manner to issues relating to money and risk. Nevertheless, the worksheets and matrices presented here attempt to recognize and take account of such behavior. For example, many investors fear a given loss more than they value an equivalent gain. With this in mind, investors need to remember that while all the worksheets and matrices presented here and elsewhere have limitations, they still can be highly useful in creating a disciplined, nuanced, and usually accurate portrayal of themselves, the markets, and the investment possibilities as investors construct and rebalance an asset allocation.

Asset-allocation worksheets and matrices are often an integral element of the asset-allocation process, yet there are other highly important aspects of asset-allocation activity that investors need to consider as well. Investors may increase the efficacy and the chances of investment success of an asset allocation by treating asset-allocation worksheets as one part of a sequential, multistage, integrated process, as depicted in Figure 9.1.

Figure 9.1 shows seven key components of the asset-allocation process that, in combination, powerfully influence investors' chances for enduring investment success. Step 1 in the figure lists three activities that can prepare investors for asset allocation: (i) a brief but reasonably complete statement of the *financial goals* they intend to achieve; (ii) *a personal financial statement*, consisting of a detailed summary of income, expenses, cash flow, and assets and liabilities in the form of a balance sheet; and (iii) *a financial plan*, which draws upon various assumptions relating to: income, expenses, and inflation; large future outlays such as education, the purchase of a home, or retirement; the returns on various assets; and other data to produce projections of net worth at various future intervals in the investor's lifespan. For many investors, Step 1 amounts to a financial checkup, which may or may not accompany a comprehensive financial review and/or an investment proposal from financial and investing sources. Steps 2, 3, and 4 in Figure 9.1 describe three areas of inquiry (that this chapter will explore in the form of detailed worksheets) which help investors choose specific assets and construct an asset allocation. The worksheet represented by Step 2, *Investor Profile*, helps analyze investors' special characteristics that may affect asset selection. The worksheet represented by Step 3, *Investment Outlook*, focuses on how the short-run and long-run outlook for financial assets may influence asset-allocation decisions. The worksheet represented by Step 4, *Investment*

Selected Determinants of Asset Allocation

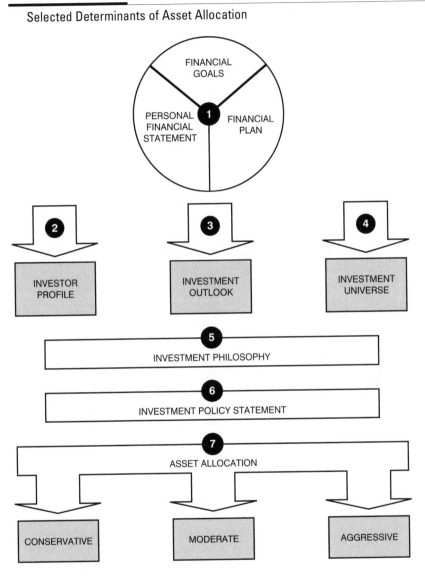

Source: The Author.

Universe, surveys the realm of potential investment opportunities that investors might consider and how this array of investment possibilities may help shape an asset allocation.

Step 5 helps investors formulate an *investment philosophy*, which investors may express in as much or as little detail as they desire, ranging from several paragraphs or pages of prose to brief bullet points jotted down on a sheet of paper. Among other considerations, an investment philosophy outlines how investors approach the whole experience of investing and navigating within financial markets, including how closely they plan to follow the financial markets and specific investments, preferred sources of information and advice, criteria for evaluating investments, and other successful styles that investors might emulate to some degree.

Step 6 describes the creation of an *investment policy statement*. In the last couple of decades, a growing number of professional and individual investors have written and adopted formal statements of investment policy to memorialize their return goals and risk tolerance, asset class preferences and exclusions, asset-allocation ranges and targets, time horizon, evaluation frequency and possible rebalancing procedures, custody and reporting arrangements, investment manager selection criteria and directives, and fees and expenses. Such formal statements can also serve as a point of reference during excessively favorable or unfavorable financial market conditions and stimulate review from time to time for possible revision.

Step 7 shows the *asset-allocation process* itself, with the portfolio invested in a conservative, moderate, or aggressive framework of domestic and/or international equities, fixed-income securities, alternative investments, and cash. These frameworks are primarily defined by investment style, quality rating, and other attributes, and are constructed according to a judicious consideration and blending of factors relating to the investor's own profile, the investment outlook, and the universe of potential investments to choose from.

ASSET-ALLOCATION WORKSHEETS IN CONTEXT

The asset-allocation worksheets—relating to an investor's profile, the investment outlook, and the investment universe—can help investors determine how: (i) their own special characteristics may affect the asset-allocation decision; (ii) special aspects about the future financial environment may affect asset-allocation decisions; and (iii) special features about a given asset class and/or a given investment may affect asset-allocation decisions. Figure 9.2 briefly summarizes the purpose of each of the seven steps diagrammed in

F I G U R E 9.2

Asset-Allocation Worksheets in Context

FINANCIAL GOALS
- The ultimate purposes of investing, including spending on self and family, transfers to heirs, or donations to charitable and philanthropic organizations
- Specific objectives such as retirement, tuition, the purchase of a home, debt repayment, the care of others, and the purchase of assets such as real estate and other property
- General timetables for achievement of goals

PERSONAL FINANCIAL STATEMENT
- Identification and aggregation of all sources of current income and expenditures
- Identification and aggregation of all real and financial assets and all liabilities, including mortgages, loans, lines of credit, and other debt
- Tracking of significant items, such as closely held businesses, options, concentrated equity positions, and tax liabilities

FINANCIAL PLAN
- Assumptions regarding income, expenses, inflation, and assets' returns
- Multiperiod views of investments, earned and unearned income, savings, and other income sources versus spending plans
- Comprehensive analyses of insurance, budgeting, trusts and estates, taxes, gift and philanthropic planning, and retirement planning

INVESTOR PROFILE WORKSHEET
- How special characteristics about the investor affect the asset–allocation decision
- The investor's aims, constraints, preferences, requirements, and current and likely future financial status

INVESTMENT OUTLOOK WORKSHEET
- How special aspects about the future financial environment affect the asset-allocation decision
- The fundamental, valuation, and psychological/technical/liquidity drivers that influence the level and direction of financial asset prices

INVESTMENT UNIVERSE WORKSHEET
- How special features about a given asset class and/or a given investment affect the asset–allocation decision
- The critical determinants of the worth of a financial asset, and the degree to which these traits can change over time

INVESTMENT PHILOSOPHY
- How the investor approaches the experience of investing and navigating within financial markets
- Preferred sources of information and advice
- Criteria for evaluating, buying, and selling investments
- Other successful investors' styles that might be emulated

INVESTMENT POLICY STATEMENT
- Written return goals and risk tolerance, asset–class preferences and exclusions, time horizon, custody and reporting arrangements, investment manager selection criteria, and other factors
- Reference resource during unusual market conditions
- Source for discussion of strategic policies and possible rebalancing decisions

ASSET ALLOCATION
- Assets invested in either a conservative, a moderate, or an aggressive framework
- Allocation of U.S. and/or non U.S. equities, fixed-income securities, alternative investments, and cash
- Asset subcategories according to market capitalization, value or growth characteristics, quality rating, and other attributes

RISK-MITIGATION MATRIX   **ASSET-ALLOCATION MATRIX**

Source: The Author.

Figure 9.1, and shows the progression of steps that investors might take to develop an appropriate asset allocation.

If at all possible, investors should list their financial goals, prepare a personal financial statement, and formulate a financial plan *before* filling out the asset-allocation worksheets in Figures 9.7, 9.9, and 9.11. They should also write a brief outline of their investment philosophy and an investment-policy statement *before* constructing an allocation of assets. The sequence of these steps is denoted by the light gray arrow running through the nine boxes in Figure 9.2. This is a suggested sequence; not all investors will complete all of these steps in the order displayed in the figure.

DRAWBACKS OF ASSET-ALLOCATION WORKSHEETS

A series of worksheets that relates the profile of investors, their investment outlook, and the investment universe to investors' asset allocation can be a highly useful tool, if used properly and with an appropriate degree of perspective. Asset-allocation worksheets are tools and guidelines; they are meant to help investors anticipate and respond appropriately to a wide range of financial market environments.

The specific answers that investors supply to the worksheets in this chapter should aim toward an asset allocation that instills sufficient confidence in investors. By and large, investors need to feel confident that their asset allocations will perform acceptably and hold up well, even under significantly unfavorable financial scenarios. At the same time, investors should not fall prey to an inappropriate feeling of certainty and predictability generated by asset-allocation models that rely on inputs from the investors and other sources.

Although the asset-allocation worksheets can help investors select asset classes that aim for specific financial goals, these worksheets do not address the issue of exactly how large the amounts need to be to attain such goals. In a similar vein, the *design* of asset-allocation worksheets can have bearing on the investor's eventual asset-allocation analysis and specific recommendations. Investors can find a variety of risk-profiling questionnaires and other worksheets at such Web sites as *financeware.com, quicken.com, decisioneering.com*, and *troweprice.com*. Others can be found at *bankofamerica.com*, *fidelity.com*, *cbs.marketwatch.com*, *scudder.com*, *vankampen.com*, *vanguard.com*, and *thestreet.com*. Some worksheets employ multiple-choice questionnaires. Others show sample asset allocations or perhaps a spectrum of possible asset-allocation outcomes, while still others use a numerical scoring system to guide investors toward a specific asset allocation depending upon a fairly quantitative interpretation of the answers. The worksheets in this chapter primarily present open-ended questions, with some amount of written commentary after the space allocated for the response. Another drawback of asset-allocation worksheets relates to the tendency of investors to overlook the possibility of earning returns from specific investments that are *well below* the long-term returns *projected* for the asset class in question. As a general rule, investors should not to be overly dogmatic about the design, content, or application of asset-allocation worksheets.

ASSET-ALLOCATION GUIDELINES

In a general sense, it is possible to develop broad asset-allocation guidelines that reflect investors' mentality, investment outlook, and chronological age, to take advantage of the relevant character-istics of the major asset classes. Figure 9.3 displays several of these guidelines.

Age Groupings

In Figure 9.3, the horizontal axis represents three broad age group-ings within the lifespan of individual investors. Assuming that investors begin investing at age 25, the first group includes the cohort ranging between 25 and 50 years old; the second age group is composed of individuals between 50 and 75 years; and the third group encompasses individuals between 75 and 100 years. Not everyone's investing and chronological life can be divided neatly into three 25-year intervals. At the same time, people on the whole are living longer and more active lives. Many individuals are working longer, often with more job mobility. Such trends can powerfully influence investors' asset-allocation and investment strategy.

FIGURE 9.3

Metality-, Outlook-, and Age-Based Allocation Guidelines

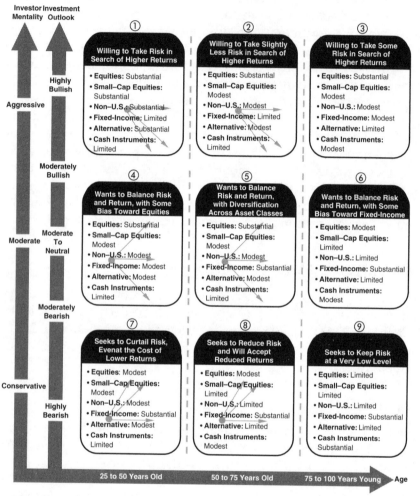

Source: The Author.

Investor Mentality

The two vertical axes in Figure 9.3 show two additional factors besides age that affect the investor's general asset-allocation guidelines. The *left-most axis* traces the spectrum of investors' mentality, ranging from *aggressive* (a willingness to accept more risk of capital loss in search of higher investment returns), to *moderate* (desire to balance risk and return somewhat evenly), to *conservative* (desire to limit the risk of capital loss, even if the latter means having to accept lower investment returns).

The *right-hand axis* (of the two vertical axes on the left side of Figure 9.3) depicts the gamut of investment outlooks that investors may hold. These range from *highly bullish* (the feeling that financial market conditions will be quite favorable for U.S. and non-U.S. stocks, bonds, and alternative investments), to *moderately bullish*, to *moderate to neutral* (neither a particularly favorable nor an unfavorable outlook for U.S. and non-U.S. financial assets), to *moderately bearish*, to *highly bearish* (the feeling that financial-market conditions will be quite unfavorable for U.S. and non-U.S. stocks, bonds, and alternative investments).

For the sake of simplicity, the two vertical axes in Figure 9.3 are in alignment; that is, when investors have an *aggressive* investment mentality, they are here also assumed to have a *highly bullish* or *moderately bullish* investment outlook. When investors have a *conservative* investment mentality, they are here also assumed to have a *highly bearish* or *moderately bearish* investment outlook.

These simplifying assumptions may not always hold true. For example, investors may have an *aggressive* investment mentality, coupled with a *moderate to neutral* or even a *highly bearish* investment outlook; or, they may have a *conservative* investment mentality, coupled with a *moderate to neutral* or *highly bullish* investment outlook.

In such instances, investors should judiciously and carefully blend the asset-allocation guidelines described in the vertical groupings of panels (panels ①, ④, and ⑦, taken together; panels ②, ⑤, and ⑧, taken together; or, panels ③, ⑥, and ⑨, taken together) to create guidelines reflecting the appropriate mix of investor mentality and investment outlook.

Shifts in Mentality and Outlook

It is also possible, and in many cases highly probable, that an investor's mentality will undergo one, several, or even many shifts during a 25-year interval. These investor-mentality shifts are by no means uniform across the rich diversity of humanity. They may be gradual or sudden. They may be sparked by changing opinions as to the relative attractiveness of: current income versus capital gains; capital growth versus the risk of capital loss; principal protection versus purchasing-power protection; or liquidity versus the long-term compounding of returns. Similarly, investors' outlook for financial markets conditions probably will shift back and forth over time.

The possibility that these shifts will occur as investors advance in age is highlighted by the series of three gray arrows within panels ①, ②, ④, ⑤, ⑦, and ⑧. For example, an aggressive, highly bullish investor in the 25- to 50-year age bracket, whose asset-allocation guidelines are summarized in panel ①, might, during his or her 50- to 75-year age interval: (i) *remain aggressive and highly bullish* (represented by the top gray arrow in panel ①, pointing to panel ③); (ii) *become more moderate in approach*, while expecting moderate to neutral financial-market conditions (represented by the middle gray arrow in panel ①, pointing to panel ⑤); or, (iii) *shift to a more conservative investment mentality*, while expecting a highly bearish outlook for financial assets (represented by the bottom gray arrow in panel ①, pointing to panel ⑧). The gray arrows in panels ②, ④, ⑤, ⑦, and ⑧ also reflect possible shifts in, or reaffirmations of, investors' investment mentalities as they progress through time.

General Asset-Allocation Guidelines

Some general asset-allocation guidelines, driven by the conjunction of investors' investment neutrality, investment outlook, and chronological age, are contained in the white-on-black text section at the top of each panel, with asset-specific guidelines spelled out in the bullet points within each panel. For example, investors in the 75- to 100-year age bracket, with a conservative investment mentality and a highly bearish investment outlook (panel ⑨), might seek to keep their risk of capital loss at a very low level. As a result, such investors' asset allocation might have limited exposure to equities, small-cap equities, non-U.S. equity and debt securities, and alternative investments, with substantial exposure to fixed-income securities and cash instruments.

At the other end of the spectrum, investors in the 25- to 50-year bracket, with an aggressive investment mentality and a highly bullish investment outlook (panel ①), might be willing to assume a higher degree of risk of capital loss in search of higher investment returns. Such investors may have a high degree of confidence that equities and equity-like investments, as long-payoff, compounding assets, will provide attractive financial returns during a long time frame—of 20 years or more—but they may have a lower degree of confidence in how equities and equity-like investments will perform over a 6-month, 1-year, 5-year, or even 10-year holding period.

For such investors to commit meaningful portions of their asset allocation to equities and equity-like investments, they must be highly confident that more volatility of returns and increased price risk will not cause high levels of anxiety, self-doubt, and an abandonment of the originally desired asset allocation *at precisely the wrong moments* in fluctuating financial market cycles. If these investors are reasonably sure of maintaining a high degree of investment patience and fortitude, their asset allocation might have substantial exposure to equities, small-cap equities, non-U.S. equity and debt securities, and alternative investments, with limited exposure to fixed-income and cash instruments.

In the middle of the spectrum, investors in the 50- to 75-year age bracket, with a moderate investment mentality and a moderate to neutral investment outlook (panel ⑤), might want to balance the risk of capital loss against the opportunity for increased investment return, with diversification across asset classes. In short, investors with these characteristics want an asset allocation with sufficient opportunities for growth to attain their financial goals, while having a sufficient degree of stability: (i) to maintain overall capital value in unfavorable financial market environments; and (ii) to yield an adequate number of positively performing investments that would shore up total return, even if some of the riskier investments should suffer temporary or permanent capital impairment. As a result, these investors' asset allocations might have substantial exposure to equity and fixed-income securities, with modest exposure to small-cap equities, non-U.S. equity and debt securities, and alternative investments, with limited exposure to cash instruments.

INVESTORS' ASSET-ALLOCATION CYCLES

During the course of an investment experience, investors probably will feel the effects of several different, usually overlapping, cycles that can affect their asset allocation. Assuming that investing activity begins in earnest sometime in the mid-twenties, an investor's experience might extend to 70 years or more. Eight of the relevant cycles affecting individual investors' asset allocation are set forth in Figure 9.4.

Investors may consider the cycles shown in Figure 9.4 as a form of financial biorhythm charts, tracing the ups and downs of life experiences. These cycles may vary widely, in both duration and degree, from the representative lengths of time highlighted for each type of cycle. As a result, the vicissitudes of investors' life patterns may be strengthened or weakened by rising and falling trends in the economy and financial markets.

The three cycles at the top of Figure 9.4 relate to external influences affecting asset allocation. *Economic Cycles* trace out periods of expansion or contraction in the domestic, global, and regional economy. Such cycles influence interest rates, profitability, and many other determinants of the value of financial assets. In response to shifting influences of a fundamental, valuation, and psychological/technical/liquidity nature, *Equity Returns Cycles* and *Fixed-Income Returns Cycles* also generate patterns of advancing and declining prices, yields, and returns. These cycles can directly bear on the success (or lack thereof) of investors' asset-allocation activity.

The five cycles in the lower two-thirds of Figure 9.4 show many of the highly personalized characteristics shaping the life, investment experience, and asset allocation of individual investors. *Personal Employment Cycles* describe the important chapters, and especially the differentiated subchapters, in pre-career, career, and retirement. These work-related cycles will often affect the levels of current income that investors may want to derive from an asset allocation, as distinguished from employment sources.

Life Needs Cycles refer to some of the significant expenditures that individual investors may contemplate during their lifetime. These major purchases may include one or more personal residences,

F I G U R E 9.4

Potential Cycles Affecting Individual Investors' Asset Allocation

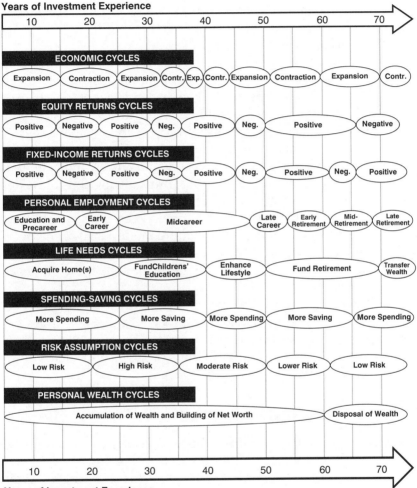

Source: The Author.

educational expenses for dependents, lifestyle enhancement, significant objects of value and/or services, saving for and spending during
retirement years, and transfers of wealth to heirs, philanthropic
causes, and other recipients.

Spending-Saving Cycles highlight periods during which investors may generally do *more spending than saving*—perhaps in the early, middle, and late years of their investing lifetime—or, alternatively, when investors might do *more saving than spending*—such as in the early to middle years, or in the middle to later years of their investing lifetime.

Risk Assumption Cycles refer to the periods when investors may be inclined to assume more risk of capital loss in pursuit of higher returns, versus periods in which investors want to reduce or avoid risk altogether, even if such behavior implies considerably lower portfolio returns. Such risk assumption and avoidance cycles may vary considerably from standard notions of investment wisdom. For example, many investment sources indicate that investors should be prepared to hold significant amounts of riskier assets in the early part of their investing lifetime. Despite such precepts, investors may very well desire to keep their portfolios at a relatively low risk level, given the more modest size of the overall portfolio, the magnitude and timing of future life needs faced, and the fact that investors may be fairly new to the experience of investing.

Personal Wealth Cycles describe the long arcs of building and adding to wealth, and then dispersing such wealth. Some investors may experience these broad cycles more than once during their lifetime, due to multiple accumulations of assets and their voluntary, or involuntary, dispersal.

SEQUENCING OF MARKET OUTCOMES

Investors would be wise to think about and visualize their portfolios over a very long time span and, as part of this process, consider possible sequences of market outcomes for various intervals during this period. Figure 9.5 diagrams one representation of such a process, with a 75-year time span of equity-market outcomes divided into five-year intervals.

The overall time span, incremental time intervals, and asset class chosen for portrayal may vary from the format in Figure 9.5. For example, investors may wish to look at fixed-income market outcomes, or alternative-investments market outcomes, over a 20- or

F I G U R E   9.5

Sequencing of Equity Market Outcomes

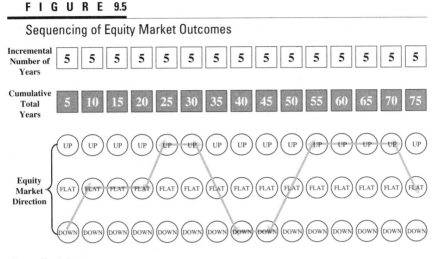

Source: The Author.

30-year span, divided into 1- or 2-year intervals. In Figure 9.5, the overall direction of equity market outcomes is shown to move in an upward, flat, or downward direction.

For the sequence of 5-year intervals shown in Figure 9.5, equity market outcomes are moving: (i) in a downward direction for 5 years; (ii) in an essentially sideways pattern for the better part of 15 years; (iii) in an upward direction for 10 years; (iv) in a downward direction for 10 years; (v) in a generally upward direction for 20 years; and (vi) have moved sideways in the most recent 5 years. If allowances are made for the fact that the *magnitudes* and *cumulative effects* of upward, flat, and downward market outcomes are not reflected in the figure, and the fact that equity market outcomes do not neatly fit into five-year intervals, Figure 9.5 may be considered as a very rough approximation of the course of U.S. equity market prices over the 1930–2005 period.

Investors should construct and approach a chart such as Figure 9.5 with care and caution, in view of the difficulty of accurately predicting the course of market outcomes for a given asset class for one year, much less for one five-year interval, not to mention a *series* of five-year intervals. Nevertheless, creating a diagram of the sequence of market outcomes for a specific asset class can furnish perspective about possible future scenarios by looking at past history. For example, Figure 9.5 shows how rare and extraordinary it is for U.S. equity market outcomes to be essentially positive for four consecutive five-year periods.

This process can also help investors distinguish between cyclical and secular bull or bear market episodes. For example, many financial analysts consider *cyclical bear markets* to be relatively short in duration (from 12 to 24 months) and in magnitude (price declines ranging from 20% to 30%), and *secular bear markets* to be relatively extensive in duration (from 5 to 10 years or more) and in severity (with price declines of 30% to 50% or more).

By visualizing the progression of investment outcomes through time, investors can become more aware of the importance of adapting their strategy for withdrawing capital from the portfolio (often referred to as "spending policy") to be more closely attuned with the actual results achieved in financial markets. Otherwise, investors run the risk of exhausting the portfolio (i.e., running out of money) well before the originally expected longevity of their fortune.

For example, Table 9.1 shows what happens to capital when investors follow a spending policy without regard to the underlying sequence of equity market outcomes.

In Sequence A of Table 9.1, the equity markets experience early *capital losses* two years in a row, with 20% price declines in each year, followed by *capital gains* three years in a row, with 12% price gains in each year. For investors who started with $100 of initial investment capital and established a spending policy of 5% of the initial investment capital, increasing by 10% (of the original 5%) each year, at the end of five years, total capital would have dwindled to $54.21.

In contrast, in Sequence B, the equity markets experience early *capital gains* three years in a row, with 12% price gains each year, followed by *capital losses* two years in a row, with 20% price declines in each year. Assuming the same $100 initial investment capital and spending 5% (with a 10% annual increase of the 5%) of the initial investment capital, at the end of five years, the total capital

T A B L E 9.1

Investment Results Under Different Equity Market Sequences

Sequence A: Early Capital Losses, Followed by Capital Gains					
	Year 1	Year 2	Year 3	Year 4	Year 5
Investment	$100.00	$75.00	$54.50	$59.99	$54.93
Times: Investment Return	−20%	−20%	+12%	+12%	+12%
Equals: End of Period Value	80.00	60.00	61.04	61.59	61.53
Less: Annual Spending[1]	−5.00	−5.50	−6.05	−6.66	−7.32
Equals: Capital Available	$75.00	$54.50	$54.99	$54.93	$54.21

Sequence B: Early Capital Gains, Followed by Capital Losses					
	Year 1	Year 2	Year 3	Year 4	Year 5
Investment	$100.00	$107.00	$114.34	$122.01	$90.95
Times: Investment Return	+12%	+12%	+12%	−20%	−20%
Equals: End of Period Value	112.00	119.84	128.06	97.61	72.76
Less: Annual Spending[1]	−5.00	−5.50	−6.05	−6.66	−7.33
Equals: Capital Available	$107.00	$114.34	$122.01	$90.95	$65.43

Note: [1]Set at 5% of the initial investment capital, increasing by 10% of the 5% each year.
Source: The Author.

would have declined to $65.43, or 21% more than the capital remaining at the end of Sequence A.

This disparity is even more pronounced when the magnitude of the capital losses increases. For example, if investors started with $100 of initial capital and spent 5% of the initial capital annually (increasing by 10% of the 5% each year), under a −30%, −30%, +10%, +10%, +10% sequence of returns, they would be left with $31.28 at the end of five years, compared with $44.35 at the end of five years with a +10%, +10%, +10%, −30%, −30% sequence of returns. The order, or sequences, of investment returns is of vital importance in investors' quest not to outlive their total assets.

ASSET-ALLOCATION MATRICES

An asset-allocation matrix shows the allocation of an investor's portfolio by asset class, by major subcategories of asset class, by region, and by currency exposure. Table 9.2 contains an example of a detailed asset-allocation matrix.

T A B L E 9.2

Investment Results Under Different Equity Market Sequences

Asset Class	United States Local Currency	United States Non-Local Currency	Canada Local Currency	Canada Non-Local Currency	Europe Local Currency	Europe Non-Local Currency	Japan Local Currency	Japan Non-Local Currency	Developed Asia[1] Local Currency	Developed Asia[1] Non-Local Currency	Emerging Markets[2] Local Currency	Emerging Markets[2] Non-Local Currency	Total
Equities													
U.S. Equities													
Large-Cap Growth	%	%											%
Large-Cap Value	%	%											%
Mid-Cap Growth	%	%											%
Mid-Cap Value	%	%											%
Small-Cap Growth	%	%											%
Small-Cap Value	%	%											%
Non-U.S. Equities													
Developed Large-Cap			%	%	%	%	%	%	%	%			%
Developed Small-Cap			%	%	%	%	%	%	%	%			%
Emerging Large-Cap											%	%	%
Emerging Small-Cap											%	%	%
Fixed-Income													
U.S. Fixed-Income													
Investment Grade -Taxable	%	%											%
Investment Grade –Tax Exempt	%	%											%
High Yield –Taxable	%	%											%
High Yield –Tax Exempt	%	%											%
Other U.S. Fixed-Income													
Developed Countries			%	%	%	%	%	%	%	%			%
Emerging Markets											%	%	%
Convertible Securities	%	%	%	%	%	%	%	%	%	%	%	%	%
Inflation-Indexed Bonds	%	%	%	%	%	%					%	%	%
Alternative Investments													
Private Equity	%	%	%	%	%	%	%	%	%	%	%	%	%
Commodities	%	%	%	%	%	%	%	%	%	%	%	%	%
Real Estate	%	%	%	%	%	%	%	%	%	%	%	%	%
Hedge Funds	%	%	%	%	%	%	%	%	%	%	%	%	%
Precious Metals	%	%	%	%	%	%	%	%	%	%	%	%	%
Art	%	%	%	%	%	%	%	%	%	%	%	%	%
Cash													
Cash and Cash Equivalents	%	%	%	%	%	%	%	%	%	%	%	%	%
Total	%	%	%	%	%	%	%	%	%	%	%	%	%

Note: [1]Includes Hong Kong, Singapore, Australia, and New Zealand.
[2]Located in Europe, the Americas, Asia, Africa, and the Middle East.

Source: The Author.

It is a good idea to make a copy of the asset-allocation matrix shown in Table 9.2, to keep on hand for notations while reviewing the Investor Profile, Investment Outlook, and Investment Universe worksheets in the next sections of this chapter. By looking at Table 9.2, investors can ascertain what percentage of their total assets is deployed in U.S. and non-U.S. equities and fixed-income securities, in alternative investments, and in cash instruments.

For each of these asset classes and their relevant subcategories, investors can also denote the percentage of the total portfolio they will allocate to the United States, Canada, Europe, Japan, developed Asia, and emerging markets, in local currency and in non-local currency terms. The gray-shaded areas denote asset categories that may not be easily obtainable or that do not exist.

Seeing an asset allocation in an organized format such as the matrix in Table 9.2 has several advantages. First, it helps investors remember that their portfolios are a mix of different kinds of assets, not all of which will generally perform *well* at the same time—nor should they all generally perform *poorly* at once. To the degree that various assets' returns have low correlations with one another, this performance rotation may even be more pronounced, as will be the offsetting effects of different asset classes' returns, at different times, on the overall financial results. Second, the matrix format can assist investors in reviewing their asset allocation at regular intervals, or after significant changes in their own circumstances, in the market outlook, or in the investment universe. Third, the rigor and discipline of such reviews, especially when conducted in a consistent period-to-period format, can help investors properly adjust their strategic asset-allocation policy and carry out tactical asset-allocation rebalancing activity. In so doing, investors can arrive at an allocation that is more likely to generate a sufficient degree of comfort with, and confidence in, the risks and rewards of the portfolio.

INVESTOR PROFILE WORKSHEET

Of all the influences affecting asset allocation, investors' own profiles—including their background, hopes, fears, dreams, and financial position—are of paramount importance. Figure 9.6 displays a summary of 10 important areas of inquiry in the Investor Profile

F I G U R E 9.6

Investor Profile Factors Affecting Asset Allocation

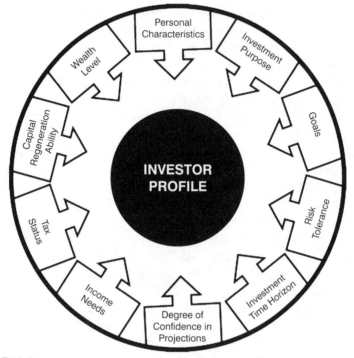

Source: The Author.

Worksheet, arranged in clockwise order as they are contained in the worksheet, beginning in the 12 o'clock position.

One of the chief purposes of the Investor Profile Worksheet summarized in Figure 9.6 is to help investors gain a deeper, somewhat organized picture of those personal traits, characteristics, and circumstances that may tilt them toward or away from a given asset class. At the same time, many of the factors spelled out in Figure 9.6 and in the worksheet are subject to a high degree of uncertainty, whether it be investors' life expectancy or the length of their working years versus their retirement years.

Many highly important investor attributes virtually defy accurate measure. For example, the investor risk profile is difficult to assess with certainty, partly because investors' risk tolerance may go through different phases over time and in response to changing financial market conditions, and partly because the linkages also vary between individuals' risk-taking behavior in the *non-financial* realm and in the *financial* realm.

Many other factors also come into play in investors' profiles, some non-financial and some financial. Among the *non-financial factors* are the investors' purpose and goals, their time horizon, and how confident they are in projections for the future. Among the *financial factors* are wealth level, tax status, income needs, and capital regeneration ability. Figure 9.7 contains an Investor Profile Worksheet with 26 questions, relating to the investor's own profile, divided into 10 key areas of inquiry: (i) personal characteristics; (ii) investment purpose; (iii) goals; (iv) risk tolerance; (v) investment time horizons; (vi) degree of confidence in projections; (vii) income needs; (viii) tax status; (ix) capital regeneration ability; and (x) wealth level. Each set of questions is followed by space for the investor to jot down answers, and then each section provides some general comments and observations discussing how each area of inquiry may affect the investor's asset allocation.

INVESTMENT OUTLOOK WORKSHEET

The overall investment outlook plays a crucial role in asset allocation. Figure 9.8 summarizes 10 important areas of focus in the Investment Outlook Worksheet, arranged in clockwise order as they are in the worksheet, beginning in the 12 o'clock position.

One of the primary aims of the Investment Outlook Worksheet summarized in Figure 9.8 is to help investors discern whether future short-term and long-term financial-market conditions are likely to be *better than, worse than*, or *the same as* recent past conditions for each asset class under consideration. In a similar vein, investors are attempting to discern how strong and how long-lasting the major trends in the investment outlook are, and the likelihood that these trends might undergo cyclical reversal.

In important ways, the overall investment outlook can influence investors' asset allocation, not only through the underlying

F I G U R E 9.7

Investor Profile Worksheet

<table>
<tr><td rowspan="7" style="writing-mode: vertical-lr;">I N V E S T</td><td>

1. Personal Characteristics

- What is the investor's age? _____

- How much time does the investor expect to work before retirement? _____

- What are reasonable expectations for the length of the retirement? _____

- How much experience does the investor have with investment and financial matters? _____

- What is the investor's proclivity for hands-on involvement with the portfolio? _____

- Whose money is the investor investing? _____
</td></tr>
</table>

I

N

V

E

S

T

Comment:

O

R

The chronological and career ages of the investor can influence the investor's ability to ride out losses in the portfolio. At the same time, the investor's age affects the number of years that assets can grow to achieve specified wealth objectives.

The investor's experience level can be long- or short-lived, deep or superficial, and may include significant positive or negative experiences that may determine asset choice. Often, the degree of an investor's experience is as important as its duration.

P

2. Investment Purpose

R

- What are the primary ultimate uses for the investor's capital? _____

O

- What are the timing and magnitudes of the investor's outlays? _____

F

- Do the investor's intended uses for his or her capital need to be prioritized? _____

I

Comment:

L

Depending upon: (i) the size of the investor's initial capital; (ii) the length of time the capital is to be invested; (iii) significant inflows and/or outflows of capital; and

E

(iv) realized rates of return for the assets held, the investor may or may not need to prioritize the intended uses for his or her capital. The investment purposes of a portfolio may include: (i) the purchase of primary, vacation, or multiple residences; (ii) investing in, buying, or starting a business; (iii) funding educational, health care, or other expenses, for children, parents, or other dependents; (iv) owning and/or collecting livestock, racehorses, art, automobiles, antiques, jewelry, and other valuables; (v) lifestyle enhancement through the purchase of multiple estates, boats, or planes; and (vi) donations to social, civic, educational, religious, and other philanthropic causes.

INVESTOR PROFILE

3. Goals

- What are the investor's goals for the portfolio? ____________________
____
____
- Is the investor aware of potential tradeoffs between multiple goals? ____________
____
____

Comment:

Investors are often asked to select and rank goals for their portfolios, among them: (i) capital growth; (ii) income generation; (iii) protection or maintenance of purchasing power; (iv) safety of principal; and (v) liquidity or accessibility of principal. At the same time, certain deep-seated, more fundamental goals must be taken into account. Expressed in succinct terms, these may include: (i) to stay wealthy; (ii) to become wealthy; (iii) not to have to worry about expenses; or (iv) not to be poor. It is useful for investors to keep in mind that some goals may have costs, and not all goals may be able to be met simultaneously. For example, focusing on capital growth may come at the cost of higher price volatility, lower income, and the potential for loss of capital.

4. Risk Tolerance

- What is the investor's ability to withstand realized or unrealized losses? ________
____
____
- How would the investor react to declines in parts or all of the portfolio of 10%, 20%, 30%, 40%, or more? ____________________________________
____
- ____

Comment:

One of the most difficult investor characteristics to assess is the investor's tolerance for risk. Not all investors have the same tolerance for risk, and many investors' risk tolerances may be different at different stages of their lives and in different financial market environments. For many investors, substantial realized or unrealized losses can inspire mood swings, panic, recrimination, paralysis, impaired judgment, and many other forms of psychological and mental turbulence; other investors may react to the prospect or actuality of loss with emotional intelligence, sangfroid, cool rationality, clear thinking, and sound reactions. A widely encountered mantra in investing states that the investor must assume higher levels of risk—and thus the possibility of suffering capital losses—to earn higher rates of return over time. Not all investors feel this way. For example, some risk-averse investors who are scheduled to receive options or shares in the future, seek ways to hedge, sell, or diversify their positions even before they receive them. Investors need to ponder and think as deeply and probingly as possible about their likely reactions to various degrees of devastating financial performance in different kinds of assets. Investors are frequently asked whether they would like to eat better or to sleep better. Unfortunately, the true answer to this question some times becomes known only under difficult circumstances for financial assets.

(*Continued*)

F I G U R E 9.7 (Continued)

Investor Profile Worksheet

---

5. Investment Time Horizon

I

N

V

E

S

T

O

R

P

R

O

F

I

L

E

- For how long is the investor likely to be investing his or her capital? _____

- When will the investor need all or a portion of his or her capital? _____

Comment:
In effect, one of the deep underlying goals of asset allocation and financial planning is not to have the investor outlive his or her assets, i.e., to run out of funds in later life. To address this challenge, it is helpful for the investor to step back and review, within a short-term, intermediate-term, and long-term context: (i) his or her own remaining lifespan; (ii) the nature, longevity, and robustness of his or her overall portfolio, as well as the key components of the portfolio; (iii) scheduled flows of capital into and out of the portfolio; and (iv) potential contingencies that may arise.

6. Degree of Confidence in Projections

- How confident is the investor about his or her short-, medium-, and long-term projections of capital inflows and outflows? _____

- How confident is the investor about the short-, medium-, and long-term investment performance of his or her assets? _____

Comment:
It is worth reiterating that an investor's overconfidence or underconfidence abou this or her projections of capital flows and capital-market conditions does not make such projections any more or less likely to occur. At the same time, the longer the interval over which the portfolio is to be invested may: (i) increase the chances of assets producing returns that are near their longer-term average rates of return; and (ii) vary the degree of certainty about the nominal or real monetary amounts of capital inflows and outflows. Computer- or model-generated projections of flows and returns may give the illusion of certainty, when in fact such forecasts are far from certain. Most individuals can roughly gauge the timing of the sizeable capital inflows and/or outflows within their lifetime, ranging from the purchase or sale of homes, to educational expenses, to retirement outlays. The investor should aim at a realistic, rather than a false, sense of security through an appreciation of probabilities and ranges of outcomes. In turn, this kind of thinking should influence the investor's: (i) affinity for complexity; (ii) frequency and degree of portfolio rebalancing activity in response to changing market conditions; and (iii) ability to focus on avoiding or correcting investment mistakes, while exercising judgment and patience, through a variety of market cycles.

7. Income Needs

- What are the likely timing and amounts of capital withdrawals from the portfolio? _
- What is the range of income needs, and how predictable are these income needs? _____
  _____

- How easy or difficult would it be to adjust the investor's projected income needs in response to changing asset allocations, investment results, and the lifespan of the investor and any beneficiaries? _____
  _____

Comment:

In general, the fixed and variable components of the investor's available income, balanced against his or her income needs, may fluctuate with, and depend upon, a blend of: (i) the asset mix of the portfolio; (ii) the projected stable, rising, or falling pattern of investment returns, investor spending rates, and capital withdrawals; (iii) increases or decreases in the general price level (such as inflation, disinflation, or deflation); (iv) the ability to postpone or not postpone certain budgeted expenses, including debt repayments, medical expenses, scheduled charitable contributions, deferrable lifestyle enhancements; and importantly, (v) the lifespan of the investor and any beneficiaries of the portfolio. Investors may need to adjust their annual spending levels to take account of the portfolio's investment results.

Otherwise, maintaining percentage annual spending levels that represent a fixed (or rising) percentage of the original portfolio, and that are insensitive to unfavorable investment results, particularly in the early years of a portfolio's life, may run the risk of exhausting all of the investor's funds many years before the expected maturity of the portfolio.

8. Tax Status

- What are the investor's current and likely future income, capital gains, estate, property, and other tax brackets at the federal, state, local, and (possibly) international level? _____
  _____
  _____

Comment:

The essence of successful investing over the long run is the ability to continuously compound the value of assets in the portfolio at respectable rates of return, year in and year out. To accomplish this, it is important that: (i) assets be owned in structures (such as 401(k), Keogh, and IRA plans, annuities, trusts, foundations, separately managed investment accounts, and related entities) that minimize, defer, or shield the portfolio from taxes; (ii) the right kind of assets be owned (such as, if appropriate, tax-exempt bonds, and investments whose returns are not highly taxed each year); and (iii) investment activities be undertaken with some degree of sensitivity toward, rather than a neglect of, their tax implications. While it may be unwise to allow tax considerations to drive investment behavior, it is equally unwise to allocate assets and execute investment policy with blithe disregard for the tax consequences of such activity. A related consideration is the tendency for many individual investors to think of their total net worth in pretax terms, rather than deducting any taxes that are currently deferred but that will eventually be payable.

(Continued)

F I G U R E 9.7 (Concluded)

Investor Profile Worksheet

9. Capital Regeneration Ability

- If it should be necessary, how easy or difficult would it be for the investor to generate additional capital? _____
  _____

I

- Is it possible that significant amounts of liquidity could be tapped at some point in the future, through borrowing against unleveraged assets, or through harvesting or converting assets into

N   monetary form? _____

V   Comment:
     Many investors who have built up fortunes by growing and selling businesses know that, if
     necessary, they could launch, build up, and sell a new business all over again. A major influence

E   on most investors' capital regeneration ability stems from the level, variability, and form of his or
     her annual occupational earnings. Other means of generating additional capital at some point in

S   the future include: (i) in heritance; (ii) earnout provisions associated with the earlier sale of a
     business; (iii) streams of royalty, endorsement, or license payments; (iv) legal settlements; or

T   (v) the sale of assets such as timber, portions of real estate, art, boats, and other properties.

     10. Wealth Level

O   - What is the magnitude of the investor's net worth? _____
       _____

R
     - What is the form of the investor's net worth? _____
       _____

     - To what degree has the investor protected his or her net worth? _____

P   _____

R   Comment:
     An investor's financial strategy and asset allocation will be greatly affected by the
     amount of money he or she has, or expects to have, available for investment. Many

O   investors start out with virtually no capital or modest sums, while others may be
     investing funds that reach hundreds of thousands, millions, or even billions of dollars.

F   In general, the greater and more liquid the investor's net worth, the wider the range of
     assets that can be considered and the greater the degree of illiquid or inefficient asset

I   classes that may be placed into a portion of the portfolio. Net worth comes in many
     forms, including: (i) income-producing activities and assets; (ii) realized capital

L   appreciation; (iii) unrealized capital appreciation (such as qualified and non qualified
     employee stock options and concentrated equity positions); (iv) various forms of
     benefits that will be payable at some future date; and (v) other liquid and illiquid

E   assets. The structure and amount of an investor's net worth are also influenced by
     potential or actual explicit, implicit, or contingent liabilities agains this or her assets.
     Such liabilities include borrowings, present and future taxes payable on embedded
     gains, and pending known or unknown payments or legal judgments. In addition, the
     investor's wealth level and income-generating ability may or may not be protected,
     through: (i) various forms of hedging, using options, other derivatives, and structured
     investment instruments; (ii) various forms of insurance, such as life, casualty, liability,
     disability, and long-term care insurance; and (iii) social security, 401(k) plans,
     profit-sharing plans, Keogh Plans, and Individual Retirement Accounts (IRAs).

F I G U R E 9.8

Investment Outlook Factors Affecting Asset Allocation

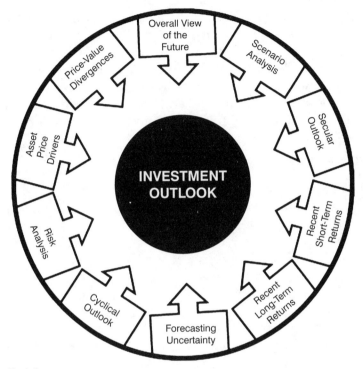

Source: The Author.

performance of each asset class under varying financial scenarios, but also through the investment approach chosen to capture positive investment returns. For instance, during the core years of a multi-year upward move in U.S. equity prices, many investors might choose to own index funds that track the price movements of a broad market average such as the Standard & Poor's 500 Index. On the other hand, during a transition period to considerably lower or even negative absolute equity returns, investors with exposure to U.S. equities might choose to emphasize active-management sector selection and individual stock selection, rather than an indexed investment approach.

Figure 9.9 contains an Investment Outlook Worksheet with 22 questions relating to the investment outlook, divided into 10 key areas of inquiry, which may affect: (i) investors' overall view of the future; (ii) scenario analysis; (iii) the secular outlook; (iv) recent short-term returns; (v) recent long-term returns; (vi) forecasting uncertainty; (vii) the cyclical outlook; (viii) risk analysis; (ix) asset price drivers; and (x) price-value divergences. Each set of questions is followed by space for investors to jot down answers, and then each section provides some general comments and observations about how each area of inquiry may affect asset allocation.

INVESTMENT UNIVERSE WORKSHEET

The set of appropriate investment options available to investors—the investment universe—can meaningfully affect asset allocation. Figure 9.10 summarizes 10 important areas of inquiry in the Investment Universe Worksheet, arranged in clockwise order as they are contained in the worksheet and beginning in the 12 o'clock position.

The Investment Universe Worksheet in Figure 9.11 aims to assist the investor in critically evaluating whether the features of the investment under consideration match the investor's goals and needs, and the exigencies of the expected investment outlook. The three fundamental decisions in asset allocation are discussed in the Investment Universe Worksheet: stocks versus bonds; U.S. versus non-U.S. investments; and conventional versus alternative instruments.

Figure 9.11 contains an Investment Universe Worksheet with 20 questions relating to the investment universe, divided into 10 key areas of inquiry: (i) equity versus debt; (ii) U.S. versus non-U.S. investments; (iii) conventional versus alternative assets; (iv) risk-return characteristics; (v) diversification and correlation characteristics; (vi) quality characteristics; (vii) liquidity characteristics; (viii) form of vehicle; (ix) tax status; and (x) costs of ownership. Each set of questions is followed by space for investors to jot down answers, and then each section provides some general comments and observations discussing how each area of inquiry may affect investors' asset allocation.

F I G U R E 9.9

Investment Outlook Worksheet

1. Overall View of the Future

- What are the key influences that are likely to shape the outlook for investment assets? _____

- What is the absolute and relative strength of these influences? _____

- When and how are these influences likely to affect the major asset classes? _____

Comment:

Investors should remember that the investment outlook will not remain static over time. Some factors in the investment landscape may exhibit a wide degree of fluctuation from period to period, while others may operate and evolve slowly, even imperceptibly, though with no less impact. Even though many asset-allocation models use fixed averages for rates of return, price inflation, standard deviation, and other variables, in practice, some or all of these parameters may undergo shifts, sometimes significant, with the passage of time. Among the important *fundamental* forces acting on investment assets are: (i) monetary policy, including money supply growth, interest-rate and currency-exchange rate targets, required reserve levels for financial institutions, and margin requirements; (ii) fiscal policy, including the forms and amounts of taxation and government spending; (iii) the economic outlook, encompassing the likely pattern of consumer, business, government, and international demand for goods and services, domestically and in other economies and regions of the world; (iv) inflationary, disinflationary, or deflationary changes in the general price level, as well as in specific areas such as labor, food, raw materials, and energy; (v) interest rate and currency trends; and (vi) geopolitical, meteorological, social, civic, demographic, regulatory, technological, and environmental trends. Among the significant *valuation* forces affecting investment assets are: (i) dividend yields and interest rates; (ii) volatility levels and risk premiums versus so-called risk-free rates of return; and (iii) profitability levels and growth rates. Among the *psychological, technical,* and *liquidity* forces affecting investment assetsare: (i) consumer, business, and investor confidence levels; (ii) supply and demand conditions in the capital markets; (iii) domestic and international portfolio and direct investment flows; (iv) volatility and price-volume patterns and conditions; and (v) recurring events, such as elections and climate shifts, and unanticipated events, such as military action, epidemics, acts of terrorism, or positive diplomatic breakthroughs.

2. Scenario Analysis

- What are the primary ultimate uses for the investor's capital? _____

- What are the timing and magnitudes of the investor's outlays? _____

- Do the investor's intended uses for his or her capital need to be prioritized? _____

Comment:

A highly valuable tool in assessing the investment out look is the process of scenario analysis. In such a process, the investor sets forth a manageable number of scenarios (perhaps from 3 to 6, or possibly as many as 10), ranging from favorable to unfavorable. It is also useful to list the fundamental, valuation, and psychological/technical/liquidity conditions that could produce each of these scenarios. Finally, an important part of scenario analysis is the ascribing of a percentage probability to each of the scenarios that has been developed. This is by no means a trivial exercise, and often demands patience, persistence, reflection, insight, logic, judgment, and seemingly, a sixth or seventh investment sense.

(Continued)

(Vertical left margin text: INVESTMENT OUTLOOK)

F I G U R E 9.9 (Continued)

Investment Outlook Worksheet

3. Secular Outlook

- Are the secular conditions affecting investment assets likely to improve or deteriorate in the future? _____

- How long are these secular influences likely to be sustained, and what new influences may emerge to reinforce, augment, or replace these influences? _____

Comment:

Many of the more successful asset-allocation and investment-strategy decisions have taken advantage of long-lived demographic, economic, political, structural, and techno-logical changes. As a result, investors may have decided to significantly increase their commitment to certain asset classes while decreasing their exposure to other asset classes. For instance, in highly generalized terms, the decades of the 1950s and the 1990s were very favorable eras to be invested in equities and equity-like assets, whereas the decades of the 1930s and the 1970s were unfavorable eras to be invested in equities and equity-like assets. Some investors are able to anticipate such periods, or to recognize them shortly after they have commenced, thereby profiting from them for the good part of their duration. Many other investors, however, realize that they are unlikely to spot and exploit these long-term shifts with lasting accuracy. As a result, these investors aim for consistency in investment performance by avoiding extreme or dogmatic commitments to individual asset classes, and even within an asset class, to specific maturity, duration, or credit categories (in fixed-income securities) or to specific market capitalization or growth/value categories (in equities). From a secular standpoint, investors should be alert for transformative periods in which returns from a given asset class shift to new levels. Such shifts should lead to meaningful changes in the way investors view, utilize, and invest in assets during the new time frame.

4. Recent Short-Term Returns

- What has been the pattern of recent short-term returns for investment assets and specific asset classes, and how do these returns compare to historical averages? _____

- What forces might lead to a continuation, or alternatively, to a cessation or reversal of such returns? _____

Comment:

It is important to attach an appropriate amount of significance to recent 1-, 3-, 5-, and 10-year returns for specific asset categories. The mere fact of high, moderate, or low recent investment returns does not imply that these returns will continue unabated, or else veer off in a new direction. The chief value of looking at the pattern of recent short-term returns is to place them in some sort of context relating to: (i) the overall cyclical and secular outlook; and (ii) the historical averages of such returns. For example, if the recent 1-, 3-, 5-, and 10-year returns for the private-equity and venture-capital asset class are very high, in the top 5 percen to fall such historical returns, such information should heighten the investor's awareness of the conditions necessary for, and the likelihood of, such returns persisting in the foreseeable future.

INVESTMENT OUTLOOK

5. Recent Long-Term Returns

- What has been the pattern of recent long-term returns for investment assets and specific asset classes, and how do these returns compare to recent historical averages? _____

- What forces might lead to a continuation, or alternatively, to a cessation or reversal of such returns? _____

_____

Comment:

Analyzing recent 10-, 20-, and 30-year returns can help the investor evaluate what the long-term performance of a set of specific asset allocations has been, but there is no certainty that such performance can be repeated. For the investor, the challenge and the opportunity of such an analysis lie in the questioning and reflection that can be prompted by this process. Over the decades of the 1980s and the 1990s, the long-term rates of return from investing in large-capitalization U.S. equities rose, from the 10–11% range to the 13–14% range. Knowledge of the true impact of this upward move in long-term returns should inspire the investor to contemplate the reasons for such a performance shift, including declining inflation and interest rates, globalization and the fall of communism, technological progress and productivity, expanding corporate profitability, lower tax rates, favorable retirement and investment flows, and the degree to which and whether these conditions might be expected to endure or reverse themselves in the future.

6. Forecasting Uncertainty

- How difficult is it to forecast the key variables affecting investment assets? _____

_____

- What are the likely consequences of a significant error in forecasting by the investor? _____

Comment:

It is prudent to regularly assess the assumptions underlying the expected outlook for each of the major asset classes. At the same time, it is important to think about the prevailing consensus views, taking care not to adopt the opposite position purely for the sake of being contrarian and without weighing such opposing views on their own merits. As part of this process, it is worthwhile to ask: (i) whether the consensus views are already reflected in asset prices; (ii) what circumstances could render the consensus views inaccurate; and (iii) what the impact of a significant upside or downside surprise relative to consensus views would be. While investment and financial outcomes in no way depend on the degree of predictability or unpredictability in forecasting the future, periods of confusion or heightened investor uncertainty can offer substantial opportunity as well as risk. In assessing a given forecast, investors should examine whether the actual outcome is more likely to exceed or fall short of expectations. Long periods of highly predictable results should not be allowed to lull the investor into a false sense of complacency about the future. Some favorable economic and/or investment trends may continue for a long time, while other investment experiences may be characterized by sudden shifts that could either turn out to be a new direction, or merely a temporary reversal in the primary underlying movement. It is frequently worth weighing what the investment consequences would be of being right for the wrong reasons, versus being wrong for the right reasons.

(Continued)

F I G U R E   9.9 (Concluded)

Investment Outlook Worksheet

7. Cyclical Outlook

- Are the cyclical conditions affecting investment assets likely to improve or deteriorate in the future? _____

- How long are these cyclical influences likely to be sustained, and how long will it take for countervailing forces to build up and potentially reverse these influences? _____

Comment:

Owing to the laws of nature, human behavior, and markets, many forces work to weaken, arrest, and reverse their seemingly uninterruptible upward or downward course. Under reasonably free-market conditions, high prices tend to dampen demand and increase supply, and low prices tend to stimulate demand and reduce supply. An integral element of successful asset allocation and investment strategy is the realization that a great many trends do not continue uninterrupted forever, but instead exhibit regular or irregular fluctuations about some general upward, downward, or sideways path. Although it is often rather difficult to foretell the onset of cyclical changes in the investment outlook, such difficulty should not prevent the investor from regularly questioning the longevity, magnitude, and likely recurrence (or disappearance) of causes, effects, patterns, and trends.

8. Risk Analysis

- What are the key risks to the investment outlook? _____

- How can these risks be monitored? _____

Comment:

Risks in the investment outlook can take several forms. From a fundamental stand point, the investment outlook can be negatively affected by: (i) *an external shock* to the existing order, usually falling on the economy or the financial system, for example, in the form of a sudden change in the price of an essential good such as oil; (ii) *an internal imbalance* that disrupts the smooth functioning of an economy, such as a lending crisis in which loans cannot be made or repaid; or (iii) *a major policy error* on the part of the executive, the legislative, or the judicial branch of government, such as prohibitively high protectionistic tariff laws, or an overly rapid expansion or contraction of the money supply by a nation's central bank. From a valuation stand point, investment risks can occur when there is a sharp contraction in valuation levels. Although such a contraction might take place when asset valuations are at extended levels, valuation shrinkages could also occur when the asset class in question is trading at modest or low valuation levels. From a psychological/technical/liquidity standpoint, investment risks can arise when: (i) investor, business, consumer, or international confidence is eroded; (ii) supply/demand relationships and price/volume relationships exhibit unfavorable trends in asset markets; and (iii) the flow of liquidity to asset market participants, investor intermediaries, and trading marketplaces is constrained or interrupted altogether. Monitoring risks in the investment outlook requires a disciplined, ongoing, comprehensive, and judicious gathering and weighing of the explicit and subtle forces that can destabilize asset markets and prices.

[Vertical margin text: INVESTMENT   OUTLOOK]

9. Asset Price Drivers

- What are the key drivers of prices within a given asset class, and its subsectors? _____

_____

_____

_____

- How do these priced rivers inter relate and operate, and what factors might increase or weaken their effects? _____

_____

_____

Comment:

By thinking about, enumerating, and ranking the key price drivers within a given asset class and its subsectors, investors can gain improved perspective as to the true causes of likely positive or negative investment performance. For example, the prices of high-yield bonds are driven by, among other factors: (i) monetary and credit conditions within the overall economy and within the principal industries raising capital by means of high-yield instruments; (ii) yields and prices on competing asset classes; (iii) funds flows to and from the major investor groups in high-yield bonds; and (iv) market-making liquidity conditions, participants' hedging strategies, and the supply of new public and private offerings of high-yield securities. Investors can substantially multiply the power of such knowledge through a systematic and thoughtful review of how asset price drivers interrelate and operate, and through thinking about what factors might increase or weaken the effects of these asset price drivers over time.

10. Price-Value Divergences

- How wide or narrow are the divergences between prices and values with in a given asset class? _____

_____

_____

- What is the likely direction of these divergences? _____

_____

_____

Comment:

At its heart, the function and purpose of most investing activity is to determine the correct relationship between the *price* of an asset and its true *value*. Often, there is spirited debate about the true value of an asset, with various theoretical models adduced to buttress either side's arguments, and with the intensity of the debate in proportion to the perceived degree of divergence. The divergences between prices and values are not uniform across asset classes nor across time, and certainly not uniform as to how long they last. At various times, the price of an asset can be much higher than its true value, approximately equal to its true value, or substantially below its true value. The investor can increase his or her chances of success in understanding the investment outlook, and thus in asset-allocation and investment strategy, by consistently endeavoring to pay at least as much attention to the *value* of an asset as to its *price*.

I N V E S T M E N T   O U T L O O K

Investment Universe Factors Affecting Asset Allocation

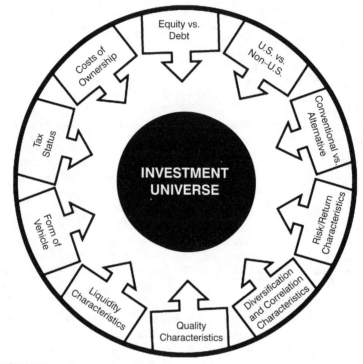

Source: The Author.

RISK MITIGATION MATRICES

Throughout the asset-allocation process, investors need to candidly and searchingly evaluate: (i) their *own tolerance to risk* (making use of question 4 in the Investor Profile Worksheet in Figure 9.7); (ii) the *risk elements in the financial market outlook* (making use of question 8 in the Investment Outlook Worksheet in Figure 9.9); and (iii) *the risk-return characteristics of specific asset classes and securities* (making use of question 4 in Figure 9.11). In this manner, investors can direct their ongoing attention to the important tasks of risk allocation, risk monitoring, and risk management.

F I G U R E 9.11

Investment Universe Worksheet

1. Equity versus Debt Investments

I
N
V
E
S
T
M
E
N
T
U
N
I
V
E
R
S
E

• How does the investor's desired degree of short- and intermediate-term nominal capital protection (for example, a low degree of expected price volatility) compare with his or her desired degree of intermediate-to long-term purchasing power protection? _____

_____

• Does the investor feel more comfortable being in the position of creditor (i.e., as a lender, or as a purchaser of an issuer's debt securities) or owner (i.e., being the ultimate recipient of claims and profit flows after fixed-income securities holders' claims have been satisfied)?

_____

_____

Comment:
The choice between equity and debt instruments is one of the most fundamental decisions in the asset-allocation and investment strategy process. As discussed in Chapter 6, each of these asset classes involves special advantages, disadvantages, potential upside and downside price movements, and analytical techniques. Each broad asset class behaves differently under varying economic circumstances, ranging from very high growth, to modest growth, to no growth, to modest retrenchment, to severe contraction. At the same time, equity and debt investments may act similarly or dissimilarly in periods of hyperinflation, high inflation, moderate inflation, moderate disinflation, severe disinflation, and deflation. Most prevailing wisdom holds that equity and equity-like investments perform best during periods of economic and profit growth, and as such, they provide the investor (who is, in effect, a business owner) with purchasing power protection because he or she is able to benefit from an increase in capital values commensurate with increases in revenues and profits as the economy grows over time. Conversely, it is generally believed that debt investments, due to the usually fixed amounts and scheduled times of their principal and interest repayments, are more likely (but not always) to provide some degree of nominal price protection, even in periods of economic contraction—more so if interest rates do not rise significantly, if the coupon payments are sufficiently high, and/or if the final maturity of the debt instrument is not too long. As with any broad set of generalizations concerning the equity and debt asset classes, there are important ingredients of truth in these perceptions, yet there are a sufficient number of exceptions that the investor should also carefully consider in allocating assets. Some equities, particularly securities whose return is primarily comprised of expected dividend or convertible-bond coupon payments, may exhibit debt-like price behavior. In like manner, some debt investments, particularly issues whose very low coupons and/or low quality ratings may lead to wide fluctuations in capital values, may effectively rise or fall in price almost like stocks. In short, at different times in the short- and long-term cycles of the economy, during differing periods of price level changes, and according to the investor's own particular circumstances, his or her asset allocation may emphasize equity more than debt investments, or vice versa.

(Continued)

F I G U R E 9.11 (Continued)

Investment Universe Worksheet

	2. U.S. versus Non-U.S. Investments
	• To what degree does the investor desire investment in and understand the pros and cons of exposure to regions, countries, companies, bond issuers, industry sectors, and currencies outside the investor's home country? _____
I	_____
	_____
N	_____
V	_____
	• How similarly or dissimilarly will non-U.S. assets in the investor's portfolio behave
E	compared with the behavior of U.S. assets? _____
S	_____
T	_____
M	_____
E	_____
N	_____
T	Comment:

How large or small a percentage of an investor's assets that is placed in U.S. versus non-U.S. stocks, bonds, alternative investments, or cash is determined by several factors, including: (i) the investor's own comfort level and experience with non-domestic investments; (ii) the relative attractiveness of foreign versus domestic investments from the standpoint of capital growth, capital preservation, and income; and (iii) whether the presence of non-U.S. investments in a portfolio can realistically, meaningfully, and positively alter the overall risk/return profile of the portfolio. Under some conditions, non-U.S. investments may behave essentially like their U.S. counterparts. In other environments, non-U.S. investments may offer distinct and not-otherwise-available economic, credit, and currency exposures that considerably enhance the upside potential and/or downward protection characteristics of a given asset allocation. Investors should think about: (i) the costs of gathering information about non-U.S. investments; (ii) the potential political and/or currency risks associated with non-U.S. investments; (iii) the accuracy, reliability, and transnational comparability of financial and economic data; (iv) the expenses associated with the transaction execution, position reporting, and custody of non-U.S. assets; and (v) the relative completeness of the array of alternatives for investing in non-U.S. investments. During eras in which the world moves toward greater integration, it often becomes easier to invest outside one's own national borders and such activity maya llow exposure to differing patterns of returns than are available domestically. At the samet ime, investors should keep in mind the fairly broad range of historic experiences, successes, risks, and shortfalls associated with investing abroad.

3. Alternative versus Conventional Investments

I N V E S T

- How willing is the investor to place his or her funds in certain kinds of alternative investments that may be characterized by high minimum a mounts, different time frames and/or procedures for measuring valuations and returns, high annual management fees and/or performance fees, and multiquarter or multiyear minimum-holding (lockup) periods, in an attempt to capture higher levels, different patterns, and different rates of return than those offered by more conventional asset classes such as stocks, bonds, and cash? _____

- How likely is it that alternative investments will provide true diversification benefits to a portfolio through returns profiles that maintain or enhance portfolio results during periods when conventional publicly traded investments may be generating unattractive returns? _____

M E N T   U N I V E R S E R S E

Comment:

Beginning in the 1980s and 1990s, alternative investments became increasingly available to qualified investors in a wide variety of sizes and types, in offshore, partnership, and separate account formats, and in various investment styles. Among the private investments universe are: (i) real property investments, including timberland and oil and gas; (ii) real estate investments, on a direct basis and in REIT (Real Estate Investment Trust) form; (iii) commodities, including gold and other precious metals, commodity futures, and commodity-trading advisors (CTAs) usually operating on a long-only or a long/short basis; (iv) arbitrage-driven strategies, generally concentrated in the areas of risk arbitrage, convertible-securities arbitrage, and capital-structure and paired-shares arbitrage; (v) venture capital; (vi) leveraged buyout investing; (vii) absolute-return, market-neutral, or relative-value strategies, involving various forms of hedging, long/short techniques, and index arbitrage; (viii) distressed securities, bankruptcy investing, and restructuring activity; (ix) hedge funds, some of which may engage in one or more of various arbitrage, sector-based, macro-oriented, or other strategies; and (x) funds of funds, which are groups of individual funds usually participating in a few or several of the disciplines within the alternative investments arena. In general terms, alternative investments tend to capture investors' attention and a portion of their asset allocations due to their attractive returns, the low correlations of their returns with traditional asset classes, and perhaps the opportunity to co-invest and tap into the specialized knowledge and focus of a skilled investment manager. In favorable periods for alternative investments, investors have sometimes overlooked many of the drawbacks associated with this asset class, including: (i) high investment minimums and lengthy minimum lockup periods; (ii) internal asset-management issues relating to valuation methodologies, transparency of approach, conflicts of interest, investment concentration and liquidity, and the robustness of the manager's investment monitoring and risk control systems; (iii) high fee structures; and in some cases, (iv) high turnover and/or tax inefficiency of returns. When considering the alternative investments asset class, investors would do well to carry out thorough due diligence of the asset manager'si nvestment processes, uses of leverage and derivative investments (if applicable), and past and expected future performance in unfavorable financial market conditions.

(Continued)

F I G U R E 9.11 (Continued)

Investment Universe Worksheet

I N V E S T M E N T M E N T U N I V E R S E	**4. Risk/Return Characteristics**

4. Risk/Return Characteristics

- What is the risk/return profile of the asset under consideration for investment, and how strong is the case for this profile? _____

_____

_____

_____

- How will the presence or absence of an asset under consideration for investment affect the overall strength of the portfolio as a whole, in good and bad markets? _

_____

_____

_____

_____

Comment:

During bull markets for major asset classes such as equities, bonds, or alternative investments, it is all too human for investors to pay undue attention to the *return* characteristics of the asset in question, while downplaying or ignoring altogether its relevant *risk* characteristics. The more highly risk-averse an investor is, and the more likely the investment markets are to experience volatility, the more frequently the investor should analyze the potential risks of an investment, assessing the circumstances, probabilities, and consequences of capital impairment or loss. In probing the risk/return profile of an asset in as pragmatic a fashion as possible, the investor should devote special care and scrutiny to what measures of risk are used, such as volatility, standard deviation, maximum drawdown (loss) during previous down market cycles, and other useful measures. Similarly, projections of the upside prospects of an investment should be firmly grounded in defensible methodologies and realistic, explicitly stated assumptions. The investor should constantly remind himself or herself that forecasts of an investment's future risk/reward profile are no more than estimates, and thus are subject to change as facts and circumstances change. The presence or absence of an asset in a portfolio can affect the overall strength of the portfolio in a variety of ways. Portfolios that have assets that hold their value or even increase in value while large remaining portions of the asset mix are declining in price may give the investor the requisite degree of fortitude and presence of mind, perhaps to maintain the asset mix, or perhaps to rebalance the asset allocation. Sometimes, a significant price decline for a given asset or group of assets, even in only a small portion of the overall portfolio, may effectively stun the investor and prevent him or her from making portfolio adjustments, however urgently they may be needed. On the other hand, holding onto an asset class that exhibits extraordinary price performance may offer the investor the mental and actual opportunity to redeploy capital to other asset classes if deemed prudent.

5. Diversification and Correlation Characteristics

I

N

V

E

S

T

M

E

N

T

- Does the asset under consideration for investment contribute to an appropriately diversified (or concentrated) asset allocation? _____

  _____

  _____

  _____

  _____

  _____

- What is the degree of returns correlation between the asset under consideration for investment and each of the other major assets in the portfolio, and what factors might cause these correlations to change over time? _____

  _____

  _____

  _____

  _____

  _____

  _____

  _____

  _____

Comment:

U

N

I

V

E

R

S

E

One of the important intellectual breakthroughs in investment theory during the past 50 years was the realization that it is not the sheer number of investment or asset classes that provides portfolio diversification, it is how the return of each major investment correlates with the return of every other major investment in the portfolio. Depending on the investor's profile and the investment outlook, each investor will generally not want the same degree of diversification (or concentration) in his or her portfolio. Thus, each asset needs to be evaluated not only on its own merits, but also on how its return and risk characteristics reinforce, neutralize, or detract from the return and risk characteristics of all the other assets considered together. Equally important is the desirability of selecting *asset managers* whose investment styles and returns are not highly correlated with one another. Most assets' returns correlations with other assets' returns correlations exhibit some degree of movement through time, influenced by the respective assets' unique and shifting responses to the vicissitudes of the global economy, price inflation, and capital-market conditions. When assets' correlations with other assets in the portfolio undergo a major upward movement, the assets' returns tend to move in the same direction. As a result, the portfolio as a whole will tend to respond as if the assets were concentrated rather than diversified. For example, in early 1987, just when diversification was most needed, Hong Kong equities' returns had a relatively low correlation, 0.42, with U.S. equities' returns. However, during the severe U.S. equity market decline of October 1987, Hong Kong equities' returns exhibited a fairly high correlation, 0.91, with U.S. equities' returns. In this case, under difficult market conditions, investors were not able to avail themselves as fully of the benefits of diversification as they thought they were going to.

(Continued)

F I G U R E 9.11 (Continued)

Investment Universe Worksheet

6. Quality Characteristics

- How is the quality of each of the assets in the portfolio measured and what is the quality of each of the assets in the portfolio overall? _____

I

- What are the likely trends in quality of each of the assets in the portfolio and how are general investment market valuations likely to reflect quality considerations? _

N

_____

V   Comment:

E   Quality is measured in different ways for different asset classes. For fixed-income securities and cash-equivalent instruments, the quality rating agencies use a blend of

S   capital-structure analyses, liquidity and debt service coverage ratios, special financial stress tests, and a variety of quantitative as well as judgmental factors developed

T   under changing market circumstances. In the world of equities, quality measurements tend to be less standardized and less broadly applied, as equity investors are usually

M   more concerned with capital appreciation opportunities than with an issuer's ability to pay off its obligations. Nevertheless, particularly during difficult economic and/or

E   financial-market conditions, equity asset quality concerns may become paramount. In such environments, a company's management performance and integrity, balance

N   sheet strength, capital resources, revenue and earnings predictability, and preferred

T   and common dividend-coverage ratios are all taken into account in assessing equity quality, as is the company's past operating and financial performance in periods of unfavorable overall economic and financial market conditions. For the disparate subcategories within alternative investments, quality benchmarks are often less

U   structured and less frequently applied than in other asset classes. In part, this is due to the difficulty of assembling, applying, and broadly disseminating asset-quality data

N   in many of the less efficient subsectors of the alternative-investments realm. Given the specialized nature of alternative investments, and the heightened degree to which

I   investors in this asset class may be exposed to the skills, judgment, and asset valuation and quality rating abilities of a single person or a small group of individuals,

V   it is equally important that investors be mindful and discerning about quality

E   considerations. In general terms, the quality characteristics of an asset may be specific to its asset class, and for many assets, quality may be improving or

R   deteriorating depending on factors external and internal to the asset class. Often, an awareness of quality characteristics, coupled with the realization that not all

S   investment approaches will be successful in all market environments, should help the investor to decide whether to retain, add to, or drop an asset class, an investment

E   position, or an asset manager. Investing styles and asset quality characteristics are often judged in extended cycles whose length and shifts in direction are especially difficult to predict. For some length of time in bullish financial environments, quality considerations tend to be ignored, or certainly may not be uppermost in judging assets, in the determination of investment strategy, and in the execution of asset allocation. Even in such times, prudent investors will not lose sight of the importance of asset quality to help preserve the value of the portfolio when less favorable investment market climates arrive.

7. Liquidity Characteristics

- How easily can the investor buy or sell a specific asset under normal investment market conditions without significantly affecting its market price? _____

  _____

I _____

  _____

N - How easily can the investor buy or sell a specific asset under unusual or abnormal investment market conditions without significantly affecting its market price? _____

V _____

  _____

E Comment:

S For a good part of the time when deciding on an asset allocation or investment strategy, most investors pay little attention to an asset's liquidity characteristics (i.e.,

T how easy or difficult it may be to buy or sell the asset without causing its price to rise or fall significantly). This relative neglect of liquidity factors stems from: (i) the usually

M manageable size of any one investor's buying or selling interest relative to the normal trading volume for a given asset; (ii) many investors' long-term buy-and-hold

E approach toward a meaningful portion of the assets in their portfolios; (iii) an underappreciation of the fact that some other investors may simultaneously decide to

N buy or sell the same asset that the investor wants to buy or sell; and (iv) a perceived lack of importance of liquidity risk to investors for long stretches of time, followed by

T short periods of low trading liquidity, succeeded again for long stretches by reasonably quiescent liquidity conditions. If the investor thinks that he or she might have to dispose of certain assets and/or purchase other assets within a short time frame, or that bouts of illiquidity may dislocate normal flows of buying and selling,

U thought should be given to how such activity or such conditions might have affected

N these assets' prices in the past or might do so in the future. It is difficult for most, if not

I all, investors to quantify with any degree of accuracy the liquidity characteristics of an asset in times of upset or distressed markets. Some possible liquidity indicators include: (i) the total monetary value of daily, weekly, monthly, and annual trading

V volume in the asset; (ii) the total supply of freely tradeable (also known as the public "float") units of the asset; (iii) the absolute price of the asset; (iv) concentrated,

E restricted, optioned, margined, or other technical conditions that might potentially affect the supply/demand balance in the asset; and not least, (v) the type,

R conventions, costs, practices, access methodologies, competing marketplaces, and settlement mechanisms associated with where and how the asset is bought and sold

S in normal times. Many assets exhibit reasonable trading liquidity in the cash equivalents markets and certain sectors of the high-grade and government/

E government-related bond markets, as well as in many large-capitalization sectors of the equity markets. In times of financial crisis, even these assets may not be able to readily be bought or sold in an organized, price-continuous manner. Some asset classes and subsectors are characterized by low or very low levels of liquidity, including many of the alternative-investment areas, as well as smaller-capitalization equities and parts of the tax-exempt, high-yield, and emerging-markets equity and fixed-income universes. When constructing or valuing a portfolio, or considering a large number of tactical adjustments to the portfolio, the investor should be aware of potentially significant costs of trading due to the market impact of buying or selling. As a result, when estimating the realizable value of a given asset allocation, it might be prudent to allow for an appropriate percentage discount from quoted prices to reflect the degree of liquidity associated with each asset.

(*Continued*)

F I G U R E **9.11 (Concluded)**

Investment Universe Worksheet

I **N** **V** **E** **S** **T** **M** **E** **N** **T** **U** **N** **I** **V** **E** **R** **S** **E**	**8. Form of Vehicle**

8. Form of Vehicle

- What are the advantages and disadvantages of the available forms of investment vehicle for each asset class being considered for inclusion in the investor's portfolio? _____

_____

- What is the desired degree of complexity in the range of vehicle forms in the investor's portfolio? _____

_____

_____

_____

_____

Comment:

The form of an investment vehicle refers to the way the investor owns a given asset, or how that asset is packaged and made available to the investor. Many investments are available in a variety of forms, while others are available in only one form or a very narrow choice of forms. Vehicle forms span the gamut from direct or beneficial ownership of an asset, to structured securities (which combine elements of more than one security type, such as a bond plus an index instrument that tracks a specific industry, such as pharmaceutical stocks), to separate account management, to pooled vehicles such as investment partnerships, open-end and closed-end mutual funds, insurance structures, wrap programs consisting of a group of asset managers, trusts, annuities, exchange funds, unit investment trusts, index funds, and exchange-traded funds (ETFs). Various fund-of-funds structures are also available, including funds of funds that invest in private partnerships within the alternative-investments asset class, and so-called asset-allocation or lifestyle funds that invest in a blend of other funds with the aim of achieving a specific asset mix or investment goal. In the late 1980s and throughout the 1990s, the high attrition and substitution rate of the components in many widely followed indices, such as the FTSE 100 index in the U.K. and the Standard & Poor's 500 index in the U.S., have steered a growing number of equity-oriented investors toward low-cost index tracking funds as a way of emulating these indices' returns. For several asset classes, the investor may be forced to hold the asset in one or a limited number of vehicle formats. For many other asset classes, the decision as to what form of vehicle in which to own the asset will be influenced by issues of: (i) cost, encompassing asset management, custody, monitoring, and reporting fees; (ii) potential access to the investment or to its asset manager; (iii) divisibility and the efficiency of buying and selling all or part of one's investment; (iv) liquidity; (v) marginability or borrowing potential; (vi) taxation; (vii) the possible multiple layering of fees (in vehicles such as fund-of-funds structures); and (viii) risk sharing. In effect, the form of vehicle for an investor's portfolio of assets is determined by the intersection of the asset's characteristics with the investor's own aversions and preferences.

9. Tax Status

- What is the current and likely future tax status of the asset and vehicle form under consideration for investment? _____

- Does the tax status of the asset and the vehicle form under consideration for investment have any effect on the overall taxation of the investor? _____

Comment:

To be successful in investing and asset allocation, the investor needs to pay careful attention to all potential forms of taxation and thus to after-tax investment returns. By doing so, the investor can gauge the possible effects of a given asset or investment vehicle form on the overall tax status of the investor and his or her portfolio. Some investments and investment vehicle structures are tax-free or partially taxed, tax-advantaged, or tax-deferred. Other investment and investment-vehicle structures may have undergone a change in tax status, with the loss of a specific tax preference following enactment of relevant tax legislation. Among the considerations that may determine the ultimate tax status of an asset are: (i) the corporate, subchapter S, partnership, or individual classification of the asset's owner filing the tax return; (ii) the tax domicile of the investor; (iii) where the assets themselves are domiciled or taxed—onshore, offshore, or within a special state, local, or another designated tax jurisdiction; and (iv) Alternative Minimum Tax (AMT) or Unincorporated Business Tax (UBT) issues. It takes skill, experience, and often a high degree of patience to properly navigate through the strictures and nuances of the tax code. Investors should consult appropriate tax counsel for advice and guidance on tax matters.

10. Cost of Ownership

- What are the initial and ongoing costs associated with the asset under consideration for investment? _____

- Are all of the explicit and implicit costs of asset ownership taken into account? ___

Comment:

The costs of owning an asset exert a direct impact on the investor's realized compound returns over time. These expenses include commissions, front-end and back-end sales loads, redemption fees and penalty charges, 12b-1 and other marketing expense recovery charges, asset management fees, performance fees, wrap fees, fiduciary and advisory fees, administration, custody, and settlement fees, transfer fees, and, not to be overlooked, record-keeping and tax-preparation fees. Some of these expenses are tax deductible, and some are not. Some of these expenses are one-time only, and some may be activity-based or may recur with the passage of time. Some of these expenses are fixed, and some may be expected to change in line with changes in the general price level and/or in the value of the portfolio. It is important for the investor to gather a complete accounting of all fees related to his or her portfolio, and then to calculate the effect of these fees on the portfolio's projected investment returns. In many cases, the fees associated with certain types of assets and/or vehicle forms can reduce the portfolio's effective annual return by a significant percentage, and in the process, considerably lower the final compounded values of the portfolio.

(left margin vertical text: INVESTMENT MENT UNIVERSE)

To help investors assess and track many of the commonly encountered risks in asset allocation, Figure 9.12 contains a Risk Mitigation Matrix.

The Risk Mitigation Matrix in Figure 9.12 describes five risks that are *investor-specific*, which relate to the worksheet questions in Figure 9.7: (i) purchasing power risk; (ii) spending shortfall risk; (iii) hedging risk; (iv) taxation risk; and (v) confidence erosion risk. In addition, the Risk Mitigation Matrix describes five risks that are *market outlook-specific*, and which relate to the worksheet questions in Figure 9.9: (i) capital loss risk; (ii) volatility risk; (iii) liquidity risk; (iv) correlation risk; and (v) systemic risk. Finally, the Risk Mitigation Matrix describes five risks that are *asset-specific*, and which relate to the worksheet questions in Figure 9.11: (i) reinvestment risk; (ii) credit risk; (iii) event risk; (iv) prepayment risk; and (v) currency risk.

Figure 9.12 briefly describes each risk and representative ways for investors to lessen or mitigate that risk. The boxes in the right-hand portion of the figure provide space for investors to note the degree to which the risk is mitigable, and the degree to which they feel they have effectively mitigated the specific risk described. For this purpose, investors may wish to use a scale ranging from 1 to 3, with 1 indicating that the risk is highly mitigable and/or has been highly mitigated, and 3 indicating that the risk is not very mitigable and/or has not been mitigated to any meaningful degree. If investors feel that it is possible to evaluate these factors more finely, they may wish instead to use a scale ranging from 1 to 5, or even 1 to 10.

The chief purposes of a Risk Mitigation Matrix such as Figure 9.12 are: (i) to remind investors of the varieties of risk; (ii) to help them recognize the interplay between different types of risk; and (iii) to sensitize them to the potential effects of multiple risks acting in combination. The list of risks in Figure 9.12 is by no means complete, as to types of risks and representative ways of mitigating risks, and is intended to give general guidance to the investor. Some investors may want to add risk categories to those portrayed in Figure 9.12, taking into account such factors as leverage risk, which relates to the different scope of risk that results when the

Risk Mitigation Matrix

Type of Risk	Brief Description of Risk	Representative Ways of Mitigating Risk	Degree to Which Risk Is	
			Mitigable	Mitigated
Investor-Specific Risks				
Purchasing Power	Underperformance of investments relative to changes in the general price level of goods and services	Emphasis on securities that keep pace with inflation, such as certain types of equities or inflation-indexed bonds	☐	☐
Spending Shortfall	Available capital and annual income flows are insufficient to meet the investor's needs	Careful monitoring and adjustment of spending rules relative to portfolio and capital market results	☐	☐
Hedging	Strategies employed to hedge the portfolio prove ineffective or produce counterproductive outcomes	Caution in the identification, application, and ongoing surveillance of hedging actions	☐	☐
Taxation	ncreases in the investor's taxes due to legislation or actions triggered by portfolio maneuvers	Regular consultation with competent sources of tax counsel	☐	☐
Confidence Erosion	Investor suffers a decline in faith in his or her own investment ability and/or in investment assets	Judicious reduction of, or pause in, exposure to capital markets; use of trusted external resources	☐	☐
Market Outlook-Specific Risks				
Capital Loss	Realized or unrealized losses due to changes in prices, interest rates, or valuation methodologies	Offsetting tactics that protect against unfavorable price movements, such as short-selling and the use of puts, calls, futures, and other instruments	☐	☐
Volatility	Wider and perhaps more frequent swings than normal in asset prices	Asset diversification and/or inclusion of assets bearing a lower degree of price volatility	☐	☐
Liquidity	Difficulty in buying or selling investments without causing unfavorable price effects	Attention to trading volumes and worst-case liquidity scenarios when establishing investment position sizes	☐	☐
Correlation	Assets whose price movements were intended to offset one another actually move in the same direction	Thorough scrutiny of the reasons for past correlation shifts and realistic assessment of future such episodes	☐	☐
Systemic	One or several components of the priced is covery, trading, lending, or settlement mechanisms ceases to function properly for some period of time	Analysis of counterparty financial health: establishment of alternative sources where possible; and creation of contingency and disaster recovery plans	☐	☐

(Continued)

F I G U R E   9.12 (Concluded)

Risk Mitigation Matrix

Type of Risk	Brief Description of Risk	Representative Ways of Mitigating Risk	Degree to Which Risk Is	
			Mitigable	Mitigated
Asset-Specific Risks				
Reinvestment	Inability to reinvest dividends in equity holdings or to reinvest coupons at original yield levels in bond holdings	Consideration of automatic dividend reinvestment plans and zero coupon bond structures	□	□
Credit	Deterioration in and/or rating-agency or market participants' downgrading of the financial strength of an investment	Scrutiny of trends in the quality and robustness of income statement, cash flow, and balance sheet data; alertness to early-warning signs of weakening finances	□	□
Event	Sudden change in the financial standing of an investment due to an event such as a merger, borrowing, spinoff, large one-time dividend, or the purchase or sale of assets	Observation of corporate behavior by other entities in the same or similar industries; pre-emptive switching into other investments	□	□
Prepayment	Premature return of all or a portion of an investment's principal value through bond callability, maturity contraction, orearlier-than-scheduled mortgage repayment	Selection of investments, such as noncallable bonds, that do not grant the issuer the option to pay back principal ahead of schedule	□	□
Currency	Decline in the domestic currency value of an investment due to depreciation in the currency of an external investment	Application of cost-effective currency hedging programs in appropriate market circumstances		

Source: The Author.

investor borrows money to finance some portion of the assets in his or her portfolio.

According to Modern Portfolio Theory, one of the overriding goals of asset allocation is to minimize uncompensated risk through diversification. With the aid of Figure 9.12, investors can recognize and work to reduce risk by distinguishing between, and responding to, risks that are: (i) forecastable and controllable; (ii) forecastable and uncontrollable; (iii) unforecastable and controllable; and (iv) unforecastable and uncontrollable.

INDEX